# Cultural Entrepreneurship in Africa

This book seeks to widen perspectives on entrepreneurship by drawing attention to the diverse and partly new forms of entrepreneurial practice in Africa since the 1990s. Contrary to widespread assertions, figures of success have been regularly observed in Africa since pre-colonial times. The contributions account for these historical continuities in entrepreneurship, and identify the specifically new political and economic context within which individuals currently probe and invent novel forms of enterprise. Based on ethnographically contextualized life stories and case studies of female and male entrepreneurs, the volume offers a vivid and multi-perspectival account of their strategies, visions, and ventures in domains as varied as religious proselytism, politics, tourism, media, music, prostitution, funeral organization, and education. African cultural entrepreneurs have a significant economic impact, attract the attention of large groups of people, serve as role models for many youths, and contribute to the formation of new popular cultures.

**Ute Röschenthaler** is Professor of Social and Cultural Anthropology at the Johannes Gutenberg University Mainz, Germany, and a member of the Cluster of Excellence "The Formation of Normative Orders" and the research program "Africa's Asian Options" at Johann Wolfgang Goethe University, Frankfurt, Germany.

**Dorothea Schulz** is Professor in the Department of Cultural and Social Anthropology at the University of Cologne, Germany.

# Routledge African Studies

# Cultural Entrepreneurship in Africa

Edited by Ute Röschenthaler and
Dorothea Schulz

Routledge
Taylor & Francis Group

LONDON AND NEW YORK

First published 2016
by Routledge

2 Park Square, Milton Park, Abingdon, Oxfordshire OX14 4RN
52 Vanderbilt Avenue, New York, NY 10017

*Routledge is an imprint of the Taylor & Francis Group, an informa business*

First issued in paperback 2019

*Library of Congress Cataloging-in-Publication Data*
Cultural entrepreneurship in Africa / edited Ute Röschenthaler and
Dorothea Schulz.
    pages cm. — (Routledge African studies ; 20)
    Includes bibliographical references and index.
    1. Entrepreneurship—Social aspects—Africa.  2. Businesspeople—
Africa—21st century.  3. Culture—Economic aspects—Africa.  4. Social
entrepreneurship—Africa.  I. Röschenthaler, Ute, editor, contributor.
II. Schulz, Dorothea Elisabeth, editor.  III. Series: Routledge African studies ; 20.
    HB615.C84 2015
    338.04096—dc23        2015025794

ISBN: 978-1-138-85166-5 (hbk)
ISBN: 978-0-367-87069-0 (pbk)

Typeset in Sabon
by Apex CoVantage, LLC

# Contents

## PART II
## Business, Pleasure, Leisure

## PART III
## Media and Popular Culture

# Figures

# Acknowledgments

Our initial idea to bring together studies on cultural entrepreneurship germinated while preparing a workshop on "media entrepreneurs", which we organized together with Tilo Grätz and which was generously funded by the German Research Council's Point Sud program. We wish to thank our editor and editorial assistant at Routledge, Max Novick and Jennifer Morrow, and Janine Murphy and the late Elliot Klein for their careful copyediting work. Dorothea Schulz offers a heartfelt thanks to Ute Röschenthaler for shouldering the main burden in shepherding this volume toward completion, and to Wilfried Hinsch for his clear-minded input into our efforts to conceptualize entrepreneurship. We gratefully acknowledge financial support from the Centre for Interdisciplinary African Studies (ZIAF) Goethe University Frankfurt and from the University of Cologne. We also benefitted immensely from discussions during panels organized on "cultural entrepreneurship in Africa" during the 2011 AAA meeting in Montréal, and during the 2011 ECAS meeting in Uppsala.

# 1 Introduction

## Forging Fortunes: New Perspectives on Entrepreneurial Activities in Africa

*Ute Röschenthaler and Dorothea Schulz*

What analytical perspective should we as scholars develop to think of African actors' daily experiences, struggles, and engagements with the postcolonial state without falling into the trap of afro-pessimistic accounts, that is, without employing the terminology of African "crisis" and victimhood? In response to this question, Simon Gikandi has recently called for a new "language" that will allow us to account for the actual lived experiences of Africans, to take seriously their capacity for innovation and invention, and hence to consider them as "subject(s) already engaged in powerful and imaginative gestures of copying and survival" (2010: xvi). Although we very much agree with Gikandi's critique of afro-pessimist accounts of Africa and Africans, we view a similar danger in overly stressing the opportunities for cultural innovation and creativity open to Africans in a historical era shaped by particular forms of globalization and neoliberalism.

The purpose of this edited volume is to move beyond the deadlock delineated by afro-pessimist and afro-positivist accounts, and instead to stress the entrepreneurial abilities shown by numerous African actors, past and present, in the face of adversity and novel opportunities. We use "entrepreneur" as a concept and a heuristic term to point to the plethora of engagements by which social actors in African societies deal with the constraints and opportunities generated by the contemporary moment, a moment shaped, although to different extents, by a neoliberal paradigm of economics and politics.

The term "cultural entrepreneurs" refers to individuals who quickly perceive the chances of the moment and seize novel opportunities to initiate new forms of generating income in the realm of cultural production. What distinguishes these entrepreneurs and their initiatives from that of other inventive individuals is that they purposefully take chances in situations of uncertainty, when failure seems to be as likely an outcome of their activities as does success. Entrepreneurs positively embrace the risk of failure. What matters to them is their strong belief that they will succeed and surmount any obstacles that will come their way.

This volume draws attention to the diverse and partly new forms of entrepreneurial practice that have emerged throughout sub-Saharan Africa since the mid-1980s, that is, in the historical period roughly associated with the times when the effects of the structural adjustment program were making themselves felt, and when, along with economic and political liberalization, the former state monopoly in the area of cultural production and media communication was weakened.

We present entrepreneurs active at the intersections between economic and cultural activities, such as entrepreneurship in media, religion, or education, illustrating that their activities encompass different trajectories of political, economic, and social success.[1] These individuals have a special nose for incipient business ventures; they generate significant economic impact, attract the attention of large groups of people, and contribute to the formation of new popular cultures. They often stand as role models for the youths aspiring to imitate their success. Because of the varied nature of these entrepreneurial activities and the paths to success they set, the entrepreneurs we portray are not necessarily representative of their country or a particular national culture. Variations in style and kinds of success may be the result of the particular historical, political, and social setting in which these entrepreneurs pursue their projects. In spite of their differences, they share an extraordinary capacity to initiate new ways of making business that have significant repercussions for their immediate surrounding or society at large, and in this sense become important actors of change and innovation.

## THE CONCEPT OF THE ENTREPRENEUR

The concept of the entrepreneur emerged in the context of industrial capitalism in the eighteenth century. It was used against predictive and prescriptive models of human behavior that paid little attention to individual economic actors (e.g., Cantillon 1775; for a critique, see Parker 2009 and Forrest 1994). Only in the early twentieth century, Josef Schumpeter (1883–1950), inspired by the second phase of industrialization in Europe, theorized the role of the individual in economic development and growth in his *Theory of Economic Development* (1912/1934, see also Schumpeter 1928, 1947). Influenced by, and simultaneously critical of, the classical economist theories of Adam Smith, James Ferguson, and Karl Marx, Schumpeter sought to stress the role of individuals in bringing about change and innovation. He coined the term "entrepreneur" for individuals, who, thanks to their personal qualities and psychological attributes, were capable of changing existing economic structures and habits. Among these personal qualities was the entrepreneur's readiness to take risks and invest his capital, his vision to recognize market niches, and his courage to create new things under conditions of uncertainty and surmount social resistance against innovation (Bude 1997: 850–855, see also McDaniel 2005). Schumpeter's "entrepreneur" capitalized on the basic means of production and commercialization, such as land, labor, capital, and transport, and, if necessary, incurred debts to transform what other people had invented into a marketable product. While Schumpeter stressed the entrepreneur's innovative and creative skills, he also portrayed him as a homeless figure whose readiness to self-sacrifice and to break with social conventions made him almost a social *enfant terrible*. Also distinctive about Schumpeter's conception of the entrepreneur was that he placed him squarely in the context of industrial production: only an owner and founder of his company was considered an entrepreneur, in contradistinction to a farmer, a trader, or an artisan, whose activities aimed at maintaining the status quo, rather than transforming it.[2]

In spite of occasional attempts to refine and rework Schumpeter's narrow conception, for decades the entrepreneur was, in William Baumol's words, "one of the most intriguing and one of the most elusive characters in the cast that constitutes the subject of economic analysis"; as a consequence, the term "entrepreneur" has remained underspecified (1968: 64). Economics and related disciplines revived scholarly debate on entrepreneurship only in the 1990s, with respect to European economies shaped by the effects of neoliberal economic reform. Here, economists celebrated "the entrepreneur" as the person capable of initiating new business opportunities and small-scale enterprises to deal with frequent bankruptcies of companies and increasing unemployment. It seems no coincidence that roughly at the same time, when the effects of the structural adjustment programs dictated by international monetary institutions were making themselves felt throughout sub-Saharan Africa, the World Bank discovered the entrepreneur as a key figure of development. Breaking with earlier depictions of African entrepreneurs as "deficient", that is, as missing essential features of the ideal-type industrial entrepreneur (Gihring 1984; Greenfield and Strickon 1981; Knutsen 2003), development economists now applied the term to various economic actors, ranging from factory owners to street vendors (Spring and McDade 1998).

In Africanist scholarship, treatments of "the entrepreneur" have also suffered from a lack of conceptual precision. Numerous historical and anthropological studies documented the long-standing existence of entrepreneurial figures and initiatives, yet they did not conceive of them as instances of entrepreneurship. Still, the studies helped identify features of entrepreneurship characteristic of non-industrial economic and political settings, in which large-scale production of goods and long-distance trade constituted major sources of wealth (Reynolds 1974 for Ghana, Amos 2001 for Togo, Denzer 1994 for Nigeria; see also Dumett 1983; Forrest 1994: 88). The trade networks and also the large-scale production of goods often implicated large numbers of clients and workers (Amselle 1977; Lovejoy 1980). Women could fare extremely well in some large-scale local industries (such as cloth-dying, pottery, oil and soap production) and also as managers and brokers in trade networks (Brooks 1997; Coquery-Vidrovitch 1983, 1994, 2002; Denzer 1994). Many of these historical examples of successful entrepreneurship combined their wealth with political influence. Some of these businesses and networks were disrupted under colonial administration

(Nwabughuogu 1982; Olukoju 2002); others were partly reconfigured and thrived with their increasing integration into colonial markets along with newly created ventures.[3]

In the first decades of post-independent politics, when the state became the principal provider of employment (MacGaffey 1987: 26)[4] yet proved increasingly unable to provide for its citizens, numerous individuals continued to seize the opportunities of the moment and to take risks under conditions of uncertainty (e.g., Grégoire and Labazée 1993; Ellis and Fauré 1995). Many of them owed their success to their apt combination of different types of social, political, and religious capital, converting their material gains into a "wealth in people" and vice versa (Grégoire 1995).

The plethora of private entrepreneurial activities that have emerged in Africa over the last three decades have been studied particularly in the economic sector. Women and men have created manifold ventures, such as cassava processing factories, breweries, flower industries, import and export businesses, gold and diamond mining, banks, supermarkets, large-scale shoe and garment industries, and cash crop plantation enterprises, among many others (Amselle 1987; Ellis and Fauré 1995; Forrest 1994; Grégoire and Labazée 1993; Hopkins 1988; Jalloh and Falola 2002; MacGaffey 1987; Meagher 2010). All these undertakings form part of what has been described as "cultures of business in Africa" (Taylor 2012), "the capitalist path to development" (Berman and Leys 1994: 1), or "the advancement of African capital" (Forrest 1994). Entrepreneurs have also become active in the cultural sector and created numerous media enterprises, churches and religious movements, universities, funeral services, and have engaged in political undertakings and various clandestine ventures all over the continent.

These entrepreneurial figures straddle the dividing lines between economic profit and other kinds of "capital" (in Bourdieu's sense), and also between the domains of cultural, social, political, and religious activity. We therefore need a concept of entrepreneur that, pace Schumpeter's narrowly conceived "industrial entrepreneur", makes room for the diverse activities initiated by African entrepreneurs, past and present, and also for the various kinds of value they generate in this process.

## THE FIGURE OF THE BIG MAN

A number of scholars, working on Melanesian, Polynesian, and African societies, have pointed to significant resemblances between the entrepreneur and the "Big Man", first described by Marshall Sahlins in reference to the Melanesian Big Man. Sahlins characterized the Big Man as a political leader who "uses wealth to place others in his debt" (Sahlins 1972: 136; see also 1963), in the form of ceremonial giveaways that aim to outrank competitors. Because only those who generously give away are socially respected and in that sense rich and powerful, for the Big Man, material wealth is not an aim in itself but serves to generate "wealth in people" (Hennings 2007). Although the "classical" Big Man bases his power on material wealth, in some societies, his competitive advantage derives from immaterial goods or capacities, such as ritual or other restricted knowledge, oratorical skills, or skills that ensure military success (Lindstrom 1984). All these capacities enable a Big Man to gather followers and to turn them into exchange partners (1984: 294).

While some authors stress genuine similarities between the entrepreneur and the Big Man (Stewart 1990), others argue that similarities between a Big Man and an entrepreneur result from the integration of local economies, in which Big Men played a leading role, into the capitalist market economy (Hennings 2007; Martin 2013; Sykes 2007).[5] In this process, Hennings argues, Big Men transform into (economic) profit-maximizing entrepreneurs who no longer invest in social relationships but in the production of goods and services.

In contrast to this restrictive view of the entrepreneur (and the Big Man) as an economic actor, authors working on "Big Men" in African societies stress that these figures draw on sources of power as varied as entrepreneurial skills (Forrest 1994), a combination of wealth and access to state resources (Lentz 1998), access to medico-religious or esoteric expertise (Bayart 1993; Médard 1992), and the mobilization of a large following through patronage and redistribution (Barber 2007: 126–127). In many cases, these individuals combine various political, economic, and social roles, as political leaders or opinion leaders, key players in trade networks, organizers of various wealth-generating activities, owners of the most valuable material objects, and sponsors of performance groups (Röschenthaler 2011) and artists (Schulz 2001; Waterman 1990). As successful businessmen, they act as role models for others yet also become easy targets for witchcraft accusations (Geschiere 2013; Rowlands and Warnier 1988). Similar to the Melanesian Big Men who use their wealth to secure followers and social support, these successful individuals use their wealth for social, philanthropic, and religious purposes and thereby convert it into more stable assets, such as respectability and "wealth in people" (Forrest 1994: 239–241; Socpa, this volume). The social dimension and impetus of their activities extends beyond the purely financial gain highlighted in economist debate on entrepreneurship, in Africa and beyond.

## THE "FIGURES OF SUCCESS"

Banégas and Warnier (2001) have coined the term "figures of success" to argue that a new type of successful political and economic actor has emerged since the 1980s, entering into competition with the salaried civil servant who, as a consequence of structural adjustment and the attendant shrinking of the state bureaucracy, no longer has the pride of place.[6] Whereas the civil servant capitalized on his privileged access to state resources, the new "figures of success" explore novel itineraries of accumulation facilitated by the liberalization of markets, a thriving informal sector, and the scramble for the appropriation of resources at the interface of the public and the private (2001: 7).

A characteristic feature of these figures of success—a feature they share with the Big Man—is that they combine a search for wealth, power, and social appreciation. Intent on the accumulation of wealth, they pursue innovative and, if deemed necessary, risky ways of making a fortune (Banégas and Warnier 2001). They are popular, prosperous, and ambitious, they strive for reputation and social and political influence, and they display a consumerist lifestyle that lends visible form to people's visions of a better life.

Popular nicknames such as _tcheb-tchap_ (in Mauritania, Ould Ahmed Salem 2001) and _feymen_ (in Cameroon, Malaquais 2001; Ndjio 2008) highlight the adventurous, risk-taking attitude of these individuals who devise new strategies of personal enrichment in times of economic crisis. The nicknames express at once awe, admiration, and shock at the combination of trickery, hustling, and smartness (_la debrouille_) that allows some of these individuals to move in the interstices of illegality and illicitness (Roitman 2008, Oldenburg, this volume). Other figures draw their success not from illicit business ventures but from their special talents, such as music-making, athleticism, or acting. In their case, too, the acquisition of wealth often serves to procure immaterial assets, such as popularity, reputation, and social support. They also impress onlookers with their display of material success and wealth, and thus act as role models of successful risk-taking, similar to the figure of the diaspora, the return migrant who valorizes his expatriation through an attitude of extravaganza (Kibora 2012; also see Gandoulou 2008; Gondola 1999; Trapido 2011).

The conspicuous consumption of these figures of success bears resemblances with the ostentatious and generous gift-giving of Big Men, yet contrasts with the attitude of many merchants who tend to downplay their wealth, and also with the cultural entrepreneurs described in this volume. Still, all the figures have in common that they operate in highly competitive contexts. Also, each of them attributes great importance to the social repercussions of their activities and wealth acquisition. Even if the Big Men, the "figure of success", and the African entrepreneur do not base their success on the support of followers to the same extent, they all treat material wealth as a means to strengthen their reputation and gain social influence. Herein consists a significant difference between these three figures and the Schumpeterian industrial entrepreneur, who invests his pecuniary means into the production process and into hiring contract workers, and not into networks of redistribution.

The cultural entrepreneurs whom we present in this volume do not clearly represent one type of these figures, but combine select features. Still, they all share a readiness for risk-taking in situations of uncertainty, where the results of the activities cannot be fully calculated and anticipated.

## TOWARD AN ANTHROPOLOGICAL CONCEPTION OF "ENTREPRENEUR"

So far, we have argued that earlier treatments of entrepreneurial figures, whether under the label of businessmen, Big Men, or "figures of success", suffered from a certain lack of systematicity and comprehensiveness and also from the fact that their emergence was not consistently related to particular historical and social settings.

Our intention is therefore to spell out important characteristics of the (cultural) entrepreneurs who have emerged throughout Africa since the 1990s and who upset narrow conceptions of the entrepreneur as either "industrial entrepreneur" or as engaging in purely economic ventures.

The first characteristic feature of "entrepreneurship" we wish to highlight is coordination, by which we refer to the capacity of individuals to bring in line business opportunities with the satisfaction of specific needs. Entrepreneurs bring together in innovative ways the means of production they have at their disposal with newly emerging business options and consumer demands and preferences.

For the second characteristic feature of the entrepreneurs under study, we draw inspiration from the economist Frank Knight's seminal distinction between "risk" and "uncertainty" in his *Risk, Uncertainty, and Profit* (1921). As Knight argued, in situations of risk, the outcomes are unknown but governed by (anticipated) probability distributions; in situations of uncertainty, in contrast, the outcomes are not known and their probability cannot be calculated.

From an anthropological point of view, "probability distributions" occur under historically and culturally specific conditions and therefore require empirical specification. We find the distinction between risk and uncertainty useful to highlight that certain personal qualities, such as an ability to make out opportunities and relate them to people's longings and concerns, are needed, but also a particular confidence to brave situations of uncertainty and turn them into successful ventures. It is these particular personal qualities that we want to highlight when studying entrepreneurs in Africa and how they deal with uncertainty and adverse conditions.

The distinctive feature of the entrepreneurs under study in this volume is that they draw on these convictions and particular personal qualities to initiate new ventures without guarantee of their success or failure. The fact that these entrepreneurs have these personal qualities helps us understand why these actors are ultimately successful under conditions of extreme adversity. The third feature regards timing and temporality: an entrepreneur's swift and timely response to new business opportunities. Fourthly, entrepreneurial initiatives often show a close affinity between "making business" and "self-making" in the sense of self-aggrandizement. But an entrepreneur works on his self-aggrandizement with a broader constituency in mind, a constituency variously composed of followers, admirers, clients, and supporters. Closely related to this point is a fifth characteristic: an entrepreneur's readiness for "social engineering", that is, for purposefully fostering social connections. The ultimate aim of such social engineering is not just to achieve personal advance and business success, but to remain or become a member of a broader social collective by redistributing some of one's own income and hence fostering webs of personal dependency. Rather than assuming a contrast between an actor's individualistic or socio-centric orientation (Grätz 2013), we insist that many entrepreneurial activities in contemporary Africa are motivated by at once personal and social ambitions. In our view, this explains why most of the entrepreneurs we describe not only draw (and depend on) a large following and simultaneously pursue a vision to change established social conventions.

Here, a word of caution seems apposite. We should be careful not to indiscriminately idealize these individuals as figures guided by an iconoclastic yet benevolent search for social and economic improvement. In fact, some of the entrepreneurs that have emerged in recent decades, often under conditions of lawlessness and disorder, are very sinister figures. A striking example is individuals in civil war-stricken DR Congo, who capitalize on the opportunities generated by a situation of general insecurity and unfettered physical coercion to exploit natural resources and to trade in ivory, gold, diamonds, coffee, cloth, and foodstuffs across the country and beyond national borders (MacGaffey 1987, 1998, 2002). Another example is the "*trafficeurs*" who snatch the new opportunities of transborder trafficking of economic and war refugees along the Mediterranean Sea. Even if entrepreneurial activities are instances of "inventiveness", they only sometimes yield socially and politically progressive consequences.

## CULTURAL ENTREPRENEURS IN AFRICA

By speaking of "cultural entrepreneurs", we highlight that these actors' knack for innovation shows itself in the realm of cultural inventiveness. Their initiatives reveal an extraordinary capacity to draw on and revise conventional cultural resources and symbolic repertoires and to turn them into new cultural forms.

Scholarly explorations of cultural entrepreneurship have referred almost exclusively to European examples, illustrating their long-standing existence in these societies.[7] The cultural entrepreneur of these studies shares certain features with the classical industrial entrepreneur (Mokyr 2014). Cultural entrepreneurs are individuals who combine innovative cultural productions with socially appreciated work in ways that grant them a reliable income and wider recognition, and secure them further support by sponsors and the advertisement industry. Very often, their work is located at the intersection between art and business, which affects the kind of art they produce (Wilson and Stokes 2002).

Although cultural entrepreneurs, in our understanding of the term (see above), have shaped African social and cultural life for a long time, in some places long before the onset of colonial rule (Röschenthaler 2011), their activities have not received systematic scholarly attention. The few studies which use the term "cultural entrepreneur" associate it with art, music, theatre, and the preservation of cultural heritage (Andrieu 2009). Our intention in this volume is at once more inclusive and more time-specific. We look at a broader range of cultural entrepreneurship, yet focus our attention on the period since the late 1980s in which, so we claim, Africans have witnessed an effervescence of new and diverse forms of cultural entrepreneurship.

Many of the entrepreneurial achievements that emerged in this period do not result from industrial production or trade capitalism but from initiatives in fields as diverse as media communication, entertainment, music production, tourism, religion, and education. Thus, in contrast to the successful trader or businessman that served as the classical model of successful (economic) entrepreneurship, the entrepreneurs covered in these chapters derive their success precisely from straddling the boundaries between cultural, political, and economic life. By combining various activities, strategies, and products, the entrepreneurs under study diversify their options and responses to the insecure and unpredictable conditions of their ventures.

Artists and musicians owe their popularity to their cultural creativity; in response to a social and normative context in which celebrity creates responsibility, they reinvest their pecuniary means in the cultural sector (Wane's chapter). Religious leaders rely on their rhetorical, organizational, and other skills to attract followers and become opinion leaders in the public arena (chapters by Sounaye, Hill, and Lauterbach; see Marshall-Fratani 2001; Schulz 2003, forthcoming; Schulz and Hinsch forthcoming; Haenni 2005; de Witte 2009; Sounaye 2012; Holder 2013). Other opinion leaders translate their visions of social and political reform into political (Socpa's chapter) or educational initiatives (O'Kane's chapter; André 2009), thereby capitalizing on new business opportunities in these domains; media entrepreneurs profit from a greater availability of audio and audiovisual recording technologies to secure new audiences and generate new consumer expectations (chapters by Ndenkop, Röschenthaler, Jedlowski and Böhme; see also Schulz 2007; Grätz 2013). Self-styled "experts" of local culture grasp tourists' scramble for an authentic Africa and thus valorize their "cultural heritage" (Scholze's chapter; see Comaroff and Comaroff 2009: 93). Other entrepreneurs devise new funeral services in response to people's wish to pay deceased family members their due respect (Lee's chapter). And yet others snatch income opportunities resulting from shadier consumer demands (chapters by Neubauer and Oldenburg). Cultural entrepreneurs also intervene in the development sector, where they found non-governmental organizations and become brokers in negotiating access to state and international financial support (Bierschenk and Olivier de Sardan 2000; Geschiere 2009).

While the chapters document very different career paths on which cultural entrepreneurs may embark, they also show that entrepreneurial success often comes about only after a series of trades learned, trajectories explored, and of (failed) business ventures. Although the domains of cultural inventiveness treated in this volume seem open and attractive to women and men, the number of successful male cultural entrepreneurs by far exceeds that of women. As some chapters suggest, this uneven representation is due, among other things, to men's and women's different chances to access credit and social support. Accordingly, women can become successful entrepreneurs only if they come up with specific strategies that ensure them social and financial support (chapters by Lauterbach and Hill). Women are also often under stronger social pressure to justify their ambitions vis-à-vis parents and in-laws, and also to defend their success in a male dominated sector (chapters by Böhme, Sounaye, Jedlowski). Some domains of entrepreneurial initiative show a clear gender-bias insofar as they either clearly privilege men (Scholze's chapter) or are only open to women (Neubauer's chapter).

## NOTES

1. We do not examine multinational companies or minority businesses of foreign or migrant entrepreneurs in Africa, or Africans abroad. Nor do we document the activities of entrepreneurial groups or "classes" (as has been proposed by Berman and Leys 1994 in an approach critical of a neoliberal development paradigm). Instead, we follow Tom Forrest's (1994: 1) call for sustained ethnographic descriptions of individual firms and for documenting life histories of entrepreneurs.
2. Schumpeter also contrasted the entrepreneur from the industrialist (as a shareholder), the president of a company, and finally, the company's manager (who avoids incalculable risks).
3. The Douala at the coast of Cameroon managed to remain entrepreneurial. They evolved from slave traders, despite colonial discouragement, to cocoa farmers and later on to property owners. During colonial times, large numbers of Bamileke left their homeland in the Cameroon Grassfields and developed economic dynamism all over the country, so that almost all successful enterprises in Cameroon are in the hands of Bamileke women and men (Warnier 1993, 1995).
4. See the studies on merchants in Burkina Faso (Şaul 1986), in Mali (Amselle 1977), in northern Nigeria (Grégoire (1986), in Congo (MacGaffey 1987), and in Togo (Cordonnier 1987); on Fulbe entrepreneurs in Sierra Leone (Jalloh (2002, 2007); and on prostitutes-cum-successful-property-owners in colonial Nairobi (Bujra 1975).
5. These authors do not clearly relate the terms "entrepreneur" and "businessman" to each other, drawing out parallels but also significant differences.
6. Banégas and Warnier (2001: 6–7) noted: "From Nouakchott to Pretoria, including Lagos, Kinshasa and Nairobi, the roles are distributed anew, and the political figures of the postcolonial era have now to share the public stage with

new figures such as the sportsman, the musician, the merchant, the religious leader, the diaspo, the feyman and the tcheb-tchap".
7. For example, creative professions (artists, architects, designers) have long since managed to produce without state support, and in the United States also important museums and theatres have emerged in the nineteenth century from private initiative (Dimaggio 1982).

## REFERENCES

Amos, Alcione. 2001. 'Afro-Brazilians in Togo: the case of the Olympio family, 1882–1945 (Les Afro-Brésiliens du Togo: l'exemple de la famille Olympio, 1882–1945)'. *Cahiers d'Études Africaines* 41, 162: 293–314.
Amselle, Jean-Loup. 1977. *Les negociants de la savane*. Paris: Éditions anthropos.
Amselle, Jean-Loup. 1987. 'Fontionnaires et hommes d'affaires au Mali'. *Politique africaine* 26: 63–72.
André, Géraldine. 2009. 'L'éducation comme entreprise. Légitimations marchande, civique et culturelle de l'école bilingue au Burkina Faso'. *Bulletin de l'APAD* 29–30: 39–54.
Andrieu, Sarah. 2009. 'Le métier d'entrepreneur culturel au Burkina Faso. Itinéraire et conditions de réussite d'un professionel du spectacle vivant'. *Bulletin de l'APAD* 29–30: 55–69.
Banégas, Richard and Jean-Pierre Warnier. 2001. 'Nouvelles Figures de la réussite et du pouvoir'. *Politique Africaine* 82 (special issue: Figures de la réussite et imaginaires politiques): 5–21.
Barber, Karin. 2007. *The Anthropology of Texts, Persons and Publics: Oral and Written Culture in Africa and Beyond*. Cambridge: Cambridge University Press.
Baumol, William. 1968. 'Entrepreneurship in economic theory'. *American Economic Review, Papers and Proceedings* 58, 2: 64–71.
Bayart, Jean-François. 1993. *The State in Africa: The Politics of the Belly*. New York: Polity Press.
Berman, Bruce and Colin Leys (eds). 1994. *African Capitalists in African Development*. Boulder and London: Lynne Rienner.
Bierschenk, Thomas and Olivier de Sardan (eds). 2000. *Courtier en developpement*. Paris: Karthala.
Brooks, George. 1997 [1976]. 'The *Signares* of Saint-Louis and Gorée: women entrepreneurs in eighteenth-century Senegal'. In: Robert Foster (ed.). *European and Non-European Societies, 1450–1800*. Vol. 2 (Religion, Class, Gender, Race). Aldershot: Ashgate, 19–44.
Bude, Heinz. 1997. 'Die Hoffnung auf den "unternehmerischen Unternehmer". Über wirtschaftliche Eliten'. *Universitas* 52: 850–858.
Bujra, Janet. 1975. 'Women "entrepreneurs" of early Nairobi'. *Canadian Journal of African Studies/Revue Canadienne des Études Africaines* 9, 2: 213–234.
Cantillon, Richard. 1775. *Essai sur la nature du commerce en général*. London.
Comaroff, Jean and John Comaroff. 2009. *Ethnicity, Inc*. Chicago: Chicago University Press.
Coquery-Vidrovitch, Cathérine (ed.). 1983. *Entreprises et Entrepreneurs en Afrique, XIXe-Xxe siècles*. Paris: Harmattan (2 Vols.).
Coquery-Vidrovitch, Catherine. 1994. *Les Africaines. Histoire des femmes d'Afrique noire du XIXe au XXe siècle*. Paris: Editions Desjonquères.
Coquery-Vidrovitch, Catherine. 2002. 'African business women in colonial and postcolonial Africa'. In: Alusine Jalloh and Toyin Falola (eds). *Black Business and Economic Power*. Rochester: University of Rochester Press, 199–211.

Cordonnier, Rita. 1987. *Femmes africaines et commerce: les revendeuses de tissu de la ville de Lomé.* Paris: l'Harmattan.

Denzer, LaRay. 1994. 'Yoruba women: a historiographical essay'. *International Journal of African Historical Studies* 27: 1–40.

De Witte, Marleen. 2009. 'Modes of binding, moments of bonding: mediating divine touch in Ghanaian Pentecostalism and traditionalism. In: Birgit Meyer (ed.). *Aesthetic Formations: Media, Religion and the Senses.* New York: Palgrave MacMillan, 183–205.

Dimaggio, Paul. 1982. 'Cultural entrepreneurship in nineteenth century Boston: the creation for an organizational base for High Culture in America'. *Media, Culture and Society* 4: 33–50.

Dumett, Raymond. 1983. 'African merchants of the Gold Coast, 1860–1905: dynamics of indigenous entrepreneurship'. *Comparative Studies in Society and History* 25: 661–693.

Ellis, Stephen and Yves-A. Fauré. 1995. *Entreprises et entrepreneurs africaines.* Paris: Karthala-Orstom.

Forrest, Tom. 1994. *The Advance of African Capital: The Growth of Nigerian Private Enterprise.* Charlottesville: University Press of Virginia.

Gandoulou, Justin-Daniel. 2008. 'Between Paris and Bacongo & Dandies in Bacongo'. In: Peter Geschiere, Birgit Meyer and Karin Barber (eds). *Readings in Modernity in Africa.* Bloomington: Indiana University Press, 194–205.

Geschiere, Peter. 2009. *Perils of Belonging: Autochtony, citizenship and Exclusion in Africa.* Chicago: University of Chicago Press.

Geschiere, Peter. 2013. *Witchcraft, Intimacy, and Trust.* Chicago: Chicago University Press.

Gihring, Thomas. 1984. 'Intraurban activity patterns among entrepreneurs in a West African setting'. *Geografiska Annaler* (Series B, Human Geography) 66, 1: 17–27.

Gikandi, Simon. 2010. 'Foreword. In praise of Afro-Optimism: towards a poetics of survival'. In: Makhulu, Anne-Maria, Beth A. Buggenhagen and Stephen Jackson (eds). *Hard Work, Hard Times: Global Volatility and African Subjectivities.* Berkeley: University of California Press, xi–xvi.

Gondola, Didier. 1999. 'Dream and drama: the search for elegance among Congolese youth'. *African Studies Review* 42, 1: 23–48.

Grätz, Tilo. 2013. 'New media entrepreneurs and changing styles of public communication in Africa: introduction'. *Journal of African Cultural Studies* 25, 1: 1–13.

Greenfield, Sidney and Arnold Strickon. 1981. 'A new paradigm for the study of entrepreneurship and social change'. *Economic Development and Cultural Change* 29, 3: 467–499.

Grégoire, Emmanuel. 1986. *Les Alhazi de Maradi. Histoire d'un groupe de riches marchands sahéliens.* Paris: ORSTOM.

Grégoire, Emmanuel. 1995. 'Commerçants et hommes d'affaires du Sahel'. In: Stephen Ellis and Yves-A. Fauré (eds). *Entreprises et entrepreneurs africaines.* Paris: Karthala-Orstom, 71–79.

Grégoire, Emmanuel and Pascal Labazée (eds). 1993. *Grands commercants d'Afrique de l'ouest.* Paris: Karthala.

Haenni, Patrick. 2005. *L'islam de marché. l'autre révolution conservatrice.* Paris: Seuil.

Hennings, Werner. 2007. ' "Big Men" or businessmen? The impact of global development on the nature of Samoan chieftainship'. *Sociologus* 57, 2: 157–175.

Holder, Gilles. 2013. 'Les Ançars de la république. La Bay'a au prisme de la laïcité malienne'. In: Gilles Holder and Moussa Sow (eds). *L'Afrique des laïcités. Etat, religion et pouvoirs au Sud du Sahara.* Tombouctou and Paris: Éditions Tombouctou and Institut de recherche pour le développement, 277–290.

Hopkins, Anthony. 1988. 'African entrepreneurship: an essay on the relevance of history to development economics'. *Genève-Afrique* 26, 2: 9–28.

Jalloh, Alusine. 2002. 'African Muslim business in post-colonial West Africa'. In: Alusine Jalloh and Toyin Falola (eds). *Black Business and Economic Power*. Rochester: Rochester Press, 311–330.

Jalloh, Alusine. 2007. 'Muslim Fula business elites and politics in Sierra Leone'. *African Economic History* 35: 89–104.

Jalloh, Alusine and Toyin Falola (eds). 2002. *Black Business and Economic Power*. Rochester: Rochester Press.

Kibora, Ludovic. 2012. 'The issue of the diaspora in Ouagadougou'. In: Hans Peter Hahn and Kristin Kastner (eds). *Urban Life-Worlds in Motion: African Perspectives*. Bielefeld: transcript, 173–186.

Knight, Frank. 1921. *Risk, Uncertainty, and Profit*. Boston: Hart, Schaffner & Marx.

Knutsen, Hege. 2003. 'Black entrepreneurs, local embeddedness and regional economic development in Northern Namibia'. *The Journal of Modern African Studies* 41, 4: 555–586.

Lentz, Carola. 1998. 'The chief, the mine captain and the politician: legitimating power in Northern Ghana'. *Africa* 68, 1: 46–67.

Lindstrom, Lamont. 1984. 'Doctor, lawyer, wise man, priest: big-men and knowledge in Melanesia'. *Man* 19: 291–309.

Lovejoy, Paul. 1980. *Caravans of Kola: The Hausa Kola Trade 1700–1900*. Zaria: Ahmadu Bello University Press.

MacGaffey, Janet. 1987. *Entrepreneurs and Parasites: The Struggle for Indigenous Capitalism in Zaire*. Cambridge and New York: Cambridge University Press.

MacGaffey, Janet. 1998: 'Creatively coping with crisis: entrepreneurs in the second economy of Zaire (The Democratic Republic of the Congo)'. In: Anita Spring and Barbara McDade (eds). *African Entrepreneurship: Theory and Reality*. Gainsville: University Press of Florida, 37–50.

MacGaffey, Janet. 2002. 'Survival, innovation and success in times of trouble: what prospects for Central African entreprenuers'. In: Alusine Jalloh and Toyin Falola (eds). *Black Business and Economic Power*. Rochester: University of Rochester Press, 331–346.

Malaquais, Dominique. 2001. 'Arts de feyre au Cameroun'. *Politique Africaine* 82: 101–118.

Marshall-Fratani, Ruth. 2001. 'Prospérité miraculeuse: les pasteurs pentecôtistes et l'argent de dieu au Nigeria'. *Politique africaine* 82: 24–44.

Martin, Keir. 2013. *The Death of the Big Men and the Rise of the Big Shots: Custom and Conflict in East New Britain*. Oxford: Berghan.

McDaniel, Bruce. 2005. 'A contemporary view of Joseph A. Schumpeter's theory of the entrepreneur'. *Journal of Economic Issues* 39, 2: 485–489.

Meagher, Kate. 2010. *Identity Economics: Social Networks & the Informal Economy in Nigeria*. Suffolk: James Currey.

Médard, Jean-François. 1992. 'Le Big-Man en Afrique: esquisse d'analyse du politician entrepreneur'. *L'Année sociologique* 42: 167–192.

Mokyr, Joel. 2014. 'Culture, institutions, and modern growth'. In: Sebastian Galiani and Itai Sened (eds). *Institutions, Property Rights, and Economic Growth*. Cambridge: Cambridge University Press, 151–191.

Ndjio, Basile. 2008. 'Evolué & feymen: old & new figures of modernity in Cameroon'. In: Peter Geschiere, Birgit Meyer and Karin Barber (eds). *Readings in Modernity in Africa*. Bloomington: Indiana University Press, 205–214.

Nwabughuogu, Anthony. 1982. 'From wealthy entrepreneurs to petty traders: the decline of African middlemen in Eastern Nigeria, 1900–1950'. *The Journal of African History* 23, 3: 365–379.

Olukoju, Ayodeji. 2002. 'The impact of British colonialism on the development of African Business in Colonial Nigeria'. In: Alusine Jalloh and Toyin Falola (eds). *Black Business and Economic Power*. Rochester: University of Rochester Press, 176–198.

Ould Ahmed Salem, Zekeria. 2001. ' "Tech-tchib" et compagnie. Lexique de la survie et figures de la réussite en Mauritanie'. *Politique Africaine* 28: 78–100.
Parker, Simon. 2009. *The Economics of Entrepreneurship*. Cambridge: Cambridge University Press.
Reynolds, Edward. 1974. 'The rise and fall of an African merchant class on the Gold Coast, 1830–1874'. *Cahiers d'Études Africaines* XIV, 54: 253–264.
Roitman, Janet. 2008. 'A successful life in the illegal realm: smugglers & road bandits in the Chad basin'. In: Peter Geschiere, Birgit Meyer and Karin Barber (eds). *Readings in Modernity in Africa*. Bloomington: Indiana University Press, 214–220.
Röschenthaler, Ute. 2011. *Purchasing Culture: The Dissemination of Associations in the Cross River region of Cameroon and Nigeria*. Trenton: Africa World Press.
Rowlands, Michael and Jean-Pierre Warnier. 1988. 'Sorcery, power and the modern state in Cameroon'. *Man* (N.S.) 23, 1: 188–232.
Sahlins, Marshall. 1963. 'Poor man, rich man, big-man, chief: political types in Polynesia and Melanesia'. *Comparative Studies in Society and History* 5: 285–303.
Sahlins, Marshall. 1972. *Stone Age Economics*. Chicago: Aldine de Gruyter.
Şaul, Mahir. 1986. 'Development of the grain market and merchants in Burkina Faso'. *The Journal of Modern African Studies* 24, 1: 27–153.
Schulz, Dorothea. 2001. *Perpetuating the Politics of Praise: Jeli Singers, Radios, and Political Mediation in Mali*. Cologne: Rüdiger Köppe.
Schulz, Dorothea. 2003. ' "Charisma and brotherhood" revisited: mass-mediated forms of spirituality in urban Mali'. *Journal of Religion in Africa* 33, 2:146–171.
Schulz, Dorothea. 2007. 'Evoking moral community, fragmenting Muslim discourse: sermon audio-recordings and the reconfiguration of public debate in Mali'. *Journal for Islamic Studies* 26: 39–71.
Schulz, Dorothea. 2014. 'Transmitting divine grace: on the materiality of charismatic mediation in Mali'. In: Heike Behrend, Anja Dreschke, and Martin Zillinger (eds). *Trance Mediums and New Media*. New York: Fordham Press.
Schulz, Dorothea and Winfried Hinsch. Forthcoming. 'Media technologies and the authentication of religious authority: a case study from Mali'. In: Felicitas Becker et al (eds). *Media, Religion and Marginality in Africa*. Columbus, Ohio: Ohio University Press.
Schumpeter, Josef. 1912. *Theorie der wirtschaftlichen Entwicklung*. Berlin: Duncker & Humblot (engl.: *The Theory of Economic Development*. Cambridge: Harvard University Press, 1934.)
Schumpeter, Josef. 1928. 'Unternehmer'. *Handwörterbuch der Staatswissenschaften* 8: 476–487.
Schumpeter, Josef. 1947. 'The creative response in economic history'. *Journal of Economic History* 7: 149–159.
Sounaye, Abdoulaye. 2012. 'God made me a preacher: youth and their appropriation of the Islamic sermon in Niamey, Niger'. Ph.D. thesis, Northwestern University, Dept. of Religious Studies.
Spring, Anita and Barbara McDade (eds). 1998. *African Entrepreneurship: Theory and Reality*. Gainesville: University Press of Florida.
Stewart, Alex. 1990. 'The Bigman metaphor for entrepreneurship: a library tale with morals on alternatives for further research'. *Organization Science* 1, 2: 143–159.
Sykes, Karen. 2007. 'The moral grounds of critique: between possessive individuals, entrepreneurs and Big Men in New Ireland'. *Anthropological Forum* 17, 3: 255–268.
Taylor, Scott. 2012. *Globalization and the Cultures of Business in Africa: From Patrimonialism to Profit*. Bloomington: Indiana University Press.
Trapido, Joseph. 2011. 'The political economy of migration and reputation in Kinshasa'. *Africa* 81, 2: 204–225.

Warnier, Jean-Pierre. 1993. *L'esprit d'entreprise au Cameroun*. Paris: Karthala.
Warnier, Jean-Pierre. 1995. 'Trois générations d'entrepreneurs bamiléké (Cameroun)'. In: Stephen Ellis and Yves-A. Fauré (eds). *Entreprises et entrepreneurs africaines*. Paris: Karthala-Orstom, 63–70.
Waterman, Christopher. 1990. *Juju: A Social History and Ethnography of an African Popular Music*. Chicago: Chicago University Press.
Wilson, Nicolas and David Stokes. 2002. 'Cultural entrepreneurs and creating exchange'. *Journal of Research in Marketing & Entrepreneurship* 4, 2: 37–52.

# Part I
# Making Moral Communities

# 2 Religious Entrepreneurs in Ghana

*Karen Lauterbach*

This chapter is concerned with the relationship between entrepreneurship and religion.[1] It examines the making of Pentecostal churches and pastoral careers as a form of entrepreneurship and discusses what the religious dimension adds to our understanding of how entrepreneurship unfolds in Africa today. The chapter analyzes in particular how striving for and attaining social and economic aspirations can be fulfilled through a pastoral career in Pentecostal churches in Ghana. What is remarkable is that young men and women are able to "become someone" in society, achieve status, and accumulate wealth through the making of pastoral careers in a general context where the possibilities for social climbing are constrained.

The argument is that there is a strong link between religious entrepreneurship and social mobility, and that religious entrepreneurs draw on local categories of status and wealth that are recognized widely in society. Pastors are entrepreneurial when making their careers, and at the same time they depend on relations with senior people (e.g., through relations of apprenticeship). The point is that becoming a pastor is not only about creating a church or making a career, but also about how this form of entrepreneurship is recognized and how it resonates with other forms of attaining social status and ascending social hierarchies. I am concerned with how pastorship is created as a form of entrepreneurship and with how becoming a pastor is a way to "become someone" in society.

Pastoral career-making involves processes of invention and creativity as well as processes of imitation and reproduction. Pentecostal pastors are creative when establishing their careers and founding new churches. They transcend social hierarchies (age-based, professional), invent new ways of being pastors, adapt the message of the Bible to the situation of their members (e.g., through their strong focus on success and wealth), create rules, and seek to establish a loyal church membership. Many also invest resources acquired through other activities in the making of new churches. Pentecostal pastors are particularly creative in their use of various media and when staging themselves as *new figures of success* (Banégas and Warnier 2001). That said, pastors also depend on social relations when constructing their careers, becoming involved in relations of apprenticeship and drawing on the legitimacy and charisma of senior pastors. They also draw on the past in the sense that the religious categories they invoke resonate within an already existing frame of reference.

Studies of entrepreneurs and entrepreneurship in Africa have traditionally focused on the economic sector (both formal and informal) (e.g., Hart 1970; Jalloh 2007; MacGaffey 2002). Some have emphasized the role of social relations, kinship, and migration networks, as well as traditional institutions in the development of new forms of capital accumulation. Anthropological studies have drawn attention to forms of entrepreneurship that unfold in cultural, social, and political spheres and outside the business sector itself (Andrieu 2009; Banégas and Warnier 2001; Fourchard, Mary, and Otayek 2005).

In this literature, however, entrepreneurship as a concept often remains undefined and implicit. The term is often used in cases where people or activities are unconventional or break with social norms. Also, entrepreneurship is thought of as occurring in times of crises and as being associated with a specific set of values. Hence, it is seen as the capacity to survive and even accumulate capital in such circumstances (MacGaffey 2002: 332; Saint-Lary 2009).

My approach to entrepreneurship lies within the broad anthropological understanding of the term. I take into consideration both recent expressions of entrepreneurship, but also acknowledge how these practices and ideas recapitulate already existing social categories, for instance the accumulation and redistribution of wealth. I see this approach as aligned with studies of social aspiration and social innovation (Barber 2006). I see creativity and inventiveness as part of social life more broadly, and not, as is commonly assumed, as based on individualism and contexts of crises. I am inspired by the approach of Ingold and Hallam (2007) on creativity and cultural improvisation.[2] They question the understanding of creativity as necessarily linked to the production of something new (as opposed to the reproduction and adaptation of something already existing) and write:

> Anthropology can best contribute to debates around creativity by challenging—rather than reproducing—the polarity between novelty and convention, or between the innovative dynamic of the present and the traditionalism of the past, that has long formed such a powerful undercurrent to the discourses of modernity. (Ingold and Hallam 2007: 2)

They suggest that improvisation as a concept (rather than innovation) better reflects the attempt to transcend the dichotomy between novelty and tradition, because improvisation alludes to the processes of cultural and social adaptation and remaking (which are also creative processes), whereas the term innovation is concerned with new products and end-results (Ingold and Hallam 2007).[3] They emphasize that creativity is relational, and challenge the idea of creativity as an individual skill.

This line of thinking fits well with the overall argument of this chapter, namely that Pentecostal pastors are making careers and churches in a way that echoes the past and has significance within a wider social field. A number of scholars have emphasized the importance of social networks when engaging in entrepreneurial activities. MacGaffey (2002: 342), for instance, stresses the importance of personal relationships and kin obligations for the success of individual entrepreneurs in retail trade. However, the above point is different and further-reaching, as it alludes not only to how entrepreneurial practices are carried out, but also to the more substantial issue of what creativity means and how it comes about. "Relational" in the present case refers both to the importance of social relationships in carrying out certain activities and to the acknowledgement of the role of the social surroundings in making sense of these practices and the ideas that underpin them.

In the rest of the chapter, I will briefly discuss the link between entrepreneurship and religion, and present the Ghanaian context in particular with regard to studies of entrepreneurship and a changing religious landscape. I will focus more specifically on an analysis of the making of Pentecostal pastoral careers and churches, and pastorship as a field of investment.

## ENTREPRENEURSHIP, ETHICS, AND RELIGION

The affinity between religion and economic strategies and rationalities is of central concern. The debate around this question is influenced by Weber's work on the protestant ethic and the rise of capitalism in Europe (Weber 2001 [1930]). Weber took interest in how religious ideas work in conjunction with a specific sociopolitical context in a way that leads to social transformation (Lambek 2002: 51). In an African context, the rapid growth of Pentecostalism has sparked renewed interest in this question (e.g., Comaroff and Comaroff 2003; Gifford and Nogueira-Godsey 2011; Meagher 2009; Meyer 2004). One strand of this literature understands the rise of the neo-Pentecostal movement as a response to the changing nature of capitalism and to the spread of a neoliberal ethic. The Comaroffs' writing on the conjuncture between the rise of millennial capitalism and the increasing occurrence of occult economies is an example of this. Their main argument lies in seeing a new protestant ethic as a response to a new spirit of capitalism where spiritual rewards come instantly and take the form of material wealth (2003). This frame of explanation accentuates the irrational and the occult as responses to life conditions marked by lack, loss, and disempowerment as well as to forces of global capitalism. And, as Coleman points out, this line of analysis seeks rational explanations as to *why* rather than trying to understand "how Faith practices articulate the connections between 'religious' and 'economic' spheres of activity" (2011: 33).

In her work on Pentecostalism in Nigeria, Marshall takes religion "as a site of action, invested in and appropriated by believers" (2009: 22), thus not viewing the Pentecostal movement as a response. However, when analyzing ethics (the prosperity doctrine), she tends to see the Pentecostal ethic as a system of ideas that is isolated from other ideological frameworks and hence to dismiss its historical appropriation and embeddedness. On a different note, Meagher draws attention to the Nigerian informal economy, where "religious movements have given rise to distinctly Weberian 'modernising tendencies'" (2009: 420). She also argues that these tendencies, to some degree, are undermined by religious entrepreneurs who seek to maximize their own benefit. By doing so, the Weberian rationalities and modernizing tendencies are diminished. Whereas Meagher is concerned with the role of religion in the economic sector itself, I am more preoccupied with the social and economic processes taking place in the religious sector.

What I find useful about a Weberian approach with regard to entrepreneurship and religion in Africa is not so much his thesis that there is an affinity between a specific protestant ethic and capitalist economic behavior, but rather the adoption of a more open and explorative approach with respect to how certain sets of ideas and values become effective forces in history and how they are drawn upon in relation to social and economic activities. I am therefore not interested in discussing whether a certain set of religious ideas is conducive to economic development or constitutes responses to new forms of capitalism. I am interested in looking into how pastoral career-making draws on local understandings of wealth and status and in particular on the processes of improvisation that are part of this.

## THE GHANAIAN CONTEXT

There is an important body of scholarship on entrepreneurs and strategies of capital accumulation in a Ghanaian context. Hart (1970, 1973) has drawn attention to the group of informal small-scale entrepreneurs. He points out that small-scale entrepreneurs contribute substantially to the Ghanaian economy, but also that they cannot be perceived as typical businessmen. They are rather "anyone who controls the management of capital which he has invested in some enterprise in order to realize profit" (Hart 1970: 107). Often these entrepreneurs are "part-time entrepreneurs", meaning that they have very diversified interests and are involved in a number of activities at the same time, for example, a university lecturer investing in a small business. What is interesting about this perspective is that the focus is on activities rather than on a specific category of people, and that entrepreneurial activities are not seen as restricted to one field, but that they criss-cross several fields of activities.

In her earlier study of migrant cocoa-farmers, Hill shows how the cocoa-farmers are "remarkably responsive to economic incentives" (1997 [1963]: 3) and "capitalist" in the sense that they pursue economic interests and the accumulation of capital. Moreover, she underlines that both ideas and institutions were flexible and adapted to the economic situation. As Austin points out in the introduction to a reprint of Hill's classic book: "her usage [of the term capitalist] was close to a common understanding of the word 'entrepreneur': connoting risk-taking, long-sighted, and innovative (at least in adoptive and adaptive senses: the exotic crop, the modified institutions)" (Austin 1997: xviii). Likewise, Hill's use of the term "capitalist" alludes to specific values and economic rational behavior and not to specific structural relations between employer and employee (1997). What is useful about Hill's approach for the present analysis is the insistence on existing institutions as flexible and conducive to undertaking entrepreneurial activities.

Another historic group of entrepreneurs were the so-called *akonkofoɔ* (businessmen in the early colonial period), who challenged prevailing ideas and norms on the consumption and recognition of wealth in Asante[4] (Arhin 1976/77, 1986). In pre-colonial Asante, there was strict social control on the redistribution and consumption of wealth. The Asante state controlled accumulation and access to wealth (McCaskie 1995). Wealth was considered to be for the benefit of the community rather than of the individual. A wealthy person's ability to reach equilibrium between accumulating for himself and the community was central in terms of legitimizing the wealth and the authority that followed on being a "Big Man" (ɔbirɛmpɔn) (McCaskie 1983). In the beginning of the twentieth century, with a changing economic context due to the introduction of a cash-based economy and a boom in commercial cocoa production, the *akonkofoɔ* managed to escape the moral constraints attached to accumulating wealth (McCaskie 1986, 2000). They insisted on accumulation for personal consumption and were against the taxes that had been imposed by the Asante state. Moreover, they were modern versions of the pre-colonial Big Man in the sense that they adapted the social norms attached to the social position of being a Big Man. Wealth was still a sign of social standing, and the public display of it was a central element in the recognition of this position (McCaskie 1986).

Allman and Parker (2005) touch upon the link between religion and entrepreneurism in their work on *Tongnaab* (a god and ancestor shrine from northeastern Ghana). They show how this shrine was taken from the Northern Territories to colonial Asante and the Gold Coast by "ritual entrepreneurs". They emphasize the flexibility of the shrine and how it was adapted to new regional contexts. The religious entrepreneurs offered protection against witchcraft, which was in increasing demand in times of growing economic activities, easier access to wealth, and social instability (due to colonialization) (2005: 128–129). Rituals for spiritual protection were commercialized, based on the understanding that people needed protection against witchcraft (*bayi*). However, the initiators of anti-witchcraft cults were not the only religious entrepreneurs in colonial times. There were a number of prophets (such as Sampson Oppong and Wade Harris) who travelled around the country and succeeded in converting many people to the established Christian churches, again with the underlying aim of providing protection against witchcraft. As Allman and Parker underline, "The spectrum of innovative ritual responses to the threat of *bayi* ranged from exotic savannah deities through growing numbers of itinerant Christian preachers and indigenous prophetic churches" (2005: 136).

More recently, accumulation of wealth, entrepreneurship, and religion have been linked to the fast-growing Pentecostal sector within Ghanaian Christianity. In Ghana, as well as in other African countries, Pentecostalism has grown significantly over the last three decades, especially the so-called neo-Pentecostal churches.[5] This particular strand of Protestant Christianity has developed from a missionary import that valued ascetics and a strong belief in the afterlife to its more recent version as independent churches that focus much more on success and wealth in this life (Asamoah-Gyadu 2005a; Gifford 2004; Maxwell 2006; Meyer 2004). These churches include both a huge number of small and independent churches, as well as a number of so-called mega-churches that in many ways resemble large business corporations.

One of the characteristics of the neo-Pentecostal churches is their apparent flat and flexible organizational structure that is little formalized and where church members and lay people have easy access to positions of responsibility and leadership. This has been termed "the democratization of charisma", which implies that ordinary church members are understood to have direct access to God without mediation by a pastor (Asamoah-Gyadu 2005a). At the same time, though, these churches are organized around one pastor (founder and leader) who has a number of junior pastors below him or her. In Ghana they are commonly known as "one-man churches", and the influence, status, and spiritual power of these pastors is one of the most dominant features of the neo-Pentecostal churches (Gifford 2004; Maxwell 2006; Meyer 2005). In many instances, the name of a pastor is a stronger brand than the name of a church, indicating that the pastor represents a personification of spiritual power. It is through contact (both physical—by the laying-on of hands—and social) that the pastor mediates spiritual power. Spiritual power is believed to be essential for obtaining success, for example, in doing business, achieving education, and being protected from evil forces. This role as a mediator between the spiritual and the material world gives the pastor a powerful position in society (Asamoah-Gyadu 2005b). There are parallels between the role played by prophets in the spiritual churches, traditional diviners, and the neo-Pentecostal pastors. In their role as religious experts they draw on their access to the divine in the provision of religious services (Asamoah-Gyadu 2005b). More generally, Christianity has played a huge social and cultural role in southern Ghana and in Asante since the beginning of the twentieth century. This aspect of the Ghanaian context has obviously also prepared the ground for the proliferation of Pentecostal churches and pastors.

Pastoral careers have to be understood in relation to the historical role of religious entrepreneurs and experts, but also in the context of the more recent socioeconomic situation. The rise of many neo-Pentecostal churches occurred at a time of economic decline and political instability (in the 1980s). During the 1990s, Ghana underwent structural adjustment programs and a liberalization of the economy. This meant a decline in employment opportunities in the public sector and consequently also access to a common way to achieve social mobility (which had long been associated with education, diplomas, and employment as a civil servant) (Osei 2004). At the same time, and with the more open and plural public sphere, new ways of social ascension were emerging. Founding a church thus represents a new way of becoming important in society, or becoming a new figure of success, as Banégas and Warnier (2001) have pointed out. Pastors, movie stars, football players, and musicians are new types of popular leaders that accumulate wealth and gain power in ways that are different from the more traditional and well-established power structures (Marshall-Fratani 2001: 27).

## PASTORSHIP AS ENTREPRENEURSHIP

The most well-known Ghanaian Pentecostal pastors (such as Mensa Otabil, Nicholas Duncan Williams, and Dag Heward-Mills) are known as charismatic, flamboyant, rich, influential, and highly visible in public space (De Witte 2003; Gifford 2004). In addition to these top pastors, there is a large group of pastors who are either associate pastors (serving one of the big pastors) or founders of smaller independent neo-Pentecostal churches. This group of pastors can be compared to other middle-level social actors, a "mobile, entrepreneurial, urban-oriented, aspiring strata" (Barber 2000: 2). In this chapter, I focus on this level of entrepreneurial pastors that aspire to religious leadership.[6] They create their pastoral careers through personal relations, by claiming access to spiritual power, and through the creation of new churches. The way in which they do this is entrepreneurial, the term understood as reinventing, adapting, and imitating already existing practices and cultural categories.[7] These up-and-coming pastors aim, moreover, to attain more status; they are socially mobile and invest dedication and resources to achieve their ambitions (Lauterbach 2010). With regard to their background or family relations, they do not belong to the highly educated elite, nor do they occupy political power positions within their home communities or extended families. Many have attended primary and secondary school and some qualify as "early school leavers". Some of the pastors have been involved in small business activities (shops, trading) and some have been employed as, for example, teachers and accountants, but have left these careers to become full-time pastors (cf. below). It should be noted, however, that not all pastors aspire to religious leadership. Some pastors work as part-time or associate pastors and pursue other pathways to generate income (e.g., farming, doing business, and education). Still, the status of pastor conveys standing and recognition.

When doing fieldwork among smaller neo-Pentecostal churches in Kumasi, I was astonished by the enthusiasm and eagerness with which young pastors created new churches. Many had been part of larger churches and had served under a senior pastor. But they all had ambitions of creating their own churches and of becoming a "Big Man of God". Some of these young people had little financial means, but they still managed to make churches in classrooms, garages, and storerooms. Some invested money from business activities, some got support from family members, and others relied on acquaintances abroad and whatever they could collect from a few church members. Their paths were not straightforward. They explored different ways of becoming a pastor, belonged temporarily to several churches, moved in and out of churches, some failed, and some eventually managed to create a church of their own. They were flexible and creative in their endeavor to become pastors.

At the same time, these pastors were largely involved in and dependent upon relationships with senior pastors and family members when establishing their careers. This dependency was about getting both material and moral support, but the social relations also served as a form of recognition of their status as pastor. In this way, there was a tension between autonomy (creating one's own church and career) and dependency (relying on others for support and respect) (Le Meur 2008).

Besides, as indicated in the introductory part of this chapter, pastors engage in processes of imitation and reproduction. They do this in two senses. First, they build on and reformulate already existing social norms and ideas that have a specific resonance in Asante, for example, concerning wealth, power, and the role of religious leaders. When staging themselves as important "men of God", they draw on a historic understanding of religious experts as persons that mediate between the physical and the spiritual worlds. Also, while accumulating wealth and referring to wealth in church services, they build on a broad understanding of wealth that makes sense in that particular context. In other words, when creating new institutions and new positions of power and status, they also introduce and rephrase existing understandings of what it means "to become someone" in society. This refers to Ingold and Hallam's (2007) point that creativity is not only a process of creating something novel, but also of improvisation. Second, pastors copy what other pastors do: how they comport themselves, how they preach, and how they present themselves publicly. As one pastor explained: "even the way I talk, the way I relate to people, the way I do my things, if you just see him [the senior pastor] you will see a bit of him in me".[8] Several pastors explained how people thought they resembled a famous pastor in the way they preached. This is seen as a sign of recognition and approval of their status.

## THE CREATION OF PASTORAL CAREERS AND NEW CHURCHES

Pastors' ambitions to start their own churches or engage in pastoral careers are often triggered and explained by a vision, a dream, or a calling from God. It is seen as a path in life, a destiny which is predetermined and cannot be refused—refusing it is understood as something that will cause failure in life. A pastoral calling is confirmed by others, and this is a way to prove the genuineness of the calling to the social milieu. A female pastor explains how her call was foreseen by someone else and thereby legitimated:

> The wife of my head pastor had a vision in 1996 about me. I owned a provision shop with things like soap. . . . People were coming in their numbers. This means I had something good to offer people. After I was told the vision my husband encouraged me to go to the Bible school to know more about God and how to deal with people.[9]

The fact that it is the wife of the head pastor who had the vision is important, as it serves as an acknowledgement of the calling by someone in a high position. It is also interesting that a link is made between being able to perform materially and being able to perform spiritually. This pastor had been successful in her business and this success is perceived as being transferable to her pastoral work. This is explained by her knowledge and skills of how to engage with people and not because she possesses special economic skills or follows a certain economic rationale. She knows the value of personal relationships and "had something good to offer people", as she says. Many pastors refer to the value of social relationships and networks in the making of their careers, and some argue that social relationships are more important than money. In this sense wealth is understood in a broad sense and includes more than money.

Another important aspect of how younger people become engaged in pastoral careers is the prospect of how fast they can rise in the hierarchy and become recognized as pastors. The smaller and more informal the churches are, the easier it is for aspiring pastors to fulfil their ambitions of becoming someone. There are two common trajectories. Some young pastors start out by serving under a senior pastor and then move away when they are mature enough to start a church on their own. Others start by joining or forming more informal groups (fellowships or prayer groups) or join newly started churches that do not have a strong leadership. This provides the possibility of obtaining a leadership position at an early stage in their careers. Within the more traditional institutions (family, chieftaincy), there is a strong age-based hierarchy where one rises, for instance, through attaining a certain life stage.

One pastor narrates his pastoral calling and why he left the church of which he was a member:

> It was something I never thought of. It was a sudden thing. I just felt the call deep within me. It tormented me for a long time, but I was stubborn because I didn't like it. The issue is that I didn't like my church, I liked the fellowship more. My church did not encourage young pastors or should I say I could not worship God the way I wanted in the church. They were old-fashioned. They weren't active. At the fellowship I was a pastor, but in my church I was recognized as a member.[10]

This pastor clearly distinguishes between being recognized as a pastor and being seen as a church member. Junior pastors working in more well-established churches would often complain that they are not allowed to preach and that the roles they are playing are "backstage" as compared to the senior pastor. They could, for instance, be responsible for certain activities, for leading prayers, and for accompanying the head pastor on trips. But they would rarely be given the responsibility of preaching, even if the head pastor was travelling. This indicates that preaching is the stage at which to prove oneself, to prove charisma, to show spiritual power, to prove knowledge of the word of God, and to prove the ability to interact strongly with the church membership: in other words, preaching is the core of being a "Big Man of God".

One pastor, who was originally a part-time pastor in the Methodist church, broke away to establish a church on his own. He explains this act both by visions indicating that he had to move, but also, more indirectly, by internal problems in the church. He accounts:

> I went to school, finished the A level and then I had the calling to enter into full-time ministry. Initially we were with the Methodist church, but at a point we had a vision to do something. . . . I decided to establish this church two years ago. We had some problems in the Methodist church, but it didn't move me to leave. We were praying for the Lord's direction. Through some prophecies and dreams I put it all together and saw the direction so I had to leave. . . . It was just some internal wrangling. It was like the pastor who came in was a new pastor and when he came he took some group of the leader, so we were divided. Some with him and others against him. It brought a lot of controversies. But really that wasn't why I left. Maybe it was a stepping stone. It made us to think and pray to God for another direction and by his grace we were led to this place.[11]

To move away involves leaving a well-established structure, finding a building, creating a new church membership, as well as making and setting up rules and institutional practices. Newly established pastors move away from their senior pastors in order to affirm their positions as "men of God", and this is often their only possibility for growing and reaching the level of being a "Big Man".

To break away involves institutional separation and a remaking of the relationship between junior and senior pastor. An apprenticeship relation that is clearly hierarchical is transformed into one of more mutual recognition and less dependency. However, younger pastors still recognize the pastors who trained them as their "spiritual fathers". In this way they draw on their legitimacy and at the same time contribute to affirming the senior pastors' position of spiritual and social authority. There is awareness from the senior pastors that up-and-coming pastors might pose a challenge to their positions. One of the pastors referred to was incited to start a church of his own (a branch church of the mother church) by his senior pastor. He explains:

> I think I went with him [senior pastor] and have been with him for about fifteen years. He then told me to pray if this was where I wanted to be so that I can get a place to start my ministry, I can go and do it, but I said I don't want to do it because I normally travel outside and come back. But he thought I was matured enough to handle a group and that there was no need to continue to stay under him, since that will be underutilizing my potential, so I should move out. So I and some few people were given the opportunity to start our ministry. So I came here to start mine. It was not easy.[12]

The senior pastor, who is the founder of one of Kumasi's biggest neo-Pentecostal churches and from a Kumasi elite family, had himself followed the same trajectory. He had trained and been an apprentice under another well-established pastor, then came to a point where he was seen by others as posing a threat to the power position of the pastor in charge. He left and created a church on his own, starting in a canteen with only nineteen members.[13]

Establishing a new church is seen as a necessary step in the trajectory of a pastoral career. It is associated with hard work and little income in the early phases. But, as mentioned earlier, it is a way for young people to achieve social aspirations and status. Drawing on the insights of Ingold and Hallam (2007), I argue that the establishment of new churches and pastoral careers is not only a matter of creating new institutions, breaking social bonds, and exploiting opportunities for individual profit-making. There are concurrently processes of imitation and improvisation at stake, for example, with regard to how social positions are recognized and legitimated and related to this the accumulation and redistribution of wealth.

This leads me to discuss how wealth is understood in this context. In the literature, the neo-Pentecostal churches are perceived as having a strong focus on money and prosperity (Gifford 2004; Meyer 1998). My argument is that it is not only the accumulation of money that is important, but the link between wealth (in a broad sense), status, and power. Pastors draw upon the historical meaning of these concepts and improvise and adapt these to new religious and socioeconomic contexts.

## PASTORSHIP AS INVESTMENT

Contrary to the picture often painted (in Ghanaian public debate and in some academic work) of pastors as being abundantly rich and accumulating capital for individual consumption, the young pastors that this chapter deals with often had little income and what they had was rarely generated from their work as pastors. At such an early stage in their careers, they were rather investing capital themselves into setting up churches or making themselves visible as pastors in the public sphere (e.g., being on radio or television, appearing on banners, and publishing books). They would use income from other sources when founding churches. As mentioned above, a young pastor created a church on his senior pastor's initiative. He explains how he managed to get finances for setting up the church:

> And then I started building this. Normally, the kinds of people I have are new converts, people who are students, people who are not working. So I had the opportunity with my background, because I go to London most of the time. I also go to Germany to go and do some programs. So when I come [back to Ghana] I use the money I have to pay for this and start the building. Because people naturally haven't enough to give. Now, people are coming gradually, but they are not financially strong. So I thought well, every money I get I will bring it in. Sometimes I bring 3,000 euro, 2,000 euro, 2,000 pounds, 1,000 pounds and just put it in. That's why we have got this far. And then I have been buying instruments. Generally, it is a cost, but if you put in your money and God bless you, things work out.[14]

This pastor's way of rationalizing builds on the principle of "giving and receiving" that is part of the neo-Pentecostal ideology (Asamoah-Gyadu 2005a; Maxwell 2006: 149). One has to plant a seed (invest money to serve God) in order to harvest (receive resources and success in return, which is seen as God's blessing). In this way of thinking, founding a church is seen as an investment. Pastors bring in various resources, construct buildings, buy instruments, and get church members. The members will eventually pay tithes and other offerings (in cash) and the investment will bear fruit. Not all pastors have capital to invest in building churches; they instead receive financial and material contributions from family members, friends, or church members living abroad. Some would be involved in other activities (e.g., poultry farming, running a canteen, running a print and photo copy shop) to generate income.

Some pastors had been accountants, shopkeepers, or civil servants before they became pastors. They abandoned these apparently attractive employments to become pastors, which implied risk-taking and a less stable income. Their strategy was instead to diversify their sources of income. They would generate money through preaching in other churches and by doing "programs" (preaching in churches at special events), starting a Bible school, and some would receive "chop money"[15] from church members that they had prayed for or had helped in any other way.

These relations of giving (investing) and receiving constitute a form of spiritual economy that is based on reciprocity, but also on ideas of rewards from God. This parallels the classical anthropological literature on gift-giving, where religious beliefs underpin gift-giving relations (Mauss 1954). In the cases presented in this chapter, it is not only the object that is being exchanged that has a religious meaning, but also the reciprocal relations of exchange themselves. These, for instance, can involve a religious leader, a church member, and God. This implies that it is not only a relation of exchange between two parties (based on social obligations), but one that also involves God. This means that a return comes not necessarily from the one who receives, but can come from God and be perceived as a reward or a blessing.

The central point is that pastoral career-making is not only an investment in financial terms. It is also an investment in one's status as pastor or religious expert. Becoming a pastor also means attaining social status that is recognized not only by members in church, but more widely in society, for example, by friends and family members. Present day Pentecostal pastors draw upon and combine features of two historic figures: the religious expert and the Big Man. On the one hand, they play the role of the religious expert, mediating between the spiritual and the material worlds, and are in this way key to people's success in life. They have the ability to bring about change and to provide protection. They possess the knowledge of the word of God, and knowledge is historically linked to power (Akyeampong and Obeng 1995). Moreover, pastors follow the model of the Big Man as they seek to attain wealth (understood in a broad sense as time, people, and money). They are concerned with how this wealth is redistributed, perceived by others, and with displaying wealth publicly (Lauterbach 2006).

## CONCLUSION

This chapter has analyzed the making of pastorship and pastoral careers as a form of entrepreneurship. I have argued that religious entrepreneurship is best understood as an intersection between changing socioeconomic circumstances and already existing ideas and practices. By seeing entrepreneurship as relational processes of improvisation rather than merely as the invention of something new, I argue that religious entrepreneurship and particularly the making of pastoral careers resonates with the past. It is a possibility of realizing aspirations and attaining social mobility that is recognized in society because it builds on and readapts (improvises) already existing ideas around being a Big Man and a religious expert.

Although the making of pastoral careers is not directly linked to economic enterprise per se, there are connections between the religious and economic spheres that can shed new light on the diverse ways in which entrepreneurship unfolds in Africa. This touches upon our interpretation of a religious ethic and the affinity with economic practices. My analysis builds on an understanding of this relationship as open and historically/

contextually defined, rather than religious ethics (or the prosperity doctrine) as a response to a certain moment in time. In this way my approach is different from that taken by, for example, the Comaroffs, but also, although in a different way, from the analytical frame proposed by Marshall. Although she emphasizes religion as a site of action that has a particular meaning for believers, her analysis comes to portray Pentecostal ethics as a system in itself and hence as isolated from other social spheres that inform ethics. This implies that the intersection between the religious and economic spheres stands out as being more schematic and less adaptive. Meagher on the other hand proposes an analysis that takes its point of departure in asking a more open question of how the economic and religious spheres influence each other and then studies, in a way more empirically informed, how a Protestant ethic is expressed.

In my analysis of pastorship as entrepreneurship, I argue that the making of pastoral careers involves both establishing new institutions and seeing the church as an area of investment, and at the same time engaging in relations of apprenticeship and dependency. In their striving for social mobility, pastors break away from senior pastors because these are seen as a hindrance to opportunities for growth. However, after establishing a new church and moving onwards in their pastoral careers, there is still a need to maintain and recreate bonds of support and dependency with senior people. This is done in a flexible way that both permits the young pastors to grow and also confers some of the credibility of senior people on the young pastors. It is a reinvention and transformation of junior-senior relationships.

Pastors draw on various social networks and are creative in the sense that they set up new churches and establish themselves as leaders by bringing in whatever resources they have at their disposal. They are often involved in several activities to gain resources to invest in their pastoral careers. Pastorship is both a way to attain social mobility and something pastors invest in, but it is moreover a life trajectory or destiny that one cannot refuse. Moreover, the investment is perceived as a gift to God and is part of a spiritual economy. Pastorship differs from other forms of economic engagement, as it involves the spiritual realm and forces that are not seen by the pastors as negotiable in the same sense as is being part of a social or economic network.

It is in particular the apparent eagerness and ease with which pastors create new churches and thereby new sources of income that make one think of Pentecostal pastors as entrepreneurial. But, as the analysis has shown, making pastoral careers is not only about following certain economic values or rationales, but also about knowledge and adaptation of social rules and conventions that are historically embedded in Asante society. Pastors combine forms of entrepreneurial and economic strategies (e.g., investment in churches) with their knowledge of and engagement in social practices so that their pastoral activities make sense in a broader social setting. Pastors are acknowledged as religious experts not only in their churches, but also in their social surroundings. Therefore the entrepreneurial dynamic lies not only in the relation between pastors and their members, but also more widely with regard to the role religious entrepreneurs play in society and the legitimacy and status with which they are ascribed. Becoming a Pentecostal pastor in present-day Ghana is therefore a way to "become someone" in society that improvises and remakes the historic figures of the religious expert and the Big Man.

## NOTES

1. The chapter is based on work for my Ph.D. dissertation (Lauterbach 2008). Fieldwork was conducted in Denmark and Ghana during 2004 and 2005. The material collected consists of 87 interviews with pastors, their family members, and church members, audiovisual material, and participation in various church activities. Additional information was obtained subsequently through phone conversations and e-mails. The ethnographic present used in the text refers to the period of fieldwork. I would like to thank the Danish Council for Development Research and The Nordic Africa Institute for financing fieldwork. The usual disclaimers apply.
2. Although the authors do not deal specifically with entrepreneurship, their unpacking of the concepts of creativity and improvisation is relevant for the present chapter, as creativity is thought of as a central characteristic of entrepreneurship.
3. Ingold and Hallam have an interesting point on innovation (as a concept) being a backward reading of society, because the focus is on innovation as "liberation from the constraints of a world that is already made" (Ingold and Hallam 2007: 3). Whereas creativity, understood as improvisation, is seen as a set of processes of adaptation to a world in the making. In other words, the term improvisation implies a more processual reading of creativity.
4. Asante refers to a pre-colonial kingdom located in central Ghana. I did most of my fieldwork in and around Kumasi, which was the center of the historic kingdom of Asante.
5. Pentecostal Christianity in Ghana can be divided into different groups. The first group—the classical Pentecostal churches—was established mainly by foreign missionaries in the first half of the twentieth century and includes churches like the Assemblies of God and the Church of Pentecost. The second group is the neo-Pentecostal churches that have been on the rise in the last three decades. These churches span from larger mega-churches to small "one-man" churches that meet in classrooms and garages. Here I deal with the latter group of churches and mostly with the small and middle-sized ones.
6. The following is based on interviews and informal conversations with thirty-seven pastors (thirty-two men and five women). The pastors had either been employed prior to becoming pastors or engaged in pastoral careers straight after leaving school. Most pastors had some formal education and had finished secondary school. A third had left secondary school after the first level, and in this group unemployment is generally high. Half of the pastors I talked to had been either to university or a technical school. Some had had public sector employment before entering into pastorship and had left these jobs to take up a full-time pastoral career. At the same time, though, some

were involved in small businesses as a supplement to their pastoral work. Many had been abroad (often as part of their pastoral training) or had aspirations to go abroad.

7. Interestingly, many pastors describe themselves as entrepreneurs. On a church's webpage, the pastor is described as follows: "Reverend Dr. Victor Osei is the visionary man of God whom God has used to establish the Family Chapel International. He is an author, entrepreneur and public speaker. He is happily married with 7 children" (http://www.familychapelint.com/#!the-spa, accessed 13 March 2013).

8. Interview, Kumasi, 22 February 2005. This pastor was responsible for a branch of one of Kumasi's biggest neo-Pentecostal churches. At the time of the interview he was thirty-two years old and married. He later established his own church. Apart from being a pastor, he was also involved in business activities and travelled a lot to Europe.

9. Interview, Kumasi, 1 September 2005. This pastor became a pastor at the age of forty-two. When I met her she was forty-seven years old. She was married to a pastor and had four children. She had been to Bible school. Before becoming a pastor, she had a small shop that one of her brothers was now looking after.

10. Interview, Kumasi, 12 September 2005. This pastor was twenty-five years old when I met him. He was leading a small and newly established church with two other young pastors. Before that he had been member of a well-established church and a fellowship. He had finished senior high school and had been to Bible school.

11. Interview, Kumasi, 24 August 2005. When I met this pastor, he was thirty-four years old, married, and had four children. He had finished high school and holds a diploma in theology. He was born and grew up in Kumasi, but his hometown is in the Brong Ahafo region.

12. Interview, 22 February 2005. See footnote 9.

13. Interview, Kumasi, 3 February 2005.

14. Interview, Kumasi, 22 February 2005. See footnote 9.

15. In a Ghanaian context, the term "chop money" means allowances to buy food and for housekeeping.

## REFERENCES

Akyeampong, Emmanuel and J. Pashington Obeng. 1995. 'Spirituality, gender, and power in Asante history'. *International Journal of African Historical Studies* 28, 3: 481–508.

Allman, Jean and John Parker. 2005. *Tongnaab: The History of a West African God.* Bloomington and Indianapolis: Indiana University Press.

Andrieu, Sarah. 2009. 'Le métier d'entrepreneur culturel au Burkina Faso'. *Bulletin de l'APAD* 29–30: 55–69.

Arhin, Kwame. 1976 [1977]. 'The pressure of cash and its political consequences in Asante in the colonial period'. *Journal of African Studies* 3, 4: 453–468.

Arhin, Kwame. 1986. 'A note on the Asante Akonkofo: A non-literate sub-elite, 1900–1930'. *Africa* 56, 1: 25–31.

Asamoah-Gyadu, J. Kwabena. 2005a. *African Charismatics: Current Developments within Independent Indigenous Pentecostalism in Ghana.* Leiden: Brill.

Asamoah-Gyadu, J. Kwabena. 2005b. ' "Christ is the answer": what is the question? A Ghana airways prayer vigil and its implications for religion, evil and public space'. *Journal of Religion in Africa* 35, 1: 93–117.

Austin, Gareth. 1997 [1963]. 'Introduction'. In: Polly Hill (ed). *The Migrant Cocoa-Farmers of Southern Ghana: A Study in Rural Capitalism*. Oxford: James Currey and International African Institute, ix–xxviii.
Banégas, Richard and Jean-Pierre Warnier. 2001. 'Nouvelles figures de la réussite et du pouvoir'. *Politique Africaine* 82: 5–21.
Barber, Karin. 2000. *The Generation of Plays: Yorùbá Popular Life in Theatre*. Bloomington and Indianapolis: Indiana University Press.
Barber, Karin. 2006. 'Introduction: hidden innovators in Africa'. In: Karin Barber (ed). *Africa's Hidden Histories: Everyday Literacy and Making the Self*. Bloomington, IN: Indiana University Press, 1–24.
Coleman, Simon. 2011. 'Prosperity unbound? Debating the "sacrificial economy"'. In: Lionel Obadia and Donald Wood (eds). *The Economics of Religion: Anthropological Approaches*. Bingley: Emerald, 23–45.
Comaroff, Jean and John Comaroff. 2003. 'Second comings: neo-Protestant ethics and millennial capitalism in Africa, and elsewhere'. In: Paul Gifford (ed). *2000 Years and Beyond: Faith, Identity and the 'Common Era'*. London and New York: Routledge, 106–126.
De Witte, Marleen. 2003. 'AlterMedia's *Living Word*: televised charismatic Christianity in Ghana'. *Journal of Religion in Africa* 33, 2: 172–202.
Fourchard, Laurent, André Mary, and René Otayek. 2005. *Entreprises religieuses transnationales en Afrique de l'Ouest*. Paris: Karthala; Ibadan: IFRA.
Gifford, Paul. 2004. *Ghana's New Christianity: Pentecostalism in a Globalizing African Economy*. London: Hurst and Company.
Gifford, Paul and Trad Nogueira-Godsey. 2011. 'The Protestant ethic and African Pentecostalism: a case study'. *Journal for the Study of Religion* 24, 1: 5–22.
Hart, Keith. 1970. 'Small-scale entrepreneurs in Ghana and development planning'. *Journal of Development Studies* 6, 4: 104–120.
Hart, Keith. 1973. 'Informal income opportunities and urban employment in Ghana'. *The Journal of Modern African Studies* 11, 1: 61–89.
Hill, Polly. 1997 [1963]. *The Migrant Cocoa-Farmers of Southern Ghana: A Study in Rural Capitalism*. Oxford: James Currey and International African Institute.
Ingold, Tim and Elizabeth Hallam. 2007. 'Creativity and cultural improvisation: an introduction'. In: Elizabeth Hallam and Tim Ingold (eds). *Creativity and Cultural Improvisation*. Oxford: Berg (ASA Monographs 44), 1–24.
Jalloh, Alusine. 2007. 'Muslim Fula business elites and politics in Sierra Leone'. *African Economic History* 35: 89–104.
Lambek, Michael. 2002. 'General introduction'. In: Michael Lambek (ed). *A Reader in the Anthropology of Religion*. Oxford: Blackwell Publishing, 1–16.
Lauterbach, Karen. 2006. 'Wealth and worth: pastorship and neo-Pentecostalism in Kumasi'. *Ghana Studies* 9: 91–121.
Lauterbach, Karen. 2008. 'The Craft of Pastorship in Ghana and Beyond'. Ph.D. thesis, Roskilde University, Denmark.
Lauterbach, Karen. 2010. 'Becoming a pastor: youth and social aspirations in Ghana'. *Young Nordic Journal of Youth Research* 18, 3: 259–278.
Le Meur, Pierre-Yves. 2008. 'Between emancipation and patronage: changing inter-generational relationships in Central Benin'. In: Erdmute Alber, Sjaak van der Geest, and Susan Reynolds Whyte (eds). *Generations in Africa: Connections and Conflicts*. Berlin: LIT, 209–235.
MacGaffey, Janet. 2002. 'Survival, innovation, and success in time of trouble: what prospects for Central African entrepreneurs?'. In: Alusine Jalloh and Toyin Falola (eds). *Black Business and Economic Power*. Rochester: University of Rochester Press, 331–346.
Marshall, Ruth. 2009. *Political Spiritualities: The Pentecostal Revolution in Nigeria*. Chicago and London: The University of Chicago Press.

Marshall-Fratani, Ruth. 2001. 'Prosperité miraculeuse: les pasteurs Pentecôtistes et l'argent de Dieu au Nigeria'. *Politique Africaine* 82: 24–44.

Mauss, Marcel. 1954 [1990]. *The Gift. The Form and Reason for Exchange in Archaic Societies.* London and New York: Routledge.

Maxwell, David. 2006. *African Gifts of the Spirit: Pentecostalism and the Rise of a Zimbabwean Transnational Religious Movement.* Oxford: James Currey.

McCaskie, Tom. 1983. 'Accumulation, wealth and belief in Asante history: Part I. To the close of the nineteenth century'. *Africa* 53, 1: 23–43.

McCaskie, Tom. 1986. 'Accumulation: wealth and belief in Asante history: Part II. The twentieth century'. *Africa* 56, 1: 3–23.

McCaskie, Tom. 1995. *State and Society in Pre-colonial Asante.* Cambridge: Cambridge University Press.

McCaskie, Tom. 2000. *Asante Identities: History and Modernity in an African Village 1850–1950.* London: Edinburgh University Press and International African Institute.

Meagher, Kate. 2009. 'Trading on faith: religious movements and informal economic governance in Nigeria'. *The Journal of Modern African Studies* 47, 3: 397–423.

Meyer, Birgit. 1998. 'The power of money: politics, occult forces, and Pentecostalism in Ghana'. *African Studies Review* 41, 3: 15–37.

Meyer, Birgit. 2004. 'Christianity in Africa: from African independent to Pentecostal-charismatic churches'. *Annual Review of Anthropology* 33: 447–474.

Meyer, Birgit. 2005. 'Mediating tradition: Pentecostal pastors, African priests, and chiefs in Ghanaian popular films'. In: Toyin Falola (ed). *Christianity and Social Change in Africa. Essays in Honor of J. D. Y. Peel.* Durham, N.C.: Carolina Academic Press, 275–306.

Osei, George. 2004. 'The 1987 junior secondary-school reform in Ghana: vocational or pre-vocational in nature?'. *International Review of Education* 50, 5–6: 425–446.

Saint-Lary, Maud. 2009. 'Introduction: des entrepreneurs entre rhétorique et action sur le monde'. *Bulletin de l'APAD* 29–30: 9–18.

Weber, Max. 2001 [1930]. *The Protestant Ethic and the Spirit of Capitalism.* London and New York: Routledge.

# 3   Let's Do Good for Islam
## Two Muslim Entrepreneurs in Niamey, Niger[1]

*Abdoulaye Sounaye*

In Niamey, the capital of Niger, promoters of reformed religiosities have almost monopolized the audiovisual media and made these platforms the central pieces of their communication strategies (Sounaye 2011b, 2013). On a Saturday morning in April 2012, a preacher had just completed the introduction to his weekly radio sermon when he said:

> Before I elaborate on the topic of our gathering, let me remind you that tomorrow you are all invited to a *wazu* [open air sermon] at the *Académie des Arts Martiaux*.[2] *Insh'allah*, it will be very beneficial to all of us. We have guests from Ghana and from other towns of Niger, so, please, people of Niamey, women and men, young and adults, tell your friends, bring your families; be there at 9 a.m. (A preacher on Radio Saraounia)

Throughout the day, TV channels, FM radios, and text messaging devices relayed this information across the city. I also received the announcement by text message from a young woman I interviewed a few weeks earlier, and who knew my research interest. Until recently, she had been part of the preacher's movement. However, she "broke up" with the community when she married a husband reluctant to let her pursue such activities. She described the event as one of the ways her former community raises money and promotes specific projects. To convince me, she concluded: "so, if you really want to know how our group functions, you should go see for yourself". I did not wait for any further invitation.

The *wazu* was called for 9:00 a.m., but the preliminary speeches began around 10 a.m. At 10:30 sermon-goers were still pouring into the *Académie* (Figure 3.1), each rushing to get a seat in this stadium-like venue. The left-hand side of the stage was reserved for women, who rapidly packed the seats. Before the end of the preliminary speeches, the organizers had to find additional mats to spread on the floor for more women who, by the end of the event, numbered at least fifteen hundred. Across from the women's section, about five hundred men were sitting in two blocks. In the middle of the two gendered sections, young boys were sitting on mats and even on the

*Figure 3.1   Académie des Arts* (Photo: Abdoulaye Sounaye)

floor. When the *wazu* reached its climax, other men joined this part of the audience to record the event on their cell phones, cameras, and camcorders.

The popularity of this event illustrates the trend of revivalism and the growing entrepreneurship that characterizes contemporary Islam in Niger.[3] In the last two decades, Islamic revival has been a major feature of the religious landscape (Alidou and Alidou 2008; Masquelier 2009; Meunier 1998; Sounaye 2005; Zakari 2009). Since the emergence of *Izala*, an Islamic reform movement, which calls for the reinstatement of the *Sunna* (tradition of the prophet Muhammad) against unlawful innovations (*bid'a*), local customs (*al a'du*), and whatever it sees as contradictory to the Qur'an and the *Hadiths*,[4] the dynamics in the religious sphere in Niger have greatly changed. *Izala's* claims of authenticity, its attempts to correct Muslim practices, and its criticism of Sufi practices eventually brought religion into the center of public life, while attacks and counterattacks became one of the modalities of interactions among Muslims (Sounaye 2009a, 2009c).

By the beginning of the 2000s, *Izala* revivalism had inspired the formation of an alternative Islamic community and had contributed to the opening up of the Islamic sphere in West Africa, within which a discourse of democratization of Islam translated into numerous learning spaces and social practices (Sounaye 2009a, 2009b). Over the years, this sphere has given Islam and Muslim actors more visibility, while the interactions among Islamic organizations, the promotion of Islamic ideologies and activities, and the socioeconomic and political spaces created for this purpose redefine the terms of being Muslim. In Niger, it is mainly within this arena that Muslims claim responsibility and obligation to serve the public and then contribute to the common good.[5] In many instances, Muslim activists used the spaces that emerged within this context to consolidate the early successes of their reform agenda (Alidou 2005; Sounaye 2009a). At the same time, *Izala* began to use audiovisual media strategically, with the objective of facilitating its popularization in both urban and rural contexts (Sounaye 2011b). As they gained ground in Niamey, particularly among traders, youth, and women, *Izala* discursive practices and communal activities favored a new Islamic culture, of which the last two social categories have become major agents (Alidou and Alidou 2008; Masquelier 2007; Sounaye 2011a, 2012). My informants and both figures I discuss in this chapter are products of these new developments in Niger.

In Niamey and across Niger, events similar to the one I referred to above have become part of the weekly *animation religieuse*, i.e., a way supporters of revivalism appropriate the public arena, fulfill their religious obligations, and pursue their wish to reform their communities. For this change to occur, Muslims require an active involvement with their institutions, their social and cultural spaces, and also with the modes of sociability they invent. Often, when they come together—as in the *wazu* at the *Académie*—in addition to the desire to live their religion in their community, the driving force behind the *animation religieuse* is the realization of a communal project. In the *wazu* at the *Académie* (Figure 3.2), the main reason for the event was a *madrasa* project for which the preacher wanted to garner support. Many organizations have used similar occasions to levy funds for dispensaries, *madrasas* (secondary Islamic learning institutions), or mosques. In the

*Figure 3.2*   View of the audience at Abdallah's *wazu* (Photo: Abdoulaye Sounaye)

past two decades, religious entrepreneurship has particularly been actively affecting these cultural, economic, and political dimensions of public life (Sounaye 2013).

From the restructuring of the religious field, to use a Bourdieusian concept (Bourdieu 1971), and the rise of new forms of Islamic organizations (*associations islamiques*), Islam experienced a politicization that made participation in religion-inspired activities a quasi-obligation for many Muslims in Niamey. These same developments also contributed to the emergence of new independent religious entrepreneurs, among whom are the *ustaz*.

*Ustaz* is an Arabic term used locally to refer to a new breed of instructors of the Qur'an and the Hadiths. They are religious entrepreneurs in the sense that they not only teach but, as individual actors, use their skills, positions, networks, connections, etc. to initiate various activities, lead communal initiatives, and mobilize segments of urban dwellers for their projects. These "God's men" generally claim to serve Islam, and in doing so set up social spaces which restructure urban socio-religious life. In the cases I present, they invent new Islamic discourses, practices, and institutions and endow them with meanings that stress the need to change and transform society. For the two young actors I introduce, this production of norms of religious life is constitutive of the way they see themselves not only as Muslims but also as authoritative figures. They develop new attitudes and practices through which they claim social roles as they create study groups and establish preaching communities to support the *animation religieuse* agenda. In this particular urban context, Islam sells as an ideological discourse that focuses on both individual and social reforms because it has an expanded consumer base (Sounaye 2011b) and because it helps many young people to deliver Islam in new ways. These newcomers have invested energy in negotiating airtime on TV and radio to make their voices heard and levying donations supposed to implement communal projects. By contrast, *ulama*, established clerics (also known as *marabouts*), are more reserved and generally little interested in acquiring visibility through the media.

Fundamentally ideological, religious formations need resources to fund their initiatives (Bruce 1992). Especially in the Islamic reform context in Niger (Grégoire 1993) and elsewhere (Osella and Osella 2010), entrepreneurial religion (cf. Feillard 2004) has developed because of this renewed interest in Islam that shapes urban lifestyles. As the need for public presence increases, promoters of reform discourses and ideologies find themselves compelled to find the necessary resources, both human and financial, in their communities. Interestingly, little has been written on these actors and the strategies they use.

In this chapter, I analyze the way in which cultural and religious initiatives are redefining Muslim practices in Niamey. I argue that religious entrepreneurship has provided many individuals with the opportunity to construct authority and organize their communities; it has also affected urban religious life, which increasingly manifests itself in informal learning spaces and cultural centers. My cases show that young Muslim actors take the lead and use alternative spaces and modes of interaction to build communities of followers as they initiate projects deemed to serve the community. The two cases I present will also show how the spread of Islam and the popularization of the *Sunna*—two justifications these public figures put forward for their initiatives—illustrate the directions religious entrepreneurship is presently taking in Niger. My examples resonate with the success stories Banégas and Warnier (2001) have called *"figures de la réussite"* (models of success) in reference to the *"opérateurs religieux"* who build on the significance of religion and illustrate the possibilities of alternative trajectories for upward social mobility in African societies. As they have shown, these success stories are not exclusively economic or political, they are also religious and highlight how individuals can capitalize on religious practices to acquire authority, expand their influence in the society, undertake communal projects, and accumulate wealth.

The two young Muslim figures whom I introduce in the following pages epitomize the entrepreneurial turn that shapes Islam in Niamey. In the first section, I focus on Abdallah, a young preacher who has become one of the personalities of *wazu* (open air sermons) in Niamey, where he has established a community that supports most of his activities. In the second section, I introduce Kadja, a young lady who has entered the world of Islamic learning more recently. She, too, has devised a particular strategy to offer what she sees as the most important good to female reform followers. Unlike Abdallah, Kadja does not have a community per se, but rather a network on which she relies for her teaching activities. I devote a final section to discussing some implications of these practices in Niamey.

My goal is to highlight some of the entrepreneurial appropriations through which a new Islamic culture manifests itself in Niamey, where I have carried out field research on Islam for the past ten years. Most of the information I use for this chapter has been collected during participant observation, interviews, and informal conversations I had while I followed the activities of young preachers and Muslim activists from 2008 to 2012. I met twice with Kadja to discuss her activities and attended three of her lessons in the Madina neighborhood in Niamey. Later, I interviewed three of her students and another group of Lycée students. As a man, the main issue I faced was the reluctance and even refusal of several of Kadja's students to have a one-on-one interview with me, as they argued that Islam proscribes conversation with an unrelated male. In those cases my only resort was a group interview. As for Abdallah, I was already familiar with his community, because I have been carrying out research on his activities for the past four years. In fact, even though he knows that I am not an *Izala*, he has regularly invited me to his sermons.

## ORGANIZING MUSLIMS: ABDALLAH'S *MADRASA* PROJECT

A relatively young preacher now in his thirties, Abdallah emerged as a personality in the religious sphere through preaching and an Islamic learning group he created in his neighborhood. After he tried unsuccessfully to pursue higher Islamic learning in Nigeria, he returned home to Niger, where he settled in Niamey's Sonni neighborhood. He never completed his degree at the neighborhood *madrasa* where his parents had sent him to learn the Qur'an, Arabic, and French. Still, he managed to have a fairly significant knowledge of Islamic texts and command of Arabic. I have heard him use Arabic in his sermons and in conversations with colleagues or former classmates, but I have rarely heard him use French. When he did, it was generally in the form of short phrases or terms that have gained popularity among youth in Niamey. As he dropped out in the early 1990s, he embraced "*adina goyo*" (literally, working for Islam), joining the *Izala* movement while he furthers his knowledge of the Qur'an with the assistance of several Muslim scholars in Niamey.

In Niamey, Abdallah has now established himself as a leading promoter of a participation ideology that calls Muslims to support their religion. When it is not financial support, participation can take many forms, including involvement in communal activities such as preaching, intermediating for the Haj and the Umra, teaching the Qur'an, fundraising, CD and DVD sermon duplication for Islamic discotheques across town, and even beyond. *Taimako* (help, assistance, in Hausa) and *gakasinay* (contribution, in Zarma) are two concepts in the local parlance, which Abdallah and his peers use to promote support to Islam. Both concepts remind fellow Muslims of their responsibility for the advancement of their reform agenda (*cigaban adini*). Abdallah often illustrates this effort at participation by referring to young preachers' commitment to spreading (*bangandi*) the *Sunna* and promoting Islamic learning. His own style has taken him on many roads across the country and West Africa. In our most recent conversation (June 2012), he complained that "this year, my schedule has been disrupted by many unexpected activities", including the opening of a TV station for which he now hosts and supervises all Islamic programs. He explained that in the last decade, he has devoted each year several months to *fattayan*, a sermon rally program destined to *da'wa* (calling to Islam).

> At this time of the year, I should be on a preaching rally on the Coast [Benin, Togo, Ivory Coast, and Ghana], but see . . . I am still around and I am not even sure I will do it this year. But, God is great . . . he knows why he hasn't made it possible this year . . . he will find a way to make it happen. (Abdallah, interview 2012)

The *fattayan* he conducts in these parts of West Africa targets Nigerien diaspora that have migrated to the coastal areas for better economic opportunities. *Fattayan* is now one of the main activities of his annual program. Many who have established successful businesses in those areas have also become major players in his preaching community because of their contributions to many of his activities. "I know I can count on them whenever we have to build a *madrasa* or a mosque," he said.

For Abdallah, however, the primary objective of *fattayan* is religious (*addina*): "Nigeriens in those countries are waiting for us every year to visit them and preach the Qur'an and the *Sunna* of the Prophet. There are only a handful of Muslims in those areas, so they usually rely on us for their religious activities". Thus, for Abdallah, a trip to the Coast equates to a religious service and has always translated into substantial contributions in support of his activities. He confesses, "Some stops on the preaching trail can be harsh and challenging, but in the end, it is always a good trip because we end up collecting a substantial *gakasinay*".

A community builder, Abdallah mobilizes and organizes Muslims with the financial assistance of other Muslims. For him, fundraising is a way to "achieve better organization" within Muslim communities; as he repeatedly stressed during his *wazu* at the *Académie*: "we raise funds so we can build whatever Muslims need. This time, it is a *madrasa*; it could be a dispensary next time". Many Islamic organizations have used the occasion of a sermon or a rally to introduce what they consider communal projects. In general, however, these initiatives are organized and carried out by charismatic leaders who have access to public spaces such as TV or radio programs on which they publicize and issue calls to their activities. Affiliated with no Islamic organization, Abdallah operates most of the time alone. With this *madrasa* project, however, he collaborates with one of his peers, Sanusi, a young Nigerien preacher who is established in Ghana. They became friends on one of Abdallah's trips to the Coast, and since then have teamed up to initiate various activities, mostly preaching. Complementarity marks their collaboration: they are both famous for their emotional style of recitation of the Qur'an; they both speak several languages, with Abdallah usually responsible for communication in Zarma, his native language, and French, the official language in Niger, while Sanusi is responsible for Hausa, a language widely spoken in Ghana and Niger, and English, the official language of Ghana.

Abdallah's philosophy of service translates therefore into a mediation that makes possible initiatives such as the *madrasa* project and other learning spaces. For example, in his neighborhood in the Quartier Sonni of Niamey, he has created several reading groups for young people from all walks of society. Today, these spaces serve as social bases for the sermons he delivers every Friday in what is now called his mosque, an open-air space used for any activity of the community, where he usually receives visitors and friends. In fact, following the sermon at the *Académie*, one of his assistants informed the audience that a "contribution box" would be placed at the mosque for anyone who was not able to contribute on the spot.

Although the wealthy businessmen and traders are the main target of his entrepreneurship, because "who has more should give more", "all Muslims have the responsibility to support Islam (*adina gayan*)", he noted. In Niamey, Abdallah receives significant contributions from women, generally civil servants, but also housewives. Those who attend his Friday night sermon, for example, contribute around 500 FCFA (about $1) every week. As he justifies his role and practices, he states:

> Muslims have the will to invest their wealth (*almano*) to help (*ga*) Islam spread, but they need leaders to show them how. Many are lucky for God has granted them extraordinary wealth, but many do not know how to invest this wealth to earn the ultimate reward. We need to tell and convince them that Islam needs their financial support. (Abdallah, interview 2012b)

Obviously, making a trip to the Coast is part of the efforts to tell Muslims "how they should invest" in Islam (*Irkoy fonda*). It is also a reminder of the role Muslims should play in the popularization of the *Sunna* in Niger and across the region, as he frequently reminds his followers during his *wazu*. Similar to many young preachers of his generation, Abdallah sees himself as a relay and a facilitator who, through his initiatives, responds to the "Islamic needs of the society" (*muradu*) and helps Muslims do good and win God's heaven (*irkoy aljanna*).

I have already made the point that the striking development in Niger in the last two decades consists in the rise of a new Islamic culture prompted by the proliferation of social, economic, and political initiatives deemed to reform Islam and create the infrastructural conditions for a proper Islamic society. This agenda has been interpreted in many ways and from various angles. In Niamey, some have emphasized preaching as a way to popularize the *Sunna* and make it available to everyone; others have used the *madrasa* to contribute to a learning culture that promotes self-reform and moral attitudes inspired by the Prophet Muhammad.

Undoubtedly, the *madrasa* project has brought to Abdallah another preoccupation, where he is investing his *savoir-faire* and capitalizing on both his popularity and the renewed interest in Islam in urban Niger. In August 2012, the project was still at the fundraising stage. When I asked him later about the result of the event he led in March, he conceded that it was a great sermon, but it did not yield enough money to start building the facility, a result many participants were actually expecting:

> After deduction of all charges related to the material organization of the sermon and the rental of the hall, we had about 500,000 FCFA (about $1,000) left. We are way short of what we need in order to begin [the construction]. So, for this reason, we are planning another activity, but we have not set any date yet. The good thing is that we have secured

some land thanks to a female sponsor who donated a 400 m²-land. Of course, with such a project, we need more space, but this will do; plus, you never know what God may throw to you. (Abdallah, interview 2012a)

Indeed, in all three conversations I had with him, he demonstrated optimism and confidence that he will complete his project. He is an inspiring young man known for his ability to captivate the attention of his audience, the main sponsor of his activities. Besides his audience, he has a network of donors who have regularly contributed to specific—although smaller—projects, such as acquiring a sound system for his sermons or transportation to a preaching rally in the outskirts of Niamey. He is aware that the materialization of his project will take energy and even bring disappointments, as he added later: "many have not kept their promises yet; we are still waiting . . . it takes time". Salimou, one of his assistants, conceded later that they are actually not expecting much from the promises people made at the sermon. He added, unless they "find a big donor for the 5,000,000 FCFA (about $10,000) they need for the construction to begin", they will require at least two more fundraising sermons. In an informal conversation the same evening, Abdallah brushed off the skepticism he sensed in my questions as I kept asking how he would collect the remainder of the funds. With confidence, he replied:

> Don't worry, we will collect the money. . . . People say Niger is a poor country; of course, many people struggle to make ends meet; many go hungry in this country, but we are a Muslim country and many more people love (*ba*) their religion (*adina*) and are ready to invest in it. They know that wealth is not an end in itself; you pray God to give you wealth and you use it to earn *aljanna*. On the day of Resurrection, only your deeds will save you. (Abdallah, interview 2012)

To understand this perspective, one has to remember that the reform discourse has particularly succeeded in promoting the idea that Islam needs Muslims' financial support. In Niamey and across Niger, wealthy traders in particular have supported the reform agenda to set up social infrastructures and disseminate the reform agenda's social and theological discourse. Two *madrasa* may illustrate this dynamic. First, the Complexe Abubakar Sadik, a *madrasa* located 35 km southeast of Niamey and funded by Himadou Sirignere, a trader who built his wealth through the import-export trade; and second, the Madrasa Mufida of Maradi, which was funded by Rabe Dan Tchadoua, another wealthy trader who was through the 2000s the main financial support of the *Izala* movement in Maradi, a town in the central part of Niger. Thousands have graduated from these institutions and many have joined social initiatives of the kind I describe here to promote the new Islamic culture.

Thus, it is not surprising that Abdallah is able to mobilize followers and garner support for his initiatives. In fact, in the last two years, as I have been following his activities, he has expanded his network of "clients" to include many civil servants, traders at the *Grand Marché* of Niamey, and high school and university students who regularly attend his preaching and learning activities. A social and cultural entrepreneur, he has opened up to many of these followers social spaces where they can contribute to both religious and social reform. As such, he provides a framework for "*adina goyo*" and a template for the kind of entrepreneurship the popularization of the *Sunna* needs in order to succeed.

As a religious figure, Abdallah would have not acquired his current status without the rise of the reform discourses and the ensuing transformation of the Islamic sphere. In effect, as the 1990s reform discourse rose, it restructured the interactions in the public sphere and created the conditions for the emergence of young *ustaz*, preachers and religious entrepreneurs in search of better social positions. It must be noted that in his case, Abdallah has also greatly benefited from his own communication skills and the training he has received in both the traditional Qur'anic learning institution (*makaranta*) and the much-structured *madrasa*.

Upon closer examination, Abdallah's case is similar to many one finds in urban Africa (Havard 2001; Malaquais 2001; LeBlanc 2012) and across the Muslim world (Feillard 2004; Osella and Osella 2010; Rudnyckyj 2009; Watson 2005). Proving that a young preacher can emerge and make a living in this context, Abdallah's story illustrates the development of a religious market and the existence of a clientele that have served him along his recent life trajectory. Certainly, his initiatives consolidate his position and make him a major figure in contemporary Islam in Niger. As the woman I mentioned at the beginning of this chapter noted, "He is at the heart of this event and like many others, not only because they are more learned, but really because they know people and know how to bring them together. God gifted them with that skill". A skill that has made him a successful Muslim leader, one of those actors urban anthropology has depicted as "*figures de la réussite*" (Ould Ahmed Salem 2001; Banégas and Warnier 2001; Havard 2001; Malaquais 2001) or religious entrepreneurs (Feillard 2004; Fourchard, Mary, and Otayek 2005; Osella and Osella 2010; Tall 2003).

## DELIVERING ISLAM: KADJA, A YOUNG *USTAZIA* ON A BIKE

At the Lycée Kassai, one of the main institutions of secondary education in Niamey, many young people have not only joined the activities their Youth Club organizes, they have also found ways to carry on the *animation religieuse* spirit beyond the confines of their school. Aissata, a young woman, for example, has persuaded two of her classmates, Jamila and Hassana, to join her to start a neighborhood Qur'an study group, *makaranta*. Aissata commented: "I used to participate in our neighborhood Islamic learning group. It was nice, but since *Ustazia* Kadja offered to meet us at home, it became easier and more convenient. She rides her bike [*porporo*] and meets us three times a week. In our group, we all appreciate her work". In Aissata's account, one could immediately sense the important bond these young women have developed with their female instructor. It is precisely while discussing these young women's learning practices that I heard about *Ustazia* for the first time.

*Ustazia* is the feminine for *ustaz*, the Arabic for teacher or instructor. In the last few years, the term has been widely used in Niamey to refer to females involved in the business of teaching Arabic, generally in informal settings, such as Qur'an study circles or even in private homes. Promoting a culture of Islamic learning that departs from the classical Qur'anic schools, they have developed teaching and learning practices that usually accommodate urban dwellers and the francophone elite (Sounaye 2011a). For that reason the term *ustaz* denotes a distinctive status in Niamey.

*Ustazia* Kadja, now in her thirties, graduated from Sabil Huda, a *madrasa* in Niamey. She began her teaching activities shortly after her first year at the Islamic University of Say, an institution located 50 km south of Niamey and mainly funded by the Organization of the Islamic Cooperation (formerly, the Organization of the Islamic Conference). Despite numerous administrative and financial challenges that almost put an end to its activities, the institution managed to offer training in Islamic sciences to many young West Africans. *Ustazia* was trained in the all-female branch of the institution now based in Niamey. After graduation, she quickly moved to serve as an assistant-teacher in a well-established neighborhood *makaranta* that the mother of a friend of hers was running. As she began to connect with more people and became comfortable in her position, she decided to start her own network of Qur'anic instruction. With no "financial resources that would have allowed me to rent or build a place", she decided "to teach the Qur'an to women in their own homes". She managed to find a bike and, like many male *ustaz*, decided to "go find" her students.

In general, attendees of this kind of learning space are expected to meet their instructor at the *makaranta*, which might be next to a mosque or under a shady roof constructed to host study sessions. *Ustazia*, however, comes to her students—reinventing the way in which Qur'anic learning is transmitted in Niamey. Her expanding network of friends, acquaintances, and relatives was supposed to serve as a sustainable base for this initiative. So far, it has, because "I have been doing this for five years now". She prides herself on the initiatives she has taken and is convinced that her decision "to go find women at home" is the main reason for her achievement: "if you want to help Muslims to learn, then make it easy for them. Growing up, I did not have this opportunity. People knew little about Islam, let alone the fact that women were nowhere to be seen in the Islamic learning institutions. Now,

I want to help my sisters and mothers". As she accommodates her clients, she has also found an innovative way to make the study of the Qur'an available to many housewives, who frequently postpone a trip to the *makaranta* because of the burden of their domestic responsibilities. Usually, "they go to the *makaranta* and . . . you know . . . sometimes they get discouraged by the walk . . . now we study in their homes, so they can have more time for their domestic responsibilities". Many of her clients meet her on a one-on-one basis. But, when she has several clients in one neighborhood, she usually groups them to save herself time, but also to create an atmosphere of comradeship that would inspire the students to meet, review their lessons, share notes, or do their homework together. "I like it this way because I don't have a *makaranta* of my own, so it works well for both sides".

A few years ago, only male instructors (*ustaz*) used this peripatetic form of Islamic learning. Women who wanted to learn the Qur'an had either to find a *makaranta* in which they could enroll, or rely on a friend already learned in the Qur'an. *Ustazia*'s initiative breaks with that classical model, as she actively seeks alternative spaces and forms of transmission of Islamic learning. She claims to promote proper Islamic practice and sees her work as a contribution to the dissemination of the *Sunna* among urban women whose role, as she stresses, is critical in spreading the values of the *Sunna* within the family. For her, every woman is "responsible for her children and even her husband". Hence her focus on women and the cultivation of Islamic learning to achieve reform: "how can people properly practice the *Sunna* if they don't know it?"

Youth organizations, in particular the *Clubs des Jeunes Musulmans*, have consistently stressed the fact that Muslim youth should "wake up and assume their responsibilities". For these discourses of awakening, youth should avoid "*Zaman kashe wondo*" (idleness) and rely on the *ulama* (Muslim clerics, also referred to as *marabouts*) to give them the meaning of the Qur'an and the Islamic tradition. As they contest the normative role of this establishment, they promote a culture of rupture and autonomy that is expected to make them better Muslims. *Ustazia* Kadja's initiative should be read within this context where, on the one hand, she departs from "*attentisme*", a French term used to depict attitudes of young people waiting for the government to provide them with job opportunities, and on the other hand, she challenges the classical model of transmission of Islamic learning in which the learners, for practical reasons and to pay respect to their instructor, meet him (or her) in the *makaranta*.

Social, economic, and cultural initiatives that respond to the call for *animation religieuse* are therefore presented as possibilities that should help young Muslims fight idleness and make them fit into the broader community.[6] For many of my interlocutors, as the case of Abdallah illustrates, participation is the primary rapport they draw and the framework within which they understand their roles and live their experiences. Along the same lines, like most female Muslim scholars, *Ustazia* could have waited in the home of her parents for a husband to come and provide her a matrimonial status. She could have chosen the security of a marriage over exposure to the public eye, which has made her now the target of many criticisms, particularly among conservative Muslim leaders, for whom she is "selling" Islam. Instead, in order to *participate*, she has decided against the cultural models she was expected to follow, arguing that as a learned Muslim, her responsibility is to transmit whatever she knows about Islam. Hence, her missionary approach to Islam and the strategies she has devised. Waithood is not for her.

Fatima, a member of another group *Ustazia* Kadja has set up, emphasizes her instructor's innovative style and notes how she breaks from the social conventions, the representation of women in religion, and more importantly, the model of the Nigerien youth who relies heavily on the state for socioeconomic integration. For Fatima, models such as *Ustazia*'s have made an impact on the lives of young Muslims because "she [*Ustazia*] knows her job and she helped us very much to read Arabic and understand the Qur'an". *Ustazia* is also groundbreaking "because she has not waited to be supported [by husband or parents]". Illustrating the self-making ideology at work, *Ustazia* has created spaces where she affects how Muslims think about and organize Islamic learning and their own lives. In fact, her "lessons" are not only based on the Qur'an: "I teach the verses, we read the *hadiths*, I preach, but we also discuss family issues". From the reactions she has received so far, she intends to maintain this practice, even when she gets married. Obviously, there could be a major challenge to her activity, as the leadership in Islamic learning consists predominantly of male figures, among whom many oppose the idea of a woman taking a public role. Thus, her approach to social life, her initiatives as a Muslim scholar, and her perception of domesticity would probably make things difficult for her, especially as she faces a conservative discourse that confines women to the domestic arena. She has already been called names because of the innovative touch she adds to Islamic learning and her promotion of a self-making ideology. "Once, a group of *ulama* appeared on TV to admonish women who are leaving their homes to teach other women. They said it is not permitted in Islam; I know one of them and I don't think he knows the *Sunna*. Women were instructors during Muhammad's era. Maybe they are unaware that Aisha [one of Muhammad's wives] taught Islam to many women". For Kadja, the example of Aisha is enough to justify her undertaking, an act she equates to the "best service a Muslim can do for Islam". This line of argument recalls what has been a central issue among the *Izala*, who promoted cultivation of Islamic learning in order to emancipate Islam and Muslims from the obscurantist attitudes of *ulama* (*marabouts*). Kadja believes she is contributing to this emancipation by spreading the *Sunna* of the Prophet Muhammad and devoting her time and energy to her study circles. "Who else than a woman is better positioned to teach other women? There are things we, as women, cannot discuss with male *ustaz*, whatever their degree of learning and open-mindedness".

Scholars of Islam in Niger have drawn attention to the rise of various forms of initiatives in particular in Islamic education (Alidou 2005; Meunier 1997, 2009). The visibility of female scholars, as Alidou (2005) shows, is one of the distinctive markers of the Islamic sphere. While Alidou focuses on figures who emerged in the 1990s and established themselves as spokespersons of Islam by the 2000s, recent developments in Islamic entrepreneurship include preaching, in particular that of women, who have now acquired a major role in the restructuring of the urban religious field in Niger (Sounaye 2011b). Presenting their religious shows through audiovisual media, these new figures have secured a presence that not only changes the gender complexity of preaching, but also draws attention to a socio-religious entrepreneurship that has reshaped Muslim practices in Niger. Although Kadja did not show much interest in initiatives that concern the mediascape, she greatly contributed to this complexity. In Niamey, as it appears, she is not alone; she belongs to a cohort of women who are now leaders of significant learning communities. However, what makes her case even more interesting is the fact that in a society still based on gerontocratic principles, i.e., precedence given to the elders and their opinions, a young single woman is able to emerge and build a Muslim public, to use Eickelman's concept, through which she promotes particular practices. Her symbolic capital as an *ustazia* makes this socio-religious entrepreneurship sustainable, now that Islam has become the authoritative language of social and political interactions (Sounaye 2007) and the promotion of the *Sunna* a norm of religious discourse.

## ISLAM, ENTREPRENEURSHIP, AND RELIGIOUS IMAGINATION

An important feature Kadja and Abdallah share is their freelance and self-made status. Neither belongs to a formal Islamic organization (*association islamique*), the type of institution that emerged in the democratization context, accentuated pluralism of discourses and practices within Muslim circles, and restructured the Islamic sphere. *Izala*, for example, has greatly benefited from this dynamic, as it went from a marginal organization at the end of the 1980s and beginning of the 1990s to a major trend that had become by the beginning of the 2000s the most mediated Islamic movement. The combination of pluralism and the appropriations of *Izala* by young Muslims eager to contribute to the popularization of the *Sunna* also provided many Muslims with the opportunity for entrepreneurship.

When considered within this context, Kadja and Abdallah illustrate a shift that affects Muslim practices in Niger. At the beginning of the 2000s, Islam was represented in the public sphere by Islamic organizations formally registered with the Ministry of Interior; after that period, the dynamics of the Islamic sphere began to change. As these organizations grew and expanded, competition intensified and ambitions clashed, diverged, and became irreconcilable, leading to conflicts and eventually to fragmentation. Among those who voluntarily left their mother organizations or were forced out, many undertook a solo career, relying on networks they had built, and more importantly, on the freedom of association consecrated by the state's non-intervention policy. Associations mushroomed openly, while individual entrepreneurs made their way into the religious arena, claiming authority and building up communities of followers and supporters. Until that period, the military and the single party rule (1974–1990) left no room for plurivocality. On the contrary, Islam was tightly controlled and only one Islamic organization (*Association Islamique du Niger*) was authorized to speak for Islam and for Muslims. Indeed, from the 1990s, the Islamic sphere lost its monolithism and opened up to all kinds of influences and appropriations, what an *alem* (pl. *ulama*) referred to as "the end of the peace". Of course, this contrasts sharply with the opinions that followers of Kadja or Abdallah would have voiced. In fact, a young supporter of Islamic entrepreneurship relentlessly stresses the major opportunity democratization has brought to Islam and religious actors. Celebrating the inscription of religious freedom in Niger's constitution, he states: "*Laïcité* [secularism] means we can freely practice our religion".

Abdallah is one of those young men who have benefited from the rise of alternative Islamic organizations; at the same time, he found no satisfaction with any of the Islamic spaces to which he previously belonged. He rejected the traditional affiliation system, which submitted a disciple to his *marabout*. Later, he cut ties with the reform organization (*Adini Islam*) he was associated with, on the grounds that it gave him little room for expression. After flip-flopping for some time, he finally resigned and decided that none of the Islamic organizations fitted his vision of Islam and the practice he envisioned to carry out. Then he started a *madrasa*, got involved in an *Umra and Haj* travel agency, and launched a preaching career, which finally seems to be the most successful of his initiatives.

With lesser public exposure, Kadja had obviously limited opportunities to initiate major projects, which would require the financial support of the kind Abdallah is receiving. Still, she managed to devise a particular strategy that allows her to satisfy her religious obligation of serving the *Sunna* (*adina gakasinay*), something dear to her, and to establish a network of learners with whom she has secured a job and social position.

Obviously, the emergence of both actors speaks for the dynamic of a religious sphere within which actors rely on personal skills and religious imagination. What I call religious imagination is how these young men and women are putting religion to work, not only for social mobility, but also as a way to organize society and promote practices, norms, and values. Thus, they can equally be viewed as social entrepreneurs who innovate in the way urban communities are built. Those who are involved in their activities are not their *talibes* (disciples), a popular concept in the literature of Islam in Africa. Most of the participants in Abdallah's activities, for example, are followers only in the sense that they regularly attend his activities. More like fans, they generally provide a major source of funding for most of the religious entrepreneurs.

Recent developments in Niger have shown a trend of both economiza-tion, to use Robertson's (1992) term, and commercialization of Islam. While claiming to serve the spread of Islam, many Muslim actors are actually enter-ing the religious sphere hoping to invest their skills and harvest any poten-tial benefit. From this perspective, the religious sphere becomes a market or a field (as defined by Bourdieu) marked by competition and antagonism, but also strategic practices that allow some actors more than others to succeed. This dynamic has prompted the constitution of an arena of production and circulation of religious norms, with its specific marketing strategies (Sou-naye 2011a). Many Muslim actors marketing the *Izala* Islamic reform, for example, have made use of techniques of social mobilization, as we see with Abdallah, who uses not only learning practices, but also preaching rallies to promote his projects. They have also introduced new ways of preaching and levying funds to assist (*gakassinay*) the spread of their reform ideology. Particularly in Niamey, preaching has become part of a religious economy that relies increasingly on individual figures and their capacity to mobilize support. Some of the features of this economy have already been described and problematized in various West African contexts, in particular by Soares (2005) and Last (1998) who, while focusing on gift-giving and mediation for blessings in Mali and Nigeria, have drawn attention to the way in which exchange of services shapes Mulsims' interactions. The Sheiks intercede in favor of their disciples, while the disciples provide the Sheiks with all sorts of gifts, financial and in kind.

Although Kadja and Abdallah belong to different social categories and illustrate modes of exchange of services, they both rely on the spaces intro-duced by this religious economy, "which treats goods and God together", to use Martin's phrase (Martin 1992). While Abdallah's God's talk and Kat-ja's domestication of Islamic learning mobilize adherents, it is important to note that the popularity of their practices resides also in the good members seek to get from attending the *makaranta* or providing financial support. In establishing a *madrasa*, Abdallah is creating an institution that will contrib-ute to the betterment of his Muslim community, as he claims. But, it also reinforces his position in society, a situation that will probably provide him with additional symbolic capital, but also material and financial benefits.

## CONCLUDING COMMENTS

Focusing on *Ustazia* Kadja and Abdallah, I wanted to stress how young pro-moters of Islamic reform in Niamey organize themselves to initiate and sus-tain their activities. This organizational work illustrates their ability to build on religious references, norms, and values to deploy a cultural infrastructure that ensures them a visibility in the public arena. In the specific case of Niamey, it is evident that these entrepreneurs have heavily influenced the current Islamic culture. Although they operate within two different registers, both actors hold similar positions in a field that is increasingly fragmented and whose modes of interaction are continuously strategized. As social and religious agents, both speak for a larger group of youth who are shaping Islam in urban Niger and for whom entrepreneurial religion has become a common idiom and a familiar practice. Calling for participation, they have reinforced their positions and expanded their social, cultural, and even economic influences.

However, in the broader socio-religious context of Niamey, it is worth noting that this entrepreneurship came with new challenges for the *ulama* establishment, which is not only called out to justify its standings on theological and political issues (Sounaye 2009b), but is also forced to find alternative strategies to maintain its status. Actually, many *ulama* have reacted by either joining forces with young religious entrepreneurs (Sounaye 2012) or revitalizing their learning centers in order to respond to the increasing demand for Islamic learning and the new modes of its transmission in an urban context. The cases I present in this chapter show how the transformation of the Islamic sphere has induced new social constructions, a reinterpretation of being Muslim in a reform context, but also new strategies, among which is entrepreneurship.

There is a significant literature on contemporary Islam, which shows that the wedding of religiosity and entrepreneurship is not specific to Niger, or even West Africa (Fourchard, Mary, and Otayek 2005; LeBlanc 2012). Rather, it seems to be a major trend in the Muslim world (Hirschkind 2006; Osella and Osella 2010; Rudnyckyj 2009), where socioeconomic and cultural processes are deeply reshaping Muslims' moral lives, interactions, and self-perception.

In the last few decades, a religious enthusiasm has favored an entrepreneurship that has resulted in various Islamic institutions in Niger (Alidou 2005; Sounaye 2011a; Zakari 2009). Particularly in Niamey, these institutions have proliferated as promoters emulate each other and seek to provide their audiences with alternative modes and spaces for Islamic learning (Sounaye 2009d). The *makaranta* phenomenon in Niamey resulted from this dynamic, which sees youth and women take the lead in reinventing Islamic learning. Thus, it is not surprising that *Ustazia* Kadja chose this field to build up her capital. For her and many other promoters of the *makaranta*, reconstructing the Islamic learning spaces is a critical move that should ensure them not only a participation in promoting a puritan Islam, but also a career. Ironically, in the 1990s, when the reform discourses emerged, they accused established *ulama* of selling their religious capital and profiting from the social positions the status of scholars earns them. This mercantilism, so to speak, was said to denature Islam; its promoters were depicted as impostors who, allegedly, paid little attention to the proper practice of Islam.

Preoccupied with the gain they could earn, the so-called impostors became the monsters to fight for the reinstatement of authentic Islam. Today, many of these critics have recourse to their status as Muslim scholars, a position key to the interactions within the new Islamic culture.

Social and cultural entrepreneurs, actors such as those I describe, seek to have an impact on their society by affecting individual behaviors and, more importantly, by infusing their communities with particular religious ideas and norms. Relying on these strategies and modes of action has been the novelty in this social context. While *Ustazia* Kadja crisscrosses the city to meet her "students", Abdallah calls on his community to fund his project. *Ustazia* Kadja goes to her students, Abdallah's followers come to him, and both claim to serve their communities and, by extension, the global *Umma* (global Islamic community).

Finally, it is also worth noting that this trend of religious entrepreneurship is not specific to Islam or Muslim societies either. As many scholars have shown, a case can be made for an ethic of entrepreneurship and prosperity that runs through religious ideologies in sub-Saharan Africa (Banégas and Warnier 2001; Bava 2003; Diouf 2000; Ebin 1993; Fourchard, Mary, and Otayek 2005; LeBlanc 2012; Tall 2003). Beyond sub-Saharan Africa, in the Americas and Asia, these trends have been noticed for quite some time already. Contemporary religious imagination seems to have comparable expressions across regions and religious traditions. In that regard, contemporary sub-Saharan Africa provides the opportunity to problematize the interactions between religious traditions, in particular Islam and Christianity, through the mediation of forms of initiatives which have been termed reformist or Pentecostal (see Lauterbach, this volume). How religious actors from these different traditions have taken their initiatives into the public arena can serve as a starting point for a comparative study of religion-inspired dynamics in contemporary Africa.

## NOTES

1. Many thanks to the Lasdel (Laboratory for the Study and Research on Social Dynamics and Local Development) of Niamey, Niger, for offering me the affiliation that facilitated my fieldwork and an inspiring intellectual environment that shaped parts of this paper.
2. A facility the government of Niger built as the country was preparing to host the Francophone games in 2005.
3. In 2012, Niger had a population of about 17 million. Over 90% of them are Muslim. The ethnic make-up of the country includes a majority of Hausa, followed by Zarma, Tuareg, and seven other ethnic groups.
4. The collection of Muhammad's sayings and deeds.
5. Scholars have attempted to theorize similar processes in resorting to the notions of Muslim publics and of the public sphere (Salvatore 2007; Hoexter, Eisenstadt, and Levtzion 2002; Eickelman and Anderson 1999; Launay and Soares 1999). Many of them stress the independence of Muslim activists and institutions from the postcolonial state. My understanding of the public

sphere refers to that of Eickelman and Salvatore, who, after they challenge the exclusive relationship between the West and the public sphere, argue that it "is the site where contests take place over the definition of the 'common good', and also the virtues, obligations, and rights that members of society require for the common good to be realized" (Eickelman and Salvatore 2002: 94). Thus, the actors I present see themselves not only as defenders of Islam, but also as contributors to the realization of the common good, hence the imperative of participation and *animation religieuse*.

6. Kadja's involvement in what she depicts as a service to her religion, *adina goya*, is not economically disinterested. The various "homes" where she teaches provide her with some of the financial resources she needs to continue her "work". As she said, "Nothing is free, and you earn the produce of your labor".

## REFERENCES

Alidou, Ousseina. 2005. *Engaging modernity: Muslim women and the politics of agency in postcolonial Niger*. Madison: University of Wisconsin Press.

Alidou, Ousseina and Hassana Alidou. 2008. "Women, Religion, and the Discourses of Legal Ideology Niger Republic". *Africa Today* 54, 3: 23–36.

Banégas, Richard and Jean-Pierre Warnier. 2001. 'Figures de la réussite et imaginaires politiques'. *Politique Africaine* 82: 5–21.

Bava, Sophie. 2003. 'De la baraka aux affaires: ethos économico-religieux et transnationalité chez les migrants sénégalais mourides'. *Revue Européenne de Migrations Internationales* 19, 2: 69–84.

Bourdieu, Pierre. 1971. 'Genèse et structure du champ religieux'. *Revue Française de Sociologie* 12, 3: 295–334.

Bruce, Steve. 1992. 'Funding the Lord's work: a typology of religious resourcing'. *Social Compass* 39, 1: 93–101.

Diouf, Mamadou. 2000. 'The Senegalese Mouride trade diaspora and the making of a vernacular cosmopolitanism'. *Public Culture* 12, 3: 679–702.

Ebin, Victoria. 1993. 'Les commerçants mourides à Marseilles et à New York 2002'. In: Emmanuel Grégoire and Üascal Labazée (eds). *Grands commerçants d'Afrique de l'ouest: logiques et pratique d'un groupe d'hommes d'affaires contemporains*. Paris: Karthala, 101–123.

Eickelman, Dale and Anderson Jon, W. 1999. *New Media in the Muslim World: The Emerging Public Sphere*. Bloomington: Indiana University Press.

Eickelman, Dale and Armando Salvatore. 2002. 'The public sphere and Muslim identities'. *Archives of European Sociology* XLIII, 1: 92–115.

Feillard, Gwenael. 2004. 'Insuffler l'esprit du capitalisme a l'Umma: la formation d'une "éthique islamique du travail" en Indonésie'. *Critique Internationale* 25: 93–116.

Fourchard, Laurent, Andre Mary, and Rene Otayek. 2005. *Entreprises Religieuses Transnationales en Afrique de l'Ouest*. Paris: Karthala.

Grégoire, Emmanuel. 1993. "Islam and Identity in Maradi." In: Louis Brenner (ed). *Muslim Identity and Social Change in Sub-Saharan Africa*. Bloomington: Indiana University Press: 105–115.

Havard, Jean-Francois. 2001. 'Ethos "bul faale" et nouvelles figures de la réussite au sénégal'. *Politique Africaine* 82: 63–77.

Hirschkind, Charles. 2006. *The Ethical Soundscape: Cassette Sermons and Islamic Counterpublics*. New York: Columbia University Press.

Hoexter, Miriam, Shmuel Eisenstadt, and Nehemia Levtzion (eds). 2002. *The Public Sphere in Muslim Societies*. Albany, NY: State University of New York Press.

## 56  *Abdoulaye Sounaye*

Last, Murray. 1988. 'Charisma and médecine in Northern Nigeria'. In: Donal Cruise O'Brien and Christian Coulon (eds). *Charisma and Brotherhood in African Islam*. Oxford: Clarendon, 183–208.

Launay, Robert and Benjamin Soares. 1999. 'The formation of an "Islamic sphere" in French colonial West Africa'. *Economy and Society* 28: 497–519.

LeBlanc, Marie Nathalie. 2012. 'Du militant a l'entrepreneur: les nouveaux acteurs religieux de la moralisation par le bas en Cote d'Ivoire'. *Cahiers d'Etudes Africaines* no. 206–207, 2: 493–516.

Malaquais, Dominique. 2001. 'Arts de Feyre au Cameroun'. *Politique Africaine* 82: 101–118.

Martin, David. 1992. 'Evangelicals and Economic Culture in Latin America: An Interim Comment on Research in Progress'. *Social Compass* 39, 1: 9–14.

Masquelier, Adeline. 2007. 'Negotiating Futures: Islam, Youth, and the State in Niger. In: Benjamin F. Soares and René Otayek, (eds). *Islam and Muslim Politics in Africa.*' New York: Palgrave. 243–262.

Masquelier, Adeline. 2009. *Women and Islamic Revival in a West African Town*. Bloomington: Indiana University Press.

Meunier, Olivier. 1997. *Dynamique de l'enseignement islamique au Niger: le cas de la ville de Maradi, Collection Etudes africaines*. Paris: L'Harmattan.

Meunier, Olivier. 1998. "Les voies de l'islam au Niger dans le Katsina indépendant du XIXe au XXe siècle : (Maradi, pays hawsa)", Mémoires de l'Institut. Paris.

Meunier, Olivier. 2009. *Variations et diversités éducatives au Niger, cultures africaines*. Paris: L'Harmattan.

Osella, Filippo and Caroline Osella. 2010. 'Muslim entrepreneurs in public life between India and the Gulf'. In: Filippo Osella and Benjamin Soares (eds). *Islam, Politics, Anthropology*. Chichester, UK: Wiley-Blackwell, 194–212.

Ould Ahmed Salem, Zekeria. 2001. '"Tcheb-tchib" et compagnie lexique de la survie et figures de la réussite en Mauritanie'. *Politique Africaine* 82: 78–100.

Robertson, Roland. 1992. 'The economization of religion? Reflections on the promise and limitations of the economic approach'. *Social Compass* 39, 1: 147–157.

Rudnyckyj, Daromir. 2009. 'Spiritual economies: Islam and neoliberalism in contemporary Indonesia'. *Cultural Anthropology* 24, 1: 104–141.

Salvatore, Armando. 2007. *The public sphere: liberal modernity, catholicism, islam*. New York: Palgrave Macmillan.

Soares, Benjamin F. 2005. *Islam and the Prayer Economy: History and Authority in a Malian Town*. Ann Arbor: University of Michigan Press.

Sounaye, Abdoulaye. 2005. 'Les politiques de l'islam dans l'ère de la démocratisation de 1991 à 2002'. In: Muriel Perez-Gomez (ed). *L'islam politique au sud du Sahara*. Paris: Karthala, 503–525.

Sounaye, Abdoulaye. 2007. 'Instrumentalizing the Qur'an in Niger public life'. *Journal for Islamic Studies* 27: 211–239.

Sounaye, Abdoulaye. 2009a. '*Izala* au Niger. Une alternative de communauté religieuse'. In: Laurent Fourchard, Odile Goerg, and Muriel Gomez-Perez (eds). *Les lieux de sociabilité urbaine dans la longue durée en Afrique*. Paris: L'Harmattan, 481–500.

Sounaye, Abdoulaye. 2009b. 'Speaking for Islam: Ulama, laïcité, and democratization in Niger'. *American Journal of Islamic Social Sciences* 23: 110–127.

Sounaye, Abdoulaye. 2009c. 'Ambiguous secularism: Islam, *Laïcité* and the State in Niger'. *Civilisations* LVIII, 2: 41–57.

Sounaye, Abdoulaye. 2009d. 'Islam, État et société: à la recherche d'une éthique publique au Niger'. In: Rene Otayek and Benjamin Soares (eds). *Islam, Etat et Société*. Paris: Karthala, 327–351.

Sounaye, Abdoulaye. 2011a. ' "Go find the second half of your faith with these women!" Women fashioning Islam in contemporary Niger'. *The Muslim World* 101, 3: 539–554.

Sounaye, Abdoulaye. 2011b. 'La "discothèque" islamique: CD et DVD au cœur de la réislamisation nigérienne'. Available online: http://www.ethnographiques. org/2011/Sounaye, accessed 22 May 2011.

Sounaye, Abdoulaye. 2012. 'Les Clubs des Jeunes Musulmans du Niger: un espace intergénérationnel'. In: Muriel Gomez-Perez and Marie Nathalie LeBlanc (eds). *L'Afrique des générations. Entre tensions et négociations*. Paris: Karthala, 166–217.

Sounaye, Abdoulaye. 2013. 'Alarama is all at once: Preacher, media savvy and religious entrepreneur'. *Journal of African Cultural Studies* 25, 1: 88–102.

Tall, Emmanuelle Kadya. 2003. 'Les nouveaux entrepreneurs en religion: la génération montante des chefs de cultes de possession à Cotonou (Bénin) et Salvador (Brésil)'. *Autrepart* 23: 75–90.

Watson, C.W. 2005. 'A popular Indonesian preacher: the significance of AA Gymnastiar'. *Journal of the Royal Anthropological Institute* 11, 4: 773–792.

Zakari, Maïkoréma. 2009. *L'islam dans l'espace nigérien*. (2 vols, *Etudes africaines*). Paris: L'Harmattan.

# 4 Entrepreneurial Discipleship
## Cooking Up Women's Sufi Leadership in Dakar

*Joseph Hill*

As formally appointed representatives (*muqaddam*s)[1] of the Fayḍa Tijāniyya Sufi movement, Adja Moussoukoro Mbaye and Aïda Thiam are both authorized to provide men and women with the mystical education (*tarbiya*) taught by the movement's founder, Shaykh Ibrahim Niasse (1900–1975), better known to his followers as "Baay" ("father" in Wolof). Both also act as spiritual leaders of large religious associations (*daayira*s) in the Dakar metropolitan area numbering well over a hundred people, through which they organize religious, educational, and other projects. Despite not having pursued an extended Islamic education, both effectively address their disciples in meetings, having learned from more formally trained leaders to quote Arabic texts alongside a Wolof gloss and then explain the quote's relevance to current situations. They are thus preachers and spiritual guides even though, like male *muqaddam*s who are not also textual specialists, they do not perform all the functions of well-known Islamic scholar-shaykhs and do not rival the prestige of more conventional male leaders who studied in traditional Islamic schools before studying at Al-Azhar University in Cairo. Both women approach discipleship not as a matter of waiting for orders from above but rather of conceiving and realizing unique projects through a combination of initiative, innovation, and a sense of unique calling. In this way, they exemplify an increasingly prevalent phenomenon that I call "entrepreneurial discipleship", although they do so in contrasting ways due to their contrasting diverse socioeconomic and educational backgrounds.

Adja Moussoukoro Mbaye is a successful entrepreneur in the conventional sense. She built a successful clothing retail business during the 1990s, but has more recently shifted her attention to importing and marketing a line of collagen-based skincare products. She is also a spiritual guide and "mother" for thousands of university students and graduates affiliated with student *daayira*s in Dakar, and has found numerous ways to invest her business success into religious capital. Although Adja Moussoukoro's economic and religious activities are complementary and she may have materially benefited from her religious networks, her livelihood does not depend on these networks. In contrast, Aïda Thiam is less economically advantaged, living in a remote and economically marginal suburb of Dakar with no steady income. A divorced mother with little formal education, she cannot depend on working relatives or formal employment for material support. Like Adja Moussoukoro, she leads a large community of disciples, yet she has no economic capital to invest in her religious activities. Instead, both her religious projects and her own subsistence rely materially on small financial contributions from disciples and others who value her contributions to the neighborhood, which include a Qurʾānic school she opened in a nearby unfinished house. Thus, although both women are religious entrepreneurs in that they creatively make use of the resources available to them in ways that increase their religious capital, religious entrepreneurship is a means of livelihood for only one of these women.

These two women are among the dozens of male and female Fayḍa disciples with no family background or training as religious leaders who, since the 1990s, have received appointments to the rank of *muqaddam* after demonstrating outstanding discipleship in some way. Until recently, and to this day in many smaller towns and villages, the rank of *muqaddam* in the Tijānī Sufi order was almost exclusively reserved for sons of important leaders who had pursued a lengthy Islamic education (Hill 2007, 2010). Over the past two decades, the Fayḍa has transformed from a marginal, largely rural movement to a mass youth movement in Dakar, its promise of universal access to a high level of mystical knowledge attracting many newly urbanized youth. The flood of new disciples has far exceeded the capacity of the relatively small numbers of formally trained leaders from clerical families to initiate and lead. Although the movement is growing far too quickly and diffusely to provide definitive numbers, I am aware of at least a dozen female and many times more male *muqaddam*s in Dakar of non-clerical backgrounds.

These formally recognized *muqaddam*s are far from being the only examples of entrepreneurial disciples. For every disciple known to act as a *muqaddam*, many others show a similar level of initiative in organizing disciple communities and religious projects and yet are not known as appointed spiritual guides. These entrepreneurial disciples organize *daayira*s and large religious meetings, open neighborhood Qurʾānic schools, found religious organizations to provide medical and economic assistance to the needy, master established repertoires of Sufi chant and compose new chants, and produce audiovisual materials and websites to publicize the Fayḍa's teachings. Disciples always seek endorsement and, if possible, sponsorship for their projects from central leaders, and they invariably describe themselves as merely "working for Baay" (*liggéeyal Baay*), often in response to Shaykh Ibrahim's personal instructions through dreams. Yet nearly all these projects are initiated by disciples themselves. Despite some efforts toward unification and centralization, the Fayḍa movement remains a collection of disparate disciple-initiated projects with a number of strong central leaders yet little centralized organization or media communications. Indeed, the movement's decentralized and polymorphous nature is precisely what drives disciples to seek new solutions to adapt it to many local situations.

Although innovative, entrepreneurial disciples' improvised solutions to contemporary problems are not born *ex nihilo* but rather depend on repertoires of skills and knowledge connected to a disciple's gender, socio-economic background, and education. A striking illustration of this observation that is central to this chapter is the fact that both women trace the moment of their recognition as religious authorities to an act of devotional cooking. Although generally overlooked in the literature on West African Muslim women, cooking is central to prevalent notions of pious Muslim womanhood in Senegal and also constitutes a significant and versatile stock of knowledge that women transpose from the household into numerous other fields. Cooking is central to women's strategies of reciprocity, collective action, and leadership in many contexts, including life-cycle rituals, large religious meetings, and individual economic activities. The consecration of cooking as a devotional activity is one crucial ingredient in Aïda Thiam's and Adja Moussoukoro Mbaye's largely improvised attempts to fill new leadership roles for a growing number of urbanizing youth who seek leadership, community, and purpose. These women exemplify entrepreneurial innovation not through inventing new doctrines or products but through such improvisations that transform aspects of conventional feminine piety into new ways of exercising religious authority.

This chapter begins with a discussion of the broader phenomenon of entrepreneurialization of religious practice in the context of recent changes sweeping West Africa. I then discuss the rapid growth of the Fayḍa movement in the context of these changes and examine the centrality of cooking as devotional practice for Fayḍa women. Finally, I characterize Aïda Thiam and Adja Moussoukoro Mbaye as entrepreneurial disciples who have gained recognition as religious leaders in response to their own initiative, with particular emphasis on their creative use of cooking to establish their religious mission and authority.

## THE DISCIPLE AS ENTREPRENEUR

Despite widespread predictions that modernity would lead to disenchantment, rationalization, and secularization (Berger 1967; Weber 1958, 1978), the neoliberal age is witnessing growing talk about a "resurgence of religion" in the public sphere (Antoun and Heglund 1987; Berger 1999; Kepel 1994), while discourses of unseen powers proliferate in Africa (Comaroff and Comaroff 1999; Geschiere 1997; West 2005). In urban African contexts, a diversity of religious movements have emerged, many headed by charismatic leaders who fashion Islamic discourses into responses to eminently contemporary problems (Schulz 2003, 2006; Soares 2004, 2005, 2010). Islamic leaders' influential roles in Senegalese life are nothing new (Copans 1980; Coulon 1981; Cruise O'Brien 1971; Villalón 1995), yet what seems to be new is the number and diversity of Islamic figures on the scene today and contrasting religious claims that bombard public spaces and everyday life. Despite the continued importance of routinized succession within the major Sufi families, many new religious figures are from non-clerical families, while the most influential leaders from clerical families are often junior or peripheral family members. If Weber is right that charismatic authority naturally arises during "moments of distress" (Weber 1978: 1111–1112), the situation of generalized and prolonged charisma we are witnessing seems to suggest a moment of generalized and prolonged distress.

The myriad charismatic Islamic leaders who in some way break the mold exemplify a more generalized trend toward what Banégas and Warnier (2001) call "new figures of success and power" that have become increasingly prevalent since the 1980s. As neoliberal policies have hollowed out state institutions and the formal economy, and state educational systems have all but collapsed, the once-dominant figure of the westernized "*évolué*" has lost much of its prestige. An assortment of new figures have emerged, whose success depends not on formal education and employment but on improvising between informal markets, global networks and flows, and contextually specific formations of knowledge and power. For example, the "*Móodu-Móodu*", or male Senegalese migrant who seeks material success through global trade, typically has little formal education and depends instead on Islamic networks mediated by charismatic Sufi leaders (Bava 2003; Diouf 2000; Kane 2011; Riccio 2004).

*Móodu-Móodu* and many other "new figures of success" are "entrepreneurs", conventionally understood as someone who uses initiative and innovation to attain a greater return on economic capital than competitors (see, for example Schumpeter 1934). Yet their economic success depends in part on investments of what Bourdieu (1971) calls "religious capital", or authority and prestige in the religious field. A complementary figure of success is the "religious entrepreneur", who in contrast converts economic capital into religious capital. For example, Kane (2003; and later Lubeck 2011) characterizes 'Yan Izala reformist preachers in northern Nigeria as religious entrepreneurs who rose to prominence through alliances with economic and political entrepreneurs, who invested their capital in the religious project. Many described as religious entrepreneurs have deftly made use of increasingly liberalized broadcast media as well as decentralized new media technologies, reaching new publics outside the confines of the religious establishment. These include popular Islamic television preachers in Egypt (Haenni 2002; Haenni and Holtrop 2002), female radio preachers in Mali (Schulz 2012), and Sufi leaders who reach a national following through audio cassettes, video discs, and the internet (Schulz 2003; Soares 2010). The designation "religious entrepreneur" applies not only to proponents of new religious movements but also to many upstart leaders within the more established Sufi obediences, whose influence may rival or far outstrip that of the obedience founder's direct descendants. For example, Senegalese Tijānī leader Moustapha Sy (Kane and Villalón 1995; Samson 2005; Samson Ndaw 2009; Villalón 2003) and Murid leader Modou Kara Mbacké (Buggenhagen 2012a; Samson Ndaw 2009) position themselves as unique leaders providing novel solutions, combining elements of personal charisma, Islamic reform, modernization, and occasional opposition to central leadership. These leaders engage in what Lubeck calls "innovative authenticity" (Lubeck 2011: 254), meaning that they claim to offer something authentically Islamic yet that breaks with other available options.

Although the literature on religious entrepreneurs in West Africa has focused on nationally renowned leaders, these leaders are a symptom of a more pervasive sense that, whether in social, economic, or spiritual matters, one can only get ahead through independent initiative, originality, and adaptation to novel circumstances. For many urban Senegalese youth disenchanted with entrenched political and religious figures' inability to provide solutions (Villalón 2003), it is not sufficient to follow the leader one's parents followed. Rather, one is responsible for seeking out the best religious path, transforming oneself into the best kind of believer, and actively organizing religious projects, whether a Sunni reform movement (Augis 2005, 2013; Gomez-Perez, LeBlanc, and Savadogo 2009), the Shīʿa movement (Leichtman 2009), or a Sufi movement like the Fayḍa that promises charismatic religious experience to any disciple.

For many Fayḍa adherents in Dakar, the entrepreneurial ethos penetrates the experience of what it means to be a disciple. Of course, religious discipleship and leadership, like the actions of economic entrepreneurs more conventionally defined, cannot be reduced to a matter of maximizing return on capital investment. Indeed, much like previous generations of disciples, the hundreds of Fayḍa adherents I have interviewed narrate their spiritual trajectories largely in terms of dreams, visions, mystical experiences, and providential encounters. Yet however numinous, any spiritual journey takes place within historical conditions that foster particular forms of religious subjectivity, agency, and material and immaterial economies. As established models of success have declined, leaving no stable alternative paths to financial and social success, many Senegalese Muslims have attempted to build their own models from the pieces of the broken models that preceded them.

## THE FAYḌA TIJĀNIYYA AS EMERGING URBAN YOUTH MOVEMENT

Since its beginnings in the 1930s among farmers in Saalum, the rural area around the regional Senegalese city of Kaolack, the Fayḍa Tijāniyya had remained marginal and stigmatized within Senegal, even while it quickly became the largest Islamic group in the rest of Africa, with followers especially concentrated in Mauritania and northern Nigeria (Gray 1998; Hiskett 1980). Since the 1990s, a period when "new figures of success" have arisen throughout Africa (Banégas and Warnier 2001), Islamic reform movements and charismatic figures have proliferated in Senegal, and the Fayḍa became a mass movement in Dakar, especially among newly urbanized youth (Hill 2010; Seesemann 2011). The Fayḍa seems in many ways tailor-made for a moment of upheaval and disillusionment, addressing contemporary contradictions and providing a combination of strong leadership, community, and tools for individual introspection and development. In its generalization of charismatic religious experience through which individuals are spiritually reborn and break with their past selves, it resembles Pentecostal movements spreading in many Christian areas during the same period (Gooren 2002; LeBlanc 2003; Meyer 1998; Robbins 2004; Lauterbach, this volume). Yet its simultaneous emphasis on complementing spiritual experience with personal edification through education and textual orthodoxy allows educated adherents to claim the level of rigor of reformist critics. Indeed, several prominent Fayḍa members I interviewed (including one of those included below) had previously been involved in the reformist group *Jamāʿat ʿIbād al-Raḥmān*.

The Fayḍa's most distinctive selling point is its unique form of *tarbiya*, or spiritual education, designed to allow any disciple in a short span to attain a direct, mystical knowledge of God at the hands of an appointed representative or spiritual guide (*muqaddam*) (Hill 2007; Seesemann 2000, 2011). In this abbreviated path to mystical knowledge, a *muqaddam* instructs the initiate to repeat and meditate on certain phrases until the initiate experiences the "obliteration of self" (*fanāʾ al-nafs*) required to experience God directly. The Fayḍa's streamlining of mystical knowledge among non-specialists popularized mystical Sufi knowledge and opened the door for male and female non-specialists to cultivate their own direct experience of God. For many disciples, this process is accompanied by conversion-style narratives of dreams, visions, and mystical states (*ḥāl*) that explain not only their journey into the movement but also how they realized what they are to do to "work for Baay" (*liggéeyal Baay*). Thus, each disciple potentially has charismatic authority to carry out a unique project. Yet at the same time, each project, whether dispensing *tarbiya*, organizing a local disciple association (*daayira*), or opening a free clinic, must be authorized by a representative of the Fayḍa's more or less routinized hierarchy. Thus, this movement perpetuates itself through reproducing a mutually sustaining relationship between charisma and routinized authority (Hill 2006).

Only since the Fayḍa's rapid expansion during the 1990s and especially since 2000 have Senegalese women in the Fayḍa acted openly as spiritual guides and leaders of religious associations (*daayiras*). Although the appointment of women as spiritual guides in the Tijānī and other Sufi orders is not new, women have only recently acted openly as spiritual guides and *daayira* leaders. Tijānī women appointed in other times and places have nearly always either refrained from acting openly as spiritual guides or have only led groups of women in order to maintain strict gender segregation (for example, Hutson 1999, 2001). Shaykh Ibrahim quietly appointed numerous women as *muqaddams*, including his own daughters and several other women who had distinguished themselves through their service. Notably, a daughter of Shaykh Ibrahim who is herself a famous leader and Qurʾān teacher, Shaykha Mariam Niasse, told me that one of these women lived in Shaykh Ibrahim's hometown of Kaolack and caught the Shaykh's attention through bringing him delicious meals. Yet it appears that the women he appointed refrained from openly acting as Sufi leaders during his lifetime (Hill 2010). Although Shaykh Ibrahim clarified in his writings that women could attain the same spiritual status as men and could in theory act as spiritual guides for men and women, it is not clear that he ever advocated that women should act openly as Sufi leaders, and his disciples express conflicting views about what he intended by appointing women as *muqaddams*. Another relevant move Shaykh Ibrahim made was to appoint many non-scholars as *muqaddams*, a title previously reserved for renowned Islamic scholars. Many of these non-specialist *muqaddams* did not end up acting as religious leaders, yet those who did focused on giving *tarbiya* to the many new disciples, leaving other Islamic leadership roles to leaders with a scholarly background.

Since the 1990s, the Fayḍa's leaders have actively adapted the movement to serve a large number of youth who came to Dakar from small towns and villages seeking education or work. For many youth living far from their families, the Fayḍa has offered an appealing combination of individual religious knowledge through *tarbiya*, social connections to other youth and through religious associations (*daayiras*), and trusted and knowledgeable authority figures in the local *muqaddam* and central leadership. *Muqaddams* and disciples have adapted these elements to suit the needs of people from diverse cultural and socioeconomic backgrounds living in diverse circumstances. Although disciples come from all economic, educational, and social backgrounds, the overwhelming majority of active *daayira* participants I have met in Dakar are young people from Senegal's villages and small towns for whom participation in a *daayira* and discipleship to a *muqaddam* are central to organizing personal and social lives in the city.

Whereas in villages there is typically one formally trained religious specialist who plays the role of *muqaddam* alongside many other roles, in Dakar there are a growing number of *muqaddams*, male and female, who have no formal religious training and who specialize in initiating and leading the steady stream of new, generally young disciples (Hill 2010). Most *muqaddams* I have met in Dakar practice some non-religious profession alongside their religious work and became *muqaddams* not through inheritance but through proving themselves as particularly active lay disciples. Although some Fayḍa adherents denigrate the "new *muqaddams*" for their lack of knowledge and claim they are hardly *muqaddams* at all, central leaders with a formal Islamic education continue to appoint them in large numbers. Locating particularly active disciples to initiate the influx of urban disciples and lead the *daayira*s that are cropping up in Dakar's neighborhoods seems the only way the movement can keep up with its growth. In many cases, the most outstanding disciple in a neighborhood without formal leadership happens to be a woman, as was the case with Aïda Thiam, discussed below.

The new *muqaddam*s, like many leading disciples who are not *muqaddam*s, are entrepreneurial disciples in that they devote their personal resources with initiative and innovation to realizing unique projects and increasing their prestige in the religious community. Each of Dakar's dozens of Fayḍa *daayira*s is simultaneously an authorized chapter of the larger Fayḍa movement, represented by the Ansaroudine Federation (*Rābiṭat Anṣār al-Dīn*),[2] and a unique initiative of its members. Each *daayira* has its title, set of goals and projects, and identifying t-shirts designed by members. Many have their own uniforms, a library of cassettes and pamphlets by their local leader, website, and page on social networking sites such as YouTube and Facebook. Various *daayira*s and other disciple organizations have organized volunteer medical clinics, Qurʾānic schools, vocational training programs, rotating credit associations, and agricultural projects. For example, students and graduates of health-related post-secondary programs in Dakar founded "Baye Assistance Médicale", while nurses at a hospital in the Parcelles Assainies founded the "Association Mame Astou Diankha", both of which collect medical supplies and offer medical services in poor villages and neighborhoods. Although *daayira* members seek a major Fayḍa leader's blessing for all projects, it is the members along with their local *muqaddam* leader who initiate the projects.

## DEVOTIONAL COOKING AND WOMEN'S ENTREPRENEURIAL DISCIPLESHIP

Aïda Thiam and Adja Moussoukoro Mbaye live in differing economic conditions and have carved out contrasting roles for themselves, yet one striking similarity is their performance of devotion and ultimately religious authority through acts of cooking. Social scientists long ago recognized the central place of culinary offerings and commensality in religious practices around the world (for example Smith 1894; Hubert and Mauss 1899), yet the uses and meanings of food offerings to those who produce them, overwhelmingly women in most parts of the world, have received little attention. Buggenhagen (2012a, 2012b) has shown that Senegalese Murid women's narratives emphasize different religious motivations than those emphasized in the male-centric literature. Women she interviewed described food offerings to religious leaders more as a means of earning religious merit (*tuyaaba*) directly from God than of earning spiritual blessing (*barke*, from Arabic *baraka*), a quality most often transmitted through and therefore emphasized by men. The narratives of Fayḍa women I interviewed suggest that they associate devotional cooking with a range of motivations in various situations, including seeking religious merit and blessing as well as perform-ing piety and devotion before fellow disciples and leaders. The two women discussed here associate cooking with religious authority within a context where cooking is a central medium through which most women participate in their own households, their kin and neighborhood networks, and the Fayḍa religious community.

In every Fayḍa household I have visited in Senegal, women have been responsible for preparing meals. Even senior women who delegate the work to hired servants and juniors insist that, as pious Muslim women, they are ultimately responsible for the state of the house and the food served in it. To explain women's natural connection to the home, many women leaders quoted the Qurʾānic verse commanding women: "And stay quietly in your houses, and make not a dazzling display, like that of the former times of ignorance" (Qurʾān 33:33). Even internationally known *shaykhas* (senior female religious leaders) and successful businesswomen insist that their domestic responsibilities are their first priority even if their actual involve-ment in domestic work is entirely symbolic. Indeed, I have found that the busier a woman is with other pursuits, the more likely she is to draw atten-tion to the fact that she keeps a clean and well-run home, thus forestall-ing accusations that she has abandoned her domestic responsibilities.[3] The short biography on the website of Shaykha Mariam Niasse, Shaykh Ibra-him's world-renowned daughter who runs four Qurʾānic schools and a large Islamic Institute in Dakar, tells how she became a well-known teacher "without ever neglecting her domestic tasks" (Dar Al Quran Al Karim). In interviews, Shaykha Mariam told me her father described her as a son when she was born and predicted that she would never do "women's work", yet she repeatedly emphasized her deference to her late husband and the fact that he worked outside the home while she carried out all her projects within the confines of her bedroom while overseeing the home.

While many women have the seniority or the financial means to rely on others' cooking labor, I have never known a Fayḍa woman to question the hegemonic notion that a woman's piety and prestige are tied to maintaining the household and feeding its members and guests. On the contrary, many women find opportunities to profit socially and economically through their cooking. A woman's ability to offer hospitality through cooking well brings praise and sometimes even monetary gifts from guests, who may explain that they want to thank her for her kindness and generosity. The extensive practical knowledge of food markets and cooking and the social networks women develop through group cooking for life-cycle rituals and religious events serve as economic and social resources. I have known a great many women, including one female *muqaddam*, who have converted their culi-nary knowledge and networks into commercial activities, such as selling raw ingredients or prepared meals at tables in the street or market. Such work can dovetail with their domestic duties, as they can feed leftovers and unsold merchandise to their families.

Cooking among Fayḍa adherents has religious significance extending far beyond feeding the household and making a living. Since the Fayḍa's beginning, women's culinary expertise has provided a basis through which they have participated in the religious community, distinguished themselves as devoted disciples, and accessed religious blessing and merit through feeding leaders. Many elder women who joined the Fayḍa movement during its early days fondly recalled their village organizing work days in fields whose produce was consecrated as an offering to Shaykh Ibrahim, who himself would visit the village during those days and pray for the disciple community. Some women would till weeds alongside the men while others would stay behind to cook lunch for the rest. A few would cook a special meal for Baay and his companions. Many rural women I spoke with placed these meals for Baay at the heart of their discipleship narratives, retelling the words with which Shaykh Ibrahim blessed the cooks and how his prayers were later realized. Interviewees from one of the early Fayḍa villages described several rural women during the 1930s as "leaders of women" and even as *muqaddamas* formally appointed by Baay.[4] My interviewees told me that their primary responsibilities were to organize women for these work days and to oversee the production of meals for workers and the special meal presented to Baay. Today disciples in some villages continue to organize such work days, with the same division of labor, for Shaykh Ibrahim's sons and other major leaders, although monetary offerings have become far more important in recent years.

Women's cooking today is also indispensable to the large meetings that *daayira*s and federations of *daayira*s organize in Dakar and throughout Senegal. In large meetings comprising hundreds of *daayira*s, such as the *gàmmu* (*mawlid*) celebrating Shaykh Ibrahim Niasse's birth in his birthplace of Tayba Ñaseen, each attending *daayira* cooks up to three meals for *daayira* members, their hosts, guests, and leaders. Before the meeting, each male and female *daayira* member pays (in my experience, usually 5,000 FCFA, around $10) to the *daayira*'s treasurer to cover transportation, food, sound system, and perhaps a commemorative t-shirt for the event. The *daayira*'s "President of the Women's Commission" distributes some of this money to *daayira* women to buy rice and vegetables, while male *daayira* members procure several sheep or goats. During the morning of the *gàmmu*, *daayira* members board a chartered bus while some of the men tie the food, the animals, a folded canvas pavilion, and a sound system to its roof. Once arrived at their host family's home in the pilgrimage site, *daayira* members set up a pavilion and sound system for their own afternoon meeting before the main overnight meeting in the central square begins. Men of the *daayira* butcher the livestock while the women gather around large bowls chopping onions and other vegetables, picking debris out of rice, and then stirring huge cauldrons of rice and meat sauce (*ceeb u yàpp*) for the collective lunch. This is a time for women, many of them schoolmates from high school, to engage in light-hearted conversation. The women invariably prepare a few special bowls to be distributed to notables, for example their host family, the *shaykh* from Medina Baay who oversees and authorizes the *daayira*, and perhaps well-known keynote speakers or visiting leaders.

Nearly every *daayira* has a male president and a female "Women's President", who gives input during the *daayira*'s general organizational meetings but whose primary responsibility is to coordinate the production of collective meals at large meetings. On a larger scale, the women's president of the Ansaroudine Federation of Dakar, which coordinates the activities of hundreds of *daayira*s in the Dakar region, is primarily responsible for organizing women's efforts to cook huge meals for attendees of several annual events in Dakar and Kaolack and to make sure visiting leaders are well-fed. The women's president during much of my research over the past decade, Ajaa Jaara Njaay, is herself a *muqaddama* who coordinates women's production of meals for large events while overseeing her own two large mixed-gender *daayira*s.

In addition to the collective meal prepared by the women of *daayira*s for general attendees and leaders, some individual women cook luxurious meals for keynote speakers and other guests of honor, each presenting a dish as an offering for an honored leader. Visiting leaders and their companions may eat a little from each bowl, often pronouncing a blessing on the women who cooked the meal. Leftovers will then be distributed to other meeting attendees, who receive blessing (*baraka*) through this indirect connection to a leader who has eaten from the same bowl.

Cooking is thus central to many women's performance of prestige and piety and easily becomes a medium for many women's entrepreneurial improvisations. Women derive significant social prestige through offering hospitality to family and guests; their participation in religious activities largely takes the form of collective and at times individual cooking for fellow disciples and leaders; and one of the most consistent ways women tell me of drawing leaders' attention is through acts of devotional cooking. It is in this context that Aïda Thiam and Adja Moussoukoro Mbaye have integrated cooking into their repertoires of entrepreneurial discipleship. Their use of cooking draws on notions of femininity presented as timeless, yet they transfigure acts of cooking into forms of spiritual authority and leadership harmonious with hegemonic notions of pious womanhood. Their narratives are in many ways very different, yet these narratives illustrate the striking regularity with which acts of devotional cooking constitute key acts in the formation of many women's moral and religious authority. This creative use of cooking in establishing religious authority illustrates the dependence of entrepreneurial innovation on gendered repertoires of action and hegemonic notions of gender roles.

## FROM THE MARKET TO SPIRITUAL MOTHERHOOD: ADJA MOUSSOUKORO MBAYE

Adja Moussoukoro Mbaye is an entrepreneur in more than one sense of the word. Not only has she established several import and retail businesses, but she has invested her economic resources and expertise into religious entrepreneurship. Adja Moussoukoro is the spiritual guide for a *daayira* comprising her own initiates as well as the spiritual guide (called "spiritual Mother") of the federation of post-secondary student *daayira*s in the Dakar area. Both organizations count at least as many male as female disciples, the vast majority of them youth of university age. Although she is stepping into roles that have almost always been reserved for men (spiritual apprenticeship, oratory, leading a religious association), she explicitly and implicitly defines herself as a spiritual mother responsible for nurturing, correcting, feeding, and otherwise taking care of a spiritual family. Diametrically opposing the classical image of the fiercely competitive entrepreneur, her gentle and elegant demeanor is a cornerstone of both her persona in the fashion and cosmetics industry and her resignification of religious authority in terms of motherhood. She traces her induction into religious leadership to a moment of culinary sacrifice, which she was able to subsidize through her independent income. She has repeated such culinary offerings many times over the years, bringing herself to the attention of many major leaders and helping university students organize collective meals at their religious events.

Born in 1960, Adja Moussoukoro was married by the age of fourteen and soon thereafter followed her husband into the Salafi Islamic reform movement *Jamāʿat ʿIbād ar-Raḥmān* (Organization of Servants of the Merciful, known in Wolof as the *Ibaadu* movement), remaining a prominent member for a decade as she raised seven children. She told me she was happy she married and had children so early because this allowed her to fulfill the task of physical motherhood early in life so she could devote the rest of her life to other pursuits. While raising her children, she avidly studied religion, psychology, and other subjects and came to experience an inexorable thirst to "know God". In 1992, a year after giving birth to her last child, she approached Fayḍa leaders and asked for mystical initiation (*tarbiya*). After her initiation, she continued to visit various Fayḍa spiritual guides to seek further spiritual instruction and became acquainted with some of Shaykh Ibrahim's children. For several years, she and her relatives testify, she was in an unstable spiritual state in which her absorption in her direct experience of God prevented her from being fully aware of her social and family obligations, and it took some time for her to learn how to juggle her mystical knowledge and these obligations. During this period, her own spiritual guide recognized that she had attained a high spiritual station and appointed her as a *muqaddam*. Her husband, who remained a leading member in a prominent Islamic movement that taught that Sufism was a forbidden innovation, could not understand her mystical journey and eventually divorced her.

One day in 1994, a group of Fayḍa students at the University of Dakar knocked on her door to seek her help. They were just starting their student *daayira*, which counted less than ten members, most of them men living in the dorms far from their families. They were organizing their first annual conference and had invited their preferred keynote speaker, Shaykh Naziiru, a senior son of Shaykh Ibrahim. Naziiru was a logical choice to address a group of students because he was widely seen as an intellectual and patron of learning and had been appointed by Shaykh Ibrahim to run his Islamic institute in the city of Kaolack, the spiritual center of the Fayḍa movement. Although they had made all the arrangements for the venue, the amplification, and the chairs, they felt unable to cook a meal worthy of presenting to such an esteemed leader. A junior daughter of Shaykh Ibrahim who was studying at the university had described Adja Moussoukoro as an excellent cook and devoted disciple and suggested approaching her for help. So they had brought her the money they had raised for the meal—18,000 FCFA Francs (at the time, shortly before devaluation, around $70). Adja Moussoukoro thanked God that they had been sent to her and prayed for the daughter of Shaykh Ibrahim who had made the suggestion. She then told them to keep the money they had raised and to use it to buy juices and soft drinks for the event. She would take care of the meal herself. From her own coffers she took twice the amount they had raised, bought a large ram and had it slaughtered, and cooked an "exquisite lunch" for the conference attendees and their honored guests.

The students presented the meal and drinks to the shaykh, and after he had eaten they introduced Adja Moussoukoro to him as the one who had provided the meal. During an interview in 2010, she described this moment as the moment when she was designated as the "mother" of Dakar's students, a role for which she is widely known today:

> He told me: I entrust you with this family of Baay [Shaykh Ibrahim] at the University. I must tell you, though, that accompanying disciples who are studying is difficult, because a disciple who studies has nothing but many needs. He said: But I tell you that you will see the day when you become the mother of the doctors, the mother of the engineers, the mother of the presidents, the mother of ministers, the mother of ambassadors, he told me, you will see a time that will be very pleasant. However, the journey will be difficult.

She confirmed that his prediction has come to pass as she saw the university *daayira*'s meetings grow from eight or ten attendees to over five hundred. Ever since then, as I observed, Fayḍa students at the university and then all of Dakar's institutions of higher learning have called her their "mother". In addition to offering the students spiritual guidance, she offers the female students the use of her kitchen, expertise, and cooking materials to prepare sumptuous meals for attendees and special guests at the large meetings they organize. During earlier interviews in 2004 and 2005, she told us that although these disciples sometimes brought her small monetary offerings (*àddiya*), she spent far more of her own money to help disciples with their problems. In interviews in 2010, she said that now whenever she goes out to take care of paperwork, almost always "there is someone there who recognizes me and comes and says 'you were my mother when I was in the student *daayira*' " and takes care of whatever she needs. If she is sick, she says, she does not need to go see a doctor, as some doctor who used to be a member of the students' *daayira* will visit her and someone else will buy any prescriptions she needs.

Adja Moussoukoro has repeated her original act of devotional cooking many times over the years. Throughout the period when I visited and interviewed Adja Moussoukoro between 2004 and 2010, I often found her hosting important religious leaders visiting from Kaolack or Mauritania and she often sent plates of food to leaders staying in other houses. Shaykh Ibrahim's then-eldest living son and Ahmed Daam Niasse (d. 2010) was ill and often stayed in Dakar for long stretches of time to be treated. Every day when he was in town Adja Moussoukoro would send him and his family a nice lunch. Whenever another important *muqaddam* from Mauritania visited Dakar, she and her husband would sometimes host him and his entourage in her own apartment (she was remarried but maintained her own apartment), and on other occasions would send their daily meals to other houses where they might stay. Additionally, she allows the young women of the *daayiras* associated with Dakar's various institutions of higher learning to use her kitchen and her extensive cooking materials to prepare meals for their *daayiras*' annual events. Before the student events I have attended in Dakar, female *daayira* members have met at her apartment to cook the collective meal and then have coordinated with the men of the *daayira* to transport Adja Moussoukoro's large pots full of cooked food to the conference venue and then, once cleaned, back to her apartment.

Adja Moussoukoro describes and surely experiences her acts of culinary devotion as part of a fundamentally spiritual narrative. Yet these acts depend on her culinary abilities and, more importantly, on subsidies from her own successful business enterprises. Not only does she come from a well-to-do family—she says her father owned around a hundred rental properties in Kaolack and many cattle, and her first husband was a successful trader—but she started her own business ventures and became financially independent during the 1990s, around the same time that she joined the Fayḍa. The first time I met her in 2004, she was running a successful clothing import business. In fact, it was the manager of one of her clothing shops, also her son-in-law and a *muqaddam* actively involved in organizing her *daayira*, who took me and my collaborators to see her. Soon after this visit, she traveled to Dubai and loaded up a container full of clothing to sell at her shops.

She has since left the clothing business to others and focuses on acting as the sole licensed importer, distributor, and public face for a line of beauty and skincare products manufactured in Côte d'Ivoire. Her products are now widely distributed throughout Senegal and her company has a presence on Facebook and on television. During my most recent interview with her in 2010, Adja Moussoukoro calmly paused the conversation and switched on the flat-screen television, turning it to the private station 2STV. The fashion program "Actumode" appeared, showing Adja Moussoukoro in her office telling the station's fashion reporter about the benefits of the collagen-based skincare products she markets. Wearing a white, golden-embroidered dress and an elegant, white headscarf similar to the one she wore during our interview, Adja Moussoukoro described the anti-aging benefits of these products and gave tips on how to prevent skin damage. She cautioned against using "aggressive" skin lighteners (*xeesal*), but reassured that collagen-based products "will take away the damage caused by skin lighteners" and reverse aging. Adja Moussoukoro's business ventures are not overtly religious, and most of her employees are not Fayḍa adherents, although she employs some graduates she met through the university *daayira* (for example, a friend of mine hired in 2009 as her accountant) as well as more manual workers, such as tailors who have recently come to Dakar.

In short, Adja Moussoukoro succeeded as an entrepreneurial disciple in creating a unique role for herself in the Fayḍa community—the "mother" of the university students and a host for major leaders in Dakar—through a combination of cultivating her own spiritual discourse and practice and investing economic capital into social and religious capital (Bourdieu 1971, 1984). Notably, she subsidized acts of devotional cooking through which she has established and maintained relationships with students and the Fayḍa's key leaders. Her business and religious activities thrive off one another in numerous ways: her religious networks feed into her employment network; she earns enough to personally sustain her own devotional cooking and to help students organize successful events; and she maintains her own home in Dakar (plus one under construction in Kaolack) where she can host important leaders, hold meetings for her disciples, and invite women from the *daayira*s to use her kitchen and tools to cook for large student meetings. Busy with work-related and religious responsibilities, she now leaves most of the cooking work to a maid and daughters, although she carefully supervises to make sure meals are up to her standards. Of course, Adja Moussoukoro's religious leadership depends on many elements aside from cooking and her business success that this chapter has not discussed, including her skillfulness in addressing young people's challenges using mystical and textual religious teachings. Yet her entrepreneurial discipleship is inseparable from both her success as an economic entrepreneur and the repertoire of gendered behaviors such as cooking and motherhood that she creatively transposes into the realm of religious authority and leadership.

## DREAMS OF A UNIQUE MISSION: AÏDA THIAM

Aïda Thiam's story resembles Adja Moussoukoro Mbaye's in some ways, yet her contrasting economic situation accompanies an opposite flow of investment between economic and religious capital. Aïda Thiam recounts similar experiences of being inexorably led by God through Shaykh Ibrahim to the mission she now carries out. Both women share certain features of their family background: both were raised in Kaolack and count Islamic educators among their ancestors although neither have religious educators or leaders in their immediate family.[5] Yet Aïda Thiam has had none of Adja Moussoukoro's (even if informal) educational or economic opportunities, and her speech is closer to that of an unschooled rural housewife than that of an urban elite or religious cleric, showing a distinct Saalum dialect and few French borrowings. Her economic situation could not be more different. As a youth, she moved with her family to Yëmbël, one of Dakar's most economically depressed and geographically marginal neighborhoods, which largely lacks electricity, running water, and paved roads and becomes an inundated swamp during the rainy season. The sprawling neighborhood is populated mainly by Senegalese fleeing rural poverty who have built largely informal housing. She married young and only briefly and then raised three children on her own: her son, who died in an accident in 2011 at the age of 24, and the younger son and daughter of her long-deceased sister.

Her *daayira* is in some ways very different from most other Fayḍa *daayira*s I have encountered in Senegal. First, it is one of the few I encountered founded as a women's organization. Also, whereas most *daayira*s were founded as youth organizations even if they include a smattering of older members, this association's founding adult women remain its core members, although over time it has come to resemble other *daayira*s demographically, as a large number of young men have joined and especially after it incorporated a nearby youth *daayira* in 2010.

While Aïda Thiam was living in Yëmbël as an adult with her mother, a devout disciple of Shaykh Ibrahim, Shaykh Ibrahim appeared to her in a series of dreams and told her to organize the disciples in the area into a *daayira* named after his own mother, Mame Astou Diankha. She emphatically declares (confirmed by other leaders I asked later) that she was the first to name an organization after Shaykh Ibrahim's mother, although several newer associations have followed suit. All these similarly named organizations were originally founded by women who intended to take Mame Astou as their model of a pious Muslim woman. Like many households in marginal areas, Aïda Thiam's household was made up of several single, divorced, or widowed women and their dependents, all Fayḍa adherents. She had met several other Fayḍa women in the neighborhood although there was no *daayira* there. In 2001, she called these women together and proposed forming a *daayira* as her dream had instructed her, and they then scoured the neighborhood to find other Fayḍa members. After they had around eight women, the group decided to become official through getting authorization from Shaykh Ibrahim's sons to found a *daayira*.

They raised 30,000 FCFA (around $60) and went to the annual *gàmmu* (*mawlid*) honoring Shaykh Ibrahim in Tayba Ñaseen, where they cooked a meal that they named "the lunch of Maam Astu Jànqa" (*añ u Maam Astu Jànqa*), presenting plates to several of Shaykh Ibrahim's senior sons.

According to Aïda Thiam, they told each of these leaders of their desire to found a *daayira* named after Shaykh Ibrahim's mother, and each leader congratulated them, telling them that Shaykh Ibrahim himself had foretold this but that they were the first to realize it. Shaykh Ibrahim's son Shaykh Màkki told them: "Thank God, praise God, perhaps the person who would do this or the time hadn't come yet, so may you all work hard". Shaykh Màkki accepted the position of the *daayira*'s "*wāṣilah*" or link to the headquarters of Medina Baay, Kaolack, and came to be the keynote speaker at their initially small annual conferences. When I visited the *daayira* in Tayba Ñaseen in 2010 on the afternoon of another *gàmmu*, I found the women of the *daayira* busy preparing their lunch as the men were butchering the goats. Soon they had prepared a bowl of rice with meat, and I accompanied Aïda Thiam as she and some of the leading women of the *daayira* personally delivered it to Shaykh Màkki's house.

At one of their annual conferences, in 2007, Màkki inaugurated the *daara* (Qurʾānic school) they had founded and asked him for authorization to open. Aïda Thiam had noticed an unfinished and un-roofed house in the neighborhood that had been collecting garbage for the past two years, so she located the absentee owner and sought permission from him and from the neighborhood chief to open a Qurʾānic school there. It is customary whenever a son or close companion of Shaykh Ibrahim visits to raise "offerings for Baay" (*àddiya Baay*), so at the school's inauguration, held as part of the *daayira*'s annual conference, *daayira* members raised 50,000 FCFA ($100) and presented it to Shaykh Màkki. He responded that he had not come to collect *àddiya* but to dedicate the school, and returned the money to her in addition to 50,000 FCFA of his own, with which they finished a room and built a roof over it and hired a teacher to begin teaching.

Aïda Thiam's *daayira* grew to the point where it had hundreds of members, including a growing number of young men, as it was the only Fayḍa *daayira* in the neighborhood. *Daayira* members are mostly migrants from Senegal's various regions who, like Aïda Thiam, came to Dakar during their youth. During these early years, new disciples who presented themselves to Aïda Thiam had to trek to another neighborhood to be initiated into the Sufi order. Yet in recognition for her feats of organization, Makki Niasse appointed her as a *muqaddam* during the *daayira*'s annual conference in 2008. Since then she has initiated many new disciples into the Fayḍa movement. In 2010, her *daayira* incorporated another *daayira* in the nearby neighborhood of Caaroy that did not previously have a resident *muqaddam*, making her the resident spiritual authority for a much larger number of young people and a large area of Dakar's suburbs. Like Adja Moussoukoro, the term she prefers to describe her relationship to all these disciples is "mother".

One major difference between Aïda Thiam and Adja Moussoukoro and most of the other "new" *muqaddam*s I interviewed is that Aïda Thiam has no source of livelihood beyond her religious activities. Her home doubles as her *daayira*'s headquarters. Until not long before I met her in 2009, she had lived in her mother's nearby house, where the *daayira* would meet in her own bedroom. The *daayira* soon outgrew this single room, and they sought a larger space. Nearby was a neighborhood for military officers (Cité Comico Yeumbeul) where many new houses were being built that were not yet inhabited. She located one of these unfinished homes (much as she had done for the Qurʾānic school) and convinced the owner (not a Fayḍa adherent) to let her live there at a nominal rent as the *daayira* used the home as their headquarters. Shortly after I visited her in 2010, she moved out of the officers' neighborhood and to a house next to her mother's house that the *daayira* is now renting. When I asked how she pays the rent, she said God provides it. Although the *daayira* members do their best to support her, most of them are young students who have no stable income of their own, and she describes much of the support she gets for her school and the *daayira* as coming not from her own religious community but from neighborhood benefactors who value her provision of religious education and a sense of moral community to at-risk young people who may not otherwise have much guidance. Her success, therefore, depends on her ability to convince both disciples and non-disciples that she offers guidance that will help young people stay out of trouble and learn good habits to help them succeed in school and in their careers.

In some ways, Aïda Thiam seems a polar opposite to classic images of entrepreneurs. Not only does she project the persona of a gentle and mild mother like Adja Moussoukoro, but she is far from a model of economic success. Yet she is a paradigmatic example of an entrepreneurial disciple in that she approaches her discipleship as a unique mission to realize something important and invests whatever capabilities she has into succeeding in this mission. While she lacks Adja Moussoukoro Mbaye's economic capital, her improvised investments in religious capital mobilize a similar stock of gendered practices surrounding cooking and motherhood as well as a mystical narrative that establishes her as having a unique and authentic mission. By performing religious authority in a way that harmonizes prevalent perceptions of feminine piety with religious leadership, Aïda Thiam improvises new, feminine leadership roles through which she has dramatically built up the Fayḍa community in a part of Dakar where the Fayḍa did not previously exist as an organized entity. Aïda Thiam illustrates a contrasting model of entrepreneurial discipleship to that of Adja Moussoukoro in that she does not invest her own economic capital in her religious mission but, on the contrary, supports herself economically—if humbly and precariously—through others' support for her religious mission. Her dramatic increase in religious capital depends on her own hard work and ingenuity purely within the religious domain, her religious work and very livelihood supported by innumerable small infusions of economic capital from those who recognize and support her religious mission—her followers, neighbors, and *shaykh*.

## CONCLUSION

In this sense, Adja Moussoukoro Mbaye and Aïda Thiam exemplify opposite relationships between religious and economic activities and thus contrasting examples of entrepreneurial discipleship. Adja Moussoukoro's successful non-religious business provides economic capital that she can invest in devotional cooking and thereby in relationships with major religious leaders as well as future professionals and leaders in her *daayira*s. Whether she materially profits from her religious roles is less important than the prestige, influence, and fulfillment she realizes through creatively establishing new religious roles for herself. In contrast, Aïda Thiam's very livelihood depends on her ability to offer religious services valued by young disciples seeking guidance and by non-disciple benefactors concerned about the neighborhood's marginalized and potentially at-risk youth. The donations that her religious projects attract to her not only allow her to carry out her religious projects but directly replace her lack of formal income, husband, or working kin who can support her.

What both women share is that, as entrepreneurial disciples, they approach discipleship as a call to fulfill a unique mission that demands realizing something new using whatever resources they have. A booming spiritual market of youth seeking spiritual guidance and community calls for new forms of leadership that these women, with their particular experience as mothers and household managers, can fulfill particularly well.

As different as these women are, it is striking that a central pillar of both women's improvisations is the creative use of the conventionally feminine act of cooking in ways that demonstrated their piety and organizational effectiveness and drew the attention of leaders such as Shaykh Ibrahim's sons. Their religious activities even after they have become religious leaders for hundreds of disciples continue to focus largely on producing communal and devotional meals with other women. Entrepreneurial innovation here clearly depends on one's specific repertoire of knowledge and capabilities gained through gendered daily practice. Although some women may reach a stage in life where they can avoid cooking on a daily basis, among Fayḍa adherents there are few domains as strongly gendered and as widely practiced by women as cooking, and nearly all women, including young women from well-to-do families, are expected to learn to cook and to engage in cooking at some point. Thus, it is not surprising that these women, despite their differences, use cooking as a primary medium for improvising new roles.

However, the acts of devotional cooking performed by the two women were not identical as social acts. Adja Moussoukoro's act indexed a material ability not only to cook well but also to finance hospitality and to support students in doing so when they did not have the means to do so on their own; on the other hand, Aïda Thiam's act indexed her ability to organize others who were equally willing to sacrifice for the religious cause. The narratives of most women I interviewed highlight such acts of devotional cooking, which perform diverse functions in their accounts. What is original in these two women's stories is not that they use cooking for social purposes but that they deploy it in new ways, reconfiguring religious authority roles typically exercised by men to make them consonant with performances of feminine piety. The constant among the many women who use devotional cooking is not the meaning or result of cooking but the fact that cooking is a shared stock of knowledge that can be mobilized for diverse purposes.

These women exemplify the growing tendency among urban Senegalese Muslims of many persuasions to approach one's religious path as an entrepreneurial endeavor, that is, to creatively use whatever resources one may have to accomplish something new and unique. In particular, Fayḍa women like Aïda Thiam and Adja Moussoukoro Mbay are becoming "new figures of success" (Banégas and Warnier 2001) through transposing conventionally feminine roles such as cooking and motherhood from the household into a religious field. These activities allow them to cultivate relationships with major leaders and to perform nurturing leadership roles for youth seeking community and a sense of purpose in an uncertain city. Notably, in taking on conventionally male leadership roles, they do not seek to overturn the patriarchal order but to build creatively on the experiences and social roles they already have, locating latent spiritual and social power within these experiences and roles. Similarly, the efficacy of their entrepreneurial innovation depends on legitimation by the Sufi hierarchy. This is not to suggest that their entrepreneurial innovations are not true breaks from the past but that all innovators are inevitably constrained and enabled by the resources available to them.

## NOTES

1. In Arabic, the feminine form is *muqaddama*, although in Wolof, which has no grammatical gender, the masculine form is used for men and women.
2. Shaykh Ibrahim Niasse prescribed the name "Ansaroudine" (Anṣār al-Dīn, "Partisans of the Faith") as the name by which his disciples should call their collective organization. It is unrelated to both the Sufi group founded by Sherif Haïdara in Mali and the militant Salafi group in northern Mali. Although the Fayḍa has Ansaroudine federations around the world, and all disciples are in theory members of the global organization Jamʿiyyat Anṣār al-Dīn (Organization of the Partisans of the Faith), when disciples throughout Senegal use the title, they are almost always referring to the federation based in the Dakar region.
3. Similarly, Hoodfar (1997) found that working-class Cairene women derived status from demonstrating that their primary responsibility was that of a housewife even if they worked full-time outside the home and earned more than their husbands.
4. Elders' accounts conflicted about whether Baay had formally appointed these women as muqaddams (Hill 2010), but the two oldest interviewees who lived during the events insisted that he had appointed them.

5. It is not uncommon for muqaddams with no religious training or close clerical relatives to list Qurʾān teachers among their ancestors, although in Western Saalum nearly all families have members who are Qurʾān teachers. It is not clear that being distantly related to Qurʾān teachers contributes to the likelihood of being appointed as a muqaddam in Dakar today.

## REFERENCES

Antoun, Richard and Mary Elaine Heglund (eds). 1987. *Religious Resurgence: Contemporary Cases in Islam, Christianity, and Judaism*. Syracuse: Syracuse University Press.

Augis, Erin. 2005. 'Dakar's Sunnite women: the politics of person'. In: Muriel Gomez-Perez (ed.). *L'islam politique au sud du Sahara: Identités, discours et enjeux*. Paris: Karthala, 309–326.

Augis, Erin. 2013. 'Dakar's Sunnite women: the dialectic of submission and defiance in a globalizing city'. In: Mamadou Diouf (ed). *Tolerance, Democracy, and Sufis in Senegal*. New York: Columbia University Press, 73–98.

Banégas, Richard and Jean-Pierre Warnier. 2001. 'Nouvelles figures de la réussite et du pouvoir'. *Politique africaine* 82, 2: 5–23.

Bava, Sophie. 2003. 'Les Cheikhs mourides itinérants et l'espace de la ziyara à Marseille'. *Anthropologie et Société* 27, 1: 149–166.

Berger, Peter L. 1967. *The Sacred Canopy: Elements of a Sociological Theory of Religion*. New York: Anchor.

Berger, Peter L. (ed.). 1999. *The Desecularization of the World: Resurgent Religion and World Politics*. Grand Rapids, Michigan: Eerdmans.

Bourdieu, Pierre. 1971. 'Genèse et structure du champ religieux'. *Revue française de sociologie* 12, 3: 295–334.

Bourdieu, Pierre. 1984. *Distinction: A Social Critique of the Judgment of Taste*. Cambridge: Harvard University Press.

Buggenhagen, Beth A. 2012a. 'Fashioning piety: women's dress, money, and faith among Senegalese Muslims in New York City'. *City & Society* 24, 1: 84–104.

Buggenhagen, Beth A. 2012b. *Muslim Families in Global Senegal: Money Takes Care of Shame*. Bloomington: Indiana University Press.

Comaroff, John and Jean Comaroff. 1999. 'Occult economies and the violence of abstraction: notes from the South African postcolony'. *American Ethnologist* 26: 279–301.

Copans, Jean. 1980. *Les marabouts de l'arachide: la confrérie mouride et les paysans du Sénégal*. Paris: Sycomore.

Coulon, Christian. 1981. *Le marabout et le prince: Islam et pouvoir au Sénégal*. Paris: Editions Pedone.

Cruise O'Brien, Donal. 1971. *The Mourides of Senegal: The Political and Economic Organization of an Islamic Brotherhood*. Oxford: Clarendon.

Dar Al Quran Karim. 2011. 'Fondatrice'. *Dar Al Quran Al Karim*. http://www.daralquranalkarim.org/fondatrice.htm.

Diouf, Mamadou. 2000. 'The Senegalese Murid trade diaspora and the making of a vernacular cosmopolitanism'. *Public Culture* 12, 3: 679–702.

Geschiere, Peter. 1997. *The Modernity of Witchcraft*. Charlottesville: University of Virginia Press.

Gomez-Perez, Muriel, Marie-Nathalie LeBlanc, and Mathias Savadogo. 2009. 'Young men and Islam in the 1990s: rethinking an intergenerational perspective'. *Journal of Religion in Africa* 39, 2: 186–218.

Gooren, Henri. 2002. 'Catholic and non-Catholic theologies of liberation: poverty, self-improvement, and ethics among small-scale entrepreneurs in Guatemala City'. *Journal for the Scientific Study of Religion* 41, 1: 29–45.

Gray, Christopher. 1998. 'The rise of the Niassene Tijaniyya, 1875 to the present'. In: Ousmane Kane and Jean-Louis Triaud (eds). *Islam et islamismes au sud du Sahara*. Paris: Karthala, 59–82.

Haenni, Patrick. 2002. 'Au-delà du repli identitaire . . . Les nouveaux prêcheurs égyptiens et la modernisation paradoxale de l'islam'. *Religioscope* 30 (November). http://religioscope.com/pdf/precheurs.pdf.

Haenni, Patrick and Tjitske Holtrop. 2002. 'Mondaines spiritualités . . . Amr Khâlid, "shaykh" branché de la jeunesse dorée du Caire'. *Politique africaine* 87: 45–68.

Hill, Joseph. 2006. 'Sufi specialists and globalizing charisma: religious knowledge and authority among disciples of Baay Ñas'. In: Kamari Maxine Clarke (ed). *Local Practices, Global Controversies: Islam in Sub-Saharan African Contexts*. New Haven: MacMillan Center for International and Area Studies at Yale, 69–99.

Hill, Joseph. 2007. 'Divine knowledge and Islamic authority: religious specialization among disciples of Baay Ñas'. Ph.D. thesis, New Haven: Yale University.

Hill, Joseph. 2010. ' "All women are guides": Sufi leadership and womanhood among Taalibe Baay in Senegal'. *Journal of Religion in Africa* 40, 4: 375–412.

Hiskett, Mervyn. 1980. 'The "Community of Grace" and its opponents, "the Rejecters": a debate about theology and mysticism in Muslim West Africa with special reference to its Hausa expression'. *African Language Studies* 17: 99–140.

Hoodfar, Homa. 1997. *Between Marriage and the Market: Intimate Politics and Survival in Cairo*. Berkeley: University of California Press.

Hubert, Henri and Marcel Mauss. 1899. Essai sur la nature et la fonction du sacrifice. *Année sociologique* 2: 29–138.

Hutson, Alaine. 1999. 'The development of women's authority in the Kano Tijaniyya, 1894–1963'. *Africa Today* 46, 3: 43–64.

Hutson, Alaine. 2001. 'Women, men, and patriarchal bargaining in an Islamic Sufi order: the Tijaniyya in Kano, Nigeria, 1937 to the present'. *Gender and Society* 15, 5: 734–753.

Kane, Ousmane. 2003. *Muslim Modernity in Postcolonial Nigeria: A Study of the Society for the Removal of Innovation and Restatement of Tradition*. Leiden: Brill.

Kane, Ousmane. 2011. *The Homeland Is the Arena: Religion, Transnationalism, and the Integration of Senegalese Immigrants in America*. Oxford and New York: Oxford University Press.

Kane, Ousmane and Leonardo Villalón. 1995. 'Entre confrérisme, réformisme et islamisme: Les mustarshidin du Sénégal: analyse et traduction commentée du discours électoral de Moustapha Sy et réponse de Abdou Aziz Sy junior'. *Islam et sociétés au sud du Sahara* 9: 119–201.

Kepel, Gilles. 1994. *The Revenge of God: The Resurgence of Islam, Christianity, and Judaism in the Modern World*. University Park: University of Pennsylvania Press.

LeBlanc, Marie Nathalie. 2003. Les trajectoires de conversion et l'identité sociale chez les jeunes dans le contexte postcolonial Ouest-africain. *Anthropologie et Sociétés* 27, 1: 85.

Leichtman, Mara. 2009. 'Revolution, modernity and (trans)national Shi'i Islam: rethinking religious conversion in Senegal'. *Journal of Religion in Africa* 39: 319–351.

Lubeck, Paul. 2011. 'Nigeria: mapping the Shari'a restorationist movement'. In: Robert Hefner (ed). *Shari'a Politics: Islamic Law and Society in the Modern World*. Bloomington: Indiana University Press, 244–279.

Meyer, Birgit. 1998. '"Make a complete break with the past": memory and post-colonial modernity in Ghanaian Pentecostalist discourse'. *Journal of Religion in Africa* 28, 3: 316–349.

Riccio, Bruno. 2004. 'Transnational Mouridism and the Afro-Muslim critique of Italy'. *Journal of Ethnic and Migration Studies* 30, 5: 929–944.

Robbins, Joel. 2004. 'The globalization of Pentecostal and charismatic Christianity'. *Annual Review of Anthropology* 33, 1: 117–143.

Samson, Fabienne. 2005. *Les marabouts de l'islam politique: le Dahiratoul Moustarchidina wal Moustarchidaty, un mouvement néo-confrérique sénégalais.* Paris: Karthala.

Samson Ndaw, Fabienne. 2009. 'Nouveaux marabouts politiques au Sénégal'. In: Gilles Holder (ed). *L'islam, nouvel espace public en Afrique.* Paris: Karthala, 149–171.

Schulz, Dorothea. 2003. '"Charisma and brotherhood" revisited: mass-mediated forms of spirituality in urban Mali'. *Journal of Religion in Africa* 33, 2: 146–171.

Schulz, Dorothea. 2006. 'Promises of (im)mediate salvation: Islam, broadcast media, and the remaking of religious experience in Mali'. *American Ethnologist* 33, 2: 210–229.

Schulz, Dorothea. 2012. 'Dis/embodying authority: female radio "preachers" and the ambivalences of mass-mediated speech in Mali'. *International Journal of Middle East Studies* 44, 1: 23–43.

Schumpeter, Joseph Alois. 1934. *The Theory of Economic Development: An Inquiry into Profits, Capital, Credit, Interest, and the Business Cycle.* Cambridge: President and Fellows of Harvard College.

Seesemann, Rüdiger. 2000. 'The history of the Tijâniya and the issue of Tarbiya in Darfur'. In: Jean-Louis Triaud and David Robinson (eds). *La Tijâniyya: Une confrérie musulmane à la conquête de l'Afrique.* Paris: Karthala, 393–437.

Seesemann, Rüdiger. 2011. *The Divine Flood: Ibrāhīm Niasse and the Roots of a Twentieth-Century Sufi Revival.* Oxford: Oxford University Press.

Smith, William Robertson. 1894. *Religion of the Semites.* London: Adam and Charles Black.

Soares, Benjamin. 2004. 'Muslim saints in the age of neoliberalism'. In: Brad Weiss (ed). *Producing African Futures: Ritual and Reproduction in a Neoliberal Age.* Leiden: Brill, 79–104.

Soares, Benjamin. 2005. *Islam and the Prayer Economy: History and Authority in a Malian Town.* Ann Arbor: University of Michigan Press.

Soares, Benjamin. 2010. '"Rasta" Sufis and Muslim youth culture in Mali'. In: Assef Bayat and Linda Herrera (eds). *Being Young and Muslim: New Cultural Politics in the Global South and North.* Oxford and New York: Oxford University Press, 241–258.

Villalón, Leonardo. 1995. *Islam and State Power in Senegal: Disciples and Citizens in Fatick.* Cambridge: Cambridge University Press.

Villalón, Leonardo. 2003. 'Generational changes, political stagnation, and the evolving dynamics of religion and politics in Senegal'. *Africa Today* 46, 3: 129–147.

Weber, Max. 1958. 'Science as vocation'. In: Hans Gerth and C. Wright Mills (eds). *From Max Weber: Essays in Sociology.* New York: Oxford University Press, 129–157.

Weber, Max. 1978. *Economy and Society: An Outline of Interpretive Sociology.* Berkeley: University of California Press.

West, Harry. 2005. *Kupilikula: Governance and the Invisible Realm in Mozambique.* Chicago: University of Chicago Press.

# 5 Social Values and Social Entrepreneurship at the University of Makeni

## An Episode in the Reconstruction of Sierra Leone

*David O'Kane*

Entrepreneurship is an activity of individuals, but the individuals who engage in that activity are never the mere *homo œconomicus* of much economic theory, even if they make rational choices based on rational economic calculation. Rather, they are always individuals whose goals, aspirations, and worldviews, and the strategic and tactical choices which flow from them, have been formed in particular social and cultural circumstances. It is in those specific social and cultural contexts, which are the product of particular historical experiences, that the patterns and outcomes of entrepreneurial activity are determined. This is true of all forms of entrepreneurial activity, including those cases where persons are engaging in forms of market exchange where the goal is the acquisition of profits through trade or manufacturing: even in those cases, rational, quantitative, pursuit of economic and monetary gain coincides with motivations of a far more qualitative and culture-bound nature. Weber's identification of the affinity between the protestant ethic and the spirit of capitalism in early modern Europe was probably the earliest recognition of this factor in social science. Value-based motivations become even more important in those cases where entrepreneurial activity is not driven by specific profit-seeking or monetary gain, but is rather motivated by desires to reconstruct a devastated society, or to enhance the educational prospects of a neglected region, or to bring about cultural changes that might enhance prospects for lasting peace and development in the country in which that entrepreneur is located. These are some of the motives and goals which have driven the founding and continuing consolidation of Sierra Leone's first private university, the University of Makeni (UNIMAK), a product of cultural entrepreneurship in the peculiarly difficult and contested context of post-civil war Sierra Leone. In this chapter, I give an account of the perspectives and worldviews behind UNIMAK's birth and development,[1] as they were revealed in interview data with the university's founder and present Vice-Chancellor, Father Joseph Turay.

The cultural entrepreneurship engaged in by Father Turay is, at the same time, a case of social entrepreneurship. The "social" and the "cultural" are not synonymous, but they are closely related: interventions in a society that are intended to change that society must mobilize cultural resources (ideas, ideologies, symbols, values, etc.) if the goals of the intervention are to be achieved. Definitions of social entrepreneurship, *qua* social, rely implicitly on a certain concept of the cultural. The "social value" which is described as the goal of social entrepreneurship will vary in its definition according to particular local cultural factors: the adaptation of novelty and innovation, and the acceptance of risk and uncertainty by social entrepreneurs are activities carried out via cultural prisms (Peredo and McLean 2006: 64).

There are cases where the task of social change and social reconstruction via cultural entrepreneurship becomes a pressing and urgent task. Sierra Leone, in the aftermath of its civil war, is one such case. In addition to the major casualty levels incurred by the population as a result of the conflict, that war also left behind a legacy of grave damage to the physical infrastructure of the country and the social fabric. Between the end of the civil war and the outbreak of the Ebola crisis of 2014,[2] steady progress toward reconstruction was made, reconstruction that involved both the restoration of prewar institutions and values, but also the introduction of social and cultural innovations. The building of the University of Makeni involves not only institutional innovation, but also social innovation, in that it adds a new aspect to the social world of a region that was historically deprived of educational institutions—and while it is not an explicitly proselytizing institution, it is still part of a wider effort by the Roman Catholic church to effect cultural change in the region. This cultural innovation is complemented by plans to encourage peacebuilding and to foster a sense of entrepreneurialism among those who form its student body, who will be encouraged to be "job-makers, not job-seekers".

The social value of building a new, private, tertiary education institution is not only that it helps to serve a need in a region which had historically been deprived of educational institutions of all sort, but that it also may help plug severe gaps in the skills and human resources available to the Sierra Leone economy. Most importantly, it may contribute to cultural change that will secure the peacebuilding and social reconstruction that has taken place since the end of the civil war in 2002. One of the major goals of Father Turay's original project was to effect a major cultural change in the northern province, and in Sierra Leone as a whole, changes that would secure and consolidate the peace of 2002.[3] In this chapter, I describe some of the values which inform the entrepreneurship of Father Turay, and other members of the community which has gathered around his brainchild, the University of Makeni. Makeni is a town in the northern region of Sierra Leone, and this region is where Father Turay spent his formative years before entering the Roman Catholic priesthood, and becoming, ultimately, the driving force behind the creation of UNIMAK. So far, the original vision which has inspired the UNIMAK project has resulted in clear, tangible results: a private university has been created, it possesses both facilities and faculty, and it has attracted several cohorts of students seeking education and qualifications suitable to a growing African economy. It is not yet possible to say if the project embarked upon at Makeni will be successful. The crisis of the Ebola epidemic (see conclusion below) has placed Sierra Leone's future in doubt once again, in spite of the very real recovery and growth which has occurred in the years since the civil war.

## FATHER JOSEPH TURAY AND THE CREATION OF UNIMAK: AN EPISODE IN THE RECONSTRUCTION OF MAKENI

Private universities and other tertiary education institutions have mushroomed across Africa in the past two decades (Jamshidi et al. 2012; Thaver 2008[4]). Even where they are intended as not-for-profit institutions, such institutions are the product of both particular entrepreneurial visions and a wider paradigm of neoliberal privatization. It is important that UNIMAK is avowedly and explicitly a not for-profit institution, and equally important that it has a certain attitude to that wider paradigm.[5] In most African countries where they have appeared, private universities have emerged in response to increased demands for higher education, which public universities could not meet. There were, however, other factors involved in the emergence of UNIMAK.

These factors were multiple and varied. They included the historic under-provision of educational infrastructure of all kinds in northern Sierra Leone, which had led to a dearth of educational opportunities in the region. As part of its evangelizing mission, the Catholic Church in Sierra Leone sought to win new adherents via the building of hospitals and schools. The most important of these factors, however, were those arising out of the civil war of 1991–2002, alluded to above, which brought massive and destructive violence to the whole country. The havoc wreaked by the civil war on Sierra Leone was not confined to the destruction of human lives or the destruction of physical infrastructure; it was also deeply destructive of civil political relations in the West African state. The challenge of reconstruction after the civil war, then, was not only to rebuild the roads, schools, hospitals and economic infrastructure of the country. It was also to recreate civil political relations within the nation-state itself, and this meant the renewal of links between individual citizens and subnational ethnic communities to which those individuals belonged.

Sierra Leone's civil war was not an ethnic or ethnoreligious conflict. Rather, all the various ethnic and religious groups that make up the Sierra Leonean nation found themselves preyed upon by the contending armies and militias. The patterns of conflict and predation which characterized the Sierra Leonean civil war were produced by the patterns of misgovernment which had characterized the Sierra Leonean state in the years after its independence from the United Kingdom in 1961. A large body of literature has documented the decline and fall of the first Sierra Leonean republic: William

Reno's work on the shadow state in Sierra Leone, for example, demonstrates how the policies of the single-party state led ultimately to the decay of that state and played a major role in the fraying of the social fabric itself (Reno 1995). By the late 1980s, there existed in Sierra Leone a substantial layer of excluded and disaffected youth who, a few years later, would be susceptible to recruitment by the rebel Revolutionary United Front (Abdullah 1998). The need to find solutions to this crisis of governance and civil relations in Sierra Leone was the major driving force in the decision by Father Turay and others with whom he was associated in the years immediately after the civil war.

In the aftermath of that war, then, UNIMAK was created out of its predecessor, the Fatima teacher training college, receiving funding from a variety of sources, including the local Catholic church, the international Catholic community, and the government of Sierra Leone (University of Makeni, n.d.). The major source of funding in recent years has been from donors outside Sierra Leone, and from students' fees.[6] In the very first years of peace, Father Turay was part of a group which tried to debate and analyze the origins of the civil war, and concluded that it lay in centralization and bad governance. UNIMAK was specifically intended to assist in the solution of the latter problem, to work around these issues. "Universities should take the lead" in these matters, he told me. For example, UNIMAK would take steps to educate paramount chiefs and other persons connected with local government in the specifics of improved administration and good governance. This was not for those persons alone, however, but part of a "bid to bring education to the community".

Born in 1966, Joseph Turay grew up in the northern region of Sierra Leone. He was first educated there, before coming to Makeni for his secondary education. In terms of the education he received, he said, "We had what we needed" in terms of good education, as "teachers were motivated". This is consistent with the views of others on the pre-war condition of the Sierra Leonean education system: for those who could access it, it did provide consistently adequate levels of educational instruction. By the time Father Turay was born, the Roman Catholic church had been engaged in evangelization activities for about a decade and a half, and a key part of those efforts had involved a contribution to the provision of educational services in the northern region. His parents were teachers (teaching materials were always present in the family home, where discussions on various topics were common), and active in the community organizations of the Catholic church; he himself developed his vocation for the priesthood after observing that priests and nuns were actively helping others in the community, working as they were in the schools and hospitals of the local area. The impressions this left had a key formative influence on him, as did his overall family background:

> In my family the opportunity for discussion and leadership was present. . . . All of that, you know, played on our own upbringing.[7]

It played on him to the point where he began to aspire to a leadership role himself: he defined leadership as the ability to set the agenda of others, to inspire others, to empower others, to work for the common good. What did this mean in the context of a post-civil war Makeni?

In Makeni in 2011, the reconstruction of the town was proceeding quickly. It was obvious, however, that the town of around 83,000 people (Workman 2011: 54) still had a great distance to travel before that reconstruction would have been complete. It had once, long before, been an administrative center of the British colonial government in what was then the "protectorate", and after Sierra Leonean independence in 1961, it had gone into decline, much like the rest of the northern region. In the time of the civil war, Makeni and its people found themselves the headquarters of the rebel Revolutionary United Front (RUF). Not only did Makeni's people suffer the effects of occupation by the RUF, it also experienced persistent fighting around and in the town, with highly adverse consequences for the civilian population. Catherine Bolten (probably the most knowledgeable foreign observer of the city and its surrounding region) records that toward the end of the war, attacks by RUF forces on Kenyan peacekeepers incited then-President Kabbah to subject the town to collective punishment, which took the form of aerial bombing that did not discriminate between RUF fighters and innocent civilians (2012: 46).

In her ethnographic work on Makeni in the years immediately after the civil war, Bolten depicts a town whose people were still suffering from the effects of poverty and underdevelopment, where citizens would say of their town, "This place is so backward" (2008, 2012). In the years immediately preceding the Sierra Leonean presidential election of 2012—the third since the end of the war, and one which appeared to consolidate and secure the new peaceful, post-war order—Makeni was showing definite signs of economic growth and even (for some people) prosperity. This was by no means the same thing as development: Makeni remains a poor community, something clearly demonstrated by the current crisis triggered by the Ebola epidemic (still ongoing at the time of writing). However, it is clear that the town is going through a phase of change, even if the course and outcome of that phase remains unknown at present. The town has been seeing numerous changes and improvements to its infrastructure, as roads were repaired, street lighting was installed, and plans were made to restore a piped water supply to the town. Most importantly, the town had finally been connected to the electricity supply provided by the Bumbuna hydroelectric plant. This allowed immediate changes to the economic life of the community, as small carpentry and metalwork shops were able to work around the clock—at least this was how one member of UNIMAK's faculty put it to me.[8]

These are the latest episodes in a long pattern in which Makeni has been opened up to outside forces and outside influences. The large mosque in the town is a testament to the long-term influence of Islam in the community, while the Catholic cathedral demonstrates the expansion of the church from its first missionary activities in the 1950s (the local Catholic radio station, Radio Maria, opens its airwaves to a one-hour broadcast by the Imam of Makeni mosque).

As for the wider region which has Makeni at its heart, it too, is being opened to external economic forces. The Azzolini highway (named after the Italian-born first bishop of the Makeni diocese), along which the main campus of UNIMAK lies, is ideally suited for the passage of the heavy transport trucks which foreign mining corporations have brought into the province. They have identified new economic opportunities, and have agreed upon long-term leases with the Sierra Leonean government. The same is true of biofuel companies such as Addaxx, a Swiss-based firm which has a number of experimental stations in the Makeni area. That area is still largely composed, however, of small villages, most of whose citizens are engaged in small-scale agriculture. During the last occasion on which I engaged in fieldwork at UNIMAK, I was told of a new plan to engage UNIMAK students as teaching assistants in schools in these villages, places where, as in the past, there are still problems with the undersupply of facilities and staff for educational provision.

The University maintains two campuses, one in Yonni (Figure 5.1), the home village of President Koroma, which lies on the periphery of Makeni city, and a main campus which stands on the Azzolini highway, at the entrance to Makeni city itself (the latter campus was the site of the Fatima

*Figure 5.1*  Yonni campus of UNIMAK (Photo: David O'Kane)

teacher training college, a predecessor to UNIMAK: teacher training still occurs via UNIMAK's department of education, but is only one of many activities of the university) (Figure 5.2). On both campuses, a greenfield site shelters a number of single-story buildings, classrooms, student hostels, staff accommodation, and administrative offices. The main campus houses a small but well-stocked library, whose collection has been built up via donations from Catholic universities in the United States (an example of the importance of international network connections to the creation and consolidation of this institution). During my last field visit to UNIMAK in 2012, several construction projects were ongoing, including the building of a new meeting hall and a two-story classroom building. The main campus is adjacent to the much older St. Joseph's Seminary, where youths aspiring to join the Roman Catholic clergy are housed and trained for the priesthood.

The University of Makeni is seeking to educate a new generation who can take management positions in the multinational firms that are entering the country.[9] It also has a developing program in agriculture and business studies, which it hopes will help modernize agriculture and breed a new generation of entrepreneurs. At the same time it remains committed to a certain type of "socially conscious" Roman Catholicism, which is by no means overtly sympathetic to unrestrained capitalism. There have already

*Figure 5.2*  A new classroom building goes up at the main UNIMAK campus, off Makeni's Azzolini highway (Photo: David O'Kane)

been incidents in which workers engaged in strike action at mines owned by foreign firms in Sierra Leone have been fired upon by police. Such incidents are inconsistent with the kind of peaceful or just society which many in Sierra Leone, including the people around UNIMAK, hope to build. The University of Makeni, therefore, sits at the center of a social and political context that is evolving in a number of potentially contradictory directions. That context must have a significant impact on the social entrepreneurship in which Father Joseph Turay is engaged. Like other social entrepreneurs, Father Turay brings a strong sense of values, informed by the Catholic faith of which he is a part, to the activities and projects in which he is engaged. In this, he follows in the tradition of other cases of social entrepreneurship by people emerging from the ranks of the Roman Catholic clergy, such as the creation of the Mondragon co-operatives in Spain, or the founding of Knock airport in the west of Ireland (Ní Bhrádaigh 2007). His entrepreneurship, however, is also informed by certain conceptions of what African culture is and what it can offer to an African country attempting to restore itself and enhance its future prospects.

## SOCIAL AND CULTURAL VALUES AND THE ENTREPRENEURIAL CREATION OF UNIMAK

Interviews with Father Turay on this matter revealed intriguing insights into the ways in which a certain set of values informed the process of policy formation that led to the creation of the university. Father Turay described a process whereby various relevant parties, both within the embryonic UNIMAK community and within the wider Makeni community, were invited to participate in the formation of the university's initial key documents. For him, policy was driven by a "vision" that cuts across society, and which in the case of contemporary Sierra Leone was very strongly influenced by the experience of the civil war and the need to address the "root causes" of the war:

> So we started with courses on good governance, begin to train leadership, and broad-based social sciences, development studies, development studies that will address the market, that will address aligning human resource and the natural resources that we have. So these are the outcomes of, I mean, outcomes engagement in producing the policies that we have. And then we had, I mean, a strategic plan. We took a year and a half to work on the strategic plan. We took actors from diverse sectors. We engaged key educational stakeholders, we engage parliamentarians, we engage—so that I mean, that whatever policy will be relevant, will address the needs of the community, will address the needs of the market, so that, I mean, you have students that eventually

will leave, they will be creative, enter, entrepreneurial, and will be able to be job-seekers, I mean job-creators and not job-seekers.

These interventions in the political life of the country are deeply cultural interventions. If successful, they will challenge deeply rooted cultural conceptions of the ways in which politics should be organized. They also involve the creation of new networks—networks of stakeholders. For Father Turay, the concept of "stakeholder" was one that extended from the administration, to staff and students, and to finally encompass the whole of Sierra Leone itself. That orientation to the wider community of which UNI-MAK was a part was repeatedly stressed throughout my interviews with him, including those that emphasized the need for UNIMAK to develop a research capacity as quickly as possible:

> You know as a university, you teach, you build community service, you orient your teaching towards community service, but also you do research, you generate new knowledge. And it's new knowledge that will, I mean, help you to build your community. I mean community, an institution, an university, a country that does not lay emphasis on research will never generate new ideas. It's new ideas that will rule the world. It's new ideas, I mean, that will help us to meet the challenges that are pressing needs. I mean if you don't do research on malaria, research on governance, research, I mean, on road construction, research on food, research on agriculture, you will not be able to generate new ideas and there will be no growth.

Pragmatic concerns and objectives of this nature were vital, but so too was the particular religious paradigm and mission borne by both the local Catholic church of which he was a part, and the wider church as a whole. Roman Catholic social teaching is concerned with a wide variety of topics, and education is one of the most important of them. For Joseph Turay, this connected with his entrepreneurial project at UNIMAK via the "search for truth" which he saw at the heart of education:

> For us, education is the search for truth, truth about man in all his dimensions. Truth about the economic, truth about politics, truth about culture, and that informs us, that guides what we are doing. Because at the end of the day, that's education, the search for truth, so that you create a better world, you create a better man, you answer the fundamental questions about human existence, about life, about death, about, I mean, our vocation, our mission as human beings to make the world a better place. . . . The concept of the common good, that's a cherished concept in our own tradition that we must create the enabling environment so that the human person may flourish, and that intermediary

bodies may flourish. . . . So these are the values that are informing, you know, our educational policies, how we run UNIMAK.[10]

The inequalities which mark Sierra Leonean society as a result of civil war and underdevelopment present obvious obstacles to the fulfillment of these goals. Aspirations toward the creation of a "better man", or to the upholding of the "common good", are difficult to achieve in conditions of persistent poverty within the wider society. One way in which the university can at least attempt to cleave to these ideals, however, involves the assertion of control over the university environment itself. One significant way, there-fore, in which those values inform the way in which educational policy is implemented at UNIMAK is in the strict prohibition on political activity by students on campus—and the even stricter prohibition on involvement in cul-tic behavior by students of UNIMAK. "Cultic", in this context, refers to the activities of secret societies formed to engage in occult ritual activity, of a kind identified as evil by the wider mainstream society. Such campus-based cults have also been associated with violence, both in Sierra Leone and elsewhere in Africa (Rotimi 2005). Violence is also a feature of student involvement in politics. During the period of the one-party state in Sierra Leone, students at the state-run University of Sierra Leone had played a role in the opposition to the dictatorship, but at the same time they had become associated with a more destructive and violent style of political activism. In the context of post-civil war reconstruction, this was deemed to be potentially disruptive to campus life at UNIMAK, and prejudicial to the university's mission. As for the ban on cultic behavior, many West African universities have experienced violence as a result of the activity of covert cultic organizations that maintain a grip on at least some members of their student bodies (Rotimi 2005). For Father Turay, this was a threat that had to be resisted in UNIMAK's case:

> You know 24 students were arrested a month ago in Njala. So, for us, from day one, we banned it, because we said, "Why cultism? When you have to study?" So we banned all the students' associations. Except associations that are strictly academic. And thank God, the response I had from parents and this was very positive, they said thank you, that you don't allow any of this nonsense in the university. Because then they begin to influence the lecturers, then they—it's a whole mess, that's why it has been banned, in all the universities, by the President himself.[11]

At a later matriculation ceremony of the university, Bishop Biguzzi (the Italian-born and then outgoing bishop of the Makeni diocese) admonished students that they were to shun such activities. Rejection of such activities and behaviors was at the heart of the university's efforts to contribute to the consolidation of peace in Sierra Leone. By the time of the third presidential election in Sierra Leone, it was becoming apparent that there was, in fact, a reasonable chance of achieving this goal. However, at least one member of the UNIMAK community expressed to me the view that a continuing problem in Sierra Leone was that "everything is politicized"—that is, everything became an object of contention between factions of the political elite and their followers among the masses.

The conflictual nature of politics in Sierra Leone was noted by many members of the UNIMAK community during the period when I witnessed the run-up to the presidential election of 2012 (Figure 5.3). During those weeks I noted a considerable amount of uncertainty and apprehension, as people feared that the coming vote would see a repeat of the violence which had marred previous elections. I was informed that members of the Mende ethnic group on the UNIMAK campus were keeping a low profile, as the country's main oppposition party, the Sierra Leone People's Party (SLPP), drew most of its support from that ethnicity. Yet at the same time, as people were expressing their views on this issue, I witnessed the local branch of the SLPP hold its election march through the town, and saw no sign of any attempt to deprive them of their rights. In the end, the election passed (more or less) peacefully, with the reelection of the incumbent president Ernest Bai Koroma, of the northern-based All-People's Congress (APC) party.

In reflections on those elections, Father Turay remarked on the relevance of the civil society to Sierra Leone. These remarks enlarged upon certain comments he had made to me in our previous interviews, when he had

*Figure 5.3*  Julius Maada Bio, presidential candidate of the SLPP, speaks at UNIMAK in the run-up to Sierra Leone's 2012 elections (Photo: David O'Kane)

stressed the need for consensual decision-making at all levels of society. This, he believed was something that had many historical precedents in precolonial African society, including precolonial Sierra Leone. In such "palaver" systems, he told me:

> People discuss and argue, everyone has a voice, even though you might say women had their own voice in a different forum. But I mean like, every young man, every adult, every member of the town, I mean, was listened to. The chief would never make a decision without listening to others. There is, I mean, that's why we have the Palaver hut, we discuss the palaver and then come to a consensus. . . . Yesterday I was preparing my talk I'm giving tomorrow in Freetown on human rights from a faith-based perspective. The concept of the individual as a moral being, as a human person, that is not subjected to the community, to the clan, to the tribe, but participates in building that, it's an area that we must work on in our culture.[12]

This effort to change the local culture, then, was one that drew on perceptions about the key organizing principles of that culture. It was also an effort that was carried out in a particular local and national context, something which contributed its own part to the forms of cultural entrepreneurship at work here.

## CULTURAL ENTREPRENEURSHIP AND NETWORK BUILDING: UNIMAK IN NATIONAL AND INTERNATIONAL CONTEXT

In the opinion of an educational adviser who regularly consults with UNIMAK's senior staff on the university's direction, Sierra Leone's paucity of private tertiary institutions is unusual in both the West African context and the context of Africa as a whole:

> I mean, Tanzania's got eighteen, Uganda's got fourteen private . . . it has become a growth industry, especially in the last ten years. There's none. I mean even Liberia, neighboring Liberia has got three private universities, and one of them goes way back to the sixties. This country had no private universities. So I think that was a breakthrough . . . in terms of the north of the country, you had two universities before, and a number of teacher training colleges alright, but there was nothing really in the north, at this level. So I think this has been a major commitment. I think it's also been helped by the fact that President Koroma is from this area, too, and he's put his weight behind it.[13]

The recent and rapid spread of private higher education in Africa is part of the wider impact of globalization on the continent, something that has been going on since the neoliberal structural adjustment policies of the 1980s. A case can be made that those policies helped create the social turmoil which would plunge countries such as Sierra Leone into civil war, through the highly disruptive effects of structural adjustment programs mandated by the international financial institutions. What those programs did not do, however, was restructure African economies and societies in ways consistent with the overall perspectives and goals of neoliberalism. Rather than producing fully marketized individuals, structural adjustment programs in Africa tended to reinforce existing political cultures and patterns of patronage and clientelism (Reno 1995: 155; Zack-Williams 1995: 60). These were the forms of distorted and perverse governance which the creation of UNIMAK was intended to overcome. Father Joseph Turay's activities as a social and cultural entrepreneur differed strongly from those which the neoliberal paradigm purported to offer. In the environment of post-conflict Sierra Leone, which like many other African countries still has to deal with the legacy of the structural adjustment era, he still had to take into account this market mechanism. There was no prior existing market for tertiary education in Sierra Leone before this time, but the conditions that would make it possible had to be taken into account by Father Turay and his collaborators.

A central proposition of the original wave of neoliberal politics in the core countries of the world economy was the contention that only a "rolling back of the state" could secure the economic future of those regions and the wider world. Such a retrenchment of state participation in the economy would, it was assumed, secure this goal through the unleashing and unshackling of entrepreneurial activity (Harvey 2005: 23). In this case, entrepreneurship was defined narrowly as profit-oriented economic activity. Social and cultural entrepreneurship contrast with this by virtue of their "embeddedness" in particular social and cultural milieus. This embeddedness serves not only to inspire the goals and strategies of social and cultural entrepreneurs, but also allow access to the various resources entrepreneurs need in order to achieve those goals. It is therefore a form of social capital, that form of reproducible wealth which takes the form of social links with others, links that facilitate "collective action for mutual benefit" (Woolcock 1998: 155). The particular modes and outcomes of such collective action are determined, however, by the fact that social entrepreneurs are motivated by particular visions and worldviews. It is these which guide their interaction with the wider social environments in which they find themselves enmeshed. The accumulation of social capital through the assiduous cultivation of network connections and their institutionalization, therefore, was an investment of cultural capital. It remains to be seen if this investment will yield dividends, especially given the disruptive effects of the Ebola epidemic (see below). Father Turay's work has, so far, been successful in building up a new institution. We do not yet know what the long-term social and mutual benefit of this project will be.

This is what qualifies Father Turay for the status of "entrepreneur", but may also complicate the meaning of that concept in his case: for Joseph Turay, the envisioning of the UNIMAK project was only the beginning. It was followed by several years in which he took several assiduous steps to make that vision a reality, and in which he assembled around himself the cadre of the new university, and around that cadre the new university itself. This was then followed by a period of consolidation of the new institution, in which the social networks created through these initiatives were maintained and extended in order to assure the continuing existence of the university and the achievement of its goals. Nor is this the only case where network connections are important in Makeni.

Catherine Bolten has, in a recent paper (2014), described the ways in which friction developed between international non-governmental organizations (INGOs) in post-civil war Makeni and those local staff employed by the INGOs, as the policies of those INGOs clashed with the moral economy adhered to by members of the social networks in which the INGOs' local staff were enmeshed.[14] Bolten's work underlines the importance of understanding social networks if the overall social dynamics of post-civil war Sierra Leone are to be properly understood. In the case described by Bolten, these include not only the local networks of kinship and other social affiliations, but also the external, global networks whose local representatives include the INGOs she describes. The networks formed via the construction of UNIMAK also involve the creation of new social networks, and this, I believe, provides the best way of understanding the creation of UNIMAK as a form of cultural entrepreneurship. When he acted as a cultural entrepreneur, Father Turay acted as an accumulator of social capital. In doing so, he was able to successfully build an institution that has, so far, avoided the conflicts and frictions that dogged the INGOs described by Bolten. In the summer and autumn of 2014, however, he and his university, like Sierra Leone and the wider West African region, found itself facing a new challenge and a new threat.

## CONCLUSION

As this chapter was being prepared, the public health crisis resulting from an outbreak of the Ebola virus in Guinea, Liberia, and Sierra Leone worsened considerably. The epidemic, which appears to have begun in Guinea in 2013, has since spread dramatically and exponentially, to the point where, as of this writing, deaths in the tens of thousands cannot be ruled out, and some observers are speaking of an ultimate casualty figure that may exceed one million. In Makeni, the virus has had acutely destructive effects, as the local healthcare system appears unable to cope with the challenges the epidemic presents (Nossiter 2014). For the community that has gathered around the University of Makeni, this presents major challenges. In the early weeks of September 2014, it was decided that the enrolment of students for the coming academic year would be suspended. Father Turay's comments on the UNIMAK website give a flavor of the way in which the university will participate in the struggle against the disease:

> I attended the district Ebola task force meeting in Makeni and we are preparing to fight this epidemic. We are confronted with many challenges: funding for sensitization, human resources to volunteer in tracing victims and suspected cases, Makeni needs urgently an ambulance only for dealing with the Ebola cases; funding for training of nurses and other health personnel etc. As a University we cannot stand aside to see so many people lose their lives and so we are engaged. (UNIMAK 2014)

Father Turay's remarks indicate one of the major problems Sierra Leone is facing in making an adequate response to the Ebola crisis. That is the problem of the lack of basic infrastructure which could guarantee the effective containment and suppression of the Ebola epidemic. Much of this infrastructure is material in nature: that is, it consists of objects such as ambulances, medical supplies, protective clothing, et cetera. Other parts of the infrastructure of public health at any time (not only in epidemic situations) are those which consist of human and intellectual capital. The catastrophic results of the failure of the public health system is not only a matter of political economy, but also a consequence of the wider social and cultural factors which have shaped political and economic outcomes in Sierra Leone. While the country's medical corps contains many highly trained and motivated medical professions, it has always been small, and unable at the best of times to provide full medical coverage to the entire population.

Since the outbreak of the epidemic, the Sierra Leone medical profession has suffered the loss of doctors dealing with Ebola at the frontline. While UNIMAK does not have a medical school, its library does contain numerous medical texts that would be useful to the bachelor's degree in public health which the university is planning to offer. A major factor in the rapid and extreme spread of the epidemic, however, if not the major factor in its spread, is the adherence of local communities to cultural practices that help to spread the virus, and which also ensure that they are highly suspicious of external forces urging them to modify those practices in the interest of containment and suppression of the disease. Among the local networks with which UNIMAK is associated is that of the primary school system, through which it is connected to many of the communities threatened by this epidemic: the university may yet come to play a crucial role in the response to the virus in the northern region. If it does, then it may become a testament to the worth of the kind of social and cultural entrepreneurship through which Father Turay has attempted to realize his vision and the values from which it derives. It also demonstrates the limits of cultural entrepreneurship.

The ultimate consequences of the present crisis in Sierra Leone and its neighbors remain unknown at the time of writing, but they are unlikely to be positive. Before this crisis struck, the country had been experiencing a respectable level of economic growth (which is by no means, as noted above, the same thing as economic development or poverty reduction, although it does suggest at least the possibility of social amelioration of some kind), and had gone through its third peaceful national election since the end of the civil war. Whatever the outcome of the present Ebola epidemic will be, it is likely to impose severe financial and social costs on Sierra Leone, in addition to the human tragedies which each death produced by the virus represents. In short, Sierra Leone will be faced with a new phase of national reconstruction to match that which it went through after the conclusion of the civil war of 1991–2002. The University of Makeni is already playing a role in the response to the crisis: the real test of the cultural entrepreneurship which has led to the creation of that university, the test which will answer the question of whether or not that university can consolidate itself and maintain itself in existence and relevance over the long-term, will come after the crisis is ended, and a new phase of national reconstruction begins.

## NOTES

1. That episode of institutional birth and development has been followed by consistent institutional growth, to the point where the university has had to introduce audit and quality assurance mechanisms to manage both its own internal systems and those of other institutions seeking to affiliate with it (O'Kane 2014).
2. The consequences of the Ebola epidemic for this process of reconstruction remain unclear as of this writing.
3. The original plan, according to informants, was for the University of Makeni to be centered around a department of Peace studies. In the end, this became a department of development studies, but the commitment to positive cultural change remains.
4. Jamshidi et al. note that "sub-Saharan Africa has come late to modern private higher education, but the growth is notable"—growth that first began in the 1980s, but accelerated in the 1990s in response to increased demand for higher education that African states could not meet (2012: 794).
5. The social teaching of the Catholic church is in many ways at odds and in conflict with neoliberal ideology (Sniegocki 2006).
6. Student fees at UNIMAK are on a sliding scale, varying according to the length and level of the degree or diploma sought. These vary from one million Leone for a teacher-training certificate, to twelve million for a Masters' degree. Additional surcharges are levied by those departments whose work requires extra material and participation in internships. These surcharges vary from two hundred thousand Leone to one million Leone (University of Makeni 2013–2014). As of 2014, the UNIMAK website claimed a figure of about 1,200 students.
7. Interview with Father Joseph Turay, 24 November 2011.
8. The bringing online of the Bumbuna plant led to an immediate reduction in the cost of electricity in Sierra Leone (Pushak and Foster 2011: 13).

9. The UNIMAK community contains a number of academic departments. The "flagship" departments are those of Development Studies and Business and Management. There are also nascent departments of Agriculture and Public Health. As in the case of other Catholic universities around the world, the church mandates and requires the inclusion of a department of Philosophy in the ranks of the university's departments, if that university is to qualify for recognition by the church as a Catholic university.

10. Interview with Father Joseph Turay, 24 October 2011.

11. Interview with Father Joseph Turay, 5 November 2011.

12. Interview with Father Joseph Turay, 24 November 2011.

13. Interview with Mr. Martin O'Reilly, 21 November 2011.

14. This friction arose, she argues, out of the contradiction between the INGOs' insistence on a western-style conception of wages as individual recompense for individual employment, and the social networks in which local employees were embedded—networks of kinship which placed heavy financial obligations on those of their members who were employed by western INGOs, receiving incomes that were high by local standards, but which were perceived by their kin-groups as signs that they should be making greater contributions to the needs of those groups (Bolten 2014). This results in severe pressure being applied on local employees of INGOs, pressure intended to make them embezzle funds or otherwise engage in malpractice that can assist the members of their social networks.

## REFERENCES

Abdullah, Ibrahim. 1998. 'Bush path to destruction: the origin and character of the revolutionary United Front/Sierra Leone'. *The Journal of Modern African Studies* 36, 2: 203–235.

Bolten, Catherine. 2008. 'This place is so backward': durable morality and creative development in Northern Sierra Leone. Ph.D. thesis. The University of Michigan.

Bolten, Catherine. 2012. *I did it to save my life: love and survival in Sierra Leone.* Berkeley: University of California Press.

Bolten, Catherine. 2014. 'Social networks, resources and international NGOs in postwar Sierra Leone'. *African Conflict and Peacebuilding Review* 4, 1: 33–59.

Harvey, David. 2005. *A Brief History of Neoliberalism.* Oxford: Oxford University Press.

Jamshidi, Laleh et al. 2012. 'Developmental patterns of privatization in higher education: a comparative study'. *Higher Education* 64: 789–803.

Ní Bhrádaigh, Eimear. 2007. 'The overlooked rugged communitarians of Ireland'. *Journal of Enterprising Communities: People and Places in the Global Economy* 1, 2: 155–161.

Nossiter, Adam. 2014. 'A hospital from hell in overwhelmed Sierra Leone'. *International New York Times,* 2 October, A1.

O'Kane, David. 2014. 'Towards "Audit Culture" in Sierra Leone?' *Max Planck Institute for Social Anthropology Working Papers Working Paper* 155.

Peredo, Ana Maria and Murdith McLean. 2006. 'Social entrepreneurship: a critical review of the concept'. *Journal of World Business* 41, 1: 56–65.

Pushak, Nataliya and Vivien Foster. 2011. 'Sierra Leone's infrastructure: a continental perspective'. *Policy Research Working Paper* (The World Bank, Africa Region, Sustainable Development Department).

Reno, William. 1995. *Corruption and state politics in Sierra Leone.* Cambridge: University Press Cambridge.

Rotimi, Adewale. 2005. 'Violence in the citadel: the menace of secret cults in the Nigerian universities'. *Nordic Journal of African Studies* 14, 1: 79–98.

Sniegocki, John. 2006. 'The social ethics of Pope John Paul II: a critique of neoconservative interpretations'. *Horizons* 33: 7–32.

Thaver, Beverley. 2008. 'The private higher education sector in Africa: current trends and themes in six country studies'. *JHEA/RESA* 6, 1: 127–142.

University of Makeni. 2014. 'UNIMAK Is Active in Fighting against Ebola Virus'. http://universityofmakeni.com/wordpress/?p=1167, accessed 23 October 2014.

University of Makeni. n.d. 'Strategic Plan, 2010–2015'. Sierra Leone.

University of Makeni. 2013–2014. 'Prospectus, Part 3, General Information'. Sierra Leone.

Woolcock, Michael. 1998. 'Social capital and economic development: towards a theoretical synthesis and policy framework'. *Theory and Society* 27: 151–208.

Workman, Anna. 2011. 'Makeni City Council and the politics of co-production in post-conflict Sierra Leone'. *IDS Bulletin* 42, 2: 53–63.

Zack-Williams, Alfred. 1995. 'Crisis and structural adjustment in Sierra Leone: implications for women'. In: Gloria Emeagwali (ed). *Women Pay the Price: Structural Adjustment in Africa and the Caribbean*. Trenton: Africa World Press, 53–61.

# 6 Political Entrepreneurship in Cameroon

*Antoine Socpa*

In Cameroon, as in many African countries, political entrepreneurship is often a circumstantial epiphenomenon that is grafted onto the careers of people who have previously not been connected to politics. This is largely attributable to the political situation in the country, the material conditions of existence, and certain modes of ideological action that encourage a particular kind of political entrepreneurship characterized by a vision to see and grasp opportunities to mobilize the masses, enhance the individual's social position, and obtain a better living at the same time. The welfare of society is thereby often a secondary consideration, if it is considered at all.

Although individuals who become political entrepreneurs mostly have no imminent political vocation, they are actors in terms of the definition offered by Michel Crozier and Erhard Friedberg: "These actors are endowed with rationality, even if it is limited; they are autonomous and come into interaction in a system that helps to structure their games" (Crozier and Friedberg 1981, quoted by Bernoux 1985). Therefore, their action is based on "political calculation" (Franklin 1975: 43) in often undeniable ignorance of professional conditions and political competence.

This chapter illustrates, using four examples of political entrepreneurship, that in Cameroon political entrepreneurship is not necessarily driven by an individuals' political vocation. Such political entrepreneurs have emerged from the professional groups of businessmen, civil servants, academic staff (serving or retired), and from diverse actors without a certain social standing yet. People from each category seize the opportunity to take advantage of the uneducated and poor rural and urban masses on one hand and unemployed graduates on the other.

This chapter explores what is required to become "political entrepreneurs", including their trajectories, motivations, and profiles. More precisely, it answers the following questions: Who is a political entrepreneur? What do they do to become political entrepreneurs? What does their community think of them? Is any politician a political entrepreneur? What is the difference between politicians who are not entrepreneurs and those who are political entrepreneurs?[1] For instance, the municipal and parliamentarian elections in September 2013 were an important political event during which most of my primary data were collected, notably during mass political campaigns organized by political leaders and contestants. During elections, public space becomes an arena in which the different political entrepreneurs compete with each other and stage themselves in various ways: personally, in the media, with banners, posters, leaflets and advertisements, by distributing gifts and refreshment, by mobilizing musicians, motorcycle taxis, and by organizing festive events such as theatre shows and football matches.

In my endeavor to depict the characteristics of political entrepreneurship in Cameroon, I will begin by discussing the concepts of economic and political entrepreneurs in order to find out what they share in common and the differences between them. I will then illustrate these reflections with examples from the four groups of businessmen, administrators, academics, and individuals without a social standing, and discuss and compare their motivations and profiles.

## ECONOMIC AND POLITICAL ENTREPRENEURS IN CAMEROON

The specificities of the concepts of political and economic entrepreneurship will provide a better understanding of the characteristics of political entrepreneurs in Cameroon. Scholars have extensively reflected on traders, businessmen, and entrepreneurs in African countries and their relation to political circumstances. Some studies focus on the entrepreneurs' farsightedness and innovative capacities, for example, when these individuals take advantage of making a business profitable in even the most chaotic political environment (MacGaffey 1987). Others emphasize the good relationships with politics as an explanation for profitable businesses (Jalloh 2007). Scholars have also drawn attention to the neglected field of big African capitalist enterprises and their contribution to development (Berman and Leys 1994; Taylor 2012). McDaniel (2005), rethinking Schumpeter's ideas, characterizes an entrepreneur as a creative innovator who not only works with the objective of making money but is also concerned with realizing change and improving life conditions by introducing his products and ideas. For Jean-Pierre Warnier (1993: 7–8), an anthropologist who studied entrepreneurial activities in the West Region of Cameroon, Schumpeter's work highlights an entrepreneur's function in the implementation of production factors and their role as a key component in economic development.

Indeed, businessmen and political entrepreneurs share in common their attempts to market a valuable good that will have a social impact. To be successful in their endeavor, they need the right dose of boldness and audacity. In contrast to the economic entrepreneur, who seeks to become big and socially respected by finding new methods of investment, production, or distribution and accumulating material wealth, the political entrepreneur's ambitions focus on becoming big by accumulating social (and also economic) power through a political position. The political entrepreneur is either selected by community members or else he places himself in a political position by subjugating those who benefit from his wealth (Laurent 2000: 169–181). His position, however, can be easily challenged by rivals or established local politicians. In contrast to such political figures, the classical economic entrepreneur does not require any larger social network of dependents in order to establish his business.

It is, however, important to note that not all politicians are political entrepreneurs. The concept of politics emerged in ancient Greece as the art of managing the "affairs of the cities". Politics refers to the set of rules and regulations that are applied to govern people in a given community or country; people should be governed in such way that their interests and rights are protected, which must be a leader's primary motivation and concern. An "ordinary politician", a politician in the usual sense of the word, is expected to behave according to good governance principles.[2]

Conditions in Cameroon's current political leadership are, however, slightly different. Corruption, embezzlement, and illicit enrichment (to use terms that derive their meaning in relation to what these "ordinary politicians" are supposed to do) have become (or have been since the introduction of the nation-state) the normal behavior that these individuals practice or feel urged to practice because of social constraints. It is also striking to note that—at least in Cameroon—civil servants and notably high-ranking state officials are often wealthier than businessmen. The major or probably unique source of this wealth accumulation is corruption (Médard 1992). In Cameroon, conversely, "normal politicians" are considered to be rather "lazy politicians" or "unfortunate politicians" because, despite their relentless political engagement, they have never succeeded at becoming wealthy. That is precisely why these politicians have become frustrated and bitter and, hence, often practice ideological flitting. They seek alternative means by creating their own political party or by moving from one political party to another and they become in this way political entrepreneurs. In Cameroon and in Africa more generally, political actors who can be termed "normal politicians" are very rare. Many scholars have therefore aptly described Cameroonian political leaders as corrupt, especially those of the second generation of politicians (see Ayissi 2008; Bayart 1989; GERDDES Cameroun 1999; Medard 1979, 1990, 1991; Socpa 2009).[3]

In the literature on political entrepreneurship, Jean François Médard (1992) compares the Sahlin's figure of the Melanesian Big Man with the African "big man politician". For Médard,

> In the African case, the political entrepreneur makes profit from the state to accumulate wealth. He then uses these accumulated economic resources to invest partly in his business and partly in the form of symbolic capital in the attraction of his followers. Therefore, the political

capital also helps, in turn, to extract more economic resources. (1992: 172, my translation)

This African Big Man politician uses political engagement as insurance to guarantee the prosperity of his business. Médard (1992: 173) also acknowledges the notion of straddling (Bayart 1989) political and economic positions, which characterizes the sociopolitical and economic nature of power. The spirit of political entrepreneurship (and indeed its economic and its religious corollaries as well), does not require intellectual or professional qualifications and is not necessarily based on any innate or natural disposition. It is important to note that political entrepreneurship is largely forged from the circumstances, constraints, and opportunities to which the individual or community is exposed.

In this political landscape, the different sectors of society are greatly intertwined (Médard 1992). Since the re-instauration of multiparty politics in the 1990s, almost all well-known economic entrepreneurs have been forced into politics, and most have become politicians against their will. Such traders or businessmen, who have developed their entrepreneurial ambitions and made enough money, are recognized by the community and referred to as a "Big Man" when they begin to redistribute their wealth through local developmental initiatives and investment in projects such as education, healthcare, water, sanitation, or road construction. Civil servants who work in the administration or belong to the intellectual elite become political entrepreneurs when they use their position as an incentive to acquire political or administrative posts from which they can easily make money, basically through corruption. They then reinvest the wealth they have accumulated in social dependants and in business, thereby becoming economic and political entrepreneurs at the same time. By playing both fields, they straddle the line between them, as Bayart (1989) notes. These circumstances urge businessmen to become politicians or political entrepreneurs and also require politicians (and other civil servants) to become political entrepreneurs and subsequently economic entrepreneurs as well. These processes are facilitated by what de Sardan (1999: 28) calls the "corruption complex", which "has become, in almost all African countries, a common and routine element of the functioning of the administrative and para-administrative apparatus, from top to bottom". Accordingly, in contemporary African societies, "corruption is then shown to be socially embedded in 'logics' of negotiation, gift-giving, solidarity, predatory authority and redistributive accumulation" (de Sardan 1999: 25).

Whereas an economic entrepreneur needs new desired goods to sell to clients and customers, a political entrepreneur depends on a large group of followers to support and elect him. This constellation brings them close to the figure of the Big Man. As the Big Man gains his followers, these entrepreneurs are required to invest their own means (or those of the government in the case of national elections), and time and energy, and create the most convincing arguments that might enhance their popularity. Their standing (as a businessman, an academic, or administrator) might help them in this endeavor. In Cameroon, in rural and urban areas, in their home community, or in society more generally, people see successful (political or economic) entrepreneurs as influential personalities, as "Big Men" or "Big Women", "who have the means", or "have succeeded". While the classical Big Men have to renew the support of their followers and their popularity persistently, politicians, after they have won an election, can be sure of their position for a specific time at least. Some, of course, also hope they can keep their political position as a life-long birth right, or even continually as a guarantee of their ethnic group. Both require a large group of followers to achieve their goal: the Big Man needs their material support, the politician their votes. Indeed, for both cases, the redistribution of wealth is a key strategy for building political support.

The notion of the classical Big Man implies the assumption that economic wealth, political and judicial power, and social status should ideally be congruent and grow simultaneously. Over the course of the past century, due to the introduction of paid labor systems, new varieties have emerged in individual trajectories. Additionally, where a Big Man has obtained his wealth and power often remains unknown, to the degree that in suspect cases people develop their own explanations that become virulent when things do not go well for them. In Cameroon, beliefs about the origin of wealth become existential when an individual is accused of belonging to a secret society (called *famla* in the Bamileke area and associated with witchcraft[4]), participating in networks of corruption, or engaging in mafia practices (sale of drugs and human organs) or sexual practices considered anti-cultural. Indeed, members of the Bamileke ethnic group from the western Grassfields of Cameroon strongly believe that many wealthy peoples "sell" their relatives for the purpose of accumulating wealth. Rumors about individuals who have died and were buried in their villages only to be found later somewhere else working tirelessly as laborers in farms or factories are rampant. People conclude that these "supposedly dead individuals" are working for the benefit of their "patron" who uses them as a kind of slave. Similarly, politicians are currently accused of being involved in the trafficking of human organs, from which they would derive both their sociopolitical power and material wealth.

Preventing or countering such accusations is another reason why entrepreneurs or men of success will show themselves to be generous, carry out development projects, and donate gifts and money to their immediate community or even the society at large. Indeed, according to Marshall Sahlins (1963: 289), "The indicative quality of big-man authority is everywhere the same: it is personal power. Big-men do not come to office; they do not succeed to, nor are they installed in, existing positions of leadership over political groups. The attainment of big-man status is, rather, the outcome of a series of acts which elevate a person above the common herd and attract about him a coterie of loyal, lesser men". Finally, the Big Man is a leader who "uses wealth to place others in his debt" (Sahlins 1972: 136).

These practices of gift-giving are particularly obvious in the context of political entrepreneurship. Individuals mobilize such practical strategies when they present gifts to their active members, followers, and voters. In Cameroon, however, their ideas and values are often ethnically oriented. Political entrepreneurs will try above all to attract people of the same ethnic origin to participate in their movements by stressing the fact that they are "sons of the soil" (belong to the original families of a place). Consequently, they expect their own people to provide them with the opportunity to represent them in the political and administrative spheres of the state, both at the local and the higher levels.

In Cameroon, issues associated with political and economic entrepreneurship are usually debated along ethnic or community lines. In this context, businessmen from certain regions are normally denied entry into political entrepreneurship due to the existence of ethno-sociological groups that hold a virtual monopoly on the national economy and the political and administrative system. This constellation influences local sociopolitical developments as well as daily relations between ethnic groups in the politico-administrative, economic, religious, and social domains.

In order to fully understand the current discourses, it is worth recalling that Cameroon only became an independent country in January 1960 after a fierce anti-colonial fight primarily between the local nationalist movement, called Union des Populations du Cameroun (UPC), and the French colonial administration. After independence, all existing political parties were banned and a single political party, the Cameroun National Union (CNU), was imposed in 1966. In 1982, it was renamed as the Cameroon People's Democratic Movement (CPDM) under Paul Biya. In the 1990s, a new multiparty political system emerged. Since then, sociopolitical and economic debates have been largely ethnically oriented due to the multi-ethnic nature and diversity of the Cameroonian population. The major ethnic groups are the Bamileke in the western Grassfields, the Beti-Fang-Boulou cluster in the south of Cameroon, and the Fulbe in the north. This ethnic distribution of the population has been replicated in the formation of political parties, which recruit their followers along ethnic lines (Nkwi and Socpa 1997; Socpa 2009; see also Van de Walle 2003).

Many people and personalities originating from the Central, South, and East Regions of Cameroon are convinced that people from other regions should be excluded from political office, arguing that this is "their turn to be in power".[5] For example, the Muslim regions in the north are often suspected[6] of wanting to "return" to power, as the first President of the Republic of Cameroon, Ahmadou Ahidjo (1960–1982), came from this region. In line with this attitude of suspicion, and even exclusion, other groups (Bassa'a, Douala, Bakweri, etc.) are qualified as "ethnic minorities", a characterization that excludes them de facto from access to the central political power.

In private and even public spaces, people often state that "it is unthinkable that Cameroon is governed by a president from an ethnic minority". For the ethnic groups in the Grassfields area (the Francophone West and the Anglophone North-West Regions), the message (based on stereotypes) is even clearer and sounds as a warning: "the Anglo-Bamileke already have economic power, it is beyond question that they aspire to power in politics". People even state that "Bamileke" and "northerners" should focus their attention on trade and economy and leave politics or administration to the Beti-Boulous aloud in the streets, in houses, and offices in Yaounde or Ebolowa.[7]

In this situation, it is wise for businessmen, as Jean-Loup Amselle states for the Malian traders,

> to convert a portion of their wealth into social or religious prestige. To proceed otherwise, would create a lack of understanding among the great mass of the population. The accumulation of wealth is indeed not reprehensible in the eyes of the people . . . what is reprehensible is their retention. If redistribution causes the blessings of those who receive, greed instead causes curses. What is more important . . . especially for the rich is to avoid being cursed as they have only one concern, that of ensuring their reputation within their social environment. (Amselle 1987: 72, my translation)

The strategy to convert economic capital into social capital (Bourdieu 1986) is not only widespread among businessmen but also among the political entrepreneurs described in the following section.

## POLITICAL ENTREPRENEURS' MOTIVES, PROFILES, AND STRATEGIES

This section explores why and how individuals become political entrepreneurs in Cameroon and reviews their profiles, motivations, and strategies. The first group consists of businessmen who have also become politicians to protect their wealth, while the second and third groups are academics and administrative staff who have become politicians to secure their posts. The fourth group comprises political opportunists who are up-comers and do not yet have anything much to secure. They all use politics as an instrument for the accumulation of wealth, whereby the first three use politics as an indirect, diverted, or less visible strategy for the accumulation of power, popularity, and prestige (more than of money), and the last simply aspire to enrich themselves. The administrative and intellectual elite are involved in a quest for political and social positions, whereas the economic entrepreneurs move into the political arena to "protect" and secure their business. For businessmen, for example, it is prerequisite to belong to the right political party when they want to protect their economic activities. They will carry out their business even more profitably when they become active politicians, often in their home regions. Affinity to (or even active campaigning for) the ruling political party is also essential for those civil servants and academic staff who need to preserve their positions and privileges or for those who are looking to be promoted to a more juicy post. Finally, the anonymous political actors have entered the political field because it offers opportunities for enrichment. They all profit from the needs and demands of society, as politicians work hard to bring social improvement and economic development and eliminate the ubiquitous status of "unemployment" for a large number of young women and men, whose situation makes them more receptive to the promises of these political entrepreneurs.

## The Businessmen

In Cameroon, two regions are particularly well-known for their successful traders and businessmen. These are the northern regions with their Hausa, Arab, and Bornu traders who have been active in long-distance trade for centuries (Mveng 1963; Roupsard 1986), and the Bamileke in the West Region who are well-known for their entrepreneurial spirit (Dongmo 1981; Geschiere and Konings 1993; Warnier 1993). Until the 1990s, entrepreneurs had not been particularly bothered when they carried out their business, provided they remained in the background in the one-party system, which changed with the introduction of the multiparty system and the economic liberalization in the 1990s. In order to protect their property, Bamileke businessmen, and northerners, had to align with the CPDM ruling party. Businessmen who at that time—the height of the politico-ideological struggle for the multiparty system—had been suspected of being associated with the opposition parties were placed in the state's tax agents' crosshairs. Often thinly veiled threats to impose high taxes were made to convince them to stand behind the ruling party, and, by reason and prudence knowing that they hold fragile eggs in their hands, businessmen were forced (despite themselves) to take registration cards from the ruling party and, worse (or better) again, to invest in or be volunteered for significant political responsibilities in the ruling CPDM party. Examples are the wealthy Mr. Victor Fotso and his henchmen, notably André Sohaing and Kadji Defosso, who are now mayors of municipal councils of their hometowns. The same opportunistic approach is observed in the northern regions of Cameroon with the entry into politics of businessmen such as Oumarou Fadhil, Alhaji Abbo, and numerous others.

Mr. Victor Fotso is a wealthy businessman who is not only well-known in Cameroon but also in other parts of Francophone West and Central Africa, where he trades in commodities and has invested in battery, lamp, and match manufacturing as well as banking. He is well respected in Cameroon and is courted by members of the ruling party as well as by the opposition leaders. In the 1990s, he discovered a new passion: politics. He ran in elections in his rural hometown, Bandjoun, in the West Region of Cameroon, where he was elected mayor. Other businessmen followed similar routes when they felt the need to demonstrate their political alignment. For example, Kadji Defosso became the mayor of Bana, Oumarou Fadhil the mayor of Douala-Bonabéri, Alhaji Abbo the mayor of Ngaoundere. A similar case can be found in Ms. Françoise Foning's engagement, as she became the mayor of Douala while remaining a businesswoman as well as a prominent activist in the ruling party. Her activism is vivid to such an extent that many Cameroonians consider her CPDM's "political mascot". Another striking example is Maidadou Saïdou, a businessman and former Vice-Chairman of the Social Democratic Front (SDF), the most well-known opposition party. In 1990, he resigned from that party and joined the National Union for Democracy and Progress (UNDP). The UNDP is another opposition party led by Bello Bouba Maigari, his "ethnic and Muslim brother" in northern Cameroon. In addition to these "party-state pundits", there is a plethora of young businessmen who try to follow in their footsteps with the ultimate goal of "protecting" their businesses and avoiding heavy taxes when they import and retail their goods.

The inclination of economic figures to engage in political entrepreneurship only gained strength following the introduction of multiparty politics in Cameroon in 1990. It occurs in a context in which these characters would usually be declared by the general public "persona non grata" or unqualified for the political game due to their incompetence and lack of political expertise, as many lack formal education.

To ensure their reputation, many businessmen from the West and Northern Regions have become entrepreneurs in local politics even if this was not their original intention. Instead, they are motivated to join politics for two reasons: first, they serve as "donors" for development activities and local policy by actively participating in the construction of social and health infrastructures such as roads, schools, health centers, or rural electrification; second, related to the first, for these businessmen entry into politics is a sort of "safety valve" that protects them against the harassment of tax officers.

These individuals can be termed political entrepreneurs because they invest their own means into the registration and campaigning for the elections. After being elected, their standing in their home community and in society at large increases. Members of their community not only consider them to be models of success but also selfish individuals who use others to obtain increased influence and material resources.

## The Intellectuals (also called the "Long Pencils")

The phenomenon of intellectuals becoming political entrepreneurs is less recent than businesspeoples' entry into politics. As early as Ahmadou Ahidjo's first regime in Cameroon and even before the independence period in the 1960s, the role of intellectuals in the political game had been well appreciated. In this chapter, however, I will only consider examples from the 1990s onward. Since the reintroduction of multiparty politics in 1990, the intelligentsia (those who are commonly called "long pencils" because they went to school and acquired extensive training and valuable diplomas) developed a politico-ideological appetite rarely seen before. Some examples will illustrate their motivations and strategies.

Maurice Kamto is a lawyer and prominent university professor of law. He is known as an excellent jurist whose popularity increased when the Hague International Court of Justice declared Cameroon's victory over Nigeria during the Bakassi border dispute. Many Cameroonians attributed this happy ending to Professor Kamto's talent and skills as he represented the state during the trial. Most likely as a reward for his efforts, Professor Kamto was appointed Vice-Minister of Justice. To much surprise, Kamto resigned from his government post and founded a political party, the Mouvement pour la Renaissance du Cameroun (MRC), only a few months before the municipal and legislative elections of September 2013. Rumor has it that he wanted to use his party to explore ways to become a full minister himself rather than play a secondary role as a deputy minister under a less-educated boss.

A contrasting trajectory has been observed in the strategies used by other personalities who have begun their own political career in the opposition party and ended up either becoming a member of the ruling party or joining another opposition party, likely allied to the ruling party. For instance, the educational scientist Miss Lydia Belle Efimba was formally the chairperson of the Liberal Democratic Alliance (LDA). She left the party after an internal dispute with other members to join the Social Democratic Front (SDF) and she later left the SDF to join the CPDM (ruling party). Currently, she is the Deputy President of the National Good Governance Program. She was rewarded for her political shift from the opposition to the ruling party with this new position. She has been able to use the privileges attached to this new position to increase her social and economic power. Similarly, Mr. George Dobgima Nyamndi, an associate professor in the English department at the University of Buea and acting leader of the Social Liberal Congress (SLC), initially emerged on the political scene as a candidate for the presidential elections in October 2012. But then, not even a year later, in September 2013, when he stood as a candidate for the municipal and parliamentarian elections, he clearly asked his followers to vote for the CPDM, as he identified that it was the best choice. He is currently the Vice-Dean for Students Affairs and Records at the University of Buea.

Such examples demonstrate that these intellectuals are not necessarily members of a clearly defined political party since they keep moving from one party to another. By doing this, it appears that they do not have any ideological conviction; they use politics as an opportunity to ameliorate their economic situation. For example, the first intellectual has a clear and personal political ambition while the second and the third are seeking administrative positions via their political activities.

Intellectuals' political entrepreneurship has been a topic of conversation for quite some time in Cameroon. Nowadays, however, the phenomenon has acquired additional strength. Many university lecturers, including some from the top of the diploma and title pedestal, think they have the expertise and insight needed to manage public or political affairs. The supporters of the regime even encourage this form of political entrepreneurship when they do not hesitate to empty university auditoriums by appointing experienced teachers to political or administrative positions. Once these intellectuals are appointed, they use their positions to their advantage, particularly as levers of strength, social protection, and economic and political advancement. In this context, the electoral period is the propitious time used to consolidate their political enterprise.

## Managers of Public Administration

The Cameroonian government is composed of various degrees of executives, senior managers, and senior clerks. The majority of these individuals work for the interest of the ruling party. Since they live in grand style, they can only run for the party in power. They enjoy all the privileges, even the most exorbitant ones, without the slightest remorse, compassion, or reserve. If they want to continue to enjoy the status quo, "high place" civil servants have no choice but to become "political entrepreneurs". Once again, as in the case of the academics, elections represent a suitable moment to show commitment, with the expectation of keeping their position or being given greater administrative responsibilities and, consequently, more fruitful privileges.

According to Maud Saint-Lary (2009: 9–17), bureaucratic and political spheres produce "big men entrepreneurs" who accumulate and divert resources from the state. In this respect, being a political entrepreneur or actor represents a political advantage for winning initiatives. Accordingly, individuals are expected to profit from their political networks in the political arena. This attitude is very common among Cameroonian small, middle, and senior-ranked civil servants and administrators. The examples are numerous; here five cases will be sufficient to illustrate the motivations and strategies of state public services managers to engage in political entrepreneurship.

The first example is Mr. Dakolé Daïsalla, the former director of the National Urban Transport Corporation of Cameroon (SOTUC), in the 1970s and the early 1980s. In 1984, he was placed under arrest and imprisoned for his alleged involvement and complicity in organizing the aborted coup d'état of April 1984. In 1990, he received a presidential pardon and regained his freedom. He then created a political party, the Mouvement pour la Défense de la République (MDR). The party ran in the 1992 parliamentary elections, during which they obtained six seats in the National Assembly. Mr. Dakolé sided with the ruling party to allow it to have the parliamentary majority. As a reward, he was appointed a minister. The most interesting thing about this personality is that he wrote a book after he was released from prison in which he fiercely criticized the CPDM regime and notably, the extremely difficult living conditions in prison (Dakolé 1993). He nevertheless was able to establish a parliamentarian alliance with this same government that he so vehemently had criticized. By siding with the ruling party, Mr. Dakolé's intention had been to make more money that he then intended to use to strengthen his own party and to satisfy his basic needs as a former "poor" prisoner.

Mr. Issa Tchiroma Bakary's case is very similar to that of Dakolé. He had been a member of the CPDM until the early 1990s, and after the introduction of the multiparty system in 1990 he resigned and joined the National Union for Democracy and Progress (UNDP). Due to internal leadership disputes within the party, he resigned again and joined another party, the Alliance for Development and Democracy (ADD). He left that party as well soon thereafter to create his own party, the Front National pour le Salut du Cameroun (FNSC). After the presidential elections in 2012, Mr. Tchiroma joined his party with the CPDM as an allied party, and was then appointed Minister of Communication in the government. The trajectory is therefore unique, moving from one party to the next and finally siding with a party that he had criticized, the CPDM party. He can therefore be considered a conqueror of posts.

The third example is Mrs. Haman Adama. She originates from the Muslim region where not many women receive formal western education. A former member of the government as the Minister of Basic Education, she was also a very active militant in the CPDM in the northern part of Cameroon. She was abruptly arrested and jailed for embezzling public funds. After several years in prison, she could pay her bail and was released in 2013. In contrast to other politically frustrated peers like Mr. Garga Haman Hadji (see below), she did not create a political party but continued to be active in the ruling CPDM party. She did not dare to create a new political party or join an opposition party because she felt that she was still under suspicion of corruption and by remaining in the ruling party, she could benefit from its protection.

Another example is Mr. Garga Haman Hadji. He was a militant of the CPDM, a Minister of Public Service and Administrative Reform, and commonly recognized in Cameroon as a committed and uncorrupted state civil servant. He did, however, resign from his post in protest of the administrative obstacles he had faced in his fight against corruption. In the media, he is usually presented as a "whale hunter", as the image of the whale refers to big and rich corrupted state civil servants. He was supposed to catch the large fortunes acquired through nepotism and corruption with his symbolic whale-boat. After his resignation, he founded his own political party and has run in several elections since. In contrast to Mr. Dakolé Daissala and Mrs. Adama, Mr. Garga Haman has completely arrived in the political opposition, trying to pave his own way to the top of the ruling power through this channel.

The last example, Mr. Jean Jacques Ekindi, used a similar strategy. He was a very active section president of the CPDM for Wouri in Douala until he left the party in the 1990s, when the multiparty system was introduced. He decided to form his own party called Progressist Movement (MP). He used to portray himself as the "lion hunter", as the lion refers to the campaign slogan of President Paul Biya who, during the 1992 presidential election, was officially presented as the "lion man". In Cameroon and elsewhere in sub-Saharan Africa, the "lion" is known as a very powerful wild animal. In Cameroon, the national soccer team, The Indomitable Lions, is named after that animal. By bearing the "lion" nickname, President Biya wanted to present himself as the "king of the forest" or the "king of Cameroon", in short, the number-one politician.

The examples of the managers of administration show that they have developed their political entrepreneurship in direct relationship to the CPDM state party. This party has shaped the purposes and the trajectories of these political entrepreneurs, and their strategies oscillate between loyalty and disloyalty to this party.

## Newcomers in the Public Scene

Beyond the economic, intellectual, and administrative personalities discussed so far, whose notoriety in political entrepreneurship was directly shaped by the existence of the CPDM state party, a number of shady actors have emerged with their own parties in the Cameroonian political arena since the 1990s. These new political actors can be qualified as a spontaneous generation consisting of a colorful crowd of individuals who have not yet become notorious in the political, social, or economic landscape. They seem to have suddenly and by enchantment discovered their new political vocation, which they hope to use to make money. This practice, which can be called "feymania" politics, is directly motivated by a desire for the opportunistic accumulation of material wealth in general and money in particular. Accumulation is essential for gaining a higher social status and these unscrupulous "politicians" quickly recapitalize their new status and the money they receive into political resources.

The emergence of these politicians seems to be related to the introduction of the multiparty system and the way in which the CPDM regime attempted to convince international donors, such as bilateral and United Nations (UN) organizations, of its sincere desire to establish an "advanced democracy"[8] with many political parties. The state provides a budget that legalized political parties are entitled to use for electoral campaigns. This has encouraged numerous self-styled politicians to create their own parties. Between 1990 and 2013, the state has allowed the creation of 250 political parties. It is therefore sufficient to create and legalize a political party and make loans here and there or receive money from the state to apply for candidature and pay the security deposit required to run in an election. The creation of such an enrichment network is therefore an easy way to gain access to state funds. This particular context of "creative chaos" (Sindjoun 1996) led, in the words of Richard Banégas and Jean-Pierre Warnier (2001: 8), to the rise of a real "economy of cunning and resourcefulness".

The presidential elections of October 2012 helped to find these individuals, who apparently had been attracted to the juicy funding the government was distributing to political parties and had been quick to create a party and submit an application. Of the thirty applications submitted, twenty-three were selected for the election. After election, more than 90% had been unable to reach 5%. These "political bandits", as they are popularly called in Cameroon, exploit the trap the ruling party set for the international community to show the vitality and dynamism of a so-called "advanced" democracy. In reality, no apparatus was implemented to limit the number of candidates. The political action of these new kinds of political activists is centered on blackmailing and they are not much different from "feymen" or "social bandits" as described by Malaquais (2001: 101).

## THE TRAJECTORIES OF THE POLITICAL ENTREPRENEURS

Three types of motivations can be identified for becoming a politician: to secure economic property, to secure positions and enhance prestige and power, and to make money. Interestingly, a political vocation with a vision to ameliorate the conditions in the country is not completely absent but does not rank first among these considerations. These motivations are part of the register of social advancement, economic and political investment, and simple enrichment (Utas 2012).

It is obvious that when administrators and intellectuals seek new statutory visibility or delay their imprisonment, many of them are particularly attentive toward "things of the political party", whereas businessmen tend to be in search of a political umbrella for their affairs. A popular diction well-known in Cameroon states that "a seller of fresh eggs does not look for trouble". Thus, among businessmen as well as academics and administrative staff, the procedure is highly conservative for these two overlapping but nested and diametrically opposed positions. In African societies, as Bayart (1989) as well as Médard (1992) note, the entanglement is a strategy to accumulate wealth and political power. The ruling elite are perceived as an entangled class (Lentz 1998: 61) in the context of a "patrimonial state" and the "politics of the belly". This ruling elite consists of a small circle of people who consider themselves "important people", "Big Men", or who are regarded as such in their home communities (Utas 2012: 1–34). As Carola Lentz (1998: 61) illustrates: "If the avenues to 'bigness' are characterized by the astute combination of different registers of power, economic and political, so are the strategies of legitimizing".

The trajectory of political entrepreneurship follows the reverse path of economic entrepreneurship. Businessmen have to invest part of their economic capital to become politicians in order to protect their businesses and raise their social status. The intellectuals and administrative staff become political entrepreneurs because they have to demonstrate their association with the state party and use the relational and economic capital accumulated during their service to promote the predominant politics in order to protect their positions and redistribute part of their wealth. In this respect, elections are an ideal time to indulge in extravagant spending and handedness shares (Veyne 1976) made in the form of campaign donations (Socpa 2000) to monetize people's votes in their ethnic and clan strongholds.

Moreover, during such occasions businessmen are solicited by senior administrative staff for their "financial firepower" to consolidate their new status as a political entrepreneur. Other village elites who are civil servants are also solicited to contribute to the project in terms of time and money. The reason for pushing civil servants to contribute is based on the assumption that because they receive a salary from the state, they should also support the party that is running state affairs. At the same time, these civil servants are expected to do what they can to bring positive results in an election in favor of the ruling party, even at the price of massive vote rigging.

This is in line with the sacrosanct principle of "njangui politics"[9] (Sindjoun 1996: 65). The benefits of successful political entrepreneurship go from extending retirement time to impunity even for physical, social, and economic crimes. It also facilitates access to training schools, tax evasion, and other unimaginable emoluments and pensions for the politicians' allies.

Political entrepreneurs' motivation seems to be far removed from that of the industrial entrepreneur who seeks to make money by investing in inventions and projects that are meant to enhance the life of people and whose realization implies taking the risk of losing one's investments. In contrast, the intellectual or administrative political entrepreneur is mostly concerned to be paid back for expenses incurred for his ascent instead of worrying about the well-being of populations.

In Cameroon, the more recent means of enrichment described above complete a long list already identified and documented by Geschiere and Konings (1993) in their seminal collection on pathways of accumulation in Cameroon. Entrepreneurship, as an economic project without the acknowledgement of the politico-ideological situation in which it takes place, is bound to potential failure, and, in turn, political entrepreneurship without economic dividend is illusory. Businessmen use policy to secure their business, while intellectuals and administrative staff use policy for social wealth and material accumulation. By giving priority to the political dimension of their investment, businessmen and administrators hope to gain economic benefits, status, and positions obtained as the reward for their political entrepreneurship. Thus, most of the political entrepreneurs' trajectories have led to the construction of the image of the "Great man" and "Big Man" widely explored in the literature (Banégas and Warnier 2001; Godelier 1986; Sahlins 1963; Utas 2012). More generally, the new growing relation between political entrepreneurs and donor organizations does not seem to be innocent. Furthermore, as Bierschenk, Chauveau, and Olivier de Sardan (2000) note, politicians gradually assume the role of "development brokers". This transition or forced passage of the status of civil servant working for the state to that of a political entrepreneur and then also that of a businessman (economic entrepreneur) has become fashionable in Cameroon, especially since the reconversion of political power into business activities after retirement is increasingly considered normal.

For businessmen especially, it seems clear that the superposition of political entrepreneur status to that of economic entrepreneur is part of an economic survival strategy in a context where the government, through its tax agents and other repressive apparatus, may decide to economically punish businessmen who might be tempted to officially support the opposition parties. The economic punishment in question here is brandished in veiled detour conversations and meetings even in the upper echelons of state decisions. To be brief, it can consist of a "Molotov cocktail" of sanctions and fiscal charges that are applied, the purpose of which is either to antagonize the "trader opponent" or to bring him back into the dominant political ideology. A tax inspector I met in Yaounde explained it quite clearly: "Well, businessmen have money but they have not gone to school. With my simple pencil, I am able to clear off all their wealth if they do not want to walk as you want".

More generally, Jean-François Médard (1992: 176) shows that for these entrepreneurial politicians, pathways to success are drawn suing the logic of "straddling" (Bayart 1989) or overlap, that is, by the occupation of multiple working positions. They can be all in one: state officials, big landowners, and businessmen. Therefore, wealth accumulation is instrumental for consolidating power (Boone 1994). Good examples are Mr. Victor Fotso and Mr. Niat Ndifendi Marcel. The former, as I have shown, is a well-known businessman turned political entrepreneur in Cameroon, who became the mayor of his hometown, the municipality of Bandjoun. The latter is a retired state minister and the general director of the state electricity company. He created an ideological movement in support of President Biya's political actions and was appointed the Senate Chamber President of Cameroon in 2013.

## CONCLUSION

The purpose of this chapter was to explore the issue of political entrepreneurship in Cameroon. My discussion was based on the notion that "the political entrepreneur" is someone with the goal of becoming a Big Man by accumulating social as well as economic power through his political position. He or she invests money and engages in moral ethnicity (Lonsdale 1996) to attract followers. The money invested by businessmen for political entrepreneurship purposes is theirs, whereas the funds spent by civil servants and academic staff come from three sources: the first and the minimal part comes from their salary; the most important part from embezzlement in the case of those who occupy lucrative positions in the state apparatus; and the third comes directly from the state, which distributes money to political parties for campaigns during elections. From previous developments, it emerges that political entrepreneurship is not a purpose in itself. Instead, it is an accidental or circumstantial epiphenomenon grafted onto careers that do not, necessarily, have a connection with politics. In Cameroon and probably in many African countries, the material conditions of existence and modes of ideological actions, policies, and career paths determine whether or not the political entrepreneur cap is used.

In the examples addressed in this study, three scenarios of political entrepreneurship have emerged. Political entrepreneurship was found among businessmen, civil servants, and academic staff. Entrepreneurs in each of these categories have used the opportunity to instrumentalize the uneducated and economically disadvantaged rural and urban masses on one hand, and graduates who are permanently or temporarily unemployed, on the other. Regardless of whether it is considered from the point of view of businessmen, civil servants, or academic staff, political entrepreneurship is a strategy that is used to secure a beneficial position or to conquer new ones. These positions are thereafter used to elevate the bearer to a higher social standing in the community.

The cases of political entrepreneurship strategies illustrate the different trajectories that these individuals follow. When these individuals are unsuccessful, they become embittered and disappointed. Very often, they "turn their coats" either by creating their own political party, or integrating it into an opposition party (phenomenon of political turncoat). In contrast, those whose political entrepreneurship is successful have access to what Bruce McDaniel (2005: 488) calls "entrepreneurial profit", which consists of the appointment to political and administrative responsibilities including a number of privileges. In this way, they become "Big Men" in their community and nationwide.

## NOTES

1. The data on which the chapter is based were collected with the methods of documentary research and direct observation during cultural and political events. I have also carried out twelve semi-structured interviews with academic

staff, civil servants, and active militants from the ruling and opposition political parties. Secondary data on such political events were collected from local newspapers and printed electoral campaign materials.

2. http://en.wikipedia.org/wiki/Politics, accessed 10 October 2014.

3. Nelson Mandela, the late South African President and hero of the anti-apartheid movement, is probably an exception that comes to mind. Cameroon occupies position 144 in the world out of 175 countries surveyed by Transparency International in 2013. Issues of bad governance and the dependency of the judiciary system are responsible for this poor performance (http://www.cameroonvoice.com/news/article-news-13490.html, accessed 4 April 2013).

4. Peter Geschiere and Francis Nyamnjoh (1998: 72) note, "Villagers tend to suspect urbanites of using the occult forces to enrich themselves, while urbanites profess to be afraid of the levelling impact of the villagers' 'witchcraft'".

5. It is necessary to recall here that the first president of the independent Republic of Cameroon was Mr. Ahmadou Ahidjo, a native of the Fulani northern region of Cameroon. After his resignation in 1982, he was replaced by Mr. Paul Biya, a native of the southern region. For ordinary Cameroonians, this transition at the top of the state is simply interpreted as a handover of ethnic rule from the Fulani to the Beti-Boulou ethnic group.

6. This suspicion has been present since 6 April 1984, when a group of coup plotters mostly from northern Cameroon tried to overthrow (unsuccessfully) Paul Biya's regime.

7. And another added: "Bamileke like to trade, so they would be willing to put the presidential palace up for rent [to have more money] if one of them were to be the tenant".

8. The concept of "advanced democracy" is an invention that only CPDM supporters can proficiently master. It could imply a democratic situation that is "full" or "complete" only if there is also something like a "simple", "average", "less-advanced", or "complicated democracy" as well.

9. "Njangui politics" means that the practice of politics is a game and share. You help me to come to power and I will in turn reward you. As the former Prime Minister of Cameroon, Achidi Achu, put it: "You scratch my back and I scratch your own".

# REFERENCES

Amselle, Jean-Loup. 1987. 'Fonctionnaires et homes d'affaires au Mali'. *Politique africaine* 26: 63–72.

Ayissi, Lucien. 2008. *Corruption et gouvernance au Cameroun*. Paris: L'Harmattan.

Banégas, Richard and Jean-Pierre Warnier. 2001. 'Nouvelles figures de la réussite et du pouvoir'. *Politique Africaine* 82: 5–23.

Bayart, Jean-François. 1989. *L'État en Afrique. La politique du ventre*. Paris: Fayard (engl.: *The State in Africa: The Politics of the Belly*. London: Longman, 1993).

Berman, Bruce and Colin Leys (eds). 1994. *African Capitalists in African Development*. Boulder and London: Lynne Rienner.

Bernoux, Philippe. 1985. *Sociologie des organisations. Initiation théorique suivie de douze cas pratiques*. Paris: Collection Points.

Bierschenk, Thomas, Jean-Pierre Chauveau, and Jean-Pierre Olivier de Sardan (eds). 2000. *Courtiers en développement. Les villages africains en quête de projets*. Paris: APAD-Karthala.

Boone, Catherine. 1994. *States and Ruling Classes in Sub-Saharan Africa: The Enduring Contradictions of Power*. Cambridge: Cambridge University Press.

Bourdieu, Pierre. 1986. 'The forms of capital'. In: John Richardson (ed). *Handbook of Theory and Research for the Sociology of Education*. New York: Greenwood, 241–258.

Crozier, Michel and Erhard Friedberg. 1981. *L'acteur et le système*. Paris: Le Seuil.

Dakolé, Daïssalla. 1993. *Libre derrière les barreaux*. Paris: Éditions du Jaguar.

De Sardan, Olivier. 1999. 'A moral economy of corruption in Africa?' *Journal of Modern African Studies* 37, 1: 25–52.

Dongmo, Jean-Louis. 1981. *Le dynamisme Bamiléké*. Yaoundé: CEPER (2 vols).

Franklin, Jean. 1975. *Le discours du pouvoir*. Paris: Union générale d'éditions.

GERDDES Cameroun. 1999. *De la Corruption au Cameroun*. Yaoundé: Friedrich Ebert-Stiftung. http://library.fes.de/pdf-files/bueros/kamerun/07798.pdf, accessed 6 October 2014.

Geschiere, Peter and Piet Konings (eds). 1993. *Itinéraires d'accumulation au Cameroun*. Paris: ASC and Karthala.

Geschiere, Peter and Francis Nyamnjoh. 1998. 'Witchcraft as an issue in the "politics of belonging": democratization and urban migrants' involvement with the home village'. *African Studies Review* 41, 3: 69–91.

Godelier, Maurice. 1986. *The Making of a Great Man: Male Domination and Power among the New Guinea Baruya*. Cambridge: Cambridge University Press.

Jalloh, Alusine. 2007. 'Muslim Fula business elites and politics in Sierra Leone'. *African Economic History* 35: 89–104.

Laurent, Pierre-Joseph. 2000. 'Entre ville et campagne : le big man local ou la "gestion coup d'Etat" de l'espace public'. *Politique africaine* 80: 169–181.

Lentz, Carola. 1998. 'The chief, the mine captain and the politician: legitimating power in Northern Ghana'. *Africa* 68, 1: 46–67.

Lonsdale, John. 1996. 'Ethnicité morale et tribalisme politique'. *Politique Africaine* 61: 98–115.

MacGaffey, Janet. 1987. *Entrepreneurs and Parasites: The Struggle for Indigenous Capitalism in Zaïre*. Cambridge: Cambridge University Press.

Malaquais, Dominique. 2001. 'Art de feyre au Cameroun'. *Politique africaine* 82: 101–118.

McDaniel, Bruce. 2005. 'A contemporary view of Joseph A. Schumpeter's theory of the entrepreneur'. *Journal of Economic Issues* 39, 2: 485–489.

Médard, Jean-François. 1979. 'L'état sous-développé au Cameroun'. Paris: L'Harmattan.

Médard, Jean-François. 1990. 'L'état patrimonialisé'. *Politique Africaine* 39: 25–36.

Médard, Jean-François. 1991. 'L'état patrimonial en Afrique noire'. In: Jean-François Bayart (ed). *Etats d'Afrique noire: formation, mécanismes et crise*. Paris: Karthala, 323–353.

Médard, Jean-François. 1992. 'Le Big-Man en Afrique: esquisse d'analyse du politician entrepreneur'. *L'Année sociologique* 42: 167–192.

Mveng, Engelbert. 1963. *Histoire du Cameroun*. Paris: Présence Africaine.

Nkwi, Paul and Antoine Socpa. 1997. 'Ethnicity and party politics: the politics of divide and rule'. In: Paul Nkwi and Francis Nyamnjoh (eds). *Regional Balance and National Integration in Cameroon*. Yaoundé: ASC and CASSRT, 138–149.

Roupsard, Marcel. 1986. *Nord-Cameroun: ouverture et développement*. Coutances: Claude Bellée.

Sahlins, Marshall. 1963. 'Poor man, rich man, big-man, chief: political types in Polynesia and Melanesia'. *Comparative Studies in Society and History* 5: 285–303.

Sahlins, Marshall. 1972. *Stone Age Economics*. Chicago: Aldine de Gruyter.

Saint-Lary, Maud. 2009. 'Introduction: des entrepreneurs entre rhétorique et action sur le monde'. *Bulletin de l'APAD* 29–30: 9–17.

Sindjoun, Luc. 1996. 'Le champ social camerounais. Désordre inventif, mythes simplificateurs et stabilité hégémonique de l'Etat'. *Politique Africaine* 64: 57–67.

Socpa, Antoine. 2000. 'Les dons dans le jeu politique au Cameroun'. *Cahiers d'Études Africaines* 157, XL-1: 91–108.

Socpa, Antoine. 2009. 'Clientélisme et ethnicité dans le jeu politique. Réflexions sur quelques mouvements thuriféraires au Cameroun'. *Revue de Sociologie, d'Anthropologie et de Psychologie* 1: 165–183.

Taylor, Scott. 2012. *Globalization and the Cultures of Business in Africa: From Patrimonialism to Profit*. Bloomington and Indianapolis: Indiana University Press.

Transparency International. 2013. *Corruption perception index.* http://cpi.transpar ency.org/cpi2013/results/, accessed 6 October 2014.

Utas, Mats. 2012. 'Introduction: Bigmanity and network governance in African conflicts'. In: Mats Utas (ed). *African Conflicts and Informal Power: Big Men and Networks*. London: Zed Books, 1–31.

Van de Walle, Nicolas. 2003. 'Presidentialism and clientelism in Africa's emerging party systems'. *Journal of Modern African Studies* 41, 2: 297–321.

Veyne, Paul. 1976. *Le pain et le cirque*. Paris: Le Seuil.

Warnier, Jean-Pierre. 1993. *L'esprit d'entreprise au Cameroun*. Paris: Karthala.

# Part II

# Business, Pleasure, Leisure

# 7 Entrepreneurship in South Africa's Emergent Township Funeral Industry

*Rebekah Lee*

In South African writer Zakes Mda's novel *Ways of Dying* (1995), Nefo-lovhodwe is a rural carpenter who seeks his fortunes in the city as a coffin-maker. In an environment where funerals are a near-daily occurrence and cemeteries are "jam-packed", Nefolovhodwe undergoes a transformation from struggling tradesman to savvy urban funeral entrepreneur. He invents what would become the cornerstone of his business's profits—the Collapsible Coffin, a flat-pack coffin which could be assembled IKEA-like in a few easy steps. For his higher-end customers to whom the Collapsible Coffin's utilitarian feel does not appeal, Nefolovhodwe markets the DeLuxe Special, a coffin made of oak and ebony and for an extra fee decorated with ivory. On the back of his success in coffin-manufacturing, Nefolovhodwe expands his business by selling tombstones, flower arrangements, and even haute couture attire for wealthy widows. Mda wryly concludes, "Nefo-lovhodwe had attained all his wealth through death. Death was therefore profitable" (1995: 124).

In a nation marked by continued economic inequality and profound AIDS mortality—with the cumulative death toll over the course of the HIV/AIDS epidemic estimated to be over 4 million (South Africa 2012)—moral questions over the profitability of the "death business" abound. Entrepreneurs like Nefolovhodwe in the nascent (and still growing) township funeral industry have faced intense scrutiny not only in popular culture but in the media and local communities as well. Rumors of unscrupulous undertakers and their "scavenger" practices circulate among township dwellers and accentuate their position as potent symbols of a broader and unseemly commercialization of death. "Conspicuous consumption is the order of the day at funerals", lamented a recent BBC News correspondent observing funerals in Johannesburg (Nkosi 2011), while another journalist soberly observed that budgeting for increasingly exorbitant funerals has left many urban African families "buried in debt" (Ballim 2013).

This chapter seeks to provide a historical and ethnographic perspective on the rise of the funeral industry and the role of funeral entrepreneurs in post-apartheid South Africa. It draws on two emergent areas of study. The first is a current surge of interest in so-called "popular economies" in South

Africa (Hull and James 2012). This turn to a popular economies approach takes into account the "hybrid" and creative character of income-generating practices, and draws from recent critiques of the "informal economy" in Africa which question simplified analytic divisions between "global" and "local" economies as well as between monetized and moral/personal exchanges (see Guyer 2004; Shipton 2007). While acknowledging the historical depth and strength of capitalist accumulation in South Africa (dating back to the growth of the mining sector in the late nineteenth century) as compared to other African contexts, Hull and James argue that the process of "formalization" of South African economies should not be over-stated or simplified. Contradictory processes are at work—including continuing reliance on the state as a redistributive mechanism, structural unemployment, as well as a broader trend toward "financialization" of the economy—which blur the boundary between formal and informal in the South African context. Social, cultural, and moral capital continue to shape transactional regimes, sometimes in unexpected ways (Hull and James 2012). Within these contradictory spaces individual strategies for accumulation can coalesce, as evidenced in James's vivid portrayals of the recent emergence of "brokers" and "loansharks" who operate within (and profit from) the interstices between institutionalized modes of authority and more fluid interpersonal relationships (James 2012, 2011). As we shall see more fully, funeral entrepreneurs' actions and motivations should be seen as embodying a similar imperative toward improvisation and innovation within this complex social and economic terrain.

The second stream of scholarship relevant to this study concerns the management and experience of death on the continent, a topic which has received much recent attention, not least in consideration of widespread HIV/AIDS mortality and its demographic and socioeconomic implications (see Lee and Vaughan 2008). In particular, social anthropologists have sought to move away from older "classical" approaches, which tended to essentialize African funerary and mortuary rituals, instead analyzing practices around death as embedded (and evolving) in a broader landscape of political and economic change (Geschiere 2005; Jindra and Noret 2011). Much of the recent literature on the commodification of funerals in Africa can be seen in this light. Although the initial emphasis of this scholarship was on the wholesale "transformation" of funerary rites (see Arhin 1994), recent work has begun to acknowledge the diverse roles that money and commodities may play in mediating African approaches to death (De Witte 2001, 2003; Lee 2011). Indeed, even processes of globalization and modernization do not necessarily empty funerals of their spiritual and social meaning. Technological innovations and money flows, in particular from migrant Africans, can help shape culturally specific and often highly localized burial practices (Noret 2004; Page 2007).

This chapter explores the development of the township funeral industry as a key "popular economy" in South Africa.[1] It draws from collected life histories, interviews, and participant observation of undertakers and their employees at work, largely in Cape Town's major African townships of Khayelitsha and Gugulethu and secondarily in the rural areas of the province of the Eastern Cape, where many ethnic Xhosa in Cape Town maintain familial connections.[2] I begin by considering the particular social, economic, and political forces at work in the transitional and post-apartheid periods, when an African-run funeral industry first began to emerge. I then turn to the distinctive features of entrepreneurship within this industry, considering both the challenges and opportunities faced by African undertakers in what is regarded as a highly competitive industry. Finally, I examine possible gendered dimensions of funeral entrepreneurship and suggest ways forward for future research.

I show that the emergence of African-run funeral parlors can be traced to a convergence of factors in the transitional and post-apartheid periods, including democratic transition, deregulation and the rise of a credit culture, the explosion of formal and informal funeral insurance, the repercussions of the HIV/AIDS epidemic, and the sharpening of ethnic allegiances in South African society. I argue that entrepreneurs' previous employment histories powerfully shaped their entry into and involvement in the funeral industry, in particular their emphasis on transport and mobility across long distances (of mourners and the deceased back to his or her natal home). In a country where high AIDS mortality, rapid political transformation, and persistent poverty and inequality have shaped the economic landscape, funeral undertakers have actively created and transformed value—in the transactional as well as moral and cultural sense—through their introduction of key technological innovations and bodily interventions (see also Lee 2011). It is this leveraging of social capital and cultural fluency, allied to a sensitive affinity to the demands of their mobile and technologically astute customer base, which characterize entrepreneurship in this particular popular economy. Ultimately, rather than viewing them as corrupt profiteers of the "death business", I argue funeral undertakers occupy a more complex and complicated role as influential mediators of the death process.

## HISTORICAL CONSIDERATIONS

The emergence of a bona fide African-run funeral industry occurred relatively recently, its entrepreneurial roots dating back to the transitional period of the late 1980s and early 1990s, when the stranglehold grip of apartheid was weakening and both the mobility and range of economic opportunities available to the black African population were increasing. Although the trajectory of this particular funeral industry itself is a relatively short one, some features that continue to mark African funeral economies in the present day have a much longer history and merit attention. For example, informal burial societies, which offer a type of community-based funeral insurance based on regular contributions from members, can be traced back to the early decades of the twentieth century, when mineworkers in the gold mines of the Rand collectively pooled meager resources to transport the deceased "home" and prevent the indignity of a mine burial (Dennie 1997; Lukhele 1990; Maloka 1998). By the mid-twentieth century, South Africanist scholars had already noted how these burial societies had become a firm fixture of life in urban African areas. Kuper and Kaplan as early as 1944 observed, "The African in town, more especially the Christianized African, is acutely conscious of the need for a 'decent burial'", noting the pride and eagerness of migrant African women in Western Native Township in Johannesburg to display their local burial society memberships (Kuper and Kaplan 1944: 185). Thus, present-day patterns of financing for death should, at least in South Africa, be understood within a longer history of communal informally based finance mechanisms.

Secondly, in particular in urban areas where apartheid spatial engineering was most acutely felt, the location of burial grounds reflected an older and highly racialized order. As Dennie shows, as early as the first decade of the twentieth century, "Sanitary Boards" empowered in urban municipalities actively sought to erase previous patterns of racially and religiously integrated cemeteries (1997: 34). The fruits of segregationist thinking can be seen to this day, as racially zoned cemetery plots continue by and large to spatially divide the city's dead. In major African townships built during the apartheid era, such as in Gugulethu and Khayelitsha, the dead were buried within township cemeteries which were often located on poorly drained land prone to flooding during the wet Western Cape winters (Settlement Planning Services 2003). During the apartheid period, the burial of urban Africans was largely handled by white and in some areas Indian undertakers. These mainly white-owned funeral parlors were modeled on those prevalent in the western world, and large commercial chains, such as Doves and Goodall and Williams, predominated. Insensitively handled funerals were a bitter pill for many urban Africans to swallow, particularly as politicized funerals of the dead in Africa's turbulent period post-Soweto riots in 1976 were themselves spaces of heightened racial tensions (Dennie 1997; Lee 2011).

The apartheid state placed heavy restrictions on African entrepreneurial activity in urban areas, even within African townships themselves. Seekings and Nattrass note apartheid era "growth path policies" strictly curtailed both informal sector activity and formalized self-employment at a time of industrial sector development and strong state intervention. Urban Africans faced considerable obstacles in obtaining trading licenses, and were restricted in terms of the location of their business premises as well as the range of goods they were able to sell. The legacy of these restrictions is a relatively small informal sector relative to other developing world contexts (Hull and James 2012: 7; Seekings and Nattrass 2005: 40, 142, 320–321). In addition, a cluster of legislation introduced in the 1950s—including the Group Areas Act, the Native Abolition of Passes and Coordination of

Documents Act, and the Urban Areas Amendment Act—effectively limited urban African mobility into and within the apartheid city, and reinforced the temporary and tenuous nature of Africans' urban existences (Lee 2009).

A specific convergence of factors created a more conducive environment for African-run funeral parlors to emerge in the urban township setting. Beginning in the transitional period of the late 1980s, there was a loosening of controls over African mobility and employment culminating in the ending in 1986 of influx control, which had severely limited African movement into and residence in urban areas (Lee 2009). At the same time, the regularizing of re-distributional payments, such as the removal of racial tiers in old-age pension payouts by the early 1990s, allowed many poor households the opportunity to obtain a regular, if limited, source of income. By 1993, one year before the formal ending of apartheid, old-age pensions constituted a major source of income for the poorest 40% of households (Ambrogi 1994; Naidoo 1996; Seekings and Nattrass 2005: 360). In addition, as James has shown, deregulation of the financial services industry in the immediate post-apartheid period led to a proliferation of lending practices, many of them unscrupulous (James 2012). Consumerism came to be seen, especially for the younger generations, as a way to exercise and display their newfound freedoms (Lee 2009). Thus, in the early years of this new democratic era, Africans found themselves more able, and willing, to spend. One can locate the rise in expenditures around funerals as part of this same trend toward mass consumerism and indebtedness.

The proliferation of funeral insurance mechanisms has exacerbated these patterns by providing ready and easily accessible capital to grieving families. As mentioned above, informal forms of funeral insurance have been in existence since the early years of urbanization on the Rand. I have elsewhere traced burial society membership among elderly African women in Gugulethu Township as far back as the 1960s. These women tended to display continuous and faithful membership to these burial societies in later decades, and simply added further forms of funeral insurance on top of this base layer when circumstances allowed (for example, after a change in residence or an added source of income). Despite these continuities with older forms of financing for death, it is evident that the funeral insurance sector had been transformed in the late 1980s and 1990s, largely by the entry of corporate funeral coverage policies marketed by the formal insurance sector. Companies such as Sanlam and MetLife, realizing the enormous market potential that had been captured by informal burial societies, began offering stand-alone funeral insurance with relatively low monthly premiums apart from their standard packages of life insurance coverage (Lee 2009). The Zionist Christian Church established a national funeral policy scheme for its members in 1989, in partnership with the insurance company African Life, but with features borrowed from informal burial societies, such as a discretionary fund which allowed for some payouts even when members had defaulted on payments (Bahre 2012). In the first decades of the twenty-first

century, funeral insurance forms continued to evolve, sometimes at a dizzy-
ing pace. In 2008, while waiting at the checkout counter at the local supermarket, I encountered a "pay-as-you-go" funeral insurance policy marketed
by Sanlam in a plastic packaged starter pack that looked exactly like the
cellphone starter packs hanging alongside. The "i-cover" funeral plan provided three "ready-to-go" policies, which could cover the policyholder's
funeral, a funeral for his family, and accidents. Monthly premiums could
be paid at the local supermarket in much the same manner as one would
purchase phone credit or pay utility bills. In 2013, Nedbank customers who
opened a "Ke Yona" checking account could benefit from funeral coverage
automatically included as part of a package of benefits. Given the range and
variety of funeral finance on offer, it is no wonder that urban African households in the last decade and a half have typically balanced a "portfolio"
of funeral policies, both formal and informal. Typically when a loved one
died, the family would make claims not only via the deceased's own funeral
policy (or policies)—it would also pool the claims from various members'
policies in which the deceased was named as a dependent. This financing
strategy greatly multiplied, even for relatively poor households, the financial
resources available for a given funeral.

Undoubtedly, AIDS mortality has also played a significant role in shaping
cultures and economies of death in post-apartheid South Africa. Much has
been written about how stigma, poor political leadership and AIDS denial-
ism, lack of access to cheap ante-retroviral therapy, gendered inequality,
and sexual violence have variously contributed to the country's HIV/AIDS
crisis (Iliffe 2006; McNeill 2009; Van der Vliet 2004). In the late 1990s, the
HIV prevalence rate quickly escalated in South Africa, and between 2002
and 2008, the HIV adult prevalence rate (individuals aged 15–49) hov-
ered between 15%–17% (South Africa 2012). By 2007, 5.7 million South
Africans were HIV positive, the largest per country number in the world
(UNAIDS 2008). Until 2005, when generic ante-retroviral therapy was made
more widely available through the government, for many of those 5.7 million having HIV amounted to a death sentence. This reality was borne out
in dramatic increases in mortality in the post-apartheid period. According to
Statistics South Africa, the number of recorded deaths in 2007 was 601,033,
which represented an increase of over 90% from ten years previous, with
deaths recorded in 1997 at 317,131 (Statistics South Africa 2010). Most
experts agree that this spike could only be explained by accounting for additional deaths from AIDS related illnesses, an observation further supported
by the disproportionate percentage of this increased mortality coming from
the 15–49 age group. The numbers certainly bear witness to a demographic
"shock" not seen on the African continent since the influenza pandemic of
the First World War and, of course, the slave trade (Lee and Vaughan 2008).

Finally, as has been observed in other postcolonial African contexts,
large-scale political transition in South Africa has been accompanied by a
shifting politics of identity (Cohen and Odhiambo 1992; Geschiere 2005).

Despite the discursive mantra of the "rainbow nation", the sharpening of ethnic allegiances has emerged as a way to leverage political and economic power in the new dispensation. This can be seen in Jacob Zuma's infamous invocation of his Zulu heritage and language during his rape trial in 2006, in the rise of a heritage tourism industry predicated around the display of "tribal" authenticity, as well as in the vagaries of a land claims process which sometimes relies on the performed recollection of ancestral knowledge on contested sites (Bank 2002; James 2009). Cultural capital based on claims to historical authenticity and notions of indigeneity have become all the more valuable (Berry 2007).

Would-be African funeral entrepreneurs thus found, in the rapidly transforming political and economic context of post-apartheid South Africa, a specific "niche of opportunity" (MacGaffey 2002: 334). The growth of a newly monied (and indebted) urban African population, an AIDS-related crisis of mortality of epidemic proportions, and a resurgent cultural politics of belonging has fed the entry and evolution of a particular type of funeral enterprise.

## KEY FEATURES OF ENTREPRENEURSHIP IN THE FUNERAL INDUSTRY

As the fledgling township funeral industry took shape in the 1990s, certain definable characteristics came to mark this sector of activity. The following vignette of one funeral business in Khayelitsha Township serves to illustrate some of these features.

> Mphumulelo Mfundisi[3] was born in the rural enclave of Lady Frere in the Eastern Cape. He migrated to Cape Town for work in the 1980s. After launching a series of informal business enterprises, he began to save money through an informal rotating credit association to grow his food vending businesses, eventually purchasing a Toyota HiAce minibus in the early 1990s. He hired out the minibus taxi to an undertaker who needed it to transport dead bodies and mourners to the Eastern Cape. Mfundisi was encouraged by the undertaker to start his own funeral business, which he eventually did in 1998. Currently, Duma Funerals—named after Mfundisi's clan—owns five vehicles and employs five staff, several of whom are family members.
>
> Duma Funerals offers an "all-in-one" service—including mortuary storage, embalming and bodily preparation, transport, burial, and repatriation (in the case of deceased foreigners). It also offers a selection of products such as coffins at various price ranges, covered chairs and a gazebo for the burial site, printed leaflets for the funeral service, and even its own branded water bottles. The transport of the deceased and mourners over long distances is a cornerstone of the business, as most of

Duma Funerals's client-base in Cape Town is made up of ethnic Xhosa who maintain kinship ties to the rural areas of Eastern Cape Province about 1000 kilometers away.

When entering the Mfundisi compound in Khayelitsha Township on a typical Friday morning, one is confronted by a somewhat jarring sense of contradictory sights and sounds. A battered and faded sign on the wall to the right of the front gate proclaims this is the site of Duma Funerals. Another sign, larger, newer, and painted a cheery red with white letters and fixed right above the front gate, says Duma's Tavern. Both signs are technically correct. Peering into the courtyard, one can view Duma Funerals employees doing final maintenance checks on a white minibus, which will be entrusted with transporting mourners and the deceased to the final burial site over the weekend. Surrounding the minibus in the courtyard area are tables and benches, slowly filling with tavern customers who are starting their weekend revelries early in the day. A converted garage at the back of the courtyard houses the tavern's pool table, further seating, and a large flatscreen TV that constantly shows music videos or sporting events. Toward the back of the converted garage, a customer can purchase from a large supply of alcoholic drinks and soft drinks available behind a small, barred window. Security cameras are fixed throughout the property, in the tavern as well as inside the family home. Duma Funerals operates from the house situated on the right of the courtyard, its front lounge functioning as the de facto "office" and reception area for any clients.

Mphumulelo's wife Nobantu currently manages the thriving tavern business. In 2008, when I first met the Mfundisis, Nobantu supported Duma Funerals as a driver and general assistant, although any involvement in the family funeral business was severely limited by her fear of looking upon dead bodies—a consequence of her beliefs as a trained traditional healer. By 2012, Nobantu had effectively distanced herself from Duma Funerals and focused her business acumen on growing the tavern trade. Their only daughter, Vuyiseka, has been a valuable support for both businesses, and moves between the two as and when her own regular job in a debt collection agency allows.

Cash flows freely between the two businesses, as can be seen when the proceeds from the Friday takings from the tavern are used to purchase fuel for the funeral vehicles' use during the weekend. However, Mphumulelo Mfundisi notes that there are important distinctions to be made between the ways the two businesses operate. For example, the tavern never offers any drinks on credit to customers, whereas he tends to be more flexible—to the detriment of his business, he attests—in allowing for extended or delayed payment in the case of funerals for particularly indigent clients. (Mphumulelo Mfundisi, interviews, 6 October 2008, 30 July 2008, January 2012; Nobantu Mfundisi, interviews, 18 September 2008, January 2012; Vuyiseka Mfundisi, interviews, 18 September 2008, January 2012)

There are elements of Mphumulelo Mfundisi's narrative which resonate with larger patterns evident across township funeral enterprises. Firstly, it is worthnoting that the "business model" for urban African funeral entrepreneurs in South Africa differs in significant ways from their counterparts in West Africa, in particular in Ghana and Nigeria where a similar commodification of burial rites has been most noted (and decried by the general public). In West Africa, as DeWitte and others have shown, funerary products and services are purchased by the grieving family from a range of separate vendors and providers (deWitte 2003). In contrast, the "all-in-one" service offered by township undertakers bears more similarity to white-owned funeral parlors in operation in South Africa. Indeed, it may be the case that some African entrepreneurs' previous work experience with white undertakers influenced the adoption of the all-in-one model at an early stage in the development of the township funeral industry. For example, Wantuntu Khanye, owner of a profitable funeral parlor in Nyanga Township and a satellite business in the coastal town of George, gained valuable firsthand experience working for the commercial funeral home Goodall and Williams before beginning his own business in 1990 (Wantuntu Khanye, 17 October 2000). Thus, African entrepreneurs in the township funeral industry situated themselves as central providers of funerary commodities and services, which as we will see, has given them a prominent role in shaping African approaches to death and the funerary process.

Secondly, funeral entrepreneurs tend to—like Mr. Mfundisi—utilize close kin as key support in the operation of their businesses. This pattern is apparent in both urban and rural-based funeral parlors. Adult children could be employed initially as general assistants and handlers of deceased bodies and, depending on training and educational attainment, could become drivers, administrators, or receptionists deployed to provide face-to-face contact with clientele. Several children of undertakers have professed to me their intentions of beginning their own funeral parlor one day, and look at their generally unremunerated work in the family business as a useful apprenticeship of sorts. Kin networks could be deployed in other manners as well. Mfundisi's use of his clan name "Duma" in the naming of his business was a conscious decision to use the strength of clan affiliations to attract a wider and loyal customer base among Cape Town's largely ethnic Xhosa population (Noncedo Masondlo and Mphumulelo Mfundisi, interview, 30 July 2008). This accords with similar strategies in evidence among rural funeral entrepreneurs as well as in other African entrepreneurial contexts (Lee 2009; MacGaffey 2002).

Funeral entrepreneurs utilize local and communal networks beyond kinship ties to aid their businesses. Word of mouth recommendations are the key form of advertisement. Interestingly, none of the undertakers I observed considered developing a social networking or other web-based profile. This is despite the fact that South Africans have increasingly used Internet based technologies such as email and facebook as well as instant messaging programs such as MxIt, all of which are easily accessible via the numerous relatively cheap smartphones flooding the domestic market in recent years. Township undertakers tend to be adept at activating their own local social networks, such as through membership in a Christian Church or a local street committee, to enhance their social capital, promote their businesses, and ensure a ready pool of clientele. Being at the center of his location's social scene through the family tavern business certainly increases Mr. Mfundisi's opportunities for informal networking. As Mr. Mfundisi asserts, "Mostly I don't advertise myself. People hear from other people that I have already helped. They say, oh, hey, Duma helped me, so go to him he will be very helpful" (Mphumulelo Mfundisi, Jan 2012). Neves and du Toit argue that rather than attempting to apply a model of entrepreneurship predicated on western notions of "rational, self-interested, utility-maximising individuals", the informal sector in South Africa should be viewed through a wider structure of exchange that includes not only strictly "economic" value regimes but also social and cultural networks and values—what they term "extra-economic factors" (2012: 132). The fluidity of capital flows between the two businesses Mr. Mfundisi operates is but one example of a seemingly "irrational" accounting practice in this funeral economy which becomes more understandable when considering that value exchanges do not simply operate on a monetary level.

The township funeral industry likewise defies neat distinctions made in the scholarship on African economic activity between the "formal" and "informal". For example, although African-run funeral parlors may be considered part of the informal economy, undertakers need to be fluent at tapping into "formal" economic networks in order to procure commodities such as coffins and marquee tents. Furthermore, African undertakers act as mediators between grieving families and the state across a variety of institutions. They work with hospitals and pathologists to organize for death certificates. They deal with municipal governance structures in the allocation of burial plots and permissions for exhumations. In the case of migrant death, undertakers comply with international regulations to organize the repatriation of remains (Nunez and Wheeler 2012). The provision of funeral finance via funeral parlors is another practice through which the boundaries between the formal and informal become blurred. As explained above, individual urban African households in the post-apartheid period had access to a range of funeral policies, both informal and formal. As individual funeral entrepreneurs entered the industry, they added additional mechanisms and channels through which funeral insurance could be provided. For example, Wantuntu Khanye's funeral home offers several different types of funeral "plans" depending on the needs and resources of his client. One of the policies is underwritten by a formal company, MetLife, which in essence makes Khanye a company broker for this particular insurance policy. However, he also offers his own in-house funeral insurance scheme, which can be joined with a regular monthly contribution. Finally, Khanye has entered into binding (although not formally contractual) arrangements with several local burial societies, whose members promise to use his funeral services in return for an agreed and discounted rate (Wantuntu Khanye, interviews, 17 October 2000; 4 October 2008).

Another characteristic feature of the township funeral industry is its close relation to the minibus transport sector, itself a loosely regulated industry known for sporadic violence and "turf wars" fueled by its cartel-like structure (Neves and du Toit 2012; Khosa 1991). Mr. Mfundisi invested the capital generated by his various food-hawking businesses to purchase a minibus taxi vehicle, which in turn aided his entry into and later establishment within the funeral industry. Undertakers' employment histories tend to resemble a sort of "transport ladder", in which the entrepreneur may begin at a relatively low rung in the transport sector (for example as a petrol station attendant) and gradually work his way up each rung until he is able to begin his funeral business in possession of one or more vehicles. Indeed, some entrepreneurs who had derived livelihoods through the taxi transport industry hastened to leave the sector when occasional violence threatened, and found in the nascent funeral industry a similarly transport-orientated yet safer working environment. Entrepreneurs have translated their affinity with transport concerns into their funeral businesses. Undertakers attest that the most profitable aspect of their businesses, over and above profits from the sale of coffins or fees for mortuary storage or embalming, is the transporting of mourners and the deceased body across long distances. Accumulated capital is usually set aside to replenish the business's stock of motor vehicles, and the more successful enterprises signal their intentions to attract an upmarket clientele through purchasing ever more outsized and glamorous hearses (Lee 2009). Yet, with the potential for heightened profits come increased risks. Road accidents during the course of a funeral, and the resultant damage to vehicular property as well as financial compensation for those mourners injured or killed, are cited as a significant financial drain on funeral businesses (Lee 2012).

This mobile orientation of the funeral industry, particularly across what I have called the "rural-urban nexus", has fostered its own type of creativity. I have shown elsewhere how embalming and exhumation are two bodily technologies funeral entrepreneurs have introduced, which were borne out of the exigencies of increased ritual traffic between Cape Town and the rural areas of the Eastern Cape (Lee 2009). Given the intensely competitive nature of the funeral industry and a changing political milieu in which ethnicity has become a powerful marker of identity, African entrepreneurs have learned to draw on and transform cultural practices as a type of "knowledge capital" to feed their businesses (Suzuki 2000). Many funeral entrepreneurs are middle-aged men who, like Mr. Mfundisi, maintain both a financial and emotional connection to their rural areas of origin, seen in their active investment of business proceeds into developing and maintaining rural homesteads. This straddling between rural and urban areas enables them to fluently translate elements of ethnic Xhosa practice into their businesses. This can be seen in their encouragement of ceremonial practices which had once been discarded, such as the wrapping of the deceased in a Xhosa traditional blanket. It can also be seen in their increasing incorporation of exhumation into their package of services—the removal of the dead from racially segregated and poorly serviced urban cemeteries and their reburial in rural ancestral land provides an opportunity to redress some of the injustices meted out by apartheid as well as to reinscribe a cultural and spiritual entitlement onto the physical remains of the body itself (Lee 2009).

Thus, a particular type of entrepreneurship premised on cultural fluency and technological innovation has emerged, shaped by the demands of an increasingly mobile customer base. In the process, funeral entrepreneurs have contributed to a powerful reshaping of funerary events in the transitional and post-apartheid period. The "problem" of mobility has long influenced the evolution of African burial rites, dating back to the early days of labor migration to the gold mines of the Rand (see Maloka 1998). However, the immense political and social transformations of the last two decades have undoubtedly contributed to fresh anxieties as to where and how to belong in this more globalized, fluid, and "un-moored" world (Simone 2004). These anxieties may be further expressed through the (mis)-handling of the dead (Ashforth 2005; Lee 2009, 2012; Whyte 2005). By enabling the transport of the deceased and mourners across vast distances, and promoting a localized cultural politics of belonging centered around a rural "traditional" pole, funeral entrepreneurs have offered an element of "anchoring" through which both the deceased and their families can navigate the ambivalent world of the dead. In this respect, undertakers' central role in the preparation of the body of the deceased—effectively replacing the role of ritual specialists and female kin—is significant, despite the continuing influence of close kin and other spiritual leaders (both Christian and traditional) in the funerary and mourning process.

## GENDERED CONSIDERATIONS

Interestingly, although scholars have attested to the feminized nature of the informal economy in South Africa (Lee 2009; Seekings and Nattrass 2005: 321), the township funeral industry is almost wholly comprised of middle-aged male undertakers. I argue this may be largely the consequence of the particular origins of urban African funeral entrepreneurship and its close association with the transport sector, itself a male-dominated environment. However, despite women's relatively low profile in this industry, their involvement has shaped the development of funeral entrepreneurship in interesting ways.

I begin with a brief vignette from a female funeral entrepreneur:

Yandiswa Ganca is a trained nurse who is employed as a medical sales representative by a major multinational food company. She spends her weekends helping her brother operate the family funeral business from the premises of a former florist's shop in Gugulethu Township. Business is modest, she admits, at about four to five funerals per month, and competition is fierce. She stressed the funeral business was a family affair—her grandfather had worked for a white undertaker during apartheid before branching off and beginning his own profitable funeral enterprise. When asked whether she encountered any challenges being a woman in a mostly male-dominated industry, she admitted her relationship with other funeral directors was "on and off. . . . It's all men. It's dominated by Men". (Yandiswa Ganca, interview, 25 November 2008)

Elements of Ganca's account are echoed by other female respondents working in the funeral industry. Women's entry into the funeral industry has been shaped strongly by familial connections, whether through marriage (as we saw in the case of Nobantu Mfundisi) or kinship relations. Noncedo Masondlo chose to become an apprentice at Duma Funerals after personally experiencing the suffering of a "botched" funeral from a corrupt undertaker—her husband had been assassinated by rival taxi members in 2005 and his body was improperly embalmed (Noncedo Masondlo and Mphumulelo Mfundisi, interview, 30 July 2008).

Women workers and entrepreneurs have encountered, as Ganca did, gendered resistance to their participation in the funeral business. When Nomfundo Khanye was sent by her father Wantuntu to front a new satellite branch of the family business in George, her position as a young female proved an impediment. Mourners were reluctant to surrender the body to her because "they said I'm a woman, so their body cannot be handled by a woman" (Nomfundo Khanye, interview, 4 December 2008). Nobantu Mfundisi expressed a similar sentiment: "In the Xhosa culture, a woman is not supposed to touch a dead person." Despite these obstacles, women claim they are able to contribute meaningfully in the running of funeral homes. They also stress that women may add value to the services offered, for example by bringing an element of sympathy, in part derived from women's "traditional" position as mourners. They "cry" together with the mourners. As Ganca attests, "It's more the caring part, that I'm able to help other people who are grieving. I'm more providing psychological treatment so that's what I enjoy most" (Yandiswa Ganca, interview, 25 November 2008). Women also claim they focus on details that their male counterparts do not, such as the presentation of the embalmed body and its clothing, as well as flower arrangements.

In particular, educated daughters of male undertakers play an influential role because of their early involvement and experience in the industry. Vuyiseka Mfundisi saw her first dead body when she visited her father's mortuary at twelve years of age and has since played an integral role in helping in all aspects of her father's business. She completed secondary school and was enrolled in a retail business management course at a local technikon—a tertiary institution which focuses on technology and trade degrees—before dropping out to start work. Although she is currently for-mally employed and cannot work full-time at Duma Funerals, her driving and computer skills remain an asset which her father utilizes when neces-sary for the family business (Vuyiseka Mfundisi, interviews, 18 Septem-ber 2008, January 2012). After finishing a secretarial course and working in various administrative positions, Nomfundo Khanye became a personal assistant and eventually junior programmer in a prominent South Afri-can insurance company, where she worked for eleven years. She admitted she was "miserable" and "frustrated" by her corporate job, and disgrun-tled by the poor pay. Turning to her father's growing funeral business in 2004 seemed, therefore, a logical step: "So I felt it's time that I helped my dad in the business and he was great about that." Nomfundo helped to establish a satellite branch of her father's successful funeral business in George, a town along the southern coast (Nomfundo Khanye, interview, 4 December 2008).

These enterprising daughters are clear-eyed and critical when assessing the relative merits and weaknesses of their fathers' businesses. Vuyiseka believes her father is missing out on potential profits by focusing too much on the "bodies" themselves and not on the marketing aspects of the busi-ness. Similarly, Nomfundo says that her father was "late" in acquiring lim-ousine hearses for his business compared to his competitors and that has hurt growth. She also thinks he needs to stress professionalism more in the services he provides, as well as pay more attention to things like the physical appearance and demeanor of his staff, which she believes affects customer satisfaction and the reputation of his business. These examples suggest that young women tend to think of the funeral parlor as a "brand" that needs to be managed. These young women have also identified ways in which the family business could maximize profits beyond the provision of basic funerary services. Nomfundo believes Khanye Funerals would save money by constructing their own mortuary storage facility, rather than its current practice of hiring storage space from someone else. Vuyiseka's future plans to improve Duma Funerals include using the Internet as a potential marketing tool and expanding the array of funeral services on offer to include catering services and hiring out tents and gazebos. Although neither daughter cur-rently has the final say on key decisions in their respective family businesses, their knowledge of the funeral industry combined with an entrepreneurial drive to modernize will undoubtedly shape and transform women's involve-ment in the "business of death" in the years to come.

## CONCLUSION

Funeral entrepreneurs are well aware that the phenomenal growth of the funeral industry has occurred in a context of deepening inequality and the long shadow cast by the HIV/AIDS epidemic. This has placed them in a precarious position. In order to thrive in an increasingly competitive environment, they need to constantly innovate and seek ways to maximize their cultural and social capital to grow their businesses. On the other hand, too much success means they are cast by the community and the media as "scavengers" who are cashing in on the "gold mine" of AIDS mortality (Mphumulelo Mfundisi, interview, January 2012; Wantuntu Khanye, interview, 17 October 2000). Many undertakers complain the image of them as exploiters preying on the flesh of the poor is inaccurate, pointing to the considerable losses their businesses absorb through unpaid or partially paid accounts, both for funerals and for in-house funeral insurance policies.

Certainly, this research has shown that African entrepreneurs face a delicate balancing of risks and opportunities within this funeral economy. They are well placed as social and cultural "insiders" within their own communities to understand as well as capitalize on the burgeoning desire to "bury expensive". They utilize kinship and social networks, such as their use of family members as employees and their activation of clan affiliations, to service the operation of their businesses as well as to widen the pool of potential clients. Undertakers creatively bridge—and exploit—the blurred boundaries between the informal and formal economies in the funeral industry, whether to augment the range of funeral insurance coverage they can offer their clients, or to help mourners navigate the complex bureaucratic apparatus of the state. Entrepreneurs' sensitivity to movement across the rural-urban nexus and previous experience in the transport sector ensure they have adopted a decidedly mobile orientation to their funeral businesses. The gradual incorporation of women into the sector has also, tentatively, begun to shape strategies of funeral entrepreneurship.

By and large, my research suggests township undertakers do not conform to the depiction of them as scavengers, and instead occupy a much more complex and pivotal role in shaping—as social and cultural "insiders"— African approaches to death. In contrast to the insensitively handled funerals and "undignified" burials available to urban African mourners during the apartheid era, township funeral entrepreneurs can offer their clientele a culturally responsive repertoire of services designed to highlight the best features of globalized "modern" lifestyles in the "new" South Africa (speed, technology, hygiene, and choice) while mitigating the effects of the worst (anonymity, dislocation). However, it is important to recognize there may be regional variations as well as variations across rural and urban areas, as research on the funeral industry in Johannesburg and in Venda suggests (McNeill 2009; Nunez and Wheeler 2012). The limited work that I have done on the rural funeral industry in the Eastern Cape appears to show that rural funeral entrepreneurship tends to be monopolized by a small number of powerful Big Men, who leverage clan affiliation and economic might over a much more impoverished and geographically spread out populace. In 2009 I witnessed the elaborate "coronation" of Gerald Fundani, a district surgeon-turned-funeral-baron, who operates a string of funeral parlors in East London and the rural areas of the Eastern Cape. The event was both a showcase for the success of his lucrative funeral business and an opportunity to consolidate his moral and ritual authority over his clan. Rather than small-scale entrepreneurism based on face-to-face communication and well-worn social and communal networks, as is evident in the township funeral industry, rural "franchises" such as Fundani's operate on a much more impersonal and potentially exploitative scale. Certainly further research on these intriguing dynamics, as well as sustained comparisons between rural and urban patterns, is necessary.

## NOTES

1. A note on terminology: I use "industry" as a collective term to denote township funeral businesses, in part following from the term's use to characterize the minibus transport sector, which has been called the "taxi industry" in both South Africanist policy and academic circles. The taxi industry and the township funeral industry share some commonalities, namely a focus on transport, the need for a relatively high threshold of start-up capital compared to other informal enterprises, and an origin rooted in processes of high consumer demand combined with state deregulation.
2. This research is drawn from a larger study of death and memory in modern South Africa, and is part of a collaborative project on death in African History with Megan Vaughan of the University of Cambridge (see www.gold.ac.uk/deathinafrica). I acknowledge the Arts Humanities Research Council of the United Kingdom for its generous support.
3. All names have been changed.

## REFERENCES

Ambrogi, Donna. 1994. 'Retirement Income of the Elderly Poor in South Africa: Some Legal and Public Policy Issues'. Unpublished report, University of Cape Town Library.
Arhin, Kwame. 1994. 'The economic implications of transformations in Akan funeral rites'. *Africa* 64, 3: 307–322.
Ashforth, Adam. 2005. *Madumo: A Man Bewitched*. Chicago: University of Chicago Press.
Bahre, Erik. 2012. 'The Janus face of insurance in South Africa: from costs to risk, from networks to bureaucracies'. *Africa* 82, 1 (Special Issue on Popular Economies in South Africa): 150–167.
Ballim, Faeeza. 2013. 'Buried in debt: high costs live on'. *Mail & Guardian*, 28 March 2013. Accessed online 23 May 2013.
Bank, Leslie. 2002. 'Xhosa in town revisited: from urban anthropology to an anthropology of urbanism'. Ph.D. Thesis, University of Cape Town.
Berry, Sara. 2007. 'Marginal Gains, market values and history'. *African Studies Review* 50, 2 (Special issue on Jane Guyer's Marginal Gains: Monetary Transactions in Atlantic Africa): 57–70.
Cohen, David and Atieno Odhiambo. 1992. *Burying SM: The Politics of Knowledge and the Sociology of Power in Africa*. Oxford: James Currey.
De Witte, Marleen. 2001. *Long Live the Dead: Changing Funeral Celebrations in Asante, Ghana*. Amsterdam: Aksant Academic Publishers.

De Witte, Marleen. 2003. 'Money and death: funeral business in Asante, Ghana'. *Africa* 74, 4: 531–559.

Dennie, Garrey. 1997. 'The Cultural Politics of Burial in South Africa, 1884–1990'. Ph.D. Thesis, Johns Hopkins University.

Geschiere, Peter. 2005. 'Funerals and belonging: different patterns in south Cameroon'. *African Studies Review* 48, 2 (Special Issue on Mourning and the Imagination of Political Time in Contemporary Central Africa): 45–64.

Guyer, Jane. 2004. *Marginal Gains: Monetary Transactions in Atlantic Africa.* Chicago and London: University of Chicago Press.

Hull, Elizabeth and Deborah James. 2012. 'Introduction: popular economies in South Africa'. *Africa* 82, 1 (Special Issue on Popular Economies in South Africa): 1–19.

Iliffe, John. 2006. *The African AIDS Epidemic: A History.* Oxford: James Currey.

James, Deborah. 2009. 'Burial sites, informal rights and lost kingdoms: contesting land claims in Mpumalanga, South Africa'. *Africa* 79, 2: 228–251.

James, Deborah. 2011. 'The return of the broker: consensus, hierarchy, and choice in South African land reform'. *Journal of the Royal Anthropological Institute* 17: 319–338.

James, Deborah. 2012. 'Money-go-round: personal economies of wealth, aspiration and indebtedness'. *Africa* 82, 1 (Special Issue on Popular Economies in South Africa): 20–40.

Jindra, Michael and Joël Noret (eds). 2011. *Funerals in Africa: Explorations of a Social Phenomenon.* Oxford: Berghahn Books.

Khosa, Meshack. 1991. 'Routes, ranks and rebels: feuding in the taxi revolution'. *Journal of Southern African Studies* 18, 1: 232–251.

Kuper, Hilda and Selma Kaplan. 1944. 'Voluntary associations in an urban township'. *African Studies* 3, 4: 176–186.

Lee, Rebekah. 2009. *African Women and Apartheid: Migration and Settlement in Urban South Africa.* London: I.B. Tauris.

Lee, Rebekah. 2011. 'Death "on the move": funerals, entrepreneurs and the rural-urban nexus in South Africa'. *Africa* 81, 2: 226–247.

Lee, Rebekah. 2012. 'Death in slow motion: funerals, ritual practice and road danger in South Africa'. *African Studies* 71, 2 (Special Issue on Death and Loss in Africa): 195–211.

Lee, Rebekah and Megan Vaughan. 2008. 'Death and dying in the history of Africa since 1800'. *Journal of African History* 49, 3 (Special Issue on Death in African History): 341–359.

Lukhele, Andrew. 1990. *Stokvels in South Africa: Informal Savings Schemes by Blacks for the Black Community.* Johannesburg: Amagi Books.

MacGaffey, Janet. 2002. 'Survival, innovation, and success in time of trouble: what prospects for central African entrepreneurs?' In: Alusine Jalloh and Toyin Falola (eds). *Black Business and Economic Power.* Rochester: University of Rochester Press, 331–346.

Maloka, Tshidiso. 1998. 'Basotho and the experience of death, dying and mourning in the South African mine compounds, 1890–1940'. *Cahiers d'Etudes africaines* 38, 149: 17–40.

McNeill, Fraser. 2009. 'From *gogos* to grave diggers: paying for funerals and reading rumours in post-apartheid Venda'. Paper presented at Popular Economies in South Africa workshop, London School of Economics, 17–18 June 2009.

Mda, Zakes. 1995. *Ways of Dying.* Cape Town: Oxford University Press.

Naidoo, Ravi. 1996. 'Pensions and investment, retirement funds and the dismantling of economic apartheid'. In: Jeremy Baskin (ed). *Against the Current: Labour and Economic Policy in South Africa.* Johannesburg: Ravan Press, 80–100.

Neves, David and Andries du Toit. 2012. 'Money and sociality in South Africa's informal economy'. *Africa* 82, 1 (Special Issue on Popular Economies in South Africa): 131–149.

Nkosi, Milton. 2011. 'The funerals that cost families dear'. *BBC News*, 26 November 2011. Accessed online 4 September 2013.

Noret, Joël. 2004. 'Morgues et prise en charge de la mort au Sud-Bénin'. *Cahiers d'Etudes africaines* 4, 176: 745–767.

Nunez, Lorena and Brittany Wheeler. 2012. 'Chronicles of death out of place: management of migrant death in Johannesburg'. *African Studies* 71, 2 (Special Issue on Death and Loss in Africa): 212–233.

Page, Ben. 2007. 'Slow going: the mortuary, modernity and the hometown association in Bali-Nyonga, Cameroon'. *Africa* 77, 3: 419–441.Seekings, Jeremy and Nicoli Nattrass. 2005. *Class, Race and Inequality in South Africa*. New Haven, CT; London: Yale University Press.

Settlement Planning Services. 2003. 'Metropolitan Cemetery Study', Report no: 1376/1 June 2003, compiled for the Cape Town Directorate of City Parks and Nature Conservation. Cape Town: Cape Town City Council.

Shipton, Parker. 2007. *The Nature of Entrustment: Intimacy, Exchange and the Sacred in Africa*. New Haven CT; London: Yale University Press.

Simone, AbdouMaliq. 2004. *For the City Yet to Come: Changing African Life in Four Cities*. Durham, N.C.: Duke University Press.

South Africa. 2012. *Global AIDS Response Progress Report: South Africa*. Submitted to UNAIDS.

Statistics South Africa. 2010. *Mortality and Causes of Death in South Africa, 2008*. Pretoria: Statistics South Africa.

Suzuki, Hikaru. 2000. *The Price of Death: The Funeral Industry in Contemporary Japan*. Stanford: Stanford University Press.

UNAIDS. 2008. *Epidemiological Fact Sheet on HIV and AIDS: South Africa 2008 Update*. Geneva: UNAIDS.

Van der Vliet, Virginia. 2004. 'South Africa divided against AIDS: a crisis of leadership'. In: Kyle Kauffman and David Lindauer (eds). *AIDS and South Africa: The Social Expression of a Pandemic*. Basingstoke: Palgrave Macmillan, 48–96.

Whyte, Susan Reynolds. 2005. 'Going home: belonging and burial in the era of AIDS'. *Africa* 75, 2: 154–172.

# 8   Sand, Sun, and Toyotas

## Tuareg Entrepreneurship in Desert Tourism in Niger

*Marko Scholze*

The study of tourism became a full-fledged subject in anthropology in the 1970s (Smith 1977). Since then, most anthropologists have focused either on the motivations and travel practices of tourists (MacCannell 1999) or the effects of tourism on local cultures (Nash 2001). Less attention has been paid to the actual interaction between hosts and guests (Van Beek and Schmidt 2012) and the entrepreneurship involved on the side of the local population. What are the motives, strategies, and resources for local actors to tap into a global business like tourism? What are the economic and sociopolitical conditions for their agency? How is entrepreneurship locally defined, and what are the reasons for economic success or failure? Which changes does the engagement of local actors in tourism generate in their own lives and their society? To deal with these questions, I will focus on Tuareg who have created their own travel agencies in the regional capital of Agadez in northern Niger. Together with their staff, they organize tours for affluent European and American tourists in the Aïr Mountains and the Tenere desert. These Tuareg belong to the social layers of the nobles (*imajighen*)[1] and vassals (*imghad*) within the hierarchical structure of Tuareg society. For these local entrepreneurs, their engagement in tourism is not obvious.

Tourism as an occupational field was introduced by Europeans in colonial times and thus initially represented a foreign cultural practice. Even today, most *imajighen* and *imghad* in northern Niger make their living from camel and goat breeding, the caravan trade, or horticulture. The latter has been increasing due to a process of sedentarization after severe droughts in the 1970s and 1980s. Nevertheless, some Tuareg who began working for European tour-operators as guides, drivers, and cooks in the 1960s quickly seized the new opportunity and became directors of their own travel agencies from 1980 onwards. They even went on to monopolize the local tourist infrastructure in Agadez and the Aïr Mountains. To do so, these Tuareg recognized that successful entrepreneurship in this economic domain requires mastering three vital aspects: the appropriation of new technical knowledge and practices; interaction with Europeans; and the commoditization of their cultural identity as being "Tuareg" and the desert as their habitat.

However, the work in tourism is not only marked by the appropriation of new competencies, locally defined as *kel azzaman* (present-day or modern). Successful Tuareg entrepreneurship, as I will argue, also depends on a fine balance between modern and traditional (*kel eru*)[2] practices, knowledge, and values stemming from their nomadic culture. Hence, success is both economically and socially defined, as the income that the local actors generate is not the sole measure of their agency. Conversely, how relatives, friends, and inhabitants of their home villages evaluate the redistribution of wealth is what counts.

*Imajighen* and *imghad* who work in tourism often describe themselves as "modern nomads", an expression with which they refer to their nomadic heritage, which they pursue with modern means. This "modernized" nomadism includes the extension of the actors' physical mobility and actual working sphere. Their movement with Toyota Landcruisers and their travels to Europe confront them with new experiences and the urban, technically enhanced world outside the Aïr Mountains. This results in a particular lifestyle that is marked by openness toward innovation and, at the same time, close attachment to their families and home villages, and to cultural values and traditions. Some of these Tuareg have acquired wealth and even political influence on the local or national level and have thus become "new figures of success and power" (Banégas and Warnier 2001), especially for the younger generations. In the following, I will refer predominately to the years between 2000 and 2006, when I conducted research on tourism in the north of Niger.

## MARGINALITY AS OPPORTUNITY

At first sight, northern Niger appears to be a destination on the periphery of global tourism.[3] The region is marginally connected to the international flight network, and tourist infrastructure like hotels, restaurants, and banks is available only in Agadez. Only a few simple guest-houses and camping grounds exist in the Aïr Mountains and the desert and tourists usually sleep under the stars. The Aïr Mountains and the Tenere desert are only accessible by off-road cars or camels (Figure 8.1). Given the harsh climatic conditions, such as extreme temperature changes between day and night, a meager water supply, no medical services at hand, and long hours of driving or walking, this destination is made for the adventurous desert pilgrim who wants to escape western civilization in search of the simplicity of life.

The conditions of travel and competition with tourism in North African countries limit the potential number of tourists. Within the market segment of Sahara tourism, Niger plays a minor role. Desert tourism in North Africa is more easily accessible to tourists and is much cheaper when compared to the high prices for flight, fuel, and imported goods that tourists in Niger consume.[4] Hence, an average of 3,000 to 5,000 tourists, predominantly

*Figure 8.1* Tour with off-road cars in the Tenere desert (Photo: Marko Scholze)

from France, Germany, Austria, Switzerland, Italy, and the U.S. visit the Aïr Mountains and the Tenere desert in the dry and cool season between November and February. With few exceptions, they book a package tour offered by a foreign tour-operator who works together with one of the local travel agencies in Agadez.[5] The tours include round trips that consist of between one to three weeks with off-road cars (65% of all tours), with camels—called a *meharee*—(30%), or by foot (5%).

While Tuareg control the local tourist infrastructure, they depend on foreign tour-operators to succeed in the market. Local agency directors have no direct access to clients, as it would be too expensive for them to open a branch agency in Europe or finance their own promotion apart from some brochures and websites. Typically the tour-operator in Europe does the advertising, acquires the clients, and organizes their flights to Niger. The local agency then carries out the voyage into the Aïr Mountains and the Tenere desert. Despite the existence of a Ministry of Tourism since 1987 and the general willingness of the state to develop tourism, the government considers it a luxury sector when compared to agriculture or education, and it therefore receives much less funding.

Generally, politics in Niger are marked by ethnic and regional affiliation. Ethnic groups, like the Hausa and Songhay-Djerma who live in the country's south, dominate Niger's political and economic spheres. They are not eager to help the north associated with the Tuareg. This unwillingness for support is further accentuated through the negative experience of the Tuareg rebellion in the 1990s and ethnic resentments that are grounded in the Tuareg's precolonial involvement in the trans-Saharan slave trade (Decoudras 1995). The actual support private entrepreneurs in the north receive can largely be attributed to the Minister of Tourism, Rhissa ag Boula's, personal engagement, as he feels "naturally" attached to his home region.[6]

Despite the handicaps and limitations that affect the Tuareg's entrepreneurial activities in tourism, they are able to draw advantage from their marginalization. Tuareg are indispensable to tourism in Niger for three reasons. First, the Sahara became a myth in Europe during the nineteenth century, grounded in the perception of the desert as a space of initiation for Europeans tired of modern civilization and an "imagined geography" (Roux 1996) that results in stereotypical aesthetic images like the delicately swayed sand dune. The Tuareg have been part of the myth as the "blue veiled men" and "knights of the desert" ever since the first descriptions of European travelers such as Henri Duveyrier in the nineteenth century. The stereotypical images of the Sahara and the Tuareg continued to be perpetuated in movies, novels, photography, and travel guides (Boilley 2000). Altogether, these images have become a natural and ethnic "marker" (Adams 1984) and part of a socially constructed "tourist gaze" (Urry 1990). This gaze dominates the tourists' perception of landscapes and cultures and represents one of the strongest incentives to travel. Consequently, tourists want to meet the myth and demand that Tuareg accompany them during their journey. Hence, Tuareg ethnic identity has become a key resource for the tourism entrepreneurs. Second, the Tuareg's dependency on foreign tour operators is mutual. Tourism in Niger is highly specialized and marked by the absence of big international tourist enterprises. Typically, foreign tour-operators that engage in Niger are small-scale enterprises that depend financially and logistically on local partners because they cannot afford to build up their own local infrastructure. Third, local knowledge of the desert and of their own culture is another important resource for Tuareg. This makes these actors perfect guides and intermediaries between the tourists and the local population.

As I will show below, the valorization of resources like ethnic identity, the establishment of long-term relations with foreign business partners, and the adjustment of local knowledge to the tourists' needs are among Tuareg entrepreneurs' key competencies in tourism and are decisive factors in economic failure or success.

## THE EMERGENCE OF NEW ENTREPRENEURS

In the 1930s, during French colonial times, a rugged form of adventure tourism developed in northern Niger. The true debut of modern tourism in the region began from 1968 onward, when two European tour-operators organized guided tours with camels and off-road vehicles for European tourists. From the beginning, they employed local *imajighen* and *imghad* as camel drivers, guides, drivers, cooks, and work aides. A few years later, these Tuareg began creating their own travel agencies in Agadez. They established relationships with European tour-operators or catered to individual tourists. They also profited from the general state-policy of "Nigerization", which led to the withdrawal of licenses for foreign travel agencies active in Niger in favor of local entrepreneurs.

The actual "era of the Tuareg" (Grégoire 1999) in tourism began with Mano ag Dayak, who founded his travel agency Temet Voyage in 1980. He had studied in New York and Paris, was married to a Frenchwoman, and disposed of an ever-growing network of contacts with tour-operators, politicians, journalists, filmmakers, and the like in Europe and North America. He succeeded in monopolizing the tourist market in Agadez and catered to 2,000 guests in 1988, which represented two-thirds of all tourists traveling on a package tour. Rhissa ag Boula became the accountant of Temet Voyage. Other Tuareg, too, created their own small enterprises.

These pioneers in tourism among the *imajighen* and *imghad* had an openness and curiosity toward Europeans and a willingness to abandon traditional economic strategies, but their professional choice was not obvious. Many considered work as caravan traders, camel herders, and gardeners to be too hard for them. Others were forced to look for alternatives because they had lost their livestock during severe droughts in the 1970s and the 1980s.

These natural disasters have also profoundly changed social relations within the hierarchical order of Tuareg society. In former times, the aristocracy (*imajighen*) stood at the top of this order, followed by the vassals (*imghad*) who were tributary to the nobles. Another social group was the Islamic scribes (*inisleman*). Further down the social ladder stood the freed slaves (*ighawelan*) and the slaves (*iklan*). The smiths (*inadan*) occupied a special status in Tuareg society. Although dependent on the nobles, they performed important functions not only as craftsmen but also in rituals and festivities.

All these social layers still exist and are of great importance for personal identity. The great droughts impoverished the aristocracy, which could no longer support its smiths. Looking for new strategies to earn a living, the smiths greatly profited from tourists and foreign traders, to whom they sold their silver jewelry. Some of them became rich businessmen with a trade network spanning from Niger to Europe and North America (Davis 1999; Scholze 2009). The smiths thus became economically independent from the nobles and this also gave them greater personal freedom. Nevertheless, most smiths, especially in the Aïr Mountains, still observe their social and ritual obligations toward the nobles in order to maintain social peace.

Tourism also opened up new opportunities for the *imajighen* and *imghad*. The pioneers among these Tuareg entered the tourism business rather accidentally through interaction with Europeans and foreign tour-operators looking for staff for their camel and four-wheel-drive tours. Additionally, European expatriates who worked for the uranium mines in Arlit asked these Tuareg to act as guides on their weekend trips into the desert.

The relatives and peers of these Tuareg initially contested their engagement in tourism. Tuareg who belong to the social layer of nobles or vassals are bound to the principles of honor (*asshak*) and shame (*tekarakit*). According to these local norms of behavior, they were not supposed to interact directly with foreigners. The smiths served as intermediaries because they were not bound to these principles and had fewer problems approaching their tourist clients. Likewise, manual work, such as the greasy maintenance of Toyota Landcruisers, was associated with the smiths and considered inappropriate for nobles and vassals. But since the smiths profited from tourism through the production of silver jewelry and other handicrafts, they had neither the intention of making their living as a driver or leader of an agency nor the skills to serve as guides.

Apart from social role contradictions, local pioneers in tourism were accused of "following the whites". Behind this criticism were the local population's fears that these actors would abandon Tuareg cultural values and—even worse—eventually convert from Islam to Christianity. However, conversion did not occur, nor did the actors completely abandon the traditions and so, with time, work in tourism became accepted for *imajighen* and *imghad*. The economic benefits for the families of the directors and staff members as well as for the population in the Aïr Mountains contributed to the acceptance of this work.

The rise of tourism came to a sudden halt when a rebellion broke out in the 1990s in which Tuareg protested against their political and economic marginalization in the state, which rendered tourism impossible. Mano ag Dayak shut down his agency and became the most prominent leader of the rebellion, making use of his European contacts to gain support for the Tuareg cause in the press and within the government in France. Likewise, Rhissa ag Boula, the former accountant for Temet Voyage, also led one of the rebel factions. Many other Tuareg who had previously worked in tourism joined the ranks of the movement or left Niger to work in other tourist destinations like Chad. Treaties in 1995 and 1997 between the different rebel groups and the state marked the end of violence.

After peace and security had been restored, Tuareg entrepreneurs quickly resumed their activities in tourism. Rhissa ag Boula became the Minister of Tourism in the government. Boula accorded licenses for new travel agencies to Tuareg in Agadez to integrate the former rebels and create employment in the north, even if they did not fulfill the legal and economic requirements to build and sustain such enterprises. This led to a boom of new agencies. In 2007, a total of 62 licensed travel agencies existed with altogether more than 500 guides, drivers, cooks, camel drivers, accountants, and guards.

All agencies are owned by men, with the exception of three women—all of them nobles—who run their own agencies. Beyond their social affiliation, the directors and their staff belong to different groups within the political organization of the Tuareg. In precolonial times, all nobles and vassals were members of a confederation or drum group (*ettebel*) that joined together for warfare. This affiliation still exists and remains of great importance for the construction of identity.[7] The directors and staff of the agencies—with rare exceptions *imajighen* or *imghad* from the Aïr Mountains and the nearby plains—belong to the confederations of the Kel Ferwan, Kel Tadele, Ifoghas, Kel Ewey, Ikazkazan, and Kel Fadey. Mano ag Dayak was affiliated with the Ifoghas. When he died in a plane crash in 1995, he left a vacuum that was initially filled by his former partners who were also Ifoghas. Later, entrepreneurs from other confederations seized their chance, and this led to a diversification of the tourism market's social and political structure and the Ifoghas's loss of monopoly.

## FROM COOK TO DIRECTOR OR HOW TO CREATE A TRAVEL AGENCY AND SUSTAIN IT

The agencies differ to a great extent in the repartition of clients, their material facilities, the number of employees, and their gross income. Seven agencies share two-thirds of the tourists, with an average of up to 350 clients per season. Another twenty-one agencies have around fifty clients and the rest have less than twenty clients per year. The leading agencies have up to twelve off-road cars—the most widespread model is the 1980s Toyota Landcruiser HJ60—and have recourse to headquarters in Agadez with an office, car park, garage, and storage rooms for spare parts, tools, camping material, and food. They employ up to fifteen Tuareg on a permanent basis as staff for the office and the tours, complemented by additional personnel hired on demand. In contrast, the majority of agencies that cater to twenty or fewer clients only have one or two Landcruisers or have no proper vehicle at all. Their offices are located at home in their living rooms and they have recourse to rudimentary material equipment only. In case of need, they hire a driver together with his own car. Likewise, these agencies have no permanent staff but hire personnel for each journey.

In terms of economic success, it is difficult to estimate the actors' annual income and profit. The directors are obliged to have accountancy, but the figures given may not be accurate or verifiable because staff members usually do not keep the books. Even if an agency has an impressive car park, well-equipped headquarters, and a lot of staff, it is difficult to judge whether this is due to their profit or to loans by friends, wives, or business partners. Nevertheless, it is possible to estimate on the basis of the average prices and costs for a voyage that a well-run agency with about 350 clients per year can make a profit of up to $150,000 pre-tax. But, as shown above, only seven out of sixty-two agencies have this number of clients. All the other agencies gain a maximum of $23,000 pre-tax or less. In fact many of the agencies do not even manage to pay their annual fees and taxes, for example, to renew their licenses. The regional tourism authority in Agadez should have shut down these agencies long ago, but its director is caught between a rock and a hard place. On one hand, the minister Rhissa ag Boula has accorded the licenses to entrepreneurs who cannot meet the formal requirements,[8] while on the other hand, these entrepreneurs approach the director with their daily problems so that he does not dare to close their agencies since "they have to feed their families". The lax policy of licensing or the good-will of local authorities, however, do not explain the differences in income but rather highlight the directors' individual capacities to grapple with the demands of a modern business like tourism. Essential to the success of an agency is that its director and staff acquire and master new competencies, as mentioned earlier, which they have to combine and balance with traditional practices, knowledge, and values.

## Technical Appropriation and Adjustment of Traditional Knowledge

No director of an agency started as such. All began to work as employees of other agencies. Since there is no formal and institutionalized apprentice-ship, training comprises a straightforward learning-by-doing approach. Normally, a new staff member begins as a cook, aide, or camel driver. He then becomes a car driver for a vehicle that transports materials alone and then later tourists. Finally, if he is eager enough, he can be promoted to work as a driver-guide.[9] All directors have learned the actual work of trav-eling with tourists before becoming a boss, while appropriating new skills and knowledge at each stage of their career. They have to deal with the state bureaucracy, renew their licenses, and get permission for each journey; complete logistical planning like water, food, and material supplies for every tour; and define the daily stages and program of the journey.

Driving a Toyota Landcruiser in a stony and sandy terrain, for example, is a complex affair that requires special skills. A driver has to choose the right gear, tire pressure, and speed to minimize the risk of getting stuck in the sand while saving fuel at the same time. Furthermore, his first concern has to be the well-being of his clients, which means avoiding accidents and driving slowly on bumpy roads so that the tourists will not hit their heads on the roof of the car or get "seasick" in the desert. The appropriation of the car includes not only the technical aspects but also the attribution of particular meanings. Daniel Miller speaks of the "humanity of the car" (2001) in this respect. Tuareg give their Toyotas typical camel names and decorate their cars with colorful woven blankets like they do for camels, as these vehicles have replaced camels as the economic basis of their enter-prise. Without the use of off-road cars tourism would simply be impossible in Niger. Hence, in analogy to the milk of the mares as the Tuareg's staple food, the money earned through the cars in tourism is called the "milk of the car" (*akhu-n-mota*). The analogy between the camel and the car neverthe-less has its limitations: cars cannot reproduce themselves; each vehicle has to be bought and maintained. Thus, the Tuareg do not measure the economic value of a car by its sheer existence like a camel but by the money they have earned using to transport tourists.[10]

Tuareg working in tourism refer to new objects like Toyota Landcruisers and competencies as *kel azzaman* (modern). They also rely on *kel eru* (traditional knowledge), which they adjust to their work in tourism. Like their homologues in the caravan trade, they use natural phenomena to orient themselves in the desert, including the color of the sand, the special formation of sand dunes created through the steady northeast trade wind, and the position of the sun and stars at night. The guides even mistrust the use of a compass or GPS, because they think they are not accurate enough. They also adjust their knowledge about the landscape, the flora and fauna, the Tuareg culture, the Aïr Mountains, and the Tenere desert for tourism when they have to find suitable places for spending the night—which have to be attractive for tourists and practical in terms of access to water and firewood—or divide the itinerary into comfortable segments to avoid danger for the often elderly tourists. To do all this, the guide has to acquire an understanding of what tourists are particularly interested in and invest this information in a way suitable for Europeans.

## Interactions with Europeans and other Tuareg

Agency directors and their employees' interaction with tourists, other directors, foreign business partners, and of local actors within the Tuareg population requires intercultural competence and at least basic skills in French.[11] Some of the Tuareg driver-guides have even learned English, Italian, or German by themselves depending on the provenance of the clients to which a particular agency in Agadez caters. The directors and their staff also have to become acquainted with the different mentalities, behaviors, and needs of tourists from various countries (Figure 8.2). They have to deal with conflicts and overtly expressed criticism by their guests, which is uncommon in Tuareg society. If conflicts arise, Tuareg will usually not confront their clients directly but will rather look away silently in order not to lose their tempers and hence their honor (*asshak*).

Another aspect of the interaction is the integration of the tourists into the status system of the Tuareg. At the onset, as they are *ikufaren* (non-believers) and outsiders, tourists become guests (*imagaren*) of a particular agency and guide who assumes the responsibility for their well-being. Sometimes, these guests can become even a friend (*amiji*), who after his or her return can help to find more clients in the future or to develop the agency further through monetary donations, internet support, or other kinds of recommendations.

Building relationships with European and American tour-operators is paramount to the success of any agency. Those Tuareg who worked closely together with Mano ag Dayak "inherited" his partners after his decease. Others have married European women who facilitate the contact with tour-operators or are even the official representative of the Tuareg agency in

*Figure 8.2*   Tourism in the Oasis of Timia (Photo: Marko Scholze)

Europe. These women also play a crucial role in counseling their husbands about the dos and don'ts vis-à-vis their business partners and clients or they invest money into the agency. Consequently, a growing number of directors are marrying European women who have come to Niger as tourists or aid workers. From a local perspective, this approach guarantees a director's ability to overcome any difficulties in building up a successful agency. There is even a saying amidst the local tourist actors that "if god takes pity on you, he will send you a Swiss wife", referring to the presumed wealth accorded to people from Switzerland. Local judgment about the relationships between Tuareg directors and European wives depends on the age of the woman: if the woman is too old to bear children, the marriage is considered to have been driven purely by the material desires of the Tuareg and qualified as *azruf* (money),[12] love can only play a role if the woman is still able to reproduce.

Another way to find a business partner is to rely on foreign friends, regardless of whether they are tourists, expatriates, filmmakers, or journalists, who can serve as intermediaries when contacting potential partners in Europe. They also help through financial and material support or the creation of a website and brochures for the agency. The support of friends and wives adds credibility to the Tuareg director in the eyes of the European tour-operators. Those who have no foreign intermediaries will hardly be able to establish a business partnership in Europe and are obliged to find their clients amidst the few individual travelers who stay in one of the hotels in Agadez.

Once a local director and a European tour-operator have established a relationship, their cooperation can be framed as a typical patron-client relationship, asymmetrical in the sense that their relation is hierarchically structured through social inequality (Weber-Pazmino 1991) and differences in access to resources. But the relationship is more complex. It is true that even if there is a certain mutual dependency between Tuareg and foreign tour-operators as stated above, the latter nonetheless have a more powerful bargaining position since the Tuareg depend on them to get clients. Additionally, given the high number of local travel agencies and the fierce competition among them, a foreign tour-operator could easily play them off against each other.

This rarely happens and hints at differences in the perception of business relationships in Niger. Tuareg nearly always conceptualize their relationship with foreign tour-operators as "friendship", wishing to bind the business partner into a framework of a locally rooted moral economy. A friend (*amiji*) is morally obliged to help another friend. Thus, were the European tour-operator to change or abandon his Tuareg partner, this would be considered locally to be a betrayal of their friendship. To build a business relationship thus means to build a friendship. Tuareg do this through gift-giving and hospitality when (potential) business partners visit Niger. The limits between a truly felt friendship and the mere instrumentalization of the concept by the Tuareg are fluid and difficult to judge.

Another point is the high self-esteem and honor of the nobles, which prevents them from feeling inferior to their foreign business partners. The foreign tour-operators are eager to become friends with the Tuareg. They have often traveled extensively in the desert and are fascinated by the Sahara and its inhabitants. They want to help their business partners and even support them in building up their agencies and offer credit so that they can buy, for example, Toyotas or camping materials. Sometimes, their assistance even goes beyond the domain of tourism. A number of tour-operators supported the rebel movement in the 1990s or initiated small-scale development projects in the Aïr Mountains. Hence, the foreign partners' exploitation of local actors is often considered a quality of patron-client relationships (Silverman 1977; White 1980) and rather absent in tourism in Niger.[13] Instead, one can observe "cross-cultural identification", as Davis (1999) has also shown for the relationship between Tuareg silversmiths and foreign traders in Niamey.

The relationship between the agency directors and family members and friends who look for work in tourism as well as between Tuareg working in tourism and the local population visited by the tourists is also important. When looking for staff, the directors of the agencies will always privilege their relatives and friends who belong to the same social layers and confederations. The director will employ Tuareg of other confederations only if his agency expands beyond the capacity of the family to provide the required staff. Recruiting the core of the staff amidst the directors' kin lends stability to the enterprise but also represents an obligation for him. Relatives and friends constantly approach the director and urge him to hire them for his agency. If he refuses, his kin and peers will criticize him, accusing him of being unfaithful, greedy, and selfish, thus putting his personal honor (*asshak*) at risk. This can pose a serious problem when the enterprise expands, since usually the director will not find enough individuals within his family who actually have the qualifications, disposition, or character needed to be trained as staff members. The director will thus employ Tuareg from other confederations at the risk of increased criticism. Directors are therefore caught between the local moral economy and the professional adjustment to the requirements of a global business. Those directors who are willing to confront this criticism and "rationalize" their enterprises complain about the fact that there "is too much sentiment" involved in the business and that qualification should determine who gets the job. A closer look at the actual recruitment practices nevertheless shows that even the adherents of a modern approach to local entrepreneurship will bow to the moral obligations involved when recruiting their staff.

The pressure of redistribution is also exerted by those family members and friends who do not look for work in tourism. Relatives and friends approach the directors to financially support them or other family members who have only a small income or none at all. The directors cannot overtly refuse these payments and their space for negotiation is limited. They rather show a demonstrative generosity to increase their reputation. Even those who make little profit will help their kin since they feel too much shame (*takarakit*) to admit this.

Under these circumstances, it is difficult to accumulate money to further expand the business even for the directors of the well-established travel agencies. The local moral economy can even become a real threat to the economic survival of the enterprise. The same difficulties hold true for the staff of agencies that only pay according to the number of days they work during the season.[14] The redistribution of jobs and financial support given to family members are two important aspects of the relation between the Tuareg working in tourism and the population. Additionally, the directors and staff of the agencies act as economic and cultural brokers for the inhabitants of the Aïr Mountains visited during the journey.

The directors and their staff bring the tourists to the villages and nomad camps where the smiths and *shasturis*[15] sell handicrafts made of local serpentine stone, silver jewelry, or objects of everyday life like woven baskets or leather bags. Most *imajighen* and *imghad* in the Aïr Mountains will not approach tourists directly to sell their objects since they feel too much shame (*tekarakit*). They give their commodities to the smith and *shasturis* to sell them on their behalf.[16] In the villages and nomad camps, the tourist group's cook also buys fruits and vegetables from gardeners and goat meat and cheese from the nomads to diversify the meals they prepare for their clients. In some villages, like Timia, men and women of all social layers gain some extra income by staging chants or dances for tourist groups, which the agencies arrange beforehand (Figure 8.3).

The agencies' staff also act as cultural brokers when they facilitate economic profits for the population and moderate the encounter between tourists and the local inhabitants. Most of the women and older men in the

*Figure 8.3*   Traditional chants and dance for tourists in Timia (Photo: Marko Scholze)

village do not speak any European languages and the guides serve as translators. Additionally, the guides accompany tourists while visiting nomad camps
and villages so that they do not stroll around alone. They provide tourists
with advice about appropriate behavior, and, in this way, foreign visitors are
socially controlled and lose much of their potential to disturb the life of the
local population. This control is possible because the number of tourists who
travel to the region is low and there is hardly any individual tourism.

The economic and intercultural brokerage of the agencies' directors and
staff is not solely driven by their attachment to their home region. If the
tourist groups do not stop in the director's or his staff's home villages, they
would be criticized for being unsocial, for wanting to keep all the profit
from tourism for themselves. Moreover, the guides would be held responsible for every disturbance that the tourists have caused, since the latter
are his guests (*imagaren*). Most of the actors observe their obligations so
that their economic and cultural brokerage helps many families in the Aïr
Mountains earn additional income. The population qualifies the work in
tourism as useful (*tumfa*), which accounts for the very acceptance of the
new profession and the "mandate for innovation" (Press 1969) local actors
thus receive from the rest of society.

## Commoditization of Cultural Identity and Habitat

Each actor's capacity to exploit the myth of the Sahara and the Tuareg is
another key competency and decisive factor for the success or failure of

an agency. Their cultural identity, foreignness, and exoticism as well as their habitat are essential commodities and resources for entrepreneurship in tourism. A master in this sense was once again Mano ag Dayak. Over the course of his studies in France and the United States, he had become well-acquainted with the stereotyped images and expectations of westerners regarding the Sahara and the Tuareg. This is reflected in the books he wrote and his interviews filled with flowery descriptions of nomads and the desert such as:

> For a whole day, I could sit on top of a sand dune and watch the magnificent spectacle. The dune moved with the hours decorating itself on and on with the most diverse colors. In front of this interleaving of sand and wind, life entered another dimension. My body did not exist anymore. It made peace with my soul. I experienced something sacred. (Dayak 1997: 59, my translation)

Mano ag Dayak also fits well into the stereotypical image of a Tuareg man both through his physiognomy and his appearance, wearing traditional clothes and the veil. Together with his openness and capacity for communication in English or French, Dayak became a Tuareg whom everyone wanted to befriend. He also knew how to promote his enterprise and Niger as a tourist destination with the aid of filmmakers, photographers, and journalists.[17]

Like Mano ag Dayak, his successors in the business present themselves—in discourse and appearance—as nomads who value their traditions and love the desert. This observation leads us to question if we are observing here a mere economic strategy to foster one's own position on the tourist market or if tourism has actually changed the natural and cultural perception of the actors. Indeed, caravan traders or traditional nomads would not talk like Mano ag Dayak and his successors. They call the desert *tenere*, which signifies a desolate, empty, and hostile space associated with fear and danger (Claudot-Hawad 1993). Tuareg actors in tourism admit that they do not travel into the desert to admire the beauty of the sand dunes or to even climb them. They do it because the tourists want to go there. In tourism, the myth of the Sahara has become translated into monetary value for the local actors.

Nevertheless, the directors and the staff of the agencies have slightly changed their perception of the desert in an affirmative way. They have begun to praise the silence and tranquility of the Tenere. This is not a sign of the tourists' influence but is rather evoked by the confrontation with urban life in Agadez, where the actors spend a great deal of their time between journeys, unlike their nomadic peers in the Aïr Mountains, who rarely visit the city.

Tourists expect to be accompanied by traditional Tuareg. These have to live up to the tourists' expectations and prove their "authenticity" even if the facts that they drive Toyota Landcruisers and are actively employed in a modern profession might appear to be contradictory. Hence, they dress in a traditional way and confirm discursively the tourists' stereotyped views of their culture. Taking into account that most actors entered tourism as a deliberate break with tradition, as stated above, it could be argued that, like the desert, cultural identity has become a mere commodity. This, however, is not the whole story.

Tuareg working in tourism are constantly exposed to the tourists' admiration. This contrasts with the negative image that most other ethnic groups in Niger attribute to them and with their conflictive relationship to the state. Furthermore, the usual stereotypes about the Tuareg in the West are related to the characteristics of the *imajighen* and *imghad*, which fits quite well with the self-perception of the actual Tuareg actors involved. Consequently, the "tourist gaze" here contributes to the affirmation of their traditional cultural identity and enhances their self-esteem.

## CHANGING LIFEWORLDS OF MODERN NOMADS

The *imajighen* and *imghad* who work in tourism call themselves "modern nomads", thus referring to their heritage as nomads. Life as a modern nomad has consequences beyond the actual sphere of work, depending on the individual profession exerted in tourism. A camel driver accompanying a *meharee* through the Aïr Mountains will return to his nomad camp after the end of the tour. For the staff and the directors of the agencies the changes are more profound. The majority of the guides, drivers, and cooks settle in Agadez's urban environment during the tourist season. Usually, they rent houses to share with several other actors. After the end of the season in March, they return to their families in the villages or nomadic camps in the Aïr Mountains. For these Tuareg, living in the city is a necessary condition for finding work at the agencies. Even if they manage to participate in several journeys, they still spend a couple of weeks in Agadez. The directors of the agencies, in contrast, spend most of their time in Agadez. They only go back to the Aïr Mountains to visit their relatives or when they occasionally accompany a tourist group. Additionally, they frequently travel to Europe between the two seasons from April to October to visit their European wives and meet their friends and business partners. During these journeys, they are confronted with modern life and foreign cultures to an even greater extent.

Most Tuareg working in tourism complain about the noise and dirt, widespread diseases like malaria or diarrhea, the higher living costs in the city, and that they have to speak Hausa, the dominant language in Agadez. In Agadez or Europe, they live in concrete houses with running water, electricity, modern bathrooms, kitchens, and television, which are unknown in their home villages. They integrate western food and dress according to their lifestyle. They also take up new pastimes like skiing or hiking while spending time in Austria, Germany, or France. In Europe, Tuareg are admired when they wear their traditional dress and confronted with totally different mentalities, behavioral norms, and practices. The growing physical distance from the villages and nomad camps in the Aïr Mountains also offers an enhanced freedom from the direct social control exerted by relatives and friends back home. The actors value this freedom because it gives them the opportunity to design their lives according to their individual needs, which forms part of their particular lifestyle.

The mobility of these modern nomads has been enhanced through the motorization of transport and the use of airplanes, which is an unusual mode of movement for Tuareg living in the remote Aïr Mountains. The use of Toyota Landcruisers when traveling with tourists in the region enables the actors to be mobile like the caravan traders but without the hardship the latter have to endure. A caravan that crosses the Tenere desert from the Aïr Mountains to the salt mines of Bilma—a distance of 500 kilometers—takes ten days of walking for sixteen hours without a break. An off-road vehicle-convoy only needs two or three days, including long breaks during the day. The Toyotas have become a status symbol and an identity marker for these "modern nomads", which is reflected in their habit of aimlessly driving around with their cars in Agadez to be recognized by their peers.

The mobile lifestyle also connotes curiosity toward the unknown. This is reflected in the term *awəzlu*, which the actors apply to their work in tourism. *Awəzlu* signifies a business journey (Spittler 1998) traditionally used for the caravan trade. Another meaning of the term is to venture across barriers from the known to the unknown when nomads extend their radius of action and experience while traveling. In this way, the journey serves the whole of society in that the latter becomes enriched through goods and knowledge brought home by the nomads (Claudot-Hawad 2002).

The new personal freedom and the aspired life of an entrepreneur have their dangers too. If a Tuareg does not succeed in the tourist market, he is condemned to live in poverty in Agadez. Out of shame (*tekarakit*), he will neither admit his failure to his relatives and friends nor will he return to the Aïr Mountains. He will thus be deprived of any support and comfort through his family network. Another danger, according to the actors living in Agadez and Europe, is to become an *anakaw*, a person who gets lost because he detaches himself too much from his cultural roots and values. A sign of such detachment is when a Tuareg working in tourism starts to drink alcohol. But this is actually an exception. More often, these actors develop a feeling of nostalgia (*asuf*) about the traditional nomadic life, combined with a growing desire to preserve their cultural heritage.

The growing conservatism of these actors who once left their villages and nomad camps precisely out of curiosity about the unknown and to deliberately break with their traditions does not mean that they wish to return to their former lives in the Aïr Mountains. It is rather a strengthened feeling of attachment to their own culture, together with the fear that this culture is threatened by the changes they observe around them and in their own lives. Similar to the integration of modern and traditional elements in their work, this attachment is expressed by integrating items of their heritage into modern homes. They decorate the walls of their rooms with traditional leather bags or mount a nomad's tent in the courtyard where they prepare tea with friends while listening to ancient chants from a tape deck.

Another expression of the actors' attachment to their culture is their wish to contribute to the preservation of traditions. In this perspective, the camel tours organized by the agencies help to sustain camel herds because the nomads can reinvest the money gained from tourism into their herds. This example, together with the involvement of Tuareg in the economic and cultural brokerage needed for tourism, indicates that while they want to live their modernized lives, they want to have personalities and be useful to their society as expressed in the term *awazlu*.

Their commitment to their society and culture contributes to the acceptance of entrepreneurship in tourism within the social layers of the *imajighen* and *imghad* and makes the Tuareg directors of the agencies and their staff "new figures of success", especially in the eyes of the younger generations. The latter no longer have to overcome the former's criticisms and seek to enter the business not accidentally but as a deliberate choice. They admire the Toyotas driven by these actors and their expensive shiny damask clothes and indigo-colored turbans, which are worn in the village only on festive occasions. The assumed wealth and recognition associated with work and tourism and, more so, the actors' entire lifestyle, constitute the attraction.[18]

## CONCLUSION: TUAREG ENTREPRENEURSHIP IN TOURISM

The agency of Tuareg nobles and vassals in tourism has contributed to the diversification of their economic options. Initially, they became entrepreneurs through the interaction with European tour-operators, tourists, and expatriates. In the course of this, they appropriated not only the western idea of tourism but also new technical skills, knowledge, and competencies. Tuareg qualify entrepreneurship in tourism as *kel azzaman*, a "modern" task. In fact, there is no generic term in *tamajeq* for this kind of entrepreneur. The Tuareg even use the expression "modern nomad" only in French. When they apply the term *awazlu* (business travel) to refer to their work in tourism, the *imajighen* and *imghad* consciously place themselves in the nomadic tradition of the caravan traders. For both professions, traveling becomes the basic occupation in order to achieve economic goals which serve the well-being of oneself, one's family, and society as a whole.

The main difference between Tuareg tourism entrepreneurs and caravan traders lies in the speed and scale of the venture. Motorization allows the Tuareg entrepreneurs to cover large distances in a short time. Those who frequently travel to Europe even widen the spatial enlargement of their agency.

Whereas the caravan traders confine their activities to Niger and northern Nigeria, tourism actors constantly seek to expand their spatial radius by visiting Europe or even North America. The interaction with Europeans is crucial for the success of the Tuareg entrepreneur. The establishment of long-lasting relationships with European tour-operators, European wives, and friends, who lend financial and material support as well as their expertise to the local director, is paramount to building up and sustaining an agency.

Scale as a quality of distinction between the caravan trader and the tourism entrepreneur thus comprises not only a spatial but also a relational and experiential connotation. Through the enhanced interaction and confrontation with different cultures in Europe, these Tuareg widen their horizon and venture into the unknown—as expressed in the term *awəzlu*—to a much greater extent than the nomad engaging in the salt caravan to Bilma.

This venture demands a certain type of entrepreneur, who is, like Mano Dayak and his followers, driven by his curiosity toward the foreign and his openness to innovation. These features helped the pioneers of this profession endure the initial contestations of their peers against their agency. Additionally, these nobles and vassals apply their traditional male ideal of being courageous and risk-taking in order to succeed in tourism entrepreneurship. Most of them have lived some time in Europe and are married to European women. They have acquired high-level communicative and intercultural competencies and are able to switch easily between different cultural codes. They manage to commoditize their cultural identity when they appear to be "real" Tuareg in traditional dress and manner in order to meet the expectations of the tourists and partners in the West.

The impact, however, that the interaction of the Tuareg entrepreneurs with Europeans has on the way Tuareg perceive their cultural identity goes beyond mere commoditization. Having rediscovered their culture and heritage with the aim of preserving it, they feel a strong attachment to their home region. They enable a maximum of Tuareg to participate in the profits generated by tourism when they meet the obligations grounded in the local moral economy. The overall result of these actors' agency is a particular lifestyle that oscillates between a sedentary urban and a nomadic life.

Some of the tourist entrepreneurs also have engaged in politics, gained political power, and obtained positions as mayors in northern Niger during the first communal elections held in 2004. Some scholars argue that the wealth and political influence of Tuareg working in tourism has led to the formation of a new bourgeoisie (Bourgeot 1992) within the social layers of the nobles and vassals. This argument, however, seems to be overstressed, as only a handful of actors might qualify for this group. The majority of agencies' staff do not live from tourism alone but combine it with other economic activities, such as working as tailors and drivers for development organizations. Others help their fathers and brothers in the garden or with the animals.

Many of the agencies' directors, however, fail to acquire the necessary funds to build up their agencies and to establish lasting relationships with European tour-operators. They also lack the comprehension of the mechanisms involved in the global tourist market. Instead of questioning their personal shortcomings and ameliorating their services and position in the market, they accuse local business rivals of having used magic to undermine their efforts. Thus, Tuareg engagement in tourism and their having become new figures of success and power is rather due to their particular lifestyle, which exerts a great attraction, especially among the younger generations, and the promise of rather than the actual accumulation of wealth and power.

The influence of local entrepreneurs on the Tuareg society should not be overemphasized. First, although work in tourism is today widely accepted in Tuareg society as an alternative economic strategy, most men still feel attached to their traditional nomadic life. Most male Tuareg nobles and vassals continue to work as camel nomads, caravan traders, and gardeners. They prefer to live a sedentary life with their families in the villages of the Aïr Mountains, raising crops in their gardens. Likewise, the engagement of Tuareg in tourism has not fundamentally changed basic cultural values and concepts as, for example, wealth continues to be measured in camels and goats. The term *ehare* for richness is synonym for herd. This perception is still valid even as the number of camel nomads and caravan traders declines. In the urban context among agency directors and their staff, ideas about monetary wealth (*tagargis-n-azruf*) and new status symbols like Toyotas are widespread. The possession of money in itself is, however, not considered a sign of wealth, since the latter can be generated only if the money is invested into goods like Toyotas, houses, or the like.

Second, tourism is a particularly fragile economic sphere. The Tuareg rebellion that broke out in 2007 led to a complete breakdown of tourism in the region. As early as the rebellions in the 1990s, some tourism actors had become leading figures in the Movement of Niger for Justice (MNJ). After peace was restored in 2009, residual groups of armed bandits continued to roam the Aïr Mountains, rendering any activities in tourism impossible until today. Most of the staff tries to survive in Agadez as drivers for local transport or as small retail traders, or are simply unemployed. The directors who are married to European wives left the country to join them for the time being. But there are also winners of this development. Some leaders of the rebellion who formerly led a travel agency in Agadez have been elected mayors in the north in the communal elections in 2011. Aghali Alambo, the president of the MNJ, became counselor of the president of the national assembly, and Rhissa ag Boula has been appointed the president's counselor. These actors, who contributed to the breakdown of the tourist market, have instead now gained political power. When the rest of the directors and their staff will be able to reclaim their lives as modern nomads remains an open question.

## NOTES

1. The terms written in italics are in *tamajeq*, the Tuareg language.
2. *Kel azzaman* literally means "the people of today". *Kel eru* means "the people of the past".
3. According to the World Tourism Organization (2002), Africa only accounts for 4.1% of worldwide tourism. Within West Africa, Niger has an inferior market share of 0.2%.
4. A package tour for three weeks in Niger costs up to $5,000.
5. Individual tourists make up only 15% of all tourists. This was different between the 1970s and the 1990s, when thousands of Europeans traveled with used cars through the desert to sell them in Niger. The violent conflicts in Algeria, the Tuareg rebellion in the 1990s, and the devaluation of the Franc CFA by 50% in 1994 brought the so-called "scrap metal tourism" to an end.
6. Rhissa ag Boula retired from his office in 2004 when he was accused of involvement in the murder of a politician in northern Niger. He was imprisoned and released in 2005 without trial.
7. A confederation is composed of several endogamous groups (*tawshiten*) of matrilineal descent.
8. The director of an agency needs to acquire sufficient material equipment, deposit a surety of 2 million FCFA (around $3,900), and pay annual fees of 500,000 FCFA ($970) and of 150,000 FCFA ($290) into a special state-owned development fund for tourism, among other payments and taxes.
9. A driver-guide receives an average of 15,000 to 20,000 FCFA per day of traveling. A driver gets 6,000 to 7,500 FCFA per day just like a cook. A camel driver earns 5,000 and an aide 3,000 FCFA.
10. Such terminological analogies appear to be widespread among pastoralists in Africa. The Tswana in southern Africa, for example, speak of money as "cattle without legs" (Comaroff and Comaroff 1991: 56).
11. All guides are drivers at the same time. The director of an agency will not hire a guide who cannot drive, as this would take up a seat in the car that could otherwise be sold to a tourist.
12. If the woman is older than her husband, then, according to local perception, she intends to rejuvenate herself through sexual intercourse.
13. Noble patrons rarely exploited the smiths—even before their impoverishment during the great droughts of the 1970s and 1980s—since they had the right to protest in public against such an abuse, thus exposing their patrons as immoral.
14. Diver-guides sometimes rent their own cars to the agency, making up to $6,300 per year whereas others do not earn more than $1,300.
15. The name *shasturis* stems from the French expression "chasser les tourists" or "hunting tourists". *Shasturis* are predominantly young smiths and nobles who work as vendors of handicrafts and other objects (Scholze and Bartha 2004).
16. Among the *shasturis* are often also adolescent nobles who deliberately break the behavioral norms valid for their social layer when they act like smiths. The elder nobles tolerate this because of their young age and usefulness as commercial intermediaries.
17. Mano ag Dayak also exploited the myth to gain political and material support for the rebellion in the 1990s in western media (Decoudras 1995).

18. School enrollment also contributes to the preference of not returning to camel herding and caravan trade.

## REFERENCES

Adams, Kathleen. 1984. 'Come to Tana Toraja, "Land of the Heavenly Kings": travel agents as brokers in ethnicity'. *Annals of Tourism Research* 11, 3: 469–485.

Banégas, Richard and Jean-Pierre Warnier. 2001. 'Nouvelles figures de la réussite et du pouvoir'. *Politique Africaine* 82: 5–21.

Boilley, Pierre. 2000. 'Sahara et Sahariens. Les Touaregs dans le regard des guides de voyage'. In: Gilles Chabaud (ed). *Les guides imprimés du XVIe au XXe siècle. Villes, paysages, voyages.* Paris: Mappemonde, 619–641.

Bourgeot, André. 1992. 'L'enjeu politique de l'histoire: vision idéologique des événements touaregs (1990–1992)'. *Politique africaine* 48: 129–135.

Claudot-Hawad, Hélène. 1993. *Les Touaregs. Portrait en fragments.* Aix-en-Provence: Edisud.

Claudot-Hawad, Hélène. 2002. 'Noces de vent: épouser le vide ou l'art nomade de voyager'. In: Hélène Claudot-Hawad (ed). *Voyager d'un point de vue nomade.* Paris: Méditerrannée, 11–36.

Comaroff, Jean and John Comaroff. 1991. '"How beasts lost their legs": cattle in Tswana economy and society'. In: John Galaty and Pierre Bonte (eds). *Herders, Warriors, and Traders: Pastoralism in Africa.* Boulder: Westview Press, 33–60.

Davis, Elizabeth. 1999. 'Metamorphosis in the Culture Market of Niger'. *American Anthropologist* 101, 3: 485–501.

Dayak, Mano. 1997. *Geboren mit Sand in den Augen.* Zürich: Unionsverlag.

Decoudras, Pierre. 1995. 'Utilisation et limite des images dans "la question" touaregue'. In: Heidi Willer, Till Förster and Claudia Ortner-Buchberger (eds). *Macht der Identität—Identität der Macht.* Münster: LIT, 209–219.

Grégoire, Emmanuel. 1999. *Touaregs du Niger. Le destin d'un mythe.* Paris: Karthala.

MacCannell, Dean. 1999. *The Tourist: A New Theory of the Leisure Class.* Berkeley: University of California Press.

Miller, Daniel. 2001. 'Driven Societies'. In: Daniel Miller (ed). *Car Cultures.* Oxford: Berg, 1–33.

Nash, Dennison. 2001. *Anthropology of Tourism.* Elsevier: Oxford.

Press, Irwin. 1969. 'Ambiguity and innovation: implications for the genesis of the culture broker'. *American Anthropologist* 71: 206–217.

Roux, Michel. 1996. *Le désert de sable. Le Sahara dans l'imaginaire des Français (1900–1994).* Paris: L'Harmattan.

Scholze, Marko. 2009. *Moderne Nomaden und fliegende Händler. Tuareg und Tourismus in Niger.* Münster: LIT.

Scholze, Marko and Ingo Bartha. 2004. 'Trading cultures: Berbers and Tuareg as souvenir vendors'. In: Peter Probst and Gerd Spittler (eds). *Between Resistance and Expansion: Dimensions of Local Vitality in Africa.* Münster: LIT, 71–92.

Silverman, Sydel. 1977. 'Patronage as myth'. In: Ernest Gellner and John Waterbury (eds). *Patrons and Clients in Mediterranean Societies.* London: Duckworth, 7–19.

Smith, Valene. (ed.). 1977. *Hosts and Guests: The Anthropology of Tourism.* Philadelphia: University of Pennsylvania Press.

Spittler, Gerd. 1998. *Hirtenarbeit.* Köln: Rüdiger Köppe.

Urry, John. 1990. *The Tourist Gaze.* London: Sage.

Van Beek, Walter and Anette Schmidt (eds). 2012. *African Hosts and Their Guests: Cultural Dynamics of Tourism*. Woodbridge: James Currey.

Weber-Pazmino, Gioia. 1991. *Klientelismus. Annäherungen an das Konzept*. Zürich: Administration & Druck AG.

White, Caroline. 1980. *Patrons and Partisans: A Study of Politics in Two Southern Italian Comuni*. Cambridge: University Press.

World Tourism Organization. 2002. Overview and Tourism Topics. www.world-tourism.org/facts/menu.htm, accessed 17 August 2002.

# 9 "I Took My Life in My Own Hands"

## The Clandestine Business of Prostitution in Bamako

*Inès Neubauer*

Prostitution in Africa, a topic of research since the 1920s (Bryk 1928: 92–102; Bujra 1975 in Nairobi), is often negatively stereotyped, troubled as it is by images of slavery (Kreutzer and Milborn 2008), poverty, the suppression of women in patriarchal social contexts (Giesen and Schumann 1980), and its prevalence in Muslim societies (Kouassi 1986: 233–235). Although the conceptualization of prostitution has become increasingly differentiated in recent years, the majority of studies on prostitution still rely on rather narrow perspectives (cf. Kiremiere 2007: 24–32).

This chapter focuses on the prostitution market in Bamako, about which very few scholarly works exist. Christine Mansfeld (2005: 212–215), for example, briefly mentions prostitution among the Dogon women who migrated to Bamako, applying a psychoanalytic rather than a socioeconomic perspective to prostitution. To fully understand the trade, however, a focus on the socioeconomic aspects of prostitution is needed, and in this chapter, I will explore the extent to which prostitution can be considered an enterprise that is a source of income that has its own market-specific dynamics. I will investigate factors that influence different forms of prostitution in Bamako and the interactions between the commodification of sex and moral perceptions in Mali that refashion prostitution into a particular form of entrepreneurship.

In Europe, prostitution is often associated with pimping, dependency, and pressure. In Bamako, the situation is different, as legal rules and the market-specific constellations that usually limit these women's trade and choices, for example the specific relationship between prostitutes and pimps, are not generally present. My research in Bamako revealed that these concepts hardly played any role in the prostitute's local reality and were instead a product of outsider imagination.[1] In Bamako, instead of an industry dominated by pimping and pressure, prostitution is a flexible informal market with versatile business options. This is not to say that such forms of prostitution do not exist in Bamako; they are, however, less common.

It is on the more common forms of prostitution in Bamako that this chapter focuses: women who operate their business independently without institutionalized constraints such as pimping or human trafficking. I will offer answers to questions about how women (re)produce their market, how they make use of sex as a resource and, above all, how they act as active business-women who do not allow others to turn them into commodities, all the while adhering to local rules of trade and supplementing them with market-specific regulations connected to the moral connotations of their trade.

As I will demonstrate, prostitution in Bamako is considered both mor-ally illegitimate behavior and a legitimate business, and these two discourses are vividly reproduced among Bamako's various inhabitants. Most of my interviewees were aware of the two interpretations and referred to them according to the specific context of my questions,[2] suggesting that they con-sider prostitutes entrepreneurs. In true business spirit, prostitutes optimize their opportunities by migrating to neighboring countries, contacting people about the industry, and weighing their different options to ensure profitabil-ity. They are consciously aware that they have a resource (their sex) at their disposition that they can invest for economic ends. When they talk about their profession, they do not see themselves as the victims of society and pov-erty, even though in other contexts, they might identify poverty as a reason for entering the field. Instead, they primarily consider themselves business-women who actively influence their economic situation by taking advantage of both their gender and sex. All participants involved negotiate this attitude through moral and social discourses, which provides a specific dynamic to this market and endows the prostitutes with an extraordinary position in the context of economic success, distinguishing them from other entrepreneurs.

The difference between prostitution and other trades obviously lies in the moral dimension of their business. They find themselves wedged between economic and moral discourses and have to adapt their behavior to these discourses and move in different social spaces with their own rules, and this influences both the prostitutes' business and private behavior. It also greatly impacts how society, including the prostitutes, evaluates and handles prosti-tutes' economic success, their labor migration, and the differentiation between their own actions and those of other women who are considered "immoral".

Prostitutes differ from other entrepreneurs in that they prefer to keep their activities secret. Their economic success is not socially acknowledged in a direct way; nevertheless, they actively fulfil their social duties. Secrecy and social isolation constitute a crucial difference between successful pros-titutes and other accomplished businesspeople. Migration from neighboring countries plays a considerable role in their endeavors, while local concepts strongly influence ideas about prostitution. The role of local discourse is particularly important, as most professional prostitutes in Bamako are migrants from various West African countries who come to Bamako to increase their opportunities and work as professionals.

My analysis is based on the field research I completed in Bamako in 2009. I conducted interviews with prostitutes and their clients, with individuals whose work has to do with prostitution, and with impartial city residents. In Bamako, I interviewed seventy-one individuals between the ages of eighteen and sixty. Additionally, I carried out participant observation in public spaces, streets, nightclubs, hotels, brothels, and with individuals and families. The results from my investigation are formulated to reflect the details my interlocutors mentioned most often and are presented using the words primarily from three of my informants, whose perspectives and biographies are described in particular detail.

## THE CONCEPT OF PROSTITUTION IN BAMAKO

In Mali, it is common for men to give presents to women who they are engaged in a sexual relationship with, and these presents can be anything from groceries to pocket money. Such gifts are similar to the European practice of inviting a woman to dinner or giving her flowers. It would, however, be misleading or insulting to offer money directly. Given the connection between gifts and sexual relations, it is difficult for non-Malians to clearly distinguish prostitution in Bamako, and identifying prostitutes is made more difficult because my informants assumed that many women take advantage of local conditions, such as engaging in sexual intercourse with the hope of receiving material payment in some form, and refer to such behavior, among others, as prostitution. When inhabitants of Bamako were asked about their understanding or definition of the term "prostitution", they explained it using a great range of interpretations that encompassed the various grey zones between private promiscuity and a commercial sex trade.

"Femmes sans morale" ("women without morals") includes all women who do not adhere to local values, including female monogamy and economic solidarity. The term can describe women who are not only promiscuous but also exploit men for personal gain, the latter of which my informants described using the term "une femme matérialiste" ("a materialistic woman"). Although such behavior is not synonymous with entrepreneurial activity, my informants sometimes referred to this as prostitution, particularly when they wanted to draw attention to the negative connotations associated with such behavior. At the same time, the professional exchange of sex for money is fully defined as prostitution (Neubauer 2014).

Informants from the trade have a much more distinguished definition of the concept of prostitution: women who exchange sex for money as part of an enterprise are referred to as *sunguruba* in Bamanakan. A *sunguruba* is "a woman who sells her body regularly" ("une femme qui se vend régulièrement") and "regularly" connotes "cinque soirées par semaine" ("five evenings a week") for some, while for others it is any exchange that happens on a regular basis if it is "une fois par mois" ("only once a month"). In a nutshell, a woman is a prostitute if she regularly sells her body in exchange for money and has sex with different men for such purposes. "Les autres ne sont pas des *sungurubaw*" ("the others are not *sungurubaw*"). Additionally, all informants agreed on the following point: the *sunguruba* trade is an economic activity that has a specific set of rules and prices and opens up various options that differ from other sexual relations and exchanges.[3]

My research focused on interviewing women who describe themselves as *sungurubaw*, those women who strive to professionalize and commodify the exchange of "sex for money". Their understanding of prostitution excludes non-professional forms of sexual exchange, such as intimate rendezvous that lack mutual agreement about the encounter and do not include a guaranteed payment for a service. Furthermore, these informants do not consider sexual relationships that have additional social dimensions beyond the sex-money exchange (such as the relationship between "sugar daddies" and young women) as professional prostitution, as such women do not apply, develop, or consider market-specific strategies.

## THE DIFFERENT FORMS OF PROSTITUTION

Prostitution in Bamako has many faces, from the corner trade to elite prostitution. The prices for each form of prostitution vary according to the clients' specific demands and the prostitute's negotiation skills. According to prices valid in 2009, the least expensive form of prostitution is corner prostitution, which ranges between 500 and 700 FCFA (about $1–1.30). In brothels, prices are generally between 1,000 and 2,000 FCFA (about $2 and $4), as women rent a room in the brothel and this justifies higher prices.[4]

The most common places for prostitution are the "bars chinois",[5] which are not only frequented by prostitutes and their clients but also by other people who might be there to watch sporting events such as soccer. In "bars chinois", the average price is 2,000 FCFA. Most often, the prostitute will rent a room in the bar for one night, and they drink beer and smoke to identify themselves as *sungurubaw*.[6]

Haggling is uncommon in the brothels, unless a client has special demands. On the corners and in the "bar chinois", clients can negotiate the price. This is similar to the process of negotiating a taxi fare in Bamako; a consensus about the appropriate price already exists, it only needs to be confirmed by the respective client and prostitute.

There are many bars in Bamako that function similarly to the "bars chinois" but are substantially more expensive.[7] Customers that frequent these bars are financially well-off, and they often prefer to take the prostitute to a hotel room that the man pays for rather than stay in the bar. This form of prostitution has a high price tag, and ranges from between 5,000 and 10,000 FCFA (about $20).[8] In the nightclubs, clients and prostitutes retreat to a hotel room or to the client's house. The call girls depicted in catalogues[9] in large hotels visit the client in his room on demand. For this form of prostitution, prices begin at 10,000 FCFA and are not restricted to a specific rate.[10]

The higher prices for the last three forms of prostitution depend on the prostitute's calculation of the clients' higher buying power. Furthermore, these meetings are very time-consuming because actors change locations and engage in more intense interactions. In contrast to brothel-prostitution, where a woman entertains clients at a frequency of one to three men per half hour, a call girl might spend the entire night with only one man and, accordingly, earn 30,000 FCFA or more.[11]

## ENTREPRENEURIAL STRATEGIES AND THE MARKET

A prostitute's income in Bamako might appear minimal, but it is important to note that during my field research in 2009, Mali's GNI was \$659.40.[12] In local terms, a prostitute's potential income is therefore remarkable.[13] Given the varying price scale for different forms of prostitution, this section focuses on why every form of prostitution, rather than just high-end prostitution, continues to exist in Bamako.

Individual prostitutes are neither required to work at certain places nor to practice a specific form of prostitution. The same prostitute can work in a brothel, while her picture might be found in a hotel catalogue.[14] It is therefore not the case that the enormous differences in earning potential varies from woman to woman but that most women are engaged in more than one form of prostitution. Prostitutes have the ability to choose the form of prostitution that will maximize the number of available opportunities as well as potential profits.

Decisions about prostitution, as the prostitutes explained during interviews, depend on demand, which fluctuates according to the day of the week they work.[15] For instance, attendance at discos is very limited during weekdays and therefore offers limited opportunity to earn money during the week. Additionally, the prostitutes added that they have to take the buying power of Bamako's inhabitants into account. In Bamako in 2010, 50.4% of its inhabitants lived below the poverty line,[16] and this is of particular importance as only one of the men I interviewed stated that he has never used the services of a *sunguruba*, and this implies that it is not an individual's expendable income that determines whether a man uses the services of a prostitute.[17]

For my interlocutors, the idea that a man can exist without regular sexual contact seemed completely absurd. For example, one interviewee explained that men need contact with the opposite sex to refuel their energy reservoir.[18] Most clients belong to Bamako's lower income groups, as my observations in bars and brothels compared to hotels and discos confirm. The more expensive the services of a prostitute are the fewer potential clients they have.[19] As such, it seems reasonable that prostitutes choose to serve the larger market with lower income clients rather than focus on high-end prostitution alone;[20] it is a matter of demand. Furthermore, prostitutes have to consider Muslim holidays like Ramadan, as such events reduce earning potential.[21]

In contrast to other entrepreneurs, prostitutes only require minor start-up capital since they do not have regular expenses. They only need to prepare for their working day, rent a room, or invest in their bodies to the extent they feel like doing so. This appears trivial but indicates that a prostitutes' financial risk is minimal.[22] Additionally, they are independent of any employer and do not need to find an investor. At the same time, however, the risk they take directly concerns their body and social standing. The prostitutes demonstrate a high degree of personal engagement to secure their daily expenses, and therefore, in Bamako they are considered "femmes qui font du business", "full-fledged businesswomen".

In Mande society, a well-performed task is directly associated with nobleness (Diawara 1996: 49).[23] This is also true for *sungurubaw*; their industriousness as well as the social value of their business is, to a certain degree, accepted. The manager (*gérant*) of a brothel explained: "elles font leur business pour nourir la famille et les villages. Ce ne sont pas des delinquents" ("they operate their business to feed their families and people in their villages. They are not criminals").[24] All informants, regardless of their social background, held similar opinions (among them a teacher and married women). They all referred to the prostitutes' activity as a "business". Professional prostitution implies that the expenses of daily life are covered by money earned from work, and prostitution is considered an income increasing activity.[25] This stands in contrast to non-professional prostitutes or women who move into prostitution grey zones in which the female body is exchanged for money and material goods alike. More importantly, there is no explicit articulation of a trade relation or a specific activity that has to be paid for. For example, the acceptance of sexual relations between men and female students are primarily materially motivated. These men can contribute to a woman's daily expenses or their concrete material desires, such as purchasing a motorcycle. Other women enter economically motivated sexual relationships when they demand various expensive presents following intercourse. Neither the professional *sunguruba* nor my other informants consider these women businesswomen, choosing instead to label them "materialists", a term that has negative moral connotations in Bamako. This, above all other considerations, determines the legitimacy and social bond of their trade and indicates a clear difference between professional prostitutes and other women who exist in the grey areas of prostitution.

The prostitutes' success therefore depends on their skills and the way in which they profit from local opportunities. Furthermore, the prostitutes need to adapt to the flexibility that Bamako's market necessitates, while the financial risk they take remains minimal. As such, they offer services based on the wide range of income obtained from prostitution to best suit the local market and optimize their access to clients.

## DEPENDENCY AND AUTONOMY—THE PROSTITUTES' NETWORKS

*Sungurubaw* work at different locations on a cyclical basis. For instance, a prostitute might work in a bar in Faladje neighborhood every Wednesday and in a club on Rue Princesse every Saturday.[26] This regularity is self-selected. The prostitutes are able to change their business choices; they are not tied to specific obligations (as employees) but act on their own behalf and rely on informal networks.

This leads to a relatively large radius of action; *sungurubaw* can determine when they work, who they work with, and the services they choose to offer.[27] If they use rooms in bars, they pay rent to the bar owner; the room is provided for the corresponding rent and there are no further obligations between the woman and the landlord. The bar owners use this revenue to pay their employees, including the bar staff that consists of bartenders, managers, and security. These individuals are, however, exclusively responsible to the bar owner and have no economic relationship with the prostitutes.

Accordingly, many prostitutes choose brothels on the basis of the personnel, i.e., whether they trust them.[28] Prostitutes are therefore not tied to a particular place or person, and this is largely the reason why dependent relationships between prostitutes and pimps, for instance, were entirely foreign for my informants.[29] They consider *sungurubaw* to be actors in a network of services rather than commodities or passive participants in a tragic economic concept.[30]

Informal work relationships are common in Bamako. In this respect, the commercial freedom of prostitutes is not unique. In contrast, the German economy is far more formalized and the notion of prostitution is attached to formally restricted parameters. Laws (ProstG[31]) on prostitution are one such formal factor, as they stipulate that prostitutes can, in terms of tax and social insurance laws, be employed (Von Galen 2004). In Germany, prostitutes are subordinated to complex and formal guidelines that are upheld on multiple levels, from the pimp to the taxman. Mali differs in this respect. Its various economic sectors are characterized by a greater informality, and this does not, interestingly, create insecurity for the prostitutes but enlarges their room to move in the trade.

## THE REGULARITIES OF THE MARKET

Prostitutes can face new decisions at any point; nevertheless, they also create regularities and reproduce a strong framework of internal regulations. This is not only connected to the service network they use but also to the rules they follow in their profession for protection. The choice of workplace depends, for example, on the quality of the location and business relationships the prostitutes have with other actors as well as, more importantly, social ties.

The regularly structured choice of workplace is an important factor for the optimization of a prostitute's success. In addition to a workplace with a good flow of customers, it is also important to have a circle of regular customers that not only provide a stable source of income but also the security that experience with these men offers.[32]

Awareness about the dangers of prostitution is always present among the women, and they therefore have to use their networks for protection. For example, one prostitute explained that her choice of workplace was tied to her preference for certain personnel, as they offered reliable protection.[33] In terms of security, the social network that exists among prostitutes also plays a role, as they use it to pass on information about clients and which men should be avoided. When prostitutes go to hotels or to homes with men, they tell their colleagues. With regard to security issues, prostitutes reproduce a tight set of rules that is fraught with moral connotations. They dictate, for example, that a prostitute does not service a client without protection from illness and attacks, and women who fail to adhere to such norms are labelled "morally corrupt" by other prostitutes.[34] The informality of prostitution is therefore not synonymous with a lack of rules. Prostitutes develop economic and social networks in order to optimize their business and to protect themselves from danger.

## MIGRATION AND SECRECY

Many of the professional prostitutes in Bamako come from other West African countries and these women move specifically to Mali to work as prostitutes and were therefore not stranded in prostitution accidentally. Some had already worked as prostitutes in their home country and wanted to increase their job opportunities by moving to Bamako, while others were advised by their friends that they could earn a lot of money as a prostitute there.[35] In this section, I focus on how prostitutes use various strategies, including migration, to optimize their market on a social level.

Labor migration is very common in West Africa (Hahn 2004; Jalloh 2007; McDougall and Scheele 2012). Prostitutes told me that they consider Bamako an attractive location for their business, as these female migrants believe that Mali is wealthier than some neighboring countries (especially Niger and Burkina Faso).[36] Furthermore, Islam is prevalent in Mali, and prostitutes from neighboring countries in the south, who consider themselves Christians, believe that the prostitution market is better in Bamako than in their home countries.[37]

The social environment is crucial for prostitute migration. Since prostitution in West Africa is heavily stigmatized, women try to keep their business secret from their families and neighborhoods. The more entangled in the profession they become, the more difficult it is for them to maintain the secret, and they therefore prefer to migrate; even prostitutes from Mali migrate to neighboring countries to maintain their secret. This does not, however, mean that there are no prostitutes in Bamako who originate from Mali as, for example, women from rural Mali come to Bamako because they assume that their secrecy is reasonably assured there.[38]

My research findings show that, while prostitution is not necessarily a result of labor migration, prostitution encourages migration. Like other entrepreneurs, prostitutes migrate to increase their business options. For these migrant prostitutes, the credo "go and try my luck elsewhere" is less important than the strategy to optimize income within the anonymity offered by a foreign country. For these women migration is an essential business strategy.

## THE MOTIVATION FOR PROSTITUTION

The notion that many African women have no other choice but go into prostitution (Kouassi 1986: 28–32) does not apply in Bamako. Although some women might have complicated life histories, they all indicated that they had previously pursued other forms of employment and could still do so; they just do not want to give up prostitution in exchange for the prospects of poor earnings associated with other jobs.[39]

In this context, financial needs range from basic sustenance to a longing for luxury. One prostitute recalled that after her father's death, she needed to find a way to pay for food and her sibling's higher education, while another said she wanted to do better than the local standard and live a luxurious life. Some indicated that they wanted to stay in prostitution only until they had reached specific goals.[40]

The interviewees emphasized that they were not forced to remain in the sex trade, and it would not be difficult for them to switch jobs. The idea that women in Africa would have limited opportunities to earn money (Tijani 2006: 81–83, 86–89) is incomprehensible for the prostitutes I spoke to. They feel that the limited amount of income they would earn from other jobs would be unacceptable. If they were not prostitutes, they would never be able to change or even maintain their standard of living. Accordingly, prostitutes consider their business in positive terms and speak of taking their lives in their own hands. As women without a university education and business contacts beyond low-income jobs, prostitution represents their chance to achieve an acceptable standard of living.[41] Given such evidence, it seems that for Bamako, the decision to become a prostitute is not synonymous with utmost economic constraints.

## A BUSINESS FOR WOMEN

In the explanations about why they chose prostitution, my informants often referred to the discourse of poverty. They assume that Africa's precarious financial situation is the cause of prostitution. Phrases like "c'est l'Afrique quoi, on est dans la misère" ("that's Africa, we are in misery")[42] underscore the fatalistic assessment of the continent's situation. In their discourses, the informants claim that women use prostitution as an opportunity to escape poverty: "Elles . . . font ça à cause de la pauvreté. Si les parents ne sont pas riches, si la fille, elle est jolie, elle va chercher à manger comme ça. La fille vient, elle donne 5,000 francs à son père—c'est l'Afrique quoi, on est dans la misère" ("They do this because of poverty. If the parents are not rich and the girl is beautiful, she uses the trade to secure food. The girl comes and gives her father 5,000 FCFA—that's Africa, we are in misery").[43] They usually ignore whether prostitution is motivated by a struggle for survival or rooted in the desire for luxury; in their minds, Africa is poor and the *sungurubaw* have therefore found a way to escape poverty.

In this sense, prostitutes give a positive connotation to their work since they are no longer subject to the "tragedy" of their continent. In contrast, my informants assume that men who have no alternative employment opportunities slip more easily into crime: "J'ai pris ma vie dans mes mains . . . un homme fait le delinquent" ("I took my life in my hands . . . [whereas] a man easily becomes a criminal").[44] It is striking that prostitutes do not feel excluded from the local labor market because of gender conceptualizations; instead, they use their gender as an additional resource. Indeed, prostitution is almost exclusively run by women, and this is in turn related to gender reversals in Bamako.

In Bamako, it is common that men give women gifts or money to express their affection regardless of the form a sexual encounter takes. This is surely not comparable to prostitution, as these couples are in a social relationship. Nevertheless, there seems to be a parallel to prostitution: all informants indicated that it is a man's duty to give women money, and men use their money to convince women to have sex with them. According to my informants, some women exploit this situation and slide into prostitution.[45]

Conversely, none of my informants saw a reason why a woman should convince a man with goods or money to enter a sexual relationship with her: Men are always "trop puissant" ("too powerful") and are therefore always looking for new women.[46] All my informants felt that it was absurd for a woman to give a man money for sex. Notwithstanding, my informants did acknowledge that there are men who allow themselves to have a "sugar mama" but these men are "pas normal" and lazy. Such behavior is an exception and not culturally accepted, as a man's duty is to take care of a woman and not vice versa.[47]

Although these statements do not fully reflect the reality in Bamako, the discourse that money flows from a man to a woman is so strong that my informants considered male prostitution in a heterosexual encounter nonexistent.[48] Only male homosexual prostitution is recognized, as in such a relationship a male customer gives money to another person. In comparison, female homosexual prostitution is considered nonexistent.[49] Prostitution therefore contributes to the preservation of a heteronormative pattern.

Although stark gender-based concepts are evident in discussions of prostitution, they are understood less as a form of women's marginalization than as an opportunity for women to earn money. MacGaffey (2002: 333) describes how local circumstances, whether social or economic, are used as an opportunity to tap into new economic niches. To an outside observer, these niches may appear chaotic or even illegitimate. Yet, according to Obbo (1980: 5), it is precisely these situations that offer new economic opportunities. Regardless of how the prostitution niche is recognized, it provides an opportunity for women to improve their economic status.[50]

## DISCOURSES ABOUT CULTURE AND CULTURAL DEGRADATION

This section focuses on the tension between legitimizing and discrediting prostitution in Bamako, and discusses the relationship between prostitution and other forms of sexual encounters. Kouassi, for example, sees a causal link between prostitution and the social heritage of "concubinage" in Ivory Coast.[51] Although prostitution may differ from place to place, my informants in Bamako emphasized the difference between "concubinage" and marriage on one hand and prostitution on the other. As I outlined at the beginning of this chapter, "concubinage" and marriage imply an ongoing social connection and social exchange;[52] they are not part of an economically defined barter. Prostitution contrasts with ongoing social exchanges insofar as the actors only engage in an economic relationship with each other and their interactions are determined by the market. The social interactions between *sungurubaw* and clients are a by-product of the trade and not part of the business model itself.

There are, of course, grey areas in prostitution as well as acts that were sometimes discredited by the informants as prostitution, such as when women enter relationships with men so that their material desires can be fulfilled. This behavior is massively condemned by prostitutes as a purely economic motivation disguised as a social one. Such behavior is considered immoral not only among prostitutes but also among other informants as well. Here, the prostitutes differentiate themselves from these women as they explicitly define themselves as businesswomen and refer to the others as materialists: "c'est des . . . matérialistes seulement, qui sont capable de tout . . . [moi] je fais mon business" ("they are just the materialists; they are capable of anything. I run my business").[53]

To be called a "materialist" is a serious insult in Mali. Such individuals are accused of turning away from local values and the associated (material) solidarity with others. The "materialistic woman" is accused of being corrupted by her affinity for money, and thereby eroding moral principles. This primarily involves the taboo associated with entering social relationships only for money (Schulz 2002: 813). That individuals would hoard resources and claim them all for themselves rather than share, or want to exploit people, is frowned upon in Bamako as well as elsewhere in West Africa (Maranz 2001: 13–15).[54]

When people in Bamako depict prostitutes in a negative light, they may also classify them as materialists. This is, nevertheless, not a prevalent opinion about them. While they are certainly accused of moral decay and of turning away from religion, they are also, at the same time, given a great deal of respect. People acknowledge that the term *sunguruba* also connotes women who sacrifice themselves for their families, share their money with others, and boost the economy. In this sense, they even settle, as Banégas and Warnier (2001: 6) argue, their "dette communautaire" ("debt to the community"). Prostitutes obtain the status of women who deal appropriately with their resources and can be trusted as business partners. Thus, my informants grant prostitutes a moral bonus and this depicts them not as exploitative individuals but as legitimate business partners.[55]

Prostitution is a double-edged sword, which is considered both immoral but also permissible within altered moral values. The sex trade, like other forms of economic exchange (Röschenthaler 2010: 161), does not exist in isolation but is always embedded in moral and cultural values. Even within the context of prostitution, there are rules that legitimize and regulate the trade. This is, according to Haller and Shore (2005), comparable to the dynamics of corruption, which is in the context of local values subjected to specific regulations and principles of conduct, despite its being classified as illegitimate.

Although prostitution is recognized as a legitimate business in terms of the market, the moral concerns of the actors cannot be ignored. My informants used positive characteristics to describe prostitution in an economic lens in the context of their employment, whereas they used negative characteristics to describe their actions in the context of morality. According to local beliefs, female sexuality is reserved for marriage and therefore the use of the female body as an economic resource represents the commodification of an inalienable good, and results in a down-conversion in Bohannan's (1962) terms, which is carried out under extreme conditions only and is negatively morally charged.[56] The moral illegitimacy of the exchange of the female body for money, as all my informants besides the prostitutes themselves explained, indicates that these women have turned away from religion, culture, and tradition, or that they were not socialized within these parameters in the first place. Some informants distinguished themselves from the *sungurubaw* to the degree that they did not even allow them to share a cultural sphere with them, as this statement exemplifies: "les femmes dans les maquis, ce sont des ivoiriennes, elles ont une autre morale, parce qu'elles ont une autre culture—au Mali, la religion interdit ça; les femmes maliennes ne font pas ça" ("the women in the nightclubs are from the Ivory Coast, and are attributed different morals because they have a different culture and religion—religion in Mali forbids Malians from doing such things").[57]

When Bamako's inhabitants judge prostitution as immoral. they contrast it with the assumed moral superiority of Malian villagers. The village is considered the place where cultural and traditional values continue to exist: "les villageois sont dans leur tradition, ils ne font pas ça [comme la prostitution]" ("the villagers live in their tradition, they do things in a way that prostitutes do not").[58] In fact, religious and cultural concepts or the relationship between local and western material culture in the villages are as mixed as they are in Bamako. In their discourses about the morality of prostitutes, my informants became blind to these circumstances and postulated instead that the villagers in Mali, with whom they themselves identified, lived up to traditional values unconditionally. Thus, the speakers discursively express (cf. Hobsbawm and Ranger 1983) their efforts to differentiate themselves from the prostitutes and fall into drastic moral judgments like: "le jour que'elle mourira, elle entrera directement dans l'enfer" ("on the day they die, they will go straight to hell").[59]

With "enfer", hell, the informants refer to a Muslim system of belief, which they use to make their negative opinion of prostitution explicit. They claim that turning away from Islam or any other religion[60] encourages an individual to become a prostitute. In contrast to such claims, some studies identify Islam as a reason for prostitution. Kouassi, for example, argues that in Abidjan, Islam excludes women from the business world, to the degree that they are basically forced to be economically reliant on prostitution (1986: 233–235). Regardless of the influence that religion may have on economic activities, in the "Mande world", no detectable causal link can be found between Islam, the displacement of women from the labor market, and prostitution. It is therefore important to develop an understanding of mixed religions: although Mali is considered predominantly Muslim, Islam is mixed with animistic worldviews and the Mande social order (De Bruijn and van Dijk 1997). Additionally, prostitutes in Bamako come from different ethnic groups, religions, and countries; as such, claims that Islam is a regulatory instrument for prostitution are only useful if Islam is considered an external factor.

Some of my informants identify that prostitution takes place outside religiously legitimate parameters. This discourse, however, has no influence on prostitutes in terms of their "dette communautaire" and the recognition of their economic role (as full-fledged businesswomen). Islam does, nevertheless, have some influence on the trade. For example, prostitutes have to cope with a decline in demand during Muslim holidays. Prayers and Islamic ablution offer the possibility to cleanse oneself of any form of sexual encounter, which is something that prostitutes' clients in particular use.[61] Thus, Islam is neither a cause of nor an impediment to prostitution, and it is also unable to condemn prostitutes beyond its moral reach because the prostitutes, independent of their religion, live in Bamako in a Muslim environment, and the behaviour of the inhabitants of Bamako and the prostitute's mostly Muslim customers influences their ideas of prostitution.

All my informants had an ambivalent attitude toward prostitution, whereby judgments about it remain complex. At the same time, they articulated the economic legitimacy and the moral illegitimacy of prostitution. These two elements exist in a moral tug of war, which, depending on the context, distorts the actors' assessment of the trade. Using different discourses, all groups differentiate themselves from each other. Thus, when prostitution is discussed and judged, it is done under the lens of local values, religion, and economic resources.

## MORALITY, PROSTITUTION, AND ITS SOCIOPOLITICAL RELEVANCE

The dynamics described above clearly indicate that prostitution is embedded in local concepts and in local parameters of judgment and meaning (Nunner-Winkler 1991: 79). Women adjust their behavior as a result of moral judgments about prostitution. They therefore develop strategies of secrecy, among which migration is one of the most common. Additionally, they often avoid contact with neighbors because they do not want to be confronted with the stigma of their profession.[62] Other women pay particular attention to not being mistaken for *sungurubaw*; they wear appropriate clothing (for example, not wearing mini-skirts) and avoid leaving their homes or going to bars at night alone.[63]

Moral judgment about prostitution is also evident in the legal framework. Most informants suggest that prostitution in Mali is illegitimate and therefore illegal. Accordingly, they fear the police and adapt their behavior in reaction to this fear. In raids, the police record the prostitutes' personal details and hold them in prison overnight at the nearest police station. If the prostitutes want to be released, they have to be ready to pay a fine of 5,000 FCFA.[64]

In fact, there is no legal regulation that defines prostitution, and police officers therefore interpret the trade to be "ni légal, ni illégal" ("neither legal nor illegal"). The police admitted that they try to curb prostitution, as it represents a "danger public" ("public danger") because the *sungurubaw* could spread disease and promote moral decay. Furthermore, the police want to give prostitutes the incentive to be tested on a regular basis and acquire a "carte de santé" ("clean bill of health"), with which they justify the fine for prostitutes who do not have one.[65]

The "carte de santé" was launched as a cooperation with the "brigade de moers" and local clinics.[66] It is a medical card that is specifically used for prostitutes and expires when the owner refuses to be regularly checked for STDs. Few prostitutes know that this card exists, and in this respect they feel harassed by the police. Prostitution is not subject to specified legal constraints and the fine for prostitution is not legally regulated but arbitrarily applied by the police.[67] Additionally, NGOs are also involved in curbing prostitution, using educational programs for girls and women to dissuade them from entering the sex trade. NGOs hold the culture and underdevelopment of the country responsible for prostitution, and paint *sungurubaw* as victims of social inequality and underdevelopment and support local development as a means to reduce prostitution.[68]

A distinctive feature of prostitution is that sociopolitical relevance does not result from the businesswomen's social action. A different dynamic unfolds among other businesspeople, such as those in the Congo, who assume a leading role in development (MacGaffey 2002: 339). In the context of prostitution, ideas about development are attached to the trade from the outside and contribute to the moral connotations associated with it.

The prostitutes do not see themselves in a political context, and in most cases they know nothing about women's rights programs that are applicable to their situation.[69] Nevertheless, in connection with prostitution, certain dynamics have emerged as sociopolitical (mis)understanding, ranging from the unsavory fines levied by the police to the feminist programs held by NGOs. In any case, prostitution gives rise to the generation of other sources of income that are not directly related to the sex trade, which profit from the local moral conception of the trade. In this context, the discourse about prostitution loses its status as a market or an opportunity to achieve a higher standard of living; instead NGOs' staff and the police merely consider the trade a social problem—as a "danger public"—or the waste product of a developing country.

## ECONOMIC AND SOCIAL SUCCESS IN CONFLICT

After the digression about the morally related interdependencies between prostitution and its environment, it is not surprising that prostitutes' socioeconomic status does not rise despite their recognition as businesswomen and their sometimes extreme success that is normally accompanied by a rise not only economically but also socially in Africa. When an individual has a lot of money, they can pay their "dette communitaire" and they thereby have (political) power and recognition in their local communities. This status is reflected in material culture, as successful individuals distinguish themselves through their clothing or other symbols, which are simultaneously used to flaunt their wealth (Banégas and Warnier 2001: 9).

In contrast, for prostitutes such characteristics of success are only evident to a limited degree. Although they have a lot of money and are able to support their families and villages and enjoy a strong reputation at home, such a reputation is only ascribed to those who are able to conceal their profession. Their success is therefore not determined in the context of the actual market. Accordingly, prostitutes do not use aspects of material culture to identify themselves as wealthy prostitutes; instead they are distinguished as wealthy women. Due to the risk of being exposed, they prefer to retreat from their own community, and primarily interact with their home village by sending money and visiting occasionally rather than interacting intensely with their homes.[70]

Regardless of the awareness of the high-level purchasing power *sungurubaw* have, prostitution is located in the context of emergency conversion.

The trade itself remains connected to the stigma of the continual plight of women ("on est dans la misère"). If prostitutes wanted to convert their economic success into social status, they would have to reinvest in different businesses—as the Kenyan prostitutes described by Bujra (1975) did by investing in property or their own children's education. My informants all felt that education is associated with the chance of high and undoubted economic success. As such, prostitutes hope that the second generation's socioeconomic status will rise.

## CONCLUSION

In Bamako, prostitution is a business subjected to special characteristics that are not created by the trade itself but influence it significantly. Everyone involved in the business understands prostitution as part of the market and adheres to the respective rules of the trade. They respect the agreements between the different service providers and the sex workers' social and economic networks and take them as seriously as in other markets.

Women make use of an economic niche, which is based on local discourses about men and women and reflected in the great demand for prostitution. To this end, they embrace a minimal financial risk, while exposing themselves to greater social and moral ramifications. They generate a relatively high purchasing power, which is only partially perceived as socioeconomic success. The moral connotations of the business, based on the principle of emergency conversion, do not allow for social recognition of the economic success that comes from prostitution. Therefore, prostitutes often hide their profession and only highlight the economic resources, and this often results in social isolation and migration.

Islam contributes to the specific local understanding of prostitution, which neither favors nor prevents the trade. I have tried to show that the economic achievement that results from prostitution is not directly associated with socially accepted success; instead it is the local discourses that decide whether a business is considered successful or not. It is important to note, however, that the prostitutes are not the pawns of locally related inequality. Above all, they are actors who have chosen to enter the trade, considering it a rational decision. *Sungurubaw* in Bamako are not passive commodities; they are instead active businesswomen.

## NOTES

1. The prostitutes and other informants answered my question about whether there was any pimping or pressure with a lack of understanding: "*je ne comprends pas bien la question*"—"I do not understand your question well". During all my interviews, only one male informant mentioned pimping at all.

2. One exception would certainly be the Wahabits, who understand themselves as strict Muslims. Notwithstanding, I have observed Wahabits who were clients in brothels.
3. *Sungurubaw* is the plural of *sunguruba*. This information comes from different prostitutes and bartenders, i.e., prostitutes from notes 6 and 8, informants 5 and 24. Additional information comes from a female prostitute who works and lives in Bamako, is between twenty and thirty years old, was born in Mali, is unmarried, and has no children. She works most often in a brothel in the Daoudabougou neighborhood.
4. Prostitute note 3.
5. The *bars chinois* are run by Chinese. The drinks are cheap and the rooms are rented to all types of guests. The room prices are about 2,000 FCFA for two hours, but the prostitutes get a price of 2,000 FCFA for the entire night, which the owners justify because the prostitutes attract clients (according to an informant, male, bartender in a hotel in Bamako, born in Bamako, 28 years old).
6. Prostitute, female, originates from Niger, works predominantly in a "bar chinois". A friend told her that she would be able to earn a lot of money if she worked as a prostitute in Bamako. She wants to move to Spain where she intends to open a hair salon. She earns her start-up capital by working as a prostitute.
7. The price of a beer in the bar Le Titan is 1,200 FCFA. In the "bars chinois", a beer does not cost more than 800 FCFA.
8. Prostitute, female, grew up in Burkina Faso, 36 years old, not married, has children, works primarily on the Rue Princesse.
9. The catalogues present photographs and short profiles of the prostitutes. The employees of the hotels mediate between the prostitutes and the clients.
10. Prostitute note 8.
11. Prostitutes notes 3, 8. It should be added that prostitutes have regular clients but these contacts do not necessarily represent long-term relationships.
12. According to the United Nations Statistics Division; see http://data.un.org/CountryProfile.aspx?crName=MALI.
13. As the prostitutes' income varies, I will not identify any concrete income but refer instead to the "potential income" from prostitution.
14. Prostitutes notes 3, 6, 8.
15. Prostitutes notes 6, 8.
16. According to the World Bank Group; see http://data.worldbank.org/indicator/SI.POV.DDAY.
17. My male informants were between 18 and 60 years old, with different socioeconomic backgrounds.
18. Informant: male, student, single, 25 years old, born in Bamako.
19. This is also reflected in the distribution of my informants, as most belong to lower socioeconomic strata.
20. In Bamako there is little sex-tourism. As such, foreign clients are rarely found. Businessmen who come to Bamako mostly reside in hotels and frequently demand the services of call girls.
21. Prostitutes note 6, 8.
22. Personal risks are explained in the section "Migration and Secrecy".
23. The "Mande world" is made up of different ethnic groups and social categories. It extends across several countries in West Africa (see, for example, Conrad and Frank 1995).
24. Informant: *gerant* in a brothel, thirty to forty years old, single, born in Senegal, grew up in Bamako.
25. Prostitutes, notes 3, 6, 8.

26. Prostitute note 8. The Rue Princesse is an entertainment district where everything is more expensive than in other districts.
27. Prostitutes notes 3, 5.
28. Prostitutes notes 3, 6.
29. Prostitutes notes 3, 6, 8. It should not be assumed that there is no forced prostitution in Bamako, but it is uncommon and was not reported by my informants.
30. Police and NGO staff are exceptions and do not agree with this statement (see section "Morality, prostitution, and its socioeconomic relevance").
31. ProstG is a law that regulates prostitution in Germany (Von Galen 2004).
32. Prostitutes notes 3, 6, 8.
33. Prostitute note 6.
34. Prostitutes notes 6, 8.
35. Prostitutes notes 3, 6, 8.
36. Prostitutes notes 3, 6, 8; informants notes 5, 18.
37. Prostitutes notes 6, 8.
38. Prostitutes notes 3, 6, 8; informant note 24.
39. Prostitutes notes 3, 6, 8.
40. Prostitutes notes 3,6, 8.
41. Prostitutes notes 6, 8.
42. Informant: male, student, 27 years old, born in Ivory Coast, but lived most of his childhood in Mali, single, no children.
43. Informant note 42.
44. Prostitute note 8.
45. Informant: female, between thirty and forty years of age, married with children, employed as a hairdresser in a salon in Bamako; prostitutes notes 3, 6, 8.
46. Prostitutes notes 3, 6, 8; informant note 18. "Trop puissant" translates as "too powerful" and implies a pronounced sexual potency.
47. Prostitutes note 3; informant note 5. Translation: "not normal", implies a deviation from what is locally considered right.
48. I met one man who identified himself as a prostitute. His clients are mostly white women.
49. Informant note 5.
50. Like other entrepreneurs, improved economic status depends on individual skills.
51. According to Kouassi (1986: 218–220), "concubinage" describes a social constellation whereby women do not have a marital bond with a man and therefore are at the disposal of men, who must in turn look out for their physical well-being.
52. Certainly women can be placed into arranged marriages in exchange for a dowry. In this sense, people enter a reciprocal agreement that includes diverse social dimensions beyond trade (cf. Camara 2002: 185–187).
53. Prostitute notes 6).
54. Informant note 24.
55. Informant note 24.
56. Here, an inalienable good is traded, or a high-value bargaining chip, which is offset by its price, the way in which family jewelry is in western countries at times of financial distress (Bohannan 1962).
57. The informant is an electronics retailer and a native of Bamako. He is married and has several children. He is between thirty and forty years of age. Indeed, a number of prostitutes are migrants from Ivory Coast.
58. The informant is a school teacher. She is between forty and fifty years old, married, has several children, and was born in Mali.

59. This informant is *gardien* of a residential building. He is a native Malian and came to Bamako looking for work. He is between twenty and thirty years old, unmarried, and childless.
60. Informant note 45.
61. Informant note 42.
62. Prostitutes notes 3, 6, 8.
63. Informant: female, unemployed, 22 years old, engaged, born in Mali but grew up in Togo, currently living in Bamako.
64. Prostitutes notes 3, 6, 8.
65. Informant: male, police commissioner, married with children, native of Bamako, 29 years old.
66. Informant: female, employee of the NGO *Danaya So;* she is between thirty and forty years old, lives in Bamako.
67. Informant note 65.
68. Informant note 66.
69. Prostitutes notes 3, 8.
70. Prostitutes notes 6, 8.

## REFERENCES

Banégas, Richard and Jean-Pierre Warnier. 2001. *Les nouvelles figures de la réussite et du pouvoir*. Politique Africaine 82: 5–21.
Bohannan, Paul. 1962. 'Introduction'. In: Paul Bohannan and George Dalton (eds). *Markets in Afrika*. Evanston: Northwestern University Press, 1–26.
Bryk, Felix. 1928. *Neger-Eros. Ethnologische Studien über das Sexualleben bei Negern*. Berlin and Köln: Marcus & Weber.
Bujra, Janet. 1975. 'Women "Entrepreneurs" of early Nairobi'. *Canadian Journal of African Studies* 9, 2: 213–234.
Camara, Ibrahima. 2002. *Le cadre rituel de l'éducation au Mali l'exemple du Wassoulou*. Paris: L'Harmattan.
Conrad, David and Barbara Frank. 1995. *Status and Identity in West Africa: Nyamakalaw of Mande*. Bloomington: Indiana University Press.
De Bruijn, Mirjam and Han van Dijk. 1997. 'Peuls et Mandingues. Dialectique des constructions identitaires'. In: Mirjam de Bruijn and Han van Dijk (eds). *Hommes et Sociétés*. Leiden and Paris: Afrika Studiecentrum, 13–29.
Diawara, Mamadou. 1996. 'Was bedeutet " arbeiten" in der Welt der Mandé?' In: Kurt Beck and Gerd Spittler (eds). *Arbeit in Afrika*. Hamburg: LIT, 49–68.
Giesen, Rose-Marie and Gunda Schumann. 1980. 'Prostitution als Emanzipation?' In: Dietlinde Gipser (ed.). *Wenn Frauen aus der Rolle fallen*. Weinheim and Basel: Beltz, 141–168.
Hahn, Hans Peter. 2004. 'Zirkuläre Arbeitsmigration in Westafrika und die "Kultur der Migration"'. *Africa Spectrum* 39, 3: 381–404.
Haller, Dieter and Chris Shore. 2005. *Corruption: Anthropological Perspectives*. London: Pluto.Hobsbawm, Eric and Terence Ranger (eds). 1983. *The Invention of Tradition*. Cambridge: Cambridge University Press.
Jalloh, Alusine. 2007. 'Muslim Fula business elites and politics in Sierra Leone'. *African Economic History* 35: 89–104.
Kiremiere, Merab Kambamu. 2007. *Prostitution in Windhoek, Namibia: An Exploration of Poverty*. Klein Windhoek: Namibia Institute for Democracy.
Kouassi, Goli. 1986. *La Prostitution en Afrique. Un cas, Abidjan*. Abidjan: Nouvelles Editions Africaines.

Kreutzer, Mary and Corinna Milborn. 2008. *Ware Frau: Auf den Spuren moderner Sklaverei von Afrika nach Europa*. Salzburg: Ecowin.

MacGaffey, Janet. 2002. 'Survival, innovation, and success in time of trouble: what prospects for Central African entrepreneurs?' In: Alusine Jalloh and Toyin Falola (eds). *Black Business and Economic Power*. Rochester: University of Rochester Press, 331–346.

Mansfeld, Christine. 2005. *Vom Dogon-Land nach Bamako. Diskurspraxen zu Gender und Migration am Beispiel der Mädchenjugend in Mali*. Frankfurt am Main: Brandes & Apsel.

Maranz, David. 2001. *African Friends and Money Matters: Observations from Afrika*. Dallas: SIL International Publications in Ethnography.

McDougall, James and Judith Scheele (eds). 2012. *Saharan Frontiers: Space and Mobility in Northwest Africa*. Bloomington: Indiana University Press.

Neubauer, Inès. 2014. *Prostitution in Bamako, Mali. Akteurinnen zwischen Geld und Moral*. Frankfurt: Brandes & Apsel.

Nunner-Winkler, Gertrud (ed.). 1991. *Weibliche Moral die Kontroverse um eine geschlechtsspezifische Ethik*. Frankfurt and New York: Campus.

Obbo, Christine. 1980. *African Women: Their Struggle for Economic Independence*. London: Zed Books.

Röschenthaler, Ute. 2010. 'Tauschsphären. Geschichte und Bedeutung eines wirtschaftsethnologischen Konzepts'. *Anthropos* 105: 157–177.

Schulz, Dorothea. 2002. ' "The world is made by talk": female fans, popular music, and new forms of public sociality in urban Mali'. *Cahiers d'Études africaines* 168, 4: 797–829.

Tijani, Hakeem Ibikunle. 2006. *Nigeria's Urban History Past and Present*. Lanham: University Press of America.

United Nations Statistics Division. 'Country profile: Mali'. *UNdata*. Accessed 1 October 2012. http://data.un.org/CountryProfile.aspx?crName=MALI

Von Galen, Margarete. 2004. *Rechtsfragen der Prostitution: Das ProstG und seine Auswirkungen*. München: C. H. Beck.

World Bank Group. 'Poverty headcount ratio at $1.25 a day'. *World Bank Data*. Accessed 1 October 2012. http://data.worldbank.org/indicator/SI.POV.DDAY

# 10 Everyday Entrepreneurs and Big Men

## Facets of Entrepreneurship in Goma, Democratic Republic of Congo

*Silke Oldenburg*

This chapter analyzes facets of entrepreneurship in Goma, DR Congo.[1] It is guided by entrepreneurs' emic understanding of vibrant economic activities that embrace innovative figures spanning a continuum from everyday entrepreneurs (*débrouillards*) to Big Men. Despite and even because of the structural voids left by the protracted armed conflict and the informalization of socioeconomic spheres, Congolese entrepreneurs act dynamically in an urban landscape characterized by complex routes to social mobility, alternative economic niches, and overlapping political, military, and economic networks of distribution. The urban elite of Big Men, often portrayed as cunning criminals, is juxtaposed to everyday entrepreneurs, who are mostly reduced to hustling for mere survival. Yet, their positions, perspectives, and social relations offer similar features while differing in the extent of their networks and resulting opportunities. Therefore, this chapter argues for an analytical openness that also includes the assumed victims of chronic political instability who nevertheless find ways to be entrepreneurial in their everyday lives. However, the ones who fail to seize opportunities are pushed out of the entrepreneurial continuum where style, self-images, and local conceptions of modernity produce a particularly local version of a protestant work ethic.

Two significant facets of entrepreneurial potential and economic activities will be presented against the background of Goma's contested urban space. Goma's economic transformation on one hand, and particularly its interpretation by entrepreneurs on the other, cannot be considered without embedding it in Kivu's turbulent history. Since the 1990s, the Kivu Provinces in eastern Congo have been the epicenter of the region's armed conflicts and are constantly confronted with changing political, military, and socioeconomic constellations. Furthermore, the high influx of humanitarian agencies led to a market of intervention,[2] a contact zone where different entrepreneurial styles and cultures meet. Consequently, Goma's economic sectors, as well as the primarily rural, so-called war economy in Goma's hinterland, create a dynamic and rapidly changing context, depicted in contrasting images of either a "cursed city" or a "boomtown".

At the slopes of the active volcano Nyiragongo, the trafficking and trade of natural resources, the geographic location as a border town, the influx of refugees, internally displaced persons (IDP), and working migrants, as well as the presence of numerous international actors, have tremendously led to a far-reaching reorganization of Goma's urban space, its power constellations and, accordingly, its economic agenda. The politically unstable urban space is, however, by no means synonymous with paralysis and apathy; instead, dynamics of armed conflict and social velocity provide Goma's population with extensive economic opportunities to increase their social status, wealth, and power (Büscher and Vlassenroot 2010; Doevenspeck and Morisho 2012; Raeymaekers 2007). However, understandings of statehood, (in)formal economic activities, and social relationships are interpreted and negotiated against the background of general unpredictability, institutional voids, and structural constraints (Greenhouse 2002; Makhulu, Buggenhagen, and Jackson 2010).

Afro-pessimistic perspectives tend to focus on the relationship between the neoliberal era, growing stagnation, and social dead ends. In such approaches, individuals are often reduced to mere extras who try to adapt and respond to their environment rather than being dynamic, creative, or transformative social actors. This is also virulent in war-torn eastern DR Congo: external perspectives that center on the allegedly disintegrating state and images of Kivu's prominent war economy promote potentially pessimistic prognostics that equate entrepreneurs with cunning criminals rather than ascribing them characteristics like effective planning and innovative action.

Reducing Kivu's economy to a war economy only fails to take into account the nuanced power dynamics and complex identities from which entrepreneurial potential can develop in the everyday even if there are huge structural constraints (Raeymaekers, Menkhaus, and Vlassenroot 2008: 12). Obviously, opportunities are not distributed equally, with only a small urban elite of Big Men (locally: *mu/bakubwa, homme d'affaires, grands patrons*) profiting in a lucrative way. Yet, the often assumed victims of this context of chronic violent conflict, the *débrouillards* or *biznizeurs*, are able due to personal skills, knowledge, and the juggling of networks to engage innovatively with Big Men who, the other way around, will provide economic possibilities as well as protection and social security.

This chapter sheds light on the social relations in what I define as an interlinked continuum of Big Men on the one side and everyday entrepreneurs on the other. These dynamics may be related to cultural, social, political, or military phenomena and most often they overlap. Goma's economic sector therefore includes a non-negligible scope of patron-client networks for a variety of actors who operate using different social resources, form alliances, and exploit or manipulate opportunities. As conflict opens up spaces for alternative political and economic structures, Goma's urban elites are not the only ones who benefit by establishing strategic alliances with armed actors from the Congolese Wars; everyday entrepreneurs also engage flexibly in new forms of patronage relations or enter a transformed service industry to approach different economic networks with different perspectives. Often, it is the Big Men who appropriate the institutional void of the formal structures by organizing control and alternative forms of governance in contexts of protracted political conflict (Utas 2012).

This chapter argues that the concept of entrepreneurship should be extended to an emic perspective of innovation and benefit-oriented economic activity that brings equally Big Men and everyday entrepreneurs to the fore. The figure of the Big Man is emically strongly associated with financial and economic success as well as social visibility, which may blend particular economic, political, and military spheres of influence. With the term everyday entrepreneurs, I am referring to those who are known locally and in literature as *débrouillards* or *biznizeurs*. Using interpretive skills, flexibility, forward-looking, and perseverance, they act in a similar fashion as *"grands patrons"*, yet with modest results and without being at the center of scholarly attention. This does not mean to overemphasize agency or the often described heroic "genius of survival" (Jackson 2010), yet demonstrates how different entrepreneurial styles emerge and reveal a local form of a protestant work ethic, which differentiates between entrepreneurial and non-entrepreneurial figures and activities in Goma. The main argument is that Big Men as well as everyday entrepreneurs accumulate, invest, distribute, perform, innovate, and are bound together through reciprocal yet flexible networks. Not only war, but also the humanitarian presence and its manifold actors enhance opportunities for getting into contact and establishing social relations. Drawing on de Boeck's description of the "urban hunter" whose primary achievement is the creation of social networks to make investments work, I illustrate facets of Goma's vibrant entrepreneurship that works despite—and even because of—the protracted armed conflict. The reformulation of social values, intergenerational conventions, and sociopolitical power relations that surround eastern Congo's natural resources will be at the center of this discussion.

This chapter consists of three parts. In the first section, I focus on Goma not as a place of shadows and struggles but as an urban fabric that stems from a range of historically based social representations of Goma's economic spheres. The second section approaches the perspectives and positions of entrepreneurs and evaluates individual actors' endeavors and missteps. It illustrates the different forms that economic engagements take and therewith underscores the range of entrepreneurial influence on the urban space. The final section focuses on entrepreneurs' analytical skills and depicts the relations between Big Men and everyday entrepreneurs. Furthermore, I demonstrate how by vilifying "non-entrepreneurial" attitudes or failure, everyday entrepreneurs in particular try to differentiate themselves by binding social status to analytical skills. While features of Weber's rational version of a capitalist work ethic are locally celebrated in the form of truisms, they are adapted to everyday life in a context of protracted armed conflict where being dynamic, smart, and boastful are no contradiction at all.

## ICI, ÇA BOUGE: GOMA BETWEEN VILLE MAUDITE AND BOOMTOWN

Goma is a hub of heterogeneous worlds and rambling aspirations, of dreams and fantasies. Paralysis and an energetic bustle are indicators of the coexistence of contradictions, including an extreme and far-reaching "social velocity" that coincides with stagnation (Mbembe and Nuttall 2004: 49). As such, Goma can be understood as a dynamic and unfolding arena in which various facets of entrepreneurship are negotiated, embodied, and are at the same time in close interplay with the conflict context, social positions, and local perspectives.

In contrast to perspectives that depict Goma as a place of shadows and struggles that feed the illusion of deviance, I approach Goma through studies that focus on the nexus of urbanity and political instability. These studies characterize the activities in the city as based on flexibility, tentative bricolage, and the prominent all-embracing catchphrase *débrouillardise* without neglecting the structural constraints (see, for example, De Boeck and Plissart 2004; De Villers, Monnier, and Jewsiewicki 2002; MacGaffey 1991, 1993; Trefon 2004). Consequently, I propose that Goma can be read less as a city of potential failure and more as a city of excessive meaning production that oscillates between threats and opportunities. This perspective contextualizes the structural limits and possibilities for entrepreneurship emerging from organizational voids in Goma's institutional realm.

"Goma? It's a well-organized disorder". This short statement from Claude, a twenty-eight-year-old traffic cop, reveals the dialectic of order and disorder in Goma. Claude exuded the ambivalence that characterizes life in Goma and suggested that the reigning disorder allows order and brings two levels of interpretation to the discussion. First, disorder is well organized, as it just works because it has some form of a system; second, disorder is also well organized because it can be profitable for those with entrepreneurial skills. This quote provides a meaningful illustration of the degree to which the context determines entrepreneurial potential, while also differentiating what entrepreneurship is—depending on how successful actors appropriate the context and interact with it. Claude's words stress the paradoxical interpretation of Goma as the epicenter of armed conflicts on one hand, while it is also an economic boomtown on the other. This apparent contradiction highlights the rich repertoire of local perceptions and social imaginations about Goma as an urban space and its economic potential. In this sense, the oxymoron of a "well-organized disorder" is fundamental for understanding the manifold activities and experiences of entrepreneurs in Goma, or as Janet MacGaffey entitled one of her articles: "How to survive and become rich amidst devastation" (1983).

MacGaffey's work has increased awareness about Congolese entrepreneurship, providing profound insight into the economic processes that led to the dissolution of "Mobutucracy". In the harsh context of extreme inflation and virtually non-existing wages during the 1980s, MacGaffey was astonished that the majority of people found their way despite shortages and precarious conditions. Furthermore, she observed that many of them were women, who developed a livelihood through entrepreneurship (Mac-Gaffey 1983). She described this social practice of *débrouillardise* (literally: resourcefulness) as a key element of the so-called "second economy", which she depicted as a highly defined yet officially undocumented phenomenon. According to MacGaffey, entrepreneurs from the second economy represent a form of resistance against the "powerful", as their actions along with the alternative economic style both work within and change the local economy (MacGaffey 1987: 23–25). *Débrouillardise* is laden with a variety of con-notations and is often interpreted as "economic disengagement from the state"; a weak state that is neither willing nor able to provide infrastructure and service for its inhabitants (MacGaffey 1988: 171). As such, *débrouil-lardise* is described primarily as a survival strategy.

Alongside the economic elites in eastern Congo, who often dominate man-ifold areas of society, everyday entrepreneurs, too, are able to find means to increase their status and to augment their access to resources and local posi-tions. This requires flexibility and versatility, concepts that Gomatraciens often use ironically, but also reflectively as guiding principles (*il faut être souple*; "you need to be flexible"). At an institutional level, this multiplic-ity implies that private or international actors and organizations take over formal state structures and establish private schools, health centers, and trade associations. These are just a few fields of action for entrepreneurial initiatives to seize opportunities in the midst of economic mismanagement and contexts of chronic crisis. Accordingly, it is necessary to understand the population's social representations of Goma, and their commentary on the pursuits and struggles of economic actors over the course of history. To document Goma's economic transformation, in the following, three indica-tors illustrate the shifts in the sociopolitical balance of power that affect likewise entrepreneurial activity.

## FROM SLEEPING BEAUTY TO BOOMTOWN: THE TRANSFORMATION OF GOMA'S URBAN SPACE

Founded as a trading post in 1910, Goma attracted working migrants and traders to the urban space. Therefore, Goma is emically described as being "cosmopolitan", a melting pot in which identity acts as a crucial fault line for misunderstandings, tensions, and conflicts. Since the end of the colo-nial period, issues of political representation and economic dominance have been articulated using the vernacular of autochthony.[3] This trend was exac-erbated by the fall of Mobutu and the onset of armed conflicts in the early 1990s that led to the emergence of complex and interdependent power rela-tions with politicians, business owners, and armed groups' manipulation of resources (Tull 2005; Vlassenroot and Raeymaekers 2004). Conflict dynamics have not only transformed access to land, resources, and political representation, they have changed urban space over the course of the last twenty years as well. Among today's estimated population of nearly one million inhabitants, the three most populous groups in Goma, the Nande, the Bashi, and the Rwanduphones, claim political and economic dominance on the basis of origin, demographic size, and economic influence.

Economic weight, in the case of Goma, is bolstered by the blending of politico-economic and military spheres. The relative absence of the state and formal regulations as well as the presence of violent conflict opened up new spaces for entrepreneurial initiatives. Such openness has provided both the Big Men and the everyday entrepreneurs with room to maneuver. However, it has also led to harsh competition, and increased intergenerational and interethnic tensions. Corruption, repression, and fraud have become an everyday and legitimized social practice, which has paved the road to great economic success and status, yet only for a small group. Prominently, "old elites" privileged by Mobutu's system became with his downfall subjected to competition. Some managed to expand their areas of activity by engaging with new actors or designing alternative economic agendas, but most of them lost gradually their influence in town to newly emerging elites, the so-called "nouveaux riches" (Büscher and Vlassenroot 2010).

As will be shown in this chapter, the amalgamation of economic and military actors, or at least their proximity, became highly accentuated over the last two decades. This interdependence is evident not only in land ownership, which underscores the degree to which conflict dynamics have transferred from the rural hinterland to urban space. Through Goma's sprawl, the result of an influx of internally displaced persons, migrant workers, international staff, and the restructuring of the urban landscape, land has become a scarce resource and a coveted commodity. Whoever can invests in land and real estate, and the business with plots is very lucrative.

## DANCE ON THE VOLCANO

Goma's development from a "sleeping beauty" to a boomtown not only indicates the transformation of urban space but also a change in the way Goma's active Nyiragongo volcano (3,470 m) is perceived. The Nyiragongo frames Goma's characteristic silhouette and its fertile soil substantiates Kivu's granary reputation. Yet, obviously, the volcano constitutes a natural risk—the volcano has erupted three times in the last hundred years: in 1894, 1977, and most recently in 2002. This sharpened the sociopolitical situation in Goma itself. For example, the eruption in 1977 led many Nande traders to draw their money from Goma to invest in the Grand Nord[4] as a means to protect themselves against further property loss. Staggered temporary labor migration from South Kivu as well as the increased visibility of Rwanda phone[5] communities fueled economic competition and heightened interethnic tensions in the aftermath.

The tremendous volcanic eruption of 2002 covered one-third of the city with lava and destroyed many Gomatraciens' livelihoods and savings. As a consequence, interurban migration broadened demographics on the outskirts of the city and forced many dwellers to move. This created new markets for entrepreneurs who provided building materials and other services needed for reconstruction. Despite the risk and probability of future volcanic eruptions and a continually tense political situation in the region, actors continue to invest in Goma. In contrast to other urban centers in the region, Goma is considered affordable, livable, and full of ambiance: *"ici pour manger, on trouve facilement"* ("you can easily find food here") or *"tu manques pas à manger"* ("you won't be short of food here"). Verbs like *manger/bouffer* and *kula* symbolize far more than the mere satisfaction of hunger or cheap food prices; they position Goma as a city of opportunities in which various forms of *bizniz*[6] are available. Volatility and a fast pace are part of the doxic experience to the degree that patience, persistence, and courage become central social values that are used to deal with the uncertainties of life and provide a basis for entrepreneurial potential in a setting of protracted violent conflict.

## GOMA'S MARKET OF INTERVENTION

With the statement, "La où toutes les rebellions commencent" ("There, where all the rebellions begin"), Valentin, a student, characterizes Goma as an important political and military center. This is particularly due to its role in the RCD[7] occupation supported by Rwanda and Uganda (1998–2002). During this period, Goma became the "siège de rebellion", with an emerging *comptoir*-economy[8] along with a fast dollarization. In the resource trade, the interdependence of various sectors becomes very obvious and demonstrates entrepreneurs' remarkable influence on the urban landscape (Vlassenroot and Büscher 2009: 6). The political economy of the comptoir (Jackson 2001: 126) is associated with the urbanization of the periphery, which has placed border regions like the Kivu at the hub of trade and exchange and makes it ideal hunting grounds for "adventurers" (De Boeck 2001: 551). The emergence of profitable mineral trade as well as the high influx of NGOs into the region catalyzed the infrastructure projects that gave Goma's construction boom its face (Oldenburg 2014: 50). Big Men operate a flourishing trade in cassiterite or coltan, and invest in land ownership, gas stations, or tourist infrastructure. Not everyone, however, has benefitted from the economic upswing to the same degree. Often the amalgamation of economic, political, and military actors is highlighted as being "mystical". Discourses about miracles, and figures from the Pétit Prédateur to the Grand Piffpaffeur (figuratively: small and big gangster) and from adventurers to fraudsters accompany stories about Goma's rise. There are allusions to "hidden interests", or those who have forged their own interests, such as importing consumer goods, technological products, or vehicles from Dubai and Mombasa.

Many of these imports are designed for international organizations, which, as a result of the presence of genocide refugees and the Congo Wars, are such dominant economic factors in Goma that Büscher and Vlassenroot (2010: 263) aptly refer to Goma as "NGOpol". The needs of the multitude of humanitarian organizations and their employees have created new economic niches and forms of employment, and, accordingly, a fresh green dollar rules over the worn bills of local currency (Oldenburg Forthcoming).

All these areas have been subjected to adjustments as a result of both the persistent armed conflict and the presence of international organizations against the background of weak formal structures. These shifts are associated with the need for interpretation and meaning allocation, and are often formulated in contradictions. Statements such as, "It is insecurity that securizes us", make the highly mobile and provisional life predictable, or as the entrepreneur Kakule states: "Money keeps Goma going". Many urban dwellers therefore consider Goma a "safe haven" precisely because many conflict actors invest in Goma or have family there. They argue that armed actors won't do harm to their "own homes", which is connected to the local perception that Goma can offer long-term benefits and a potential stability to its population, even if this is not equally distributed.

## *Vita ni bizniz tu . . .:*[9] Self-Image, Status, and Entrepreneurial Style

*"Le Congo est un Pays Mystique. Les Plus Riches Sont Les Plus Affameés".*[9]
Along with war, "modernity" is evident in luxury hotels, expensive supermarkets, discotheques, or large jeeps, which are visible yet unaffordable in most residents' daily consumption practices. These projections of modernity are perceived through the encounter between the market of intervention and the industry of ambiance where Big Men and expatriates' lifestyles provide an illusion of progress and prosperity that is out of reach for the vast majority of the population. Modernity is articulated in a moral conversion by which even the "rich" present themselves as "needy". With this polemic, Moise, a twenty-four year-old motorcycle taxi driver, laments the greed of Goma's Big Men and their monopolization of power and economic resources, which hints at limited social mobility and unequal distribution of wealth in Goma. This perception is based on a strong asymmetry that has been translated into the social distribution of resources, as the few have a great deal while the many have little. The ascribed overindulgence of the elites adds to the sense of an "economy of grabbing," a social practice of seizing opportunities wherever they arise. Described as *"économie morale de*

*la ruse et de la débrouille*" (Banégas and Warnier 2001: 8) or "dirty tricks" (Bayart, Ellis and Hibou 1999: 70) in other contexts, they generate new entrepreneurial values and morals that exist alongside the classical Weberian protestant working ethic. Fraud (*escroquerie*), unscrupulousness (*idéologie ya costeau*), or repression (*tracasserie*) create an "urban jungle" in Goma, which functions according to the principle of the "survival of the fittest". As socio-biological rhetoric, *homo homini lupus est*,[10] or the social figure, the "*petit prédateur*" (Devisch 1998: 449), allude to the rules of the jungle, where particular measures must be applied in order to profit and make ends meet. It thus seems that Goma's urban world is inhabited by figures and shaped by moral values that form part of what de Boeck calls the "hunter's landscape" (2001: 550), where alternative morals and ethics of accumulation, expenditure, and redistribution exist as the next example shows:

> A great *homme d'affaires* who had been able to build up assets under Mobutu through the benefit of a flourishing transport industry, trade with resources, and investment in the industry of ambiance invested in land ownership in Goma. Following the fall of Mobutu and the looting that happened during the wars, he lost his possessions outside Goma and began to focus on new business opportunities in the city. With Goma's occupation by the RCD in 1998, his land was expropriated; the RCD sold part of it and offered him the chance to buy back the remaining part and get involved in RCD politics.

This example demonstrates the merging of engagements and activities of supposedly "purely" military or economic actors. It becomes obvious how social relations are established and networks of dependence and influence are created. It highlights the seeming importance of Big Men for armed movements who could potentially bring in resources as well as their own loyal network of followers. However, this may manifest itself in even more extreme rivalries, as illustrated by the following example.

Shortly after the beginning of my field research in 2008, one of the most well-known and visible entrepreneurs, who had accumulated and extended his wealth during Mobutu's regime, was murdered in Goma. At the time he had been murdered, he was topic of conversation number one on *radio trottoir* (sidewalk radio) where questions about power and morality, and "sociability, leadership, and agency" were raised (White 2004: 188). To date, the murder remains unsolved. Next to political conspiracy theories, one of the main lines of discourse was that a second big businessman, a local nouveau riche, had given the order to murder the patron so he could acquire some of his large possessions on Lake Kivu. The rumors that accompanied this dispute pertained particularly to the profits entrepreneur B could access after the death of A, as entrepreneur A was the owner of a prestigious and at the time traditionally rich hotel, and entrepreneur B was building a more modern and elegant hotel in Goma. Local perception therefore frequently referred to a rivalry between the two. In the local analysis of Goma's inhabitants, discussing these issues demonstrates first the high social status of the two Big Men, and second, that the entertainment sector is a prominent feature in the urban landscape and of particular interest in terms of the self-identification of Goma's population, as it brings the nexus of entrepreneurship, status, and lifestyle to the fore.

Obviously not all bars are owned by the urban elites, but the most fancy and important ones (including restaurants and hotels) are owned by Big Men and are well known throughout the city; their businesses attract a clientele of various stripes.[11] Investment in the hotel industry often leads to a competition of superlatives. Even "the diaspora" follows up on these events and discusses them on the social media. So, it is what I call "the industry of ambiance" that generally provides a platform for entrepreneurs to showcase themselves and their wealth, to demonstrate their power, to attract followers, to establish networks, and to strengthen their reputation. Additionally, the tourism sector, which blossomed under colonialism and during the Mobutu era, is a still cherished nostalgic memory that offers a platform of commonality, yet also a stage upon which to present oneself. Therefore, concepts like "conspicuous consumption", or verbs like *se vanter* or *kuonyesha* (brag, show off) reflect a starkly discussed dimension of local entrepreneurship: the need to display success and wealth in order to increase one's social status (Banégas and Warnier 2001: 14; Godelier 1986: 163).

However, not only the display, but also the (re)distribution of resources is crucial. The murder in 2008 offered plenty to talk about in terms of both entrepreneurs' distributive power, whereby the population in particular evaluated their investment in local infrastructure and in the population itself. Distribution creates dependencies and loyalty. As Utas writes, "Bigness is measured in status symbols and the ability to fill that Big Man role according to social criteria" (2012: 7). In this sense, scholarships for students, commitment to the environment, or sponsoring local football teams serve as arguments in favor of entrepreneurs' credibility and respectability, which, at the same time, underscore the social recognition of successful entrepreneurs.

The most sought-after plots are built on the shores of Lake Kivu and the names of their owners are common knowledge, as they mark the urban landscape. Yet, with the dynamics of the market of intervention, multi-story villas have sprung up like mushrooms in Goma's city center, which point to the level of dollarization that transforms the city's appearance noticeably. This is why many Gomatraciens now proudly speak of Goma as a *"ville de chateaux"* ("city of castles"), ascribing a new level of meaning to entrepreneurship.

Another component of this example is found in the reflection on the origin and identity of entrepreneurs. As Goma's Big Men are, because of their high profile and publicly visible investments, topics of conversation, various myths have grown up around their sources of fortune, their construction projects, and potential hidden agendas. In times of protracted armed conflict, cleavages like autochthony are strongly amplified and the presumption is that anyone who has alliances with the "Rwandans" might be selling off Congolese resources. Accordingly, Stephen Jackson (2001) refers to the reversal of interpretive practices that stem from the conflict context as well as the aggravating antagonisms of identity. Under Mobutu, the exploitation of mineral resources was interpreted as the *"mode d'entrepreneuriat congolais pour survivre"* (Jackson 2001: 130). Today, this exploitation is interpreted through networks questioning who is organizing mining, trading, and distribution with whom. This local analysis (*il faut analyser*) often proceeds normatively and refers to the fierce competition between the "autochthonous" and the "newcomers" for power, profit, and protection (Vlassenroot and Raeymaekers 2004). Furthermore, competition among generations is an equally crucial factor in Goma, as the next section shows.

## RECYCLAGE DES ELITES AND THE ECONOMY OF GRABBING

The derisive phrase *"recyclage des elites"* evokes intergenerational conflicts, which were already present under Mobutu's paternalistic rule because he tried to create a bridge to precolonial times. Vansina frames this as "lineage ideology" that refers to the gerontocratic order whereby young people will eventually replace their elders (Vansina 1990: 175f.). While this did not introduce generational replacement, it did create a perpetuation of structural inequalities through the renewal of elites. Schatzberg (2001) calls this "generational rotation", which remained firmly rooted in the experience of Goma's population.[12] The renewal of elites excluded the majority of the population—primarily the youth—from social participation and prosperity. As such, intergenerational tensions emerged between the young Gomatraciens and the "dinosaurs", the "old Mobutists" who did not make any room for the younger generation because they wanted to not only maintain their power but also avoid having their access to resources run dry. Ironically, such recycling reproduces itself. For instance, while the formative players in a children and youth-related NGO are older than eighteen years of age, they are looking for ways to legitimize their extended stay. One afternoon, there was a scandal in this organization which illustrates internal rivalries on one hand and the continuity of cleptocratic practices on the other hand: one NGO member provoked his colleague (both were seventeen years old) when he asked for a receipt for his laptop. The accused, irritated, reacted and replied:

> You have been in this NGO long enough, *débrouille toi-même*. Everyone has the chance to make contacts. Everybody does that. Just be a bit smart.

This can be understood as mimetic routine, the copying and reinterpreting of historically grown practices like "grabbing" (Callaghy 1984: 190). Grabbing refers to Mobutu's well-known policies based on dependencies and loyalties that allowed those to whom he was partial to ascend rapidly; this could, however, also lead to a steep descent when an individual lost Mobutu's favor. Such arbitrariness led to a social practice whereby individuals tried, as directly, effectively, and extensively as possible, to use the system before they were met with disapproval. That this is not a path to sustainability is obvious; it has, nevertheless, remained unchanged after the end of Mobutu's rule. The tense and nervous climate that emerged under Mobutu continues today in the "economy of grabbing" in a context of violent conflict, volcanic eruptions, and humanitarian crisis. Anticipation and equally, the recourse to experience, facilitate the grabbing of every opportunity before it evades. As said before, it is not necessarily about large sums, but grabbing means for the everyday entrepreneur often the first step to capital which can be (re)invested innovatively and rationally.

Faustin, for example, was the manager of an acquaintance's bar (*Nganda*). Faustin had a deal with his neighbor, who sold reusable bottles. He took the empty bottles and cases, which he presented to his boss as goods sold, and he shared the profit with his neighbor who was putting Faustin's share in a small kiosk for his wife. As his boss became aware of this, he called him a thief and canceled for two weeks the travel money he received to go to his remote neighborhood. When I asked my friend, the bar's owner, about this, and about whether he thought to look for a new manager, he looked at me, irritated, and said: "Anyone who is clever will try to find a way to cheat you. And I do not want to have any idiots working for me".

This anecdote illustrates the socially accepted nature of *débrouillardise*. Faustin's diversification strategy, which was driven by the skill and the resourcefulness to secure money for his own pocket, was considered by my acquaintance to be "clever" as well as common. It is therefore closely related to "street wisdom" and the search to outwit the law, employers, or even just the next person. It is about grabbing opportunities before they might disappear. Paradoxically, my friend legitimized Faustin's behavior by characterizing it as understandable and therefore elevating cleverness to the level of a social value.

Furaha, a student, also saw her chance. With two friends she had been exploring ways to get involved with the lucrative trade with international organizations. At the same time, she had been in a year-long relationship with a Belgian logistician. Through her boyfriend, she was able to secure her first contract using the start-up capital provided by her father. She explained: "If you have an eye for business, everything runs smoothly".

An "eye for business" and the right connections dynamize business ideas and entrepreneurial spirit. Faustin and Furaha are prime examples of those who I refer to as everyday entrepreneurs. They take the initiative (*faut être dynamique*) and have the will as well as the creativity needed for business.

Through their own initiative, they seek out markets and cooperation partners. On the other hand, they rely on networks to provide start-up funding (like a friend's car or shared tasks) or gain access to capital through trickery. The contact zones between everyday entrepreneurs and the Big Men are clearly evident in their cooperation and their ability to identify and access opportunities. The example of Faustin illustrates that everyday entrepreneurs can cleverly use their position to make a profit, creatively seizing the opportunity to put some money aside and invest it in a new income strategy (the kiosk) for his household. It is therefore not only to the Big Men that Goma offers opportunities for status and success.

Despite big entrepreneurs' monopolization of the most lucrative spheres and particularly their complex involvement in various economic, political, and military networks, it is also possible for everyday entrepreneurs to invest and accumulate wealth. Their profits are also reinvested in turn, regardless of whether it is in hedonistic pleasures (to impress and gain status with the peers or the neighborhood) or by investing in a *bizniz* in their kinship network. In a volatile context like Goma, an economic climb is made less through specialization in a specific field than it is through diversification, flexibility, and the "eye" for opportunities, which are equally available to Big Men and everyday entrepreneurs. It is the specific volatile situation of humanitarian crisis, natural risk, and man-made political conflict that makes Goma's urban dwellers innovative yet not always successful. However, the complex market of intervention offers manifold economic niches and new patrons to engage with. Whether it is worth the while to take a specific chance or a risk will depend on a particular actor's assessment of the situation.

## ENTREPRENEURS AS ANALYSTS OF A COMPLEX ENVIRONMENT

Goma is a city with excessive meaning production and compact communication structures, and such conditions require flexibility, improvisation, and vision. Baudouin, who imports and sells construction material, explains:

> I analyze exactly what people need. You have to go with the times; you have to be dynamic, always alert. You have to cover as many different spheres as possible, because the demand is always there. (Baudouin, Shi, late thirties, school education but no diploma)

As an "urban jungle", Goma presents complex challenges for the cognitive abilities of entrepreneurs, who see nevertheless more potential in Goma than afro-pessimistic perspectives suggest. In contrast to a focus on criminal or irrational actors who are consumed with sheer survival, entrepreneurs explain their success as well as the failure of others in terms of an understanding of the complex relationships that comprise Goma's social environment. The interchange between diverse networks and the evaluation of information makes entrepreneurs analysts as they emphasize self-confidently: "*on est malin*" ("one is clever"), "*mayele*" ("clever" [Lingala]), "*je sais analyser*" ("I am able to analyze"), "*je suis un intellectuel*" ("I am an intellectual"), "*je suis sage*" ("I am wise"), "*Niko na kichwa*" ("I have brains"), or "*Niko na mawazo*" ("I think things over").

These concepts are part of a vernacular that reflects trust, or an illusion of it, in one's own intelligence, wisdom, clear-mindedness, and vigilance. They are intersubjectively staged to situate themselves in the sociopolitical structure but also to identify, track down, and exploit opportunities. The same is true for both Big Men and everyday entrepreneurs alike, as both groups need to negotiate and convince other sociopolitical actors of their value. This demonstrates the usefulness of understanding these social relations as a continuum. It highlights the flexible positions in the social network, as a Big Man may have their own Big Man and even a boy might have his boy (Utas 2012: 8f.). Suggesting proximity, then, is connected to verbal skills, the rhetorical ability to convince others, to pretend, and to make people believe if direct access to wealth is denied (Oldenburg 2012). Bob White (2004) illustrates that rumors about local celebrities offer an important source of information about how Kinshasa's urban culture is organized. Also in Goma, the ability to pretend as if one is in close contact with the powerful, the influential, the stars, the politicians, or the rebels is a widespread means used to position oneself.

The pursuit of success or the favor of, proximity to, and attention from successful figures is typical for everyday entrepreneurs. For instance, during our first meeting, Thierry tried to position himself by telling me about the Big Men he knew in Goma: he sought to present himself as an influential person in the right light and through specific details ("the governor drinks whiskey") to prove his credibility. Thierry described himself as a *débrouillard*. At thirty-one, he was studying International Relations and has been interested in politics from an early age. He was a member of the *Conseil de la Jeunesse* at the provincial level, and he represents his ethnic community in university politics as a *porte-parole*. In this function, he quickly came in contact with important local Big Men, and he was taken on by one well-known patron who paid for his studies, brought him into his network, and supplied him with contacts.

The patron was a big name in business in eastern Congo under Mobutu, whom he later criticized at the end of his regime, and he is now an influential politician. By funding Thierry, he hoped to gain influence with the student body. Thierry acted as an errand boy for him, and partly as a chauffeur. He was also able to conduct some business so that he could put aside some money and get a car. In his position with the Conseil de la Jeunesse, he had a travel budget, and as long as he did not use those funds and used his patron's networks to travel, he could put aside a large sum each half year.

As a social actor, Thierry was well aware of how he ought to behave toward whom and how to plan strategically. He was able to judge which contact in which situation would be most beneficial and how to approach someone in order to form an alliance. Large cost calculations are normal in political networks and, in particular, the large distance from eastern Congo to the capital, Kinshasa, is milked in this context. His patron advised him to invest in land. Due to Thierry's success, the generational hierarchy in his family has been reversed, and he referred to himself proudly as the *"grand"* of his family. His parents lived in South Kivu, but he acted autonomously and has helped his two younger siblings attend school.

Today, the range of possibilities for patronage has been significantly differentiated by war and humanitarian organizations and has opened up new business relations. Thierry, as an everyday entrepreneur, and his patron, as a Big Man, demonstrate the complexity of patron-client relationships: although Thierry was dependent on his patron, his patron also benefitted from Thierry's influence on his peers. In the kin context, Thierry has reversed intergenerational relations, whereby he, instead of his father, was able to provide for his younger siblings, and furthermore, was able to invest his earnings in various sectors to diversify and enlarge his chances of success.

### *"Tulamuke!"*[14]—From Pursuits to Missteps

> Kimanuka and his friends are debating how Rudy had managed to arrange such a good deal with a well-known trader. Kimanuka paces back and forth. He laughs nervously. Pushing his hands together, he says: "But we are sleeping! We need to wake up (*tulamuke*) because we are still asleep". (Fieldnotes, 7 September 2009, at a petrol station, Himbi)

Sharp senses are needed for good business. One must not sleep or celebrate but should instead focus on the right moment. Opportunities arise through networks and communication. Stable and manifold relationships are therefore particularly important in order to explore the market. Similarly, verbal skills are needed to draw in potential patrons, to deceive potential victims, or to enter into alliances with complex political, military, and humanitarian actors. Support is largely provided on the basis of "personality". In this sense, *débrouillardise* seems to catalyze a specific version of a protestant work ethic in entrepreneurs. Even if trickery and boasting by "astutely calculated generosity" (Godelier 1986: 163) seem to contradict the rational dynamics of Weber's definition, Goma's entrepreneurs use normative instructions to test a person's will, courage, and dynamic ability (*faut avoir la volonté/ être courageux/ être souple*).

At the same time those who fail are vilified, so that the social polarization along with the ethnic fragmentation of Goma accelerates processes of "inclusive exclusion" (Hansen and Stepputat 2005: 17). This can be illustrated by semantic shifts, like that which occurred for the "bandit" figure, but which also appear in adjectives like *pourri* ("rotten"), *muvivu* ("lazy"), the figure of the *voyou* ("rogue"), or an apathetic person with crossed arms (*il a des bras creuses*), which contradict the entrepreneurial spirit. As such, those who act like a *yuma* ("idiot") are referred to as villagers or *nyama* (fresh meat) and are displaced from the "civilized" or the "developed world". Here, the local differentiation between everyday entrepreneurs and those dwellers who are disregarded because of their non-entrepreneurial potential becomes obvious. It seems that the emic, highly touted recourse to a "protestant work ethic" (which is expressed by rules like *"faut être dynamique"*), particularly in times of political instability, plays a central role.

These rules are closely intertwined with a social imagination that is translated into concepts of power, protection, and control in Goma. This is also exemplified and substantiated by narratives of success and failure that entrepreneurs themselves perceive and produce, as well as the characteristics that have been attributed to them by their social environment. In this way, a Nande trader who effectively combines both economic and political sectors explained his perspective on successful entrepreneurship: "It must flourish. We do not love free things. We want to create things ourselves. You have to work hard in life".[13] Such a focus on morality and power(lessness) and on the belief in one's own creativity and assertiveness provides a basis and a self-understanding of entrepreneurship that, in particular, young people emulate:

> A young person in a village wakes up in the morning and goes to his field. That is his only concern. But in the city, a person has to contemplate how he can pursue his projects and how he can get ahead. Therefore, one is civilized in the city. (Moise, twenty-four, singer, painter, student, UJADP, Nande)

The civilized life of a city dweller that Moise painted in this example resembles a form of "metropolitan arrogance", which Walter Benjamin used to describe Berlin at the turn of the century (2009 [1928]). It requires determination, analysis, and creativity, in order to choose between a multitude of options and to evolve. The desire for progress is also found in young people's desire to participate in consumption possibilities and to gain social status. Locally implicit references to the protestant work ethic, by which everyone can "make one's own luck", mask structural limitations and obscure unequal access to resources. It therefore might seem surprising that a belief in social mobility is relatively strong in Goma. Emically, each individual explains his own success by referring to characteristics such as perseverance, patience, dynamism, versatility, or flexibility, which express the pursuit of wealth and status. Analyzing social relations and the social environment allows the urban dwellers to hope and simultaneously to keep an eye on upcoming opportunities.

CONCLUSION

The contextual meaning binds past experiences and anticipation, the need to keep looking forward while maintaining some focus on the past. Accordingly, entrepreneurship forms a continuum which is generated by, strengthened by, and used by informal networks. The locally oft-cited values of a capitalist work ethic are frequently thwarted by fraud, corruption, and violence. Nevertheless, innovation, pragmatism, and patience to take risks or to save money are part of the central entrepreneurial values for both Big Men and everyday entrepreneurs (MacGaffey 2002: 333). In contrast to Big Men, *débrouillards* and *biznizeurs* are rarely associated with entrepreneurship. However, they often have much more than pure "survival" in mind and use creative entrepreneurial skills. In this sense, I consider everyday entrepreneurs to be soldiers of fortune that pursue, similar to Don Quixote, their goal with perseverance and with the hope that one day they will have a successful business. The oft-quoted saying in Goma, *"On vit par miracle"* is in this context not just a fatalistic reflection on one's own life or the country's economy, but also reflects the perceived hypothetical nature of chronic crisis where everything might be possible despite social inequality and high constraints. In Goma, it is not a straight path that leads to one's destination but rather many small side streets that point the way to a meal, a small sum, or even status, wealth, and power.

NOTES

1. This analysis is based on ethnographic research and empirical material that I have collected in Goma since January 2008. The data is primarily qualitative and is based on interviews and participant observation, which was intensified by my staying with a Big Man's family. For security reasons, names of my research informants and concrete places have been made anonymous.
2. I consider the market of intervention as a space where a broad range of flexible transactions, interdependent actors, and temporary arrangements of power coexist. It is a social space where different actors meet, offer, praise, pretend, bargain, buy, sell, gossip, clash, and finally exchange ideas and emotions. The market serves as a metaphor of supply and demand, vision and velocity, emerging opportunities and dwindling chances. Furthermore, I understand these "contact zones" between the local population, armed actors, and members of humanitarian missions as being characterized by "highly asymmetrical relations of power" (Pratt 1992: 4) that shape socioeconomic conditions and give rise to "parallel" economies (see Oldenburg forthcoming).
3. Questions about citizenship, exclusion, and political representation, along with access to land, resources, and security, have been issues for the Kivu since the colonial construction of ethnic identities. Autochthony (Greek: from the soil itself) serves as an arbitrary form of articulation to frame political debates and enhance the production of self and otherness (Geschiere 2009).
4. North Kivu is divided into the *Grand* and *Petit Nord*. The *Grand Nord* includes Beni/Lubero and Walikale and the *Petit Nord* comprises Masisi und Rutshuru.

5. This stems back to the politics of representation that made eastern Congo a time bomb for years. During the Belgian colonial period, most of Goma's members of the provincial parliament were primarily from the well-educated Rwandophone communities. The Rwandophones are not an ethnic group; instead the term is used to denote all Kinyarwanda speakers (Hutu and Tutsi), who are differentiated territorially in North Kivu as the Banyamasisi and Banyarutshuru (Banya = people from). They competed with the *Grand Nord* represented by the Nande and more recently with the Bashi, considered to be from South Kivu.

6. Temporary employment is a field of tension between the "official" and "unofficial" economy and is emically called *bizniz,* on *s'arrange* or *on coop.* All of these terms point to cooperation and deals, which can coincide with collusion and trickery.

7. RCD stands for Rassemblement Congolais pour la Démocratie.

8. A *comptoir* is a nodal point for the trade and commerce of mineral resources (in Goma mostly coltan and cassiterite).

9. "War is also only a business".

10. "The Congo is a mystical country. The richest are at the same time also the hungriest" (Moise, motorcycle taxi driver, Hutu, 15 August 2008).

11. According to my observations, students in particular like to bring this Hobbesian statement up, first to describe the situation in the Kivus and second to emphasize their own eloquence and intellect.

12. For example, some young people frequented the restaurant of a businessman who was reputed for his support of the CNDP (Congrès National pour la Défense du Peuple). There, they told me, they could drink a beer in quiet and remain undetected. However, I observed several times their strenuous attempts to catch the attention of certain actors trying to gain the favor of a prominent Big Man.

13. When I returned to Goma in 2009, I asked several people if Laurent Nkunda, the leader of the CNDP who had been living under house arrest in Rwanda, would return to Goma, and the response was unanimous: "No, no one has ever made it twice in the Congo. But maybe his son". This view is underscored by the experience that after the end of Mobutu's dictatorship, four prominent "sons" ran as candidates during the 2006 elections, including the sons of Laurent-Désiré Kabila, Mobutu, Lumumba, and Kasavubu (Turner 2007: 168).

14. "Let's wake up!"

15. "*Ça doit être florissant. On n'aime pas les vitu ya bure. On veut créer nous-même. Il faut bosser dans la vie*" (Bertin, forty-six years of age, ex-RCD politician, ex-advisor to the governor, today UNDP).

## REFERENCES

Banégas, Richard and Jean-Pierre Warnier. 2001. 'Nouvelles figures de la réussite et du pouvoir'. *Politique Africaine* 82: 5–21.

Bayart, Francois, Stephen Ellis, and Béatrice Hibou. 1999. *The Criminalization of the State in Africa.* Oxford: James Currey.

Benjamin, Walter. 2009 [1928]. *Einbahnstraße.* Frankfurt: Suhrkamp.

Büscher, Karen and Koen Vlassenroot. 2010. 'Humanitarian presence and urban development: new opportunities and contrasts in Goma, DRC'. *Disasters* 34, 2: 256–273.

Callaghy, Thomas. 1984. *The State-Society Struggle: Zaïre in Comparative Perspective*. New York: Columbia University Press.

De Boeck, Filip. 2001. 'Garimpeiro worlds: digging, dying and "hunting" for diamonds in Angola'. *Review of African Political Economy* 28, 90: 548–562.

De Boeck, Filip and Marie-Françoise Plissart. 2004. *Kinshasa: Tales of the Invisible City*. Ghent: Ludion.

De Villers, Gauthier, Henri Monnier, and Bogumil Jewsiewicki. 2002. *Manières de Vivre: Économie de la Débrouille dans les Villes du Congo Zaïre*. Paris: L'Harmattan.

Devisch, René. 1998. 'La violence à Kinshasa, ou l'institution en négatif'. *Cahiers d'Études Africains* 28: 441–469.

Doevenspeck, Martin and Nene Mwanabiningo Morisho. 2012. 'Navigating uncertainty: observations from the Congo-Rwanda border'. In: Bettina Bruns and Judith Miggelbrink (eds). *Subverting Borders: Doing Research on Smuggling and Small-Scale Trade*. Wiesbaden: VS Verlag, 85–106.

Geschiere, Peter. 2009. *The Perils of Belonging: Autochthony, Citizenship, and Exclusion in Africa and Europe*. Chicago and London: The University of Chicago Press.

Godelier, Maurice. 1986. *The Making of Great Men: Male Domination and Power among the New Guinea Baruya*. Cambridge: Cambridge University Press.

Greenhouse, Carol. 2002. 'Introduction: altered states, altered lives'. In: Carol Greenhouse, Elizabeth Mertz, and Kay Warren (eds). *Ethnography in Unstable Places: Everyday Lives in Contexts of Dramatic Political Change*. Durham and London: Duke University Press, 1–34.

Hansen, Thomas Blom and Finn Stepputat. 2005. *Sovereign Bodies: Citizens, Migrants, and States in the Postcolonial World*. Princeton: Princeton University Press.

Jackson, Stephen. 2001. ' "Nos richesses sont pillees!" Économies de guerre et rumeurs de crime au Kivu'. *Politique Africaine* 84: 117–135.

Jackson, Stephen. 2010. 'It seems to be going: the genius of survival in wartime DR Congo'. In: Anne-Maria Makhulu, Beth Buggenhagen, and Stephen Jackson (eds). *Hard Work, Hard Times: Global Volatility and African Subjectivities*. Berkeley: University of California Press, 48–68.

MacGaffey, Janet. 1983. 'How to survive and become rich amidst devastation: the second economy in Zaire'. *African Affairs* 82: 351–366.

MacGaffey, Janet. 1987. *Entrepreneurs and Parasites: The Struggle for Indigenous Capitalism in Zaïre*. Cambridge: Cambridge University Press.

MacGaffey, Janet. 1988. 'Economic disengagement and class formation in Zaire'. In: Donald Rothchild and Naomi Chazan (eds). *The Precarious Balance: State and Society in Africa*. Boulder: Westview Press, 171–188.

MacGaffey, Janet (ed.) 1991. *The Real Economy of Zaïre: The Contribution of Smuggling and other Unofficial Activities to National Wealth*. James Currey: London.

MacGaffey, Janet. 1993. ' "On se debrouille": reflexions sur la "deuxieme économie" au Zaire'. In: Tshonda Omasombo (ed). *Le Zaïre à l'épreuve de l'histoire immédiate*. Paris: Karthala, 143–159.

MacGaffey, Janet. 2002. 'Survival, innovation, and success in time of trouble: what prospects for Central African entrepreneurs?' In: Alusine Jalloh and Toyin Falola (eds). *Black Business and Economic Power*. Rochester, N.Y: University of Rochester Press, 331–346.

Makhulu, Anne-Maria, Beth Buggenhagen and Stephen Jackson (eds). 2010. *Hard Work, Hard Times: Global Volatility and African Subjectivities*. Berkeley: University of California Press.

Mbembe, Achille and Sarah Nuttall. 2004. 'Writing the world from an African metropolis'. *Public Culture* 16, 3: 347–372.

Oldenburg, Silke. 2012. 'A Goma On Sait Jamais. Jugend, Krieg und Alltag in Goma, DR Kongo'. Ph.D. thesis, University of Bayreuth.

Oldenburg, Silke. 2014. 'Liebe in Zeiten humanitärer Intervention. Sex, Geschlechterbeziehungen und humanitäre Intervention in Goma, DR Kongo'. *Peripherie* 133: 46–70.

Oldenburg, Silke. 2015. 'The Politics of Love and Intimacy in Goma, Eastern DR Congo: Perspectives on the Market of Intervention as Contact Zone.' In: *Journal of Intervention and Statebuilding.* DOI: 10.1080/17502977.2015.1054660.

Pratt, Mary Louise. 1992. *Imperial Eyes: Travel Writing and Transculturation.* London: Routledge.

Raeymaekers, Timothy. 2007. 'The Power of Protection: Governance and Transborder Trade on the Congo-Ugandan Border'. Ph.D. thesis, Ghent University, Belgium.

Raeymaekers, Timothy, Ken Menkhaus, and Koen Vlassenroot. 2008. 'State and non-state regulation in African protracted crises: governance without government?' *Afrika Fokus* 21, 2: 7–21.

Schatzberg, Michael. 2001. *Political Legitimacy in Middle Africa: Father, Family, Food.* Bloomington: Indiana University Press.

Tegera, Alois and Dominic Johnson. 2007. *Rules for Sale: Formal and Informal Cross-Border Trade in Eastern DRC.* Goma: Pole Institute (Regards Croisés 19).

Trefon, Théodore (ed.). 2004. *Reinventing Order in the Congo: How People Respond to State Failure in Kinshasa.* London: Zed Books.

Tull, Denis. 2005. *The Reconfiguration of Political Order in Africa: A Case Study of North Kivu (DR Congo).* Hamburg: Institut für Afrikakunde.

Turner, Thomas. 2007. *The Congo Wars: Conflict, Myth and Reality.* London: Zed Books.

Utas, Mats. 2012. 'Introduction: Bigmanity and network governance in African conflicts'. In: Mats Utas (ed). *African Conflicts and Informal Power: Big Men and Networks.* London: Zed Books, 1–31.

Vansina, Jan. 1990. *Paths in the Rainforests: Toward a History of Political Tradition in Equatorial Africa.* London: James Currey.

Vlassenroot, Koen and Karen Büscher. 2009. 'The city as frontier: urban development and identity processes in Goma'. *Crisis States Research Centre Working Paper Series* (London) 61.

Vlassenroot, Koen and Timothy Raeymaekers (eds). 2004. *Conflict and Social Transformation in Eastern DR Congo.* Gent: Academia Press.

White, Bob. 2004. 'The elusive Lupemba: rumors about fame and (mis)fortune in Kinshasa'. In: Theodore Tréfon (ed). *Reinventing Order in the Congo.* London: Zed Books, 174–191.

# Part III
# Media and Popular Culture

# 11 Entrepreneurial Trajectories and Figures of the Cameroonian Mediascape

*Olivier Atemsing Ndenkop*

## INTRODUCTION: FROM PRESS ORGANS TO MEDIA ENTERPRISES

Roughly twenty-five years after the liberalization of social communication in Cameroon (1990), several studies were published on the media of this Central African country with its twenty million inhabitants. These studies, however, are exclusively interested in macrostructural aspects of communication and consequently in general and transverse problems such as press freedom, the status of journalists, and the sociopolitical role of media (Djimeli 2012; Kouleu 2007; Ndongo 1993; Okala 1999; Tjade 2001). They neglect the microstructures, i.e., the media enterprises (newspapers and audiovisual media) and their initiators. After the liberalization, a manifold media landscape has emerged in Cameroon due to the creativity, perseverance, and boldness of private entrepreneurs who challenge the dominant public media—Cameroon Radio and Television (CRTV) and the *Cameroon Tribune*—and create diversity and plurality of information.

These media entrepreneurs differ essentially from the classical industrial entrepreneurs. Contrary to the industrial entrepreneurs who work with the novel ideas of inventors and the money they borrow from banks to build up their industrial enterprises, the media entrepreneurs in Cameroon, aspiring to become successful, are obliged to play the role of the inventor, the bank owner, and the entrepreneur at the same time. This accumulation of roles can partly be ascribed to the refusal of the banks to finance the media due to their precarious situation and the poor buying power of the country's citizens. These two shortcomings have forced aspiring media entrepreneurs to search for capital among family members, friends, and even with *njangis* (rotating saving and credit associations).

It is not easy for media entrepreneurs, particularly those in audiovisual media, to render their investments profitable given the piracy of images by dishonest cable distributors and the reduced number of enterprises who are able to pay the radio or television stations for broadcasting their publicity.

Despite the existence of the law that liberalizes communication, the state has become well-known for its multiple forms of open or veiled censorship

(Nyamnjoh 2004). With the aim of reducing the number of audiovisual media entrepreneurs, the authorities have, for example, imposed a broadcasting license that costs 100 million FCFA (about $192,000) that is valid for ten years. Every individual who wants to start a private TV channel is obliged to acquire such a license. With the same intention of limiting information, gendarmes and policemen often raid newspaper houses to intimidate journalists, some of whom are even arrested and kept in police custody (Zoe-Obanga and Ekambi 2006: 31). These constraints make any success in the Cameroonian media sphere a heroic deed.

This study retraces the trajectories of four Cameroonians who have become successful despite the a priori unfavorable circumstances. They have built up viable and enviable media enterprises in their country to the point that they have become role models for others to follow. These four entrepreneurs were also chosen based on Cameroon's linguistic and ethnic diversity. The examination of their strategies and the evaluation of their individual success stories will be preceded by an outline of the history of media in Cameroon. This study profits from my double status as a scholarly research fellow and practicing journalist. As a research fellow in social sciences and without pretending to be exhaustive, I have studied the existing works on Cameroonian media. As a practicing journalist for nine years, I have myself experienced the persistent changes in the Cameroonian media landscape. I personally know many of the media actors on all different levels (entrepreneurs and employed journalists). It is from this perspective that I will explore the "secrets of success" of the initiators of the daily *Le Jour*, the Radio Equinoxe, and the television stations, Canal2 and STV.

## THE HISTORY OF MEDIA ENTERPRISE IN CAMEROON

From 1903 onward, the Cameroonian mediascape was firmly in the hands of foreign actors, beginning with missionaries followed by colonialists. After independence in 1960, the administration and national entrepreneurs progressively built up media enterprises.

### The Colonial Media Aiming at Assimilation

The German missionaries introduced the first newspapers to Cameroon, including *Das Evangelische Monatsblatt* (The Evangelical Newsletter) which was circulated from 1903 onward as one of the instruments the German missionaries intended to use to convert Cameroonians to Christianity (Ndombo 1997: 267). When the Germans left following their defeat in the First World War, the French controlled the colony and created newspapers to disseminate French culture in the country. In September 1922, commissioner Marchand created *La Gazette du Cameroun*, a bimonthly that was written by emancipated Africans (Tudesq 1999: 133). The nationalist party,

Union des Populations du Cameroun, created in 1948, also produced a newspaper known as *La voix du peuple du Cameroun*.

Newspapers in this period (1900–1950), however, were not enterprises, as the information they provided was not considered part of a commercial service. The Europeans who edited these newspapers knew that the majority of the local population were exploited and poorly paid by the expatriates and their limited wage made it impossible for them to pay however small a sum in exchange for culture like books and newspapers.

## The Media as an Instrument of Claims

The Africans who followed in the footsteps of the Europeans in creating newspapers also did not consider them a commercial product tied to modern management rules or profit. They promoted cultural, ideological, and sociopolitical gains only. For them, a newspaper had to fulfil three missions: to contest established opinions that infantilized Africans, to insist on recognition in the absence of equality with the colonial masters; and third, to allow African newspaper publishers' social ascent beyond their compatriots. Thus, it is not surprising that the first African newspapers were rather weapons to conquer identity and to claim the space of liberty rather than commercial products that followed the logic of returning investment. A focus on profit marks the point where an entrepreneur becomes "above all an undertaker, that is, someone who begins" (Provost 1986: 165, my translation).

The first known media enterprise, *La presse du Cameroun*, was created in Cameroon in 1955 by the Frenchman Michel De Breteuil. It was an "economic and judicial unit that produced goods and services for sale with the objective of creating benefits" (Capul and Garnier 2005: 170, my translation).

The evolution of media was long and strenuous. After Cameroon's independence (1960), the new powers tried, first and foremost, to maintain a state monopoly on communication in general and the press in particular. The state-owned newspaper (*Cameroon Tribune*) was created in 1974, and the national TV channel began broadcasting a decade later. Until 1996, all private newspapers published in Cameroon were censured by the Ministry of Territorial Administration, which decided upon what was to be published and what was considered tendentious.

Over the course of the following two decades, due to an advance in education, the number of Cameroonians able to read and write increased markedly. Trying to control them more efficiently, the state integrated all young journalism diploma holders automatically into public service. Indeed, almost all of them wanted to become *Gomna* (an individual embodying state authority such as a mayor, tax collector, or policeman) and benefit from the advantages that this status offered, i.e., a decent and regular salary, social security, and diverse benefits. This period was one of glory, what the authors of "Les nouvelles figures de la réussite en Afrique" ("The new figures of success in Africa") have called "the established equation between study, salary, and social success" (Banégas and Warnier 2001: 6, my translation).

After the creation of the first private media enterprise in 1955 by a Frenchman, Cameroonians waited until 1974 when an African, Abodel Karimou, founded a veritable newspaper in Cameroon, *La Gazette*. Employing professional journalists and subscribing to the criteria of profitability, *La Gazette* is the ancestor of the private newspapers that have since been established by Africans in Cameroon (Tjade 1986: 31).

## The Awakening of Private Entrepreneurs

Following Cameroon's independence in 1960, the new authorities did not prioritize communication. Instead, the leitmotif of the first president, Ahmadou Ahidjo, was "National Unity". Accordingly, Ahidjo required more soldiers to fight against nationalists, abusively called "maquisards", than journalists to describe his authoritarian policy. In this unfavorable political environment, private initiatives were very rare. Before the liberation of communication, very few private initiatives, including *Le Combattant*, *Le Quotidien*, and *Le Messager*, were launched in Cameroon. Created in 1979, *Le Messager* was the oldest survivor of those post-independence media.

The veritable "entrepreneurial turn" (Djimeli 2012) came at the turn of the 1990s for two reasons: the democratic opening and the economic crisis that obliged many so-called underdeveloped states to accept the conditions of the International Monetary Fund (IMF), known as the privatization of public enterprises, the dismissal of personnel, the freeze on further recruitment of new civil servants, and so forth. This "liberalization provided new itineraries of accumulation" (Banégas and Warnier 2001: 6, my translation) and caused the myth of the *Gomna* to vanish and make way for new actors with diverse motivations who began to promote different trajectories.

Since 1990, the press in Cameroon has encouraged the reshaping of society in the sense that it has helped to forge a citizens' consciousness that has allowed citizens to claim their rights in a more articulated and ordered way (Ngayap 1999). The press has also furthered mobilization and sensitization concerning illnesses such as HIV/Aids, cholera, and others (Kouleu 2007). At present, with 600 newspapers, a hundred radio stations, and more than fifty television channels, Cameroonian media has progressively adapted the rules of modern management to the socio-anthropological and politico-economic realities of investment. The new media entrepreneurs appear to understand that "an enterprise is above all . . . a relatively autonomous organization, supplied with human, material, and financial resources and the objective to carry out an economic activity in a stable and organized way" (Cohen 2001: 129, my translation).

This paradigm change allowed this generation of media entrepreneurs to become different from their predecessors. The resulting success in terms of new, better organized, and economically more viable media enterprises was admired and fostered hope in an African environment where people still look for a local model of success to combat the ubiquitous pessimism. It is important to add that the present vitality of media enterprises in Africa generally and in Cameroon in particular can also be attributed to cooperation between three key actors (state, entrepreneurs, bankers), as these actors are increasingly involved in and work together to organize the African press through the *African Media Initiative* (AMI), which explores ways to finance all kinds of projects. The number of participants at the different meetings reveals the importance attributed to the development of veritable media enterprises in Africa.

The agreement between the media entrepreneurs, the state, and bankers is rooted in the transformation that Cameroon society has undergone since the 1993 academic reform that facilitated intellectual growth of a great number of citizens. Additionally, the growing number of television sets and the availability of images from cable distributors in almost all urban families made the authorities believe they could use the media as an instrument of mass socialization. The commitment of great media moguls also played a role. Paul Fokam Kenmogne, the owner of the principal banking network in Cameroon (MC2, Afriland First Bank), is the perfect example. Fokam finances the creation of media enterprises and has created a proper television channel: Vox Africa.

We have thus left the Africa that Christian Brincourt and Michel Leblanc paint in *Reporters*, a continent where "the simple word of reportage was synonymous of a heroic deed and those who carried it out, although journalists, were above all adventurers" (Brincourt and Leblanc 1970: 15, my translation). With the goal of strengthening and ameliorating the media sectors, almost all countries of the continent have created media regulatory bodies (Tudesq 2002: 25).

## The Challenge of Finance for the Cameroonian Press

The liberalization of social communication and the creation of regulatory bodies for the media are alone not sufficient to make media enterprises viable. For media enterprises to be viable, they require the spending power of the citizens who are potential consumers and the support of public authorities. As Cameroonian journalists are carrying out a public service (informing, educating, and entertaining citizens), they demand subventions from the state (Sipa 2010: 33). This would not be an exclusive right. Having studied the press in the West, Patrick Le Floch and Nathalie Sonnac recognize that "the collective character of a good is often that which constitutes the main justification of public intervention as far as its production, consumption, and availability for the public are concerned" (Le Floch and Sonnac 2013: 15, my translation).

Facing the scarcity of classical financing, some media entrepreneurs have returned to *njangis*, while others search for patrons to help them publish a newspaper. When a newspaper is sponsored by a patron, disputes become more common because a sponsor can easily become the real editor-in-chief of the newspaper, reading the entire manuscript so that he can erase the articles that may present one of his friends in an unfavorable light before providing the money for printing. He can also ask to include an article that brings a business competitor or a political opponent into disrepute.

The consequences are immediately visible. Potential readers will quickly qualify the newspaper as a "local rag". They will be careful not to waste their money on such prescribed news. But instead of surrendering to such a paid-for press at the expense of journalistic ethics and deontology, certain Cameroonians were able to establish media enterprises that are able to position themselves in the web of national economy. They interest those readers who are convinced that information is a commercial good or service, which is sold only after the careful study of the market.

Beyond its external difficulties, the Cameroonian press is also largely a victim of the newspaper founders' own abuses. It begins with porosity. In Cameroon, there are no restrictions as to who can become a journalist, no national organization responsible for training, the provision of certificates, and upholding of ethical rules and the professional deontology. This opens the door for all kinds of abuses. Consequently, a kind of para-journalism has emerged, the chasms of which are represented by the "*journalistes du Hilton*", those individuals who attend press conferences and seminars at Yaounde's hotels under the pretence that they are journalists. They pick up the documents, help themselves to the buffet, eat the food reserved for invited guests, and ask the organizers to pay them a daily allowance. In Douala, the country's economic capital, those who practice such dishonorable acts of deceit are called "journalistes de la Rue Mermoze" ("journalists of Mermoz Street", one of Douala's well-known boulevards).

## THE ITINERARIES OF BIG MEN IN CAMEROONIAN MEDIA

This part will present details of four major entrepreneurs' success in the Cameroonian mediascape.

## Haman Mana: The New Model of Success for the Newspaper Sector

Over the course of the past twenty years, Haman Mana's name has become synonymous with achievement in the Cameroonian press. Most of his newspapers were, and still are, successful. His involvement in media began in the early 1990s, when Cameroon passed the law that liberalized social communication. After one year of studying history at the Faculty of Arts, Lettres et Sciences Humaines at the University of Yaounde (which was at that time the only university in the country), the young Pépin Haman Mana decided to become a journalist. He applied for admission to the school of journalism in Yaounde. After two years of training, he was recruited by the Société de presse et d'Édition du Cameroun, which published the governmental daily *Cameroon Tribune*, created in 1974. Not much later, in 1993, Haman Mana left the governmental newspaper and joined *Le Messager*, the principal private newspaper in terms of readership and sales at that time.

He left *Le Messager* to pursue his dream of becoming a press patron himself. With the experience that he acquired working at both newspapers (*Cameroon Tribune* and *Le Messager*) in two different economic spheres (private and public), Pépin Haman Mana came to the decision that there was sufficient space for a new journal. He wanted to satisfy an audience that had been neglected by the state media on the one hand and misunderstood by private newspapers that seemed to have conflated public interest (durable by nature) and the interest of the public (ephemeral by definition) on the other.

Rejuvenating the Cameroonian press, Haman Mana created a newspaper called *Ozone*, which specialized in environmental issues. While Cameroonian readers liked the new media product, the founder quickly came to the realization that his venture would not pay off, as the newspaper was not selling. As such, he decided to abandon *Ozone* in favor of another project, but lacked the means to do so. This was compounded by the fact that he was unemployed because he had already left the *Cameroon Tribune* and *Le Messager*.

As a means of survival, Haman Mana, who has married in the meantime, had become a *taximan* (taxi driver), driving a taxi during the day and working on his media projects at night. At that time, he designed a new newspaper to revolutionize the Cameroonian media scene. In July 1996, when he was thirty years of age, Pépin Haman Mana launched another newspaper, *Mutations*. Its slogan was an entire program: *vif dans le ton, sérieux dans la tenue, iconoclaste dans les positions, culturel dans la vision* ("vivid in its tone, serious in its claim, iconoclastic in its positioning, cultural in its vision"). With the newspaper, he has two trumps: he only worked with trained journalists and he declared his independence from political power.

Before his appearance, the Cameroonian press had been greatly inhibited. Trained journalists had been integrated into the public sector, where they forgot the values of objectivity, neutrality, and impartiality they had learned in school (Nyamnjoh 2005). Additionally, private newspapers focused on maintaining the profession's ethical and deontological rules without, however, being able to keep to them, because those men and women who worked for them had never had the opportunity to learn these rules.

The mere fact that Pépin Haman Mana launched the newspaper *Mutations* with four diploma holders (Alain Blaise Batongue, Emmanuel Gustave Samnick, Emmanuel Mbede, and Serges Alain Godong) from the Ecole supérieure des sciences et techniques de l'information (ESSTI) based in Yaounde was a revolution. It was also a token of success, as before Haman

Mana, private media in Cameroon was essentially produced by journalists who had not received training in that domain. Certainly, before the creation of *Mutations*, the wealthy Fadil family had already bought back the newspapers *Dikalo* and *Challenge Hebdo* that were published by some trained journalists. But the Fadils obviously lacked the slightest experience in managing a media enterprise and were soon abandoned by their educated journalists because of "incompatibility of theirs and the patron's sense of humor". The content of the newspaper *Mutations* differs from existing journals. This novel weekly publishes detailed research reports about civil servants' performance and interesting stories from within society. His readership is able to note that the newspaper respects its slogan: the language of *Mutations* is lively and pleasant, its claims are serious, its positions iconoclastic, and its vision cultural. His readers accept it and his sales corroborate the fact that it is a success.

Haman Mana is the son of a leading general of the Cameroonian army who originates from the north of the country. The revenues from the sale of his newspaper had yet to satisfy his ambitions and he wanted to grow it. As such, responding to the high demand of his readership, the young publisher changed the periodicity of *Mutations* from a weekly at its creation in 1996 to a daily in 2002. As soon as the newspaper stabilized, Haman Mana came in contact with a financier. Protais Ayangma Amang, the owner of the insurance company *La Citoyenne*, began to provide the necessary financial support for printing the daily and the salaries needed to pay its staff. With this change, *Mutations* became the first Cameroonian daily in terms of sales. His employees are not only well trained but also well paid. Many young diploma holders from the school of journalism have applied to work with him and several of Cameroon's most prominent media personalities began their career with *Mutations*, including Cheta Bilé, Aimé Robert Biyina (CRTV), and Dominique Mbassi (Repères).

As an astute entrepreneur, the publishing director of *Mutations* decided to diversify his products with the objective of occupying the empty spaces available on the information market. As such, Haman Mana created the newspaper *Situations* to satisfy the need to participate in social events, and he created *Ndamba* for the country's sports fans of the Lions Indomptables. Until that time, intellectuals also did not have their own journal. The indefatigable entrepreneur therefore developed *Les Cahiers de Mutations*, a monthly that analyzes topics on a deeper level to increase understanding about them. To oversee production of those titles (*Mutations*, *Situations*, *Ndamba*, and *Les Cahiers de Mutations*), he united them under one roof, the South Media Group.

Suddenly, in 2007, a serious crisis arose between Haman Mana and his financial partner Protais Ayangma Amang in a fight about the ownership of the journals *Mutations*, *Situations*, *Ndamba*, and *Les Cahiers de Mutations*. Indicative of the anticipatory capacity that only a proper visionary has, Haman Mana underwent a new entrepreneurial transformation and sacrificed the South Media Group and launched the daily *Le Jour* the next day. Less than a decade later, Protais Ayangma Amang was forced to admit that he could not continue the journals he had taken from Haman Mana, and in 2014, *Ndamba*, *Les Cahiers de Mutations*, and *Situations* ceased to exist.

In contrast, Haman Mana's *Le Jour* has become the country's first private daily in terms of sales and notoriety. As an untiring creator of enterprises, Haman Mana founded his seventh newspaper, *La Pointe du Jour*. This thematic periodical with an intellectualist focus fills the empty space that the disappearance of *Les Cahiers de Mutations* has left.

Differing from the vast majority of media entrepreneurs who think that the under-financing of the Cameroonian media can be described as an exogenous problem, Haman Mana believes that media patrons are the victims of their own depravity. In Cameroon, there were, for example, no newspapers that specialized in sport, literature, or entertainment. When he was invited to talk about the under-financing of the Cameroonian media in the framework of the Press Club of the Friedrich Ebert Foundation in Yaounde on 19 July 2008, Haman Mana stated without wasting time that "the management of journals has not yet sufficiently explored the possibilities of profitability that these media offer", continuing that "the journalists should work to be accepted by the quality of their newspapers" (Djimeli 2012: 106, my translation). Haman Mana made his daily *Le Jour* and his periodical *La Pointe du Jour* profitable. He also deserves praise for the informative content of his products.

With the aim of diversifying his sources of income, Haman Mana created a publishing house (Éditions du Schabel) in 2009. His daily, *Le Jour*, and his company, Schabel, both based in Yaounde, have become a success. In 2011, this new publishing house was chosen by MTN, the most important mobile telephone company in Cameroon, to publish the book that commemorated its founding ten years prior (Anon, 2011). With Mireille Bisseck, Haman Mana wrote and published *Rois et royaumes bamiléké* (*Kings and Kingdoms of Bamileke*, 2011) which traces the history of the traditional chiefdoms in west Cameroon. This book received a great deal of attention both on the national and the international levels.

The details outlined above suggest that Haman Mana's profile does not correspond with that of a classical entrepreneur who invests the money he borrows from a bank to buy a patent and construct an industrial enterprise producing commodities. As a trained journalist, he worked with newspapers, drove a taxi to earn a living, and created his first newspaper. This was followed by the creation of a second newspaper, then a third, and several more. Once Haman Mana had created his newspapers, he assumed the double role of manager and publisher. During the World Cup in Brazil in 2014, for example, Haman Mana wrote a column every day, *La chronique du DP*, in his daily *Le Jour* and he closely observed the daily production of the journal.

The secret of Haman Mana seems to reside in the fact that he is the principal commercial agent of his journal. He personally meets the patrons of public and private enterprises and asks them to advertise with him. He chats regularly with the newspaper sellers to know what the Cameroonians love to read. The answers he receives serve as the basis for research and coverage that he asks to be carried out and published a few days later. His journal has become a veritable bridge between the supply of and demand for information in Cameroon. Haman Mana is the only patron of a daily who has signed the collective national agreement of journalists and professionals related to social communication, adopted on 12 November 2008 (Tchakoua 2010: 50), which obliges patrons of the press to pay their employees a decent salary.

## Sévérin Tchounkeu: The Initiator of the Group La Nouvelle Expression

Originating from the West Region of Cameroon, Sévérin Tchounkeu came to the press in the aftermath of the efforts of democratization and the multiparty system. In 1991, Sévérin Tchounkeu, while he was still studying political science in Paris, decided to travel to his home country, which, by that point, had changed drastically since he had left, particularly with the implementation of free social communication that had been passed a year earlier.

During his return to Cameroon, Tchounkeu engaged in the political debate that had just begun in society as the country was preparing for the presidential elections planned for 1992. This election was important, as it marked the first time since 1982 that President Paul Biya had to run to secure his position and faced other candidates who were representing newly formed parties. People were eager not to miss any bit of this democratic swing and the election was continually reported on in the press (Ndongo 1993). The young Sévérin Tchounkeu distinguished himself among the crowd of journalists with his pertinent analyses of the situation.

Facing this success, he requested financial help from his senior brother, an established trader in the economic capital of Cameroon (Douala), so that he could create a weekly, *La Nouvelle Expression*. This new journal quickly became successful. Encouraged by his success, Sévérin Tchounkeu purchased a rotary press and opened printers at Douala to produce his own newspapers and reduce production costs. *La Nouvelle Expression* became a daily in 2004 in order to satisfy his readership and above all some clients who wanted to publish their advertisements daily in the newspaper. Being a *"bon bamiléké"*, as people say in Cameroon to characterize those who take the initiative, Sévérin Tchounkeu did not hesitate to find a way to profit from the decree N°2000/158 of 3 April 2003 *"fixant les conditions et les modalités de création et d'exploitation des entreprises privées de communication audiovisuelle"* ("fixing the conditions and modalities of creation and exploitation for private enterprises of audiovisual communication") signed by the Cameroonian Prime Minister. This decree has facilitated Tchounkeu's extension of his economic empire.

When he noticed that his daily *La Nouvelle Expression* became a success, Séverin Tchounkeu decided to diversify his media products, beginning with audiovisual media. Article 34 of the law N°90/052 of 19 December 1990 on social communication in Cameroon declares in Paragraph 2 that "a license is required whenever a private enterprise wants to create or exploit a radio or television station. The conditions and modalities of reception of the license, as specified in Paragraph 2, are regulated according to the recommendations of the Conseil National de la Communication". The conditions and modalities of reception were published by the decree N°2000/158 of 3 April 2000 "fixing the conditions and modalities of creation and exploitation for private enterprises of audiovisual communication" (CRTV 2000, my translation).

To be able to better counter the "power of sound and image" (Airault 2004: 47, my translation), the Cameroonian government institutionalized a license for audiovisual exploitation. Article 15 of Decree of 3 April 2000 sets the amount that has to be paid for the license as follows: commercial radio stations pay 10 million FCFA (about $19,200) and non-commercial radio stations pay 5 million FCFA, commercial television stations pay 100 million FCFA ($192,000) and non-commercial television stations pay 25 million FCFA (about $48,000). These licenses are valid for ten years for a television station and for five years for a radio station.

Convinced that these amounts were discouraging when compared to the economic level of the country, the authorities created the so-called principle of "administrative tolerance". Theoretically, it enabled the state to allow entrepreneurs to open and run a radio or television station while they were still waiting for their license. However, as Alexandre T. Djimeli (2012) states, as this administrative tolerance was "applied in a discriminatory way—it did not work out for potential media people in the same way—it became a kind of Damocles sword" that threatened the media entrepreneurs. It was sufficient to make a broadcast or reportage that the authorities did not like and they closed the studio for "illegal exercise of the profession".

To cope with such a closed opening, the economic actors needed to develop their imaginativeness or intelligence in the sense that they were required to successfully manage the authorities' desired censorship and the expression of their opinion in public. In reality, they face a double challenge: how to satisfy the curiosity of their audiences who want to know what the authorities hide from their eyes and ears, without, in turn, suffering from the authorities' retaliations. Only those entrepreneurs who have found good solutions for these challenges have been able to achieve success in the audiovisual media sector.

Despite this juridico-administrative and politico-economical confusion, Séverin Tchounkeu prepared his application papers to open Equinoxe

Télévision. On 10 October 2006, the Minister of Communication, Ebénézer Njoh Mouelle, judged the application favorably. Having obtained the permission of the minister, Tchounkeu was among the first media entrepreneurs in Cameroon to have a daily newspaper (*La Nouvelle Expression*), a radio station (Radio Equinoxe), a television station (Equinoxe Télévision), and a printing press. Most importantly, however, he not only created all these enterprises, he also made them profitable. Tchounkeu followed the trajectory of French journalist Edwy Plenel, paying attention to prior research and giving a voice to the voiceless. As Plenel suggested earlier, Séverin Tchounkeu understood that if he wanted to be distinct, his broadcast would have to "do research in the school, on poverty and the conditions of life as much as on political and financial scandals" (Hunter 1997: 113–114, my translation).

To be able to survive in this competitive environment, Radio Equinoxe focused on interactive broadcasts. Instantly, its audience in Douala, where the station is based, felt it was taken seriously by his radio broadcast. Tchounkeu developed a quiz show in which members of the audience were compensated for good answers to the questions posed by the radio presenters in the broadcast, *Jambo* (game of chance), which was moderated by the humorist Tchop-Tchop.

This interactive innovation enabled the young entrepreneur Séverin Tchounkeu to beat the public media that ruled Cameroon's media scene for decades and had been content with the hardly value-increasing praxis that Michel Eoné Tjade calls the "seated journalism (*journalisme assis*) that gives preference if not exclusivity to government reports and basically covers institutional events" (2001: 25). Equinoxe, which asks the public to participate in the broadcast, was rather baptized "the people's radio" because Equinoxe was the first interactive radio station in Cameroon. It gave people the opportunity to express themselves by calling the station when they wanted to participate in the broadcast *Jambo*. To date, this station remains close to the ordinary people and is referred to with the slogan "the people's radio". This approach toward the voiceless constitutes the major added value that has allowed Séverin Tchounkeu to gain a foothold in this media universe, which is governed by economical Darwinism in which big enterprises devour the small ones in order to survive.

To survive, however, an entrepreneur needs the necessary means. The means are in the banks that refuse to lend money, arguing that media are not profitable. Public media live from the audiovisual fee that is deducted monthly from civil servants' salaries. Private media, however, have for a long time accepted the refusal of the banks and have not asked for credit to finance their ventures and those who did generally submitted low-grade applications. The patron of the group La Nouvelle Expression was able to persuade the banks with his well-prepared application and received financial support from two banks.

Obviously, Séverin Tchounkeu's status as an entrepreneur can be attributed to his capacity to seize opportunities and pull ashore appropriate projects. In 1991, jumping on the law that liberalized social communication in Cameroon, he launched the newspaper *La Nouvelle Expression*. At the time, he had no support from the banks but asked his family to give him money. Mr. Tchounkeu has not remained with just one journal; he has diversified his products and created a radio and a television station. He was not only busy with his management tasks, connected with his entrepreneurship, but often wrote the editorials in his daily newspaper, *La Nouvelle Expression*, himself.

In 2014, Séverin Tchounkeu is the only media entrepreneur in Central Africa who owns a daily (*La Nouvelle Expression*), a radio station (Radio Equinoxe), and a television station (Equinoxe TV). He has united all his enterprises in the group La Nouvelle Expression, which currently employs almost 300 people. To better understand the success of Séverin Tchounkeu, it is important to get beyond his entrepreneurial intuition and analyze his management strategy. He has not even paid the 100 million FCFA (about $192,000) for the broadcasting license for his television station and the 10 million (about $19,200) for the radio station yet, but Equinoxe TV and Radio Equinoxe function well under the regime of the "administrative tolerance" which enables media entrepreneurs to function while waiting to fulfil their fiscal obligations. In 2008, when the "hunger riots" broke out in Cameroon, thousands of youths went out into the streets to protest the price increase of petrol and foodstuffs. The authorities reacted by sending policemen, gendarmes, and the military to stop the demonstrations. Equinoxe documented the cruelty of the forces of order when they fired at the defenseless youth. Its journalists described the situation in detail. The authorities were unhappy and decided to close Equinoxe's radio and TV studios for several months.

## Emmanuel Chatué's Canal2 International: Television for the Public and the Authorities

Emmanuel Chatué was born in Bandjoun in the West Region of Cameroon and holds a diploma in telecommunication sciences. He became known to the Cameroonian public due to his television channel Canal2 International and his radio station Sweet FM, both based in Douala. As is the case with most Cameroonian entrepreneurs, Emmanuel Chatué's past remains a mystery. His economic activities are, however, well known, and both the entrepreneur and his followers talk with ease about them.

Chatué's entrepreneurship began with the cable distribution enterprise TV+. This start-up enterprise sells images that are broadcast by foreign, mostly western, television channels. At that time, when satellite dishes still cost about 1.5 million FCFA (about $2,880), television owners had access to journals, serialized stories, and soap operas from abroad only when they subscribed to TV+, and in Douala and Yaounde, the number of subscribers grew quickly.

When the Decree of 3 April 2000 was issued to regulate the modalities of the creation and exploitation of audiovisual enterprises, Emmanuel Chatué decided to create his own television channel, Canal2. He began to produce and sell his own images. However, only two years later, Canal2 closed its doors, as its organizational structure was weak. At that point, Chatué decided to become a real entrepreneur. He had to rethink the project, find the means to get it going again, and above all make his incipient enterprise profitable.

In 2004 the enterprise opened its doors again and advertised its new ambition: to expand globally. Canal2's transformation into Canal2 International marked the ground zero for Chatué's great innovations. First of all, he connected his television channel to satellites; in September 2004, Canal 2 International was connected to the satellite W3A and in November 2005 to the satellite NSS7. In February 2006, the channel was integrated with the group Canal Satellite, and later the ADSL network in Europe (Free, Neuf, Orange, Numéricâble, etc.). In his home country, Canal2 International broadcasted clear images on channel 25 of the UHF band in Cameroon's big cities and by cable in the remaining towns. Two years after it reopened, the channel was moved to its own premises in 6 Rue Njo-Njo in Douala.

Canal2 International is the first private television channel that covers the entire country. Becoming successful, its owner also benefited from the weariness of the audience. Indeed more generally in Africa, "since the end of the 1980s, the intensification and aggravation of the economic and social crisis, of poverty and inequalities, made populism and corruption intolerable, and led to protests against single-party regimes while the state media were affected by a crisis of legitimacy and losing credibility in the eyes of their audiences" (Tudesq 2003: 71, my translation). Furthermore, the Cameroonian audience felt increasingly disappointed with the CRTV's "monochrome images", which were, above all, preoccupied with serving the president of the Republic and his ministers.

The demand, therefore, already existed and waited only for supply. In such a situation, the quality of the supply did not matter much for a Cameroonian public that had yet to develop reliable criteria for its appreciation. Emmanuel Chatué profited from this favorable environment and dynamized his channel's commercial service. He received advertisements and public relations reportage from all corners of society, including public administration and private enterprises. Chatué's development strategy included opening offices in other countries as well, namely in Europe and West Africa (Abidjan).

In 2007, the Minister of Communication, Ebénézer Njoh Mouelle, issued three licenses of media exploitation "on credit" for Emmanuel Chatué. The first was for his radio station (Sweet FM), the second for his television channel (Canal2 International), and the third for his cable distribution society (TV+). After he obtained his license in 2007, the channel was enlarged by six other departments (Department of Human Resources, Commercial

Department, Department of Information, Department of International Cooperation, Technical Department, Program Department) and broadcasted both the government's and Paul Biya's Cameroon Peoples Democratic Movement (CPDM) party's activities. CPDM meetings are often shown live for hours. The audience eventually baptized Canal2 "CRTV2", and its owner did not even seem overly shocked by this name. Chatué inaugurated the TV business in Cameroon when he opened his studios for all those who were able to pay for a television screen. Everyone came to him, from the small street sellers to the big importers, from the charlatans to all the other sorcerers who promise to heal the mentally ill and alleviate the pains of the victims of disappointed love with the magic of their enchanted images.

In a report on the functioning of radio and television stations in Cameroon, the journalist Justin Blaise Akono came to the conclusion that "in Cameroon, the private media [are] in chains (*enchaîné*)" (Akono 2014: 7–10).

## STV: The Visible Face of the Muketes

Without a doubt, the Muketes are not just a family, they are an entire enterprise: this aristocratic family from the Anglophone Region of South-West Cameroon functions exactly as an enterprise listed on the stock market. They meet each year, as all modern enterprises do, when they have their annual board meeting. Over the course of a century, the Muketes have constructed an empire that includes everything from agro-industry to media and telecommunication. The creation of the television channels STV1 and STV2 marks the entrepreneurial expansion of one of the Muketes's descendants, Colin Ebarko Mukete.

The creation and function of STV can be best understood through the lens of another enterprise that emerged one century earlier. The saga of the Muketes begins in 1910 when Abel Mukete created extensive plantations in southwest Kamerun (written with a "K" by the Germans who arrived in 1884, before the arrival of the British and French after the First World War). In 1928, the plantation Abel Mukete had created became known as A. Mukete and Sons Plantations. Today, A. Mukete and Sons Plantations has become Mukete Plantations Ltd and Mukete Estates Ltd and all of Mukete's sons are shareholders in this empire. This family enterprise specializes in raising oil palms, hevea, and cocoa trees. In the 1970s, Godfrey Mbe Mukete, the first Cameroonian diploma holder from the University of Yale, enlarged the plantations and diversified the crops when he was 59 with the help of credit from the Caisse centrale de coopération économique française (Juompan-Yakam 2011).

According to the Muketes's family tree, Abel Mukete is the father of Victor Essimi Mukete, the present paramount chief of the Bafaw in the South-West Region of Cameroon. Due to his good relationship with the Cameroonian authorities, Essimi Mukete was nominated senator on 8

May 2013 by President Paul Biya. His children include Godfrey Mbe (the manager of Mukete Estates Ltd), Jacob Diko (departmental manager of the African Development Bank), Colin Ebarko (founder of STV and president of the advisory board of MTN Cameroon), Ekale (mayor of Kumba I), John Akpo (owner of Amtrade), and Ekoko (the manager of Spectrum).

Since its establishment in Cameroon in 2001, the Muketes have owned 30% of the mobile phone company (MTN), which marked the family's entry into the field of new information and communication technologies. Gradually, the Muketes created a family-owned advertisement agency (Spectrum) and a television channel in 2007, which revolutionized the Cameroonian audiovisual landscape again. The creation of STV represents the materialization of the Muketes' entrepreneurial expansionism with its name, Spectrum Television (STV), being part of the prolongation of the family's advertisement agency.

One man is behind all these developments: Colin Ebarko Mukete. He is very discreet and hardly ever appears in public, not even on his own television channel (STV). Colin Ebarko Mukete lives between New York and Johannesburg. His last public appearance was on 18–19 November 2010 when the persistent entrepreneur took part in the third African Media Leaders Forum at Yaounde. These meetings of African media leaders are organized by the African Media Initiative, which allows an open and direct exchange between media entrepreneurs, the authorities, and bankers. Speaking at this forum, Colin Ebarko Mukete stated that the "Local National Organizing Committee of this Forum is happy to host this event because we believe that a professional and sustainable media can play a critical and transformational role in the economic, social, and political lives of nations". Colin Ebarko Mukete's assertion proves his desire to create STV, and, without doubt, to gain money, but also to ameliorate life as well as the relationships between the citizens and the nations, as he confirmed himself.

Fundamentally, STV is a media group that began with two television channels. The first, STV1, provides music and entertainment. The target audience is the youth. The second, STV2, is a more practical channel that broadcasts information (with several daily news programs), music, talk shows, and discussions. The STV television channels are broadcast for free and are unencrypted. STV1 and STV2 can be watched via antenna or satellite for direct reception at home, and via the cable network in Cameroon and beyond. STV's daily programs are based on locally produced content and target all social groups.

After its creation, STV recruited a well-versed journalist, the Senegalese Mactar Silla, as its manager. Mactar Silla holds a Ph.D. and he is the author of several books on communication. He also collected extensive professional experience. Before he joined the group STV, he was the manager of the national Radio Télévision in Senegal, manager of TV5 Afrique, manager of Worldspace Afrique, and regional manager of *AfricaOnline*. Due to his extensive experience, he successfully facilitated STV's emergence in the

Cameroonian context where the beginnings of competition were already visible. STV is broadcast on Intelsat 4 on band C since 1 October 2004 and distributed on the satellite NSS since March 2007. In the same year, the minister of communication, the philosopher Ebénézer Njoh Mouelle, issued a license for the STV Group.

To maintain its audience, STV acquired the exclusive distribution rights of the Barclays Premier Football League (United Kingdom) and La Liga (Spain) for Cameroonian territory in August 2007. In the country of the Indomitable Lions, where football has been baptized a "royal sport", STV was successful enough to acquire the financial means to secure the broadcasting rights for the British and Spanish championships. Every week, the television channel offers the audience in Cameroon and beyond two matches by direct transmission. The channel also offers a weekly program about the activities of African stars abroad, such as Samuel Eto'o, Didier Drogba, and others, and a weekly summary of the opportunities for goals of these two captivating champions.

The public was surprised by the innumerable innovations of this television channel, based in Douala in Cameroon and at the same time present at all the big global events. STV has become the channel for anyone who is passionate about football. This means that almost all families watch this channel, particularly when it broadcasts major football events.

Over the course of a decade, with its diversity of programs and the spontaneity of its information, STV has left its footprint in the Cameroonian media landscape and beyond. Always trying to diversify its products, the Muketes have succeeded in launching a new television channel specialized in music and show biz. They have also managed to create three television channels in only one decade. With roots in the advertising business, the Muketes have supplied the media landscape with the television channels STV1, STV2, and BoomTV. This diversification also reflects the vitality of the new media entrepreneurs in Cameroon.

## THE FOUR MAJOR CAMEROONIAN MEDIA ENTREPRENEURS COMPARED

This section compares the four entrepreneurs that were presented above: Haman Mana (*Le Jour*), Emmanuel Chatué (Canal2 International), Séverin Tchounkeu (Group La Nouvelle Expression), and Colin Ebarko Mukete (STV and BoomTV). I will begin with what they have in common, and continue with what makes each individual trajectory a success.

With the promotion of liberalization, Cameroon underwent profound changes concerning its ideological and political domains as well as its socio-economic infrastructure. The authorities had to accept political and social movements, and this reduced the president's power, installed a multiparty system, and launched the democratic process (Ngayap 1999: 7–22). As far as the media are concerned, the law N°90/052 of 19 December 1990 had a huge impact. It allowed entrepreneurs to freely invest in the creation of media. It was complemented by the decree N°2000/158 of 3 April 2003 that regulated the conditions and modalities of the creation and exploitation of private audiovisual media enterprises. These two legal regulations constitute the judicial and regulatory basis for the foundation of the four media enterprises that have been discussed in this chapter. This starting point unites the undertakings of Haman Mana, Emmanuel Chatué, Séverin Tchounkeu, and Colin Ebarko Mukete. This judicial regulation is tied to the logic of liberalism (economy, politics, moral) that has been catching on globally. Whether they are working in the print or audiovisual sector, the Cameroonian media entrepreneurs have to cope with the lack of advertisement, which in turn is due to the weak industrial fabric of the country. With the exception of mobile phone companies, breweries, cosmetics companies, and agro-industrials (subsidiaries of multinationals), only very few national companies have the means to launch veritable advertising campaigns. Notwithstanding, the revenues from advertisement remain the principal source of financing for the audiovisual media.

The four enterprises have also contributed to social transformation by providing information and education, and heightening the awareness of the citizens (Kouleu 2007). Media entrepreneurs in Cameroon also share the fact in common that they keep the sources of their capital and the strategies of their enterprises' development a secret. Despite these things in common, each of the four entrepreneurs discussed in this chapter have become successful due to their personal ingenuity. According to their focus of interest, their vision of the world, and their capital, they have to deliver a specific supply to the public's general demand for information.

Comparing the four entrepreneurial trajectories, singularities are evident in each of the success stories. Their choice for the name of their enterprises already distinguishes them from one another. They chose these names according to their respective interests. With the objective of marking the new era with which he began his entrepreneurial career, when Haman Mana decided to create his media group in 2007, he named his newspaper "*Le Jour*". Séverin Tchounkeu created "*La Nouvelle Expression*" with the intention of realizing his new vision and breaking with the partisan type of journalism prevalent in Cameroon before 1991. A spirit of rupture with existing practices and a need for innovation spurred the particular entrepreneurial activities of these two visionary men.

The entrepreneurs are also distinct in the way they find access to financial means. Séverin Tchounkeu and Colin Ebarko Mukete both began with the financial aid of their families. Haman Mana worked as a taxi driver and this enabled him to continue his journalism project, until he eventually succeeded in receiving financial help from Protais Ayangma Amang to create his newspaper, *Mutations*. Emmanuel Chatué began with cable distribution before he was able to create his television channel, Canal2, and later,

Canal2 International. These trajectories represent "itineraries of accumulation" (Banégas and Warnier 2001: 6) of media entrepreneurs and illustrate the diversity of ways that were pursued to create some of the more important structures that characterize the Cameroonian media landscape in the twenty-first century.

Each of the four media entrepreneurs chose his own strategy to expand his enterprise. Haman Mana created several newspapers (*Ozone, Mutations, Le Jour*) to diversify his media products and raise their revenues. Part of the strategy of diversification was to create his own publishing house. Confronted with the same problem, Séverin Tchounkeu rather decided to invest in audiovisual media and open a radio station (Radio Equinoxe) and a television channel (Equinoxe TV). Emmanuel Chatué and Ebarko Mukete had already found success in other entrepreneurial sectors, for example, agricultural food production in the case of Mukete and the commercial distribution of images by cable in the case of Chatué. For them, the creation of STV and Canal2 International respectively, formed part of their diversification strategies.

Finally, this comparison shows that the creation of the big Cameroonian media entrepreneurs was spurred by the judicial opportunities that notably the law of 19 December 1990 and the decree of 3 April 2000 provided. Furthermore, each entrepreneur defined his own strategy to make the enterprises that they had created viable and expand their economic empires.

## CONCLUSION: THE SIGNS OF VITALITY

This chapter has discussed the appearance of new media entrepreneurs in Cameroon. It has identified that they have positioned themselves in public space since the adoption of the law N°90/052 from 19 December 1990 which redefined social communication in Cameroon. Differing from industrial entrepreneurs who combine the novel ideas of inventors with the means that they borrow from banks to create their enterprises, the four media entrepreneurs who have been presented in this chapter are at the same time inventors, financiers, and managers of their own projects. The chapter began with the history of the Cameroonian mediascape in order to better situate the trajectories of the four big media entrepreneurs in their sociohistorical environment. This history recalled that the first newspapers were introduced to Cameroon by German missionaries at the beginning of the twentieth century, precisely in 1903. In Cameroon, these religious journals had no vision of profitability. In 1955, the production of newspapers was turned into an enterprise by the Frenchman Michel de Breteuil and further developed in 1974 by Abodel Karimou, the founder of the weekly *La Gazette*. Only a quarter century later, profiting from the efforts of democratization and the economic liberalization, four Cameroonians—Séverin Tchounkeu (La Nouvelle Expression), Colin Ebarko Mukete (STV), Emmanuel Chatué (Canal2

International), and Haman Mana (*Le Jour*)—revolutionized their country's media landscape, demonstrating an extraordinary entrepreneurial spirit. In conclusion, the success of media enterprises depends on objective and subjective conditions. The media entrepreneurs who have succeeded in the media sector are those who have carefully studied the social, political, and economic environment and knew how to constantly adapt the products they were able to supply to the specific demands of their readers, their listeners, and their TV audience.

## REFERENCES

Airault, Pascal. 2004. 'Des journaux en quête de lecteurs et d'annonceurs'. *Jeune Afrique l'Intelligent* 2277 (29 August–4 September): 42–43.
Akono, Justin-Blaise. 2014. 'L'audiovisuel enchaîné au Cameroun'. *Mutations* 3620 (3 April): 7–10.
Anon. 2011. *MTN Un ami de 10 ans*. Yaounde: Éditions Schabel.
Banégas, Richard and Jean Pierre Warnier. 2001. 'Nouvelles figures de la réussite et du pouvoir'. *Politique africaine* 82: 5–23.
Bisseck, Mireille and Haman Mana. 2011. *Rois et royaumes bamiléké*. Yaounde: Éditions Schabel.
Brincourt, Christian and Michel Leblanc. 1970. *Les reporters, Coulisses et secrets d'un métier. Cent journalistes racontent . . .* Paris: Robert Laffont.
Capul, Olivier and Jean Yves Garnier. 2005. *Dictionnaire d'économie et de sciences sociales*. Paris: Hatier.
Cohen, Elie. 2001. *Dictionnaire de gestion*. Paris: La découverte.
CRTV. 2000. *Journal radio*. Broadcast at 5 p.m.
Djimeli, Alexandre T. 2012. *Le capital contre le journalisme. La presse camerounaise entre missions sociales et obligations de rentabilité*. Yaoundé: Ifikiya.
Hunter, Mark. 1997. *Le journalisme d'investigation*. Paris: PUF.
Juompan-Yakam, Clarisse. 2011. 'Les grandes familles du Cameroun'. *Jeune Afrique*. www.jeuneafrique.com, accessed 12 juin 2014.
Kouleu, Ferdinand Chindji. 2007. *Communication et mobilisation sociale au Cameroun*. Yaoundé: Saagraph.
Le Floch, Patrick and Nathalie Sonnac. 2013. *L'économie de la presse*. Paris: La découverte.
Ndombo, Kale McDonald. 1997. 'Deconstructing the dialectics of press freedom in Cameroon'. In: Festus Eribo and William Jong-Ebot (eds). *Press freedom and communication in Africa*. Asmara: Africa World Press, 263–289.
Ndongo, Valentin Nga. 1993. *Les médias au Cameroun. Mythes et délires d'une société en crise*. Paris: l'Harmattan.
Ngayap, Pierre Flambeau. 1999. *L'opposition au Cameroun. Les années de braise*. Paris: l'Harmattan.
Nyamnjoh, Francis. 2004. 'Global and local trends in media ownership and control: implications for cultural creativity in Africa'. In: Wim van Binsbergen, Rijk van Dijk, and Jan-Bart Gewald (eds). *Situating Globality: African Agency in the Appropriation of Global Culture*. Leiden: Brill, 57–89.
Nyamnjoh, Francis. 2005. *Africa's Media: Democracy and the Politics of Belonging*. London: Zed Books.
Okala, Jean-Thobie. 1999. *La télévision africaine sous tutelle. L'exemple camerounais*. Paris: L'Harmattan.

Provost, Joël. 1986. *Les mots de l'économie*. Paris: Ellipses.

Sipa, Jean Baptiste. 2010. 'La précarité de la presse camerounaise et la nécessité d'un plaidoyer pour une intervention de l'Etat'. In: *La viabilité des entreprises de presse au Cameroun: situation et perspectives*. Collection of papers of a conference organized by the Syndicat des journalistes employés du Cameroun from 18 to 19 February 2010 in Yaoundé.

Tchakoua, Jean Marie. 2010. 'Le statut du salarié de l'entreprise de presse au Cameroun'. In *La viabilité des entreprises de presse au Cameroun: situation et perspectives*. Collected papers of the conference organized in Yaounde from 18–19 February 2010 by the Syndicat des journalistes employés du Cameroun.

Tjade, Eoné Michel. 1986. *Radios, publics et pouvoirs au Cameroun. Utilisations officielles et besoins sociaux*. Paris: l'Harmattan.

Tjade, Eoné Michel. 2001. *Démocratisation, libéralisation et liberté de communication au Cameroun. Avancées et reculades*. Paris: l'Harmattan.

Tudesq, André-Jean. 1999. *Les médias en Afrique*. Paris: Ellipses.

Tudesq, André-Jean. 2002. *L'Afrique parle, l'Afrique écoute. Les radios en Afrique subsaharienne*. Paris: Karthala.

Tudesq, André-Jean. 2003. *Radio: Africa's Major Media*. www.african-geopolitics. org, accessed 31 January 2005.

Zoe-Obanga, Jean Samuel and Jacqueline Moutome Ekambi. 2006. *Ethique et communication au Cameroun*. Yaoundé: Édition Clé.

## Journals and Official Documents

Décret N°2000/158 du 03 avril 2000 "Fixant les conditions et les modalités de création et d'exploitation des entreprises privées de communication audiovisuelle". Published by the Service du Premier ministre du Cameroun (Yaounde).

Loi N°90/052 du 19 décembre 1990 régissant la communication sociale au Cameroun. Published by CRTV, Yaounde.

# 12 Aspiring to Be Praised with Many Names

## Success and Obstacles in Malian Media Entrepreneurship

*Ute Röschenthaler*

In 2013, Mande Massa, a popular radio presenter in Bamako, told me that he had started his own radio station that he called "Radio Dakan, la voix du destin" ("Voice of Destiny") because, as he explained, he had dedicated his professional life to the radio and creating media products was his destiny. He founded his own station in order to fully commit his energy to this venture, be independent, and benefit from his work without being exposed to the constant friction associated with the radio's asymmetrical employment relationships. Opening a new radio station was a risky enterprise because, since the early 1990s, a high number of private radio stations had been founded in the country, which competed for audiences and influential merchants' needs for publicity. Mande Massa nevertheless decided to invest his energy and money so that he could have his own station. Although radio is his central concern, he also produces films, television shows, and cloths with his image and organizes concerts and other public events. Mande Massa embodies many of the qualities of an entrepreneur but, from the local Malian perspective, is not regarded as such. Indeed, such individuals are in Bamako referred to as a praised person. From a scholarly perspective, he comes closer to what Banégas and Warnier (2001) refer to as a "figure of success", albeit with a large followership and a wish to enhance social life and preserve Mande family values.

This chapter will analyze the grounds on which Mande Massa's success is based.[1] It explores diverging notions of entrepreneurship, the lens of Mande Massa's career, and his products. I will begin by discussing the concept of the classical entrepreneur in relation to local concepts of successful individuals. I will then contextualize his career, which began in the early 1990s, in Bamako's bustling mediascape, followed by a discussion of the decisive steps he took in his professional life and the development of his media products and enterprise. The chapter concludes by examining his entrepreneurial skills from the local perspective.

## THE CONCEPT OF THE ENTREPRENEUR AND FIGURES OF SUCCESS IN MALI

When I asked people in Bamako about entrepreneurs and successful individuals, most described these individuals using various words but did not seem to have a clear idea of what being an entrepreneur entailed. Mande Massa also hesitated to call himself an entrepreneur, preferring instead to define himself as a *tógotigi*, somebody praised with many names. Indeed there is no word in Bamanakan that reflects the concept of "entrepreneur". This has to do with the history of the term: the classical entrepreneur as a figure emerged during industrialization and is largely linked to the production of commodities and services with economic aspirations. As such, social compatibility and respect of cultural values remain in the background.

Bamanakan, the language widely spoken in Bamako and southern parts of Mali, has several words that refer to successful individuals. They connote entrepreneurial activities but also include other concepts of popular, rich, and socially influential personalities. The *tógotigi* is a popular person, a celebrity that has received many names (*tógo*) from the public to praise him, while *dáwulatigi* refers more to rich, famous, successful, and popular persons with renown beauty, prestige, and glory (*dáwula*). Both terms place more emphasis on social appreciation than entrepreneurial capacities. The term for patron, *báaratigi*, comes closer to this. It not only connotes supervising workers (*báarakela*) and financial means but also reflects spiritual and occult capacities. Although entrepreneurs and merchants are often grouped together, the Bamanakan term for merchant, *jàgókèla* (a person that makes commerce, *jàgò*), does not pertain to being a master or patron or inducing social veneration and glory.[2] Indeed, the *jàgòkela* often acts as a sponsor or financier, and is in this sense an entrepreneur, who searches for advertising space to enhance the popularity of his products and image among potential clients. Becoming a figure of success always implies constant struggles and the awareness that success is dynamic and cannot be permanent.

The personality of the classical entrepreneur, as characterized by Schumpeter, embodies many of the attributes I will identify in Mande Massa's career: innovation, strength to resist social pressure, visions for the future, the conviction that he can bring projects to fruition, and the capacity to find the means to do so, that is, the willingness to take risks and accrue debt (Bude 1997; Schumpeter 1934). Nevertheless, while Mande Massa embodies these qualities, he still differs from this kind of classical entrepreneur in several ways: he is also a creator, artist, and film actor himself, and is also his own producer. He has a large audience that gives him prestige and popular appeal that the classical industrial entrepreneur only rarely receives. As Heinz Bude states, the entrepreneur does not depend on large crowds of followers but on credit (1997: 870). Popular personalities such as Mande Massa often embody the conviction of investing their energy in the service of the community, striving to preserve the values of Mande culture and identity, and stabilizing society in times of rapid cultural change in the urban environment and a globalizing world.

Mande Massa acts not as the parasite of an inventor,[3] but is a mediator between sponsors or patrons and the audience in a process enhancing prestige. This combination makes him resemble the figures of success that Banégas and Warnier (2001) describe and which many other African entrepreneurs also embody. Mande Massa has the courage to realize his visions, finds new formats for broadcasts, and discovers ways to work as an independent media presenter in Bamako; he looks for credit and invests his own money. He also has properties of Lindstrom's (1984) Big Men, who focus on the particular skills necessary to attract large crowds of followers that have to be convinced and continually beguiled. As I will illustrate in this chapter, Mande Massa embodies the qualities of all three concepts and additionally has the wish of enhancing society and preserving the Mande values, activities for which he is "praised with many names" by his audience.

## THE MEDIA SITUATION IN BAMAKO SINCE THE 1990S—A SUITABLE SPRINGBOARD

Most of the literature on mass media in Africa focuses on various aspects of media consumption and its potential for development, nation-building, and democracy (Abu-Lughod 2004; Askew 2002; Bourgault 1995; Fardon and Furniss 2000). Far less attention has been paid to founders of radio stations and creators of media products (for an exception see the special issue of the *Journal of African Cultural Studies* 25.1, 2013). Conversely, most scholarly work on entrepreneurship is concerned with industrial production and trade, documenting its diversity in the economic domain (Ellis and Fauré 1995; Jalloh and Falola 2002), the challenges of entrepreneurship in uncertain environments (MacGaffey 1987, 1998), and entrepreneurship's role in development (Spring and McDade 1998). The entrepreneurial aspects of media persons, religious leaders, and wealthy artists are usually not the focus of attention.

Many regions of Africa have cultivated a rich repertoire of media cultures, long before the colonial introduction of the printing press and electronic media. Such cultures include praise singers, drummers, dance groups, and theatre specialists, some of which developed great entrepreneurial qualities (Röschenthaler 2011). Although this aspect will not be developed here, it is important to mention that some of these media actors continue to be of importance in the urban context and elements of such outputs are incorporated into present-day electronic media practices. Mande Massa's radio theatre, *Baroni*, for example, draws on such performances, although he himself emphasizes the novelty of his radio broadcast.

Initially, colonially introduced media, such as newspapers and radio stations, were monopolized by independent governments for nation-building. Independent media entrepreneurship was therefore barely possible in Mali, as well as in many other African countries.[4] This situation changed with reforms that took place in the early 1990s, which created a favorable environment for media entrepreneurs. Already a year before the new media law was passed in October 1992, the first private radio station in Bamako, Radio Bamakan, began its broadcasts. Soon thereafter, numerous private media emerged, including independent newspapers (Keita 1992), radio stations (Myers 2000; Schulz 1999), some television stations (Dioh 2009), and internet cafés. In 1997, sixty-five officially registered local radio stations of various statuses (commercial, religious, communal, rural) already existed in Mali, fifteen of which were located in the capital of Bamako (Schulz 1999: 165). In 2013, their number had grown to several hundred in the country with more than twenty located in the capital.[5]

This liberated media situation created a hitherto nonexistent entrepreneurial atmosphere. The degree to which founders of radio stations were entrepreneurial depended largely on their financial situation and institutional affiliation. Some were part of a larger organization, such as a religious institution, a political party, or a development body. Others had initially received support from foreign donors, especially in the form of equipment and training, but were then left alone to survive and suffer from a constant lack of financial resources. Despite their popularity and large audiences, such independent radio stations are only able to generate a limited income through advertisements and other private sector services. They do not earn enough to cover their expenses and are in a state of constant financial insecurity. In large cities, such as Bamako, radio stations can at least hope for support from merchant advertising and sponsorship; but in rural areas people lack the buying power to invest in publicity and therefore radio stations need to locate alternative forms of support (Schulz 2002: 154).

From the 1990s on, private television stations also appeared on the market, among them the French channel Canal+ Horizons, followed by local stations like Télé Klédu and Multicanal SA (Dioh 2009). In 2004, a Malian entrepreneur, Ismaïla Sidibe, opened the television station Africable in Bamako, and Mande Massa began to collaborate with the station soon after.[6] As a media entrepreneur, Sidibe also works with a number of merchants who advertise with him.

Many of the new activities are intertwined, including the creation of private radio and television stations, the emergence of advertising agencies, the trade and commerce with new locally created or imported brand name products. Opportunities—real or imagined—give the growing city its specific attraction and appeal and showcase it as a privileged place for cultural invention and for the creation of popular cultures (Barber 1987; Falola and Salm 2005). Indeed, over the course of the past couple of decades, Bamako has doubled its population and is currently approaching two million inhabitants.[7] In this cultural and political environment, many people sensed a new era of entrepreneurial activity. It was also during this period that Mande Massa came to Bamako and began his media career.

## MANDE MASSA'S CAREER AS RADIO PRESENTER

Mande Massa's family background and the prospects offered by his formal education did not inspire his inclination for the media. He discovered his creative talents and sense of achievement as a radio presenter rather casually while looking for employment in Bamako. His biography supports claims made by entrepreneurial theories that see a certain number of entrepreneurs in every society rather than the capacities inherited from family traditions or ethnic affiliation that may be important in other contexts.

Boubacar Konaté—alias Mande Massa—was born in 1970 in a village near Kayes in western Mali, the son of a Malinke father and a Wolof mother. After school, he first engaged in petty trade along the railway between Kayes and Senegal. Trying to improve his and his parents' economic condition in the village, he moved to Bamako to study transit business and accounting. During a period of unemployment following graduation, he discovered his love for the radio as he became fascinated with the radio presenter at ORTM, actor and filmmaker Moussa Keïta. Mande Massa recalled: "Whenever I listened to him, I loved the radio . . . and I said to myself, this is my destiny. I have to follow it . . . and it became my passion to be a radio presenter" (interview May 2013). He began to push his luck and try his hand at radio.

The early 1990s were favorable for such a decision: new independent radio stations were being established everywhere in the country, and young talented presenters in demand. He applied for a traineeship with Radio Guintan, a newly founded radio station with a predominantly female audience, and in November 1995 he began to work there. After some months of training, the director and founder of the radio—one of the few females to create a radio station[8]—asked him to help open a branch station in another region of Mali. He agreed, and opted for Mopti, where in 1996 Guintan remained the first private radio station. Here, Mande Massa created his radio broadcast *Baroni*, a serialized radio theatre staged using a small team of actors.

*Baroni* means small discussion (*petite coserie*) among friends. Mande Massa's *Baroni* combines the idea of the small discussion (*baroni*) with a humorous and entertaining role play (*koteba*), including advice or moral lessons that should be learned from it.[9] Differing from *koteba*, the audience does not see actors, but hears them discussing as if they were in a play. The audience is no longer physically present and female roles are played by women (and not young men). In his *théâtre radiophonique*, as Mande Massa calls it, a group of actors sits around a table and discusses topics in the local language, Bamanakan. Each actor plays a role related to the topic and is projected into the royal environment in which the women represent the different wives and Mande Massa plays the Mande king (*masa*). According to Mande Massa, at that time his *Baroni* differed from that of other radio presenters as he used a serialized story form that continued for several weeks.

His broadcast soon became very successful. However, when he was not—despite being promised he would be—promoted director of Radio Guintan's Mopti branch, he decided to return to Bamako in 2000, where he worked with Radio Donko, another private radio station, and a new team of actors. One year later, he moved on to Radio Liberté, as its broadcast covered the entire city. The director gave him two hours of broadcast time twice a week. *Baroni* quickly became popular and, at the behest of the audience, his broadcast was shifted to the early morning hours.

*Baroni* thematizes problems that can arise between spouses and co-wives in polygamous families, and offers the reflection and advice the audience longs to hear. Mande Massa attributes the success of his *Baroni* to its role in responding to its predominantly female audience's daily concerns. According to his own estimation, women between forty and ninety years of age comprise 90% of his audience. These women like to listen to his broadcast when he talks about situations and experiences similar to their own.

As Mande Massa explained:

> Via the *Baroni* I can communicate many messages to the women. . . . Sometimes the women call me. One of them told me: "I was already about to divorce my husband, but because of your broadcast . . . I am again on good terms with him. I listened carefully to you". It [the *Baroni*] educates, it is a broadcast that sensitizes, but I challenge people's ways of thinking. And you feel that you are concerned. . . . When I take the issue "conflict between two co-wives", you see that the husband is involved with only one, and no longer cares about the other. And you, you have lived through all this, you listen, and it makes you think about your past. Or you are about to experience this in that very moment when I talk in the broadcast, and you feel that this is your situation. Some of the women then raise the volume so that their husbands will have to listen to it. (interview May 2013, all interview translations are mine)

So, instead of fighting for the rights of the women, he seeks to help them understand and master their situation as well as their husbands better and continue their matrimonial life in the compound. Mande Massa intends to preserve the Mande values, the *dànbe*,[10] and educate both women and their husbands.

His success reached an apex in 2006. *Baroni* was ranked as the most listened to broadcast in Bamako among female audiences and Mande Massa was selected the best radio promoter of the year. The minister for the Promotion of Women, the Family, and the Child invited him to receive the highly desired trophy, the Tamani d'Or, which all radio presenters aspire to win.[11] He received the trophy in the presence of Amadi Toumani Touré, the former president of Mali, and his wife, Mme Touré Lobo, in the Palais de la Culture on 8 March, International Women's Day. Mande Massa was duly proud that he had received the award and that his popularity and the social impact of his broadcast had been officially acknowledged by his audience. In the same year, Radio Liberté also made him program director.

Until 2006, Mande Massa was a successful radio presenter, whom people addressed as *tógotigi*, a popular figure, referred to with many praise names.

He was, however, not yet an entrepreneur. This next career step was triggered by the award, which strengthened his vision and set his conviction to become an independent media producer in motion. He felt that he had worked long enough for others without receiving a fixed salary, living from the bits and pieces that were offered to him by the radio directors for whom he had worked. He was not the only radio presenter who lived under such conditions; most private radio stations lacked financial resources and were forced to survive on more or less nothing with the exception of the revenue from a few advertisements.

In March 2007, Mande Massa organized his first concert in the Palais de la Culture. The hall—with 3,500 seats—was filled with women from far and wide. His concerts follow a specified plan: Mande Massa invites his *jèliwba* (great family praise singers) and other locally known griottes, popular singers, and entertainers to contribute and they perform the first couple of hours before Mande Massa arrives in the concert hall. For each concert he appears in a special way. In 2009, for instance, he entered the hall on a horse, while in 2010 in a beam of light from his royal chamber. In 2011, he arrived in a saloon projected for the audience on a video screen. Before his appearance in the hall, his favorite griotte sings his special praise song (*fàsa*), "Mande Massa, the Mande king, the descendant of Sunjiata's son, Sunjiata Keïta, the descendant of the Mande". She sings as if he was the Mande king himself. While she performs his praise song, Mande Massa appears to the public, waving his royal scepter. After the singers have performed and praised him sufficiently, Mande Massa stages a piece of the *Baroni* with his team, another highlight of the concert. With the *Baroni*, the concert comes to an end.

In 2008, he felt that there was more to gain from the concert and created a cloth that had photographs of him and his team on it so that women could use it to tailor dresses to wear to the event. Mande Massa invested his means to gain more, combining what is useful for him with something exciting for his audience. He convinced the director of Radio Liberté that the cloth should not only bear the radio station's logo but a photograph of Mande Massa and his team (Figures 12.1 and 12.2). Then he ordered a certain quantity of the decorated cloth from the privatized Malian company BATEX-CI in Bamako. Half of the production costs were paid in advance, the other half after delivery.[12] He took the cloth to the radio station and announced its sale, and then: "[He whistles and claps his hands] In one day, I sold more than a hundred bales. He [the director] was satisfied because now he had money. We have sold more than three hundred, four hundred, five hundred, one thousand [pieces]; can you imagine the result?" Women came to the concert in their newly made dresses. The success was enormous, and the gains as well. Concerts in 2009 and 2010 (Figure 12.3) were similarly successful: he sold innumerable pieces of cloth that had a different design and color each year.

The cloth and the concert go together, and the cloth is, according to Mande Massa, a highly effective means to advertise the concert and his broadcast (Röschenthaler 2015). According to Mande Massa, only

*Figure 12.1* The Cloth of 2010 with Mande Massa in the center, his team at the top, and the logo of Radio Djekafo (Photo: Ute Röschenthaler)

*Figure 12.2* Woman at the market wearing a dress with the Mande Massa cloth of 2009 (Photo: Ute Röschenthaler)

*Figure 12.3*   The Mande Massa concert of 2011 with Mande Massa in an expensive boubou with a red cap, surrounded by singers and entertainers (behind the right speaker) (Photo: Ute Röschenthaler)

10% of the women who buy the cloth attend the concert. The other 90% do not attend because of age, of disabilities, or because their husbands do not allow them to attend alone.

In 2009, Mande Massa began to document his concerts. At first, DVDs were given as presents to some of his audience, friends, and supporters. In 2012, he began to sell the DVDs for a moderate price of 1,000 FCFA (about $2) at the radio station, so that women who were unable to attend the concert could come and purchase a DVD. Mande Massa has organized seven concerts and ordered six editions of cloth to date. The coup in March 2012, a few weeks after that year's concert, bitterly interrupted the organization of events.

## BECOMING AN ENTREPRENEUR, "LA VOIX DU DAKAN", AND THE MALIAN CRISIS OF 2012

In December 2008, Mande Massa decided to talk to the director of Radio Liberté about the unacceptable financial situation in which he worked. He had worked four years for Radio Liberté without a salary and he had he not received any money for the transport to the radio station for himself and the team of four women (at the time) he was paying himself. The only revenue he received at this point was a certain percentage of the advertising money his broadcast attracted. This was not enough to make a living, pay his team, care for his family and house, and support his extended family in the village. The radio director responded that he was unfortunately unable to pay him even a small regular salary.

Mande Massa therefore chose to leave Radio Liberté and create his own media company, Mandemassa Production. He decided to continue the *Baroni* with Radio Djekafo, not as a radio presenter but as an independent broadcast producer with his own team. The director agreed and suggested that he sell him an hour of airtime for 150,000 FCFA per month (about $300). Mande Massa asked for a reduction and eventually decided, despite the considerable monthly costs, to give it a chance. They signed a one-year contract, according to which Mande Massa was to pay 125,000 FCFA monthly for the airtime needed for his *Baroni* broadcast, under the condition that all revenues from the advertisements the broadcast attracted would go to him.

Mande Massa would have preferred advanced production and to sell the program, but was unable to do so at the time. He therefore continued to produce *Baroni* live in the studio. Although the first year, 2009, was difficult, he considered it the beginning of his independence. He paid for the airtime and his team, and survived on the revenues from the advertisements his broadcast brought to the station. His audience followed him to Radio Djekafo. Nevertheless, it was a difficult time financially:

> The women supported me when I left Radio Liberté to begin with Djekafo. The women always said: "we will die behind you, Mande Massa, we will never fail you". These women, I can never fail them either. . . . If you have this kind of success, you always have problems. I had this success until I believed that it is all over. [Because] when the women are behind you, then you have problems with the men. (interview May 2013)

The constant moral support and approval he received from his family, friends, and audience encouraged him to continue. Friends and listeners said: "truly, this [the radio] is your destiny", and when he did not perform the *Baroni* even for one day, people told him that the women were not happy because he had not given them consolation.

In 2010, the bouillon cube company, Maggi, came in as a sponsor of the broadcast, paying for six months of airtime. The other six months were supported by local merchants who paid him monthly for publicity. Maggi felt that the results of its advertisement were favorable. In 2011, the third year of Mandemassa Production, Maggi paid for the entire year's airtime, along with the other local advertisers.[13] In the fourth year, Maggi also sponsored the concert, but when the coup came in March 2012, all merchants refrained from placing advertisements due to the crisis.

We can see that despite Mande Massa's huge success in Bamako, he was initially unable to obtain a salary that would be enough to live on: "In full success, without any salary, with nothing, yes! I did not have the choice, because as a radio presenter at a private radio station, I live off publicity only". This was not the result of the radio directors' hardheartedness, but confirms instead the difficult situation independent radio stations face. Notwithstanding, hundreds of such stations continue to exist today, largely surviving because of the people's excitement for the medium.

The success he already enjoyed enabled Mande Massa to emancipate himself from this situation and become an independent entrepreneur. Not all radio presenters were able to do this.

> The difference between us is the popularity I have. My audience, you have seen the concert, it was full, full to bursting. . . . When I make the cloth, I know that those who come to the Palais will pay for it. And there are thousands of women who buy the cloth but do not come to the Palais. (interview May 2013)

A number of other personalities also produce cloths with images (Röschenthaler 2015): politicians do this before their campaigns as do religious leaders, such as Haidara when they celebrate Maouloud (Schulz 2012) and artists before concerts, such as Oumou Sangare, Salif Keita, Babani Kone, and Djeneba Seck, among others. Selling textiles works for certain people, but not for everybody, as Mande Massa explained:

> Everyone has his market. There are people for whom it did not work, and who now have problems. They invest the money, and then it does not work. But I have sold more than fifty bales, a hundred bales, because . . . when you have the support of the women . . . who wear the dresses, you see, this is because . . . the name Mande Massa, the success, it can sell all this. . . . If you do not have a certain greatness, and when it does not work, your money is gone just like this. (interview May 2013)

Mande Massa's success with his cloths indicates his entrepreneurial vision. He invested his money and risked losing it, in the conviction that it would work out and women would pay for the product. The same is true for the decision to pay for airtime and look for sponsors. According to Mande Massa, he is the only radio presenter who pays for his own airtime.

> There is no other radio presenter in Bamako who pays for his own airtime, because I know that it will pay and I know that it will work. But others cannot do this. . . . I know that I can pay. Others have begun and they were unable to continue. (interview May 2013)

His successful radio broadcast, name, and image, and the support he receives from women as well as the certainty that it will be rewarding to try new paths motivated his drive to become an independent media entrepreneur and popular personality (*tógotigi*).

Following the creation of his own media production company, Mande Massa also developed other media products. In 2009, he created a television show, *Mande Massa ka Bara Mùsow* (*The King and his Favorite Wife*). Twelve young Malian women entered a competition for several weeks and the woman who most perfectly represented Mande values was eventually selected as the queen. The show was broadcast live via satellite by Africable, the independent television station, which provided worldwide accessibility. The competition was well attended and very popular and was therefore repeated in 2010 and 2011. In 2010, the competition took place in Paris, where five women from the Malian diaspora participated.[14]

In 2012, Mande Massa conceptualized a television film, *Solo*. The film is also about Mande cultural values and calls for harmony in polygamous families. Mande Massa was the main actor in the film but, for the first time, did not play the Mande king, thereby giving the film the advantage of his great popularity in Bamako.[15] Mande Massa discussed the project with his friend, the director of Africable, who considered it a promising proposal and expressed his interest, coming up with a budget of around 17 million FCFA (about $35,300), which resulted in a contract between the two and allowed shooting to begin. The film is broadcast by Maicha TV, owned by Africable's director, in the form of a serialized story (*feuilleton*) containing 52 episodes, which is also accessible on satellite, playing on the fact that imported telenovelas, most often from Latin America, are generally very popular among Malian audiences (Gärtner 2008).

2012 began as a promising year for Mande Massa, but quickly became complicated by the political crisis that followed the March coup, only a few weeks after that years' concert. The crisis reduced the cultural life of Bamako. People had to respect a ban on public assembly, nightclubs were closed, and concerts were prohibited. Mande Massa was therefore unable to organize a concert in 2013, print his cloth, or hold the *Mande Massa ka Bara Mùsow* competition. For him and all musicians and artists, political instability resulted in substantial revenue loss. Although radio stations continued to broadcast, merchants stopped airing commercials. Although Mande Massa's radio broadcast continued, hardly any advertisements were used to generate income.

The coup again confirms that entrepreneurs are wise not to specialize in one field but rather to remain flexible and turn to different ventures if necessary. Since Mande Massa left Radio Liberté in 2009, he tried to find ways to realize his dream of having his own radio station. A first step in this direction was the decision to become independent from employers and create his media production company. This provided the basis to negotiate with radio directors and sell his productions. In a second step, he found the means to acquire the equipment to start a radio station—in earlier years, donors had provided this for many radio stations—and apply for an FM frequency and authorization from the Malian government to broadcast. The political crisis slowed this process down and his application has not been processed to this day. Nevertheless, in July 2013, he left radio Djekafo, rented a house, installed the equipment and, after the *karem* (end of Ramadan) celebrations, Radio Dakan began its broadcast with news, the *Baroni*, griot music, information, and entertainment. Mande Massa had realized his long cherished dream despite financial difficulties—the radio house needed to be maintained and his team has increased—albeit on a different level. The political crisis in Mali, the lengthy procedure of receiving the license from the ministry, and the shift in audience illustrate the dynamics that make media entrepreneurs', including Mande Massa's, survival a risky and uncertain undertaking that has to be renegotiated daily.

## MANDE MASSA AS AN ENTREPRENEUR: SUCCESS AND OBSTACLES

Mande Massa has achieved his success through talent, persistency, and hard work. Discovering his talent as a radio presenter and creating his broadcast *Baroni* were initial steps toward recognition, and he directly connects his success on the radio to his personality:

> The talent I have comes first of all from my personality . . . and I have many ideas, I work with my head . . . I will not sit beside somebody and ask: explain how this should be done, no, no, no! I know how to create myself . . . I know that my creativity makes me progress. This is a talent that I have, and I work with my voice at the radio, the language I use, I know that I am good at talking, I know how to talk, I have a beautiful voice on the mic . . . I have the courage and love for my job . . . I don't know how to explain this. I have nobody who has taught me this. It is a gift from God.

Mande Massa sees his capacities as a talent and divine gift that he makes use of without any formal training or advice from others. Such personal success often remains a conundrum. Many people asked him how actually he produces his *Baroni*:

> Many people have asked me this question: "How do you do this, who produces your broadcast, who writes it, how do you prepare this before it is broadcast?" I say: "I have never prepared this before it is broadcast". I arrive at the studio, [I say:] "now, the ladies, this is the topic of this morning, we continue where we ended yesterday. I will explain

to you . . . you do this, you do that, and you make this, and then, we begin!" (interview May 2013)

The topic of the day is developed spontaneously. Most of the topics deal with family conflicts, wicked women who refuse to raise their co-wives' children, or a man who makes his wives suffer because wealth has made him arrogant. This on-the-spot staging requires that both Mande Massa and his team have the talent to improvise.

In his artistic work, a combination of ingredients is recurrent: the *Baroni* as a story told in sequels, his concern for women as well as the Mande values, combined with his role as Mande Massa, the Mande king, which became his artist name and his brand. The figure of the Mande king is not only a role that he plays, it is also derived from the Mande social fabric. As a descendant of the ancient Mali kingdom's royal families, his family name, his artist name, and his role are all intertwined with his identity. His family is connected to a griot family, the Kouyaté, some members are also integrated into his projects, and those that he developed later recombine these elements: the concert that enhanced his popularity among Bamako's artists; the cloth that provided women with the opportunity to decorate themselves with his image; the *Bara Mùsow* show which took up the sequels, the Mande values, and the image of the king, while the film episodes, as is the *Baroni*, are about Mande values and succeed because of his popularity as the main actor. At the root of all this is his gift of talking in an entertaining manner that is highly appreciated by his audience.

*Baroni* has become the brand name that is firmly associated with Mande Massa's work. A number of other radio presenters have also appropriated the baroni format, but Mande Massa considers this a positive development, as it further advertises his name:

> *Baroni?* Everybody says that it comes from the concert of Mande Massa! Therefore, it is publicity for me, even when you present your own baroni on your radio station. Everybody says that it was my idea. It is my original idea. This cannot be changed. . . . I have received prizes for *Baroni*; I have made concerts with *Baroni* . . . all my creations have been derived from the idea of *Baroni*; even the film that I have made emerged from the idea of *Baroni*. . . . These are my traces. (interview May 2013)

There are numerous media entrepreneurs in Bamako, and many more radio presenters. Some have imitated his successful broadcast and also use a form of baroni; others have tried to follow his entrepreneurial concept and founded their own media company and communication agency, but they have not branded their name and connected it with a new concept and company. Obviously there is more to it than simply the *Baroni* and the concept:

Mande Massa's success is wedded to his personality, his conviction, and his oratory skills. The best example is the sale of his cloths and his ability to attract advertisers. Indeed, the cloth represents a measure of success, as many other personalities have a similar textile product but nobody, with the exception of the religious leader Haidara, has ever sold as many bales of cloths as Mande Massa has. Most radio presenters are media producers; they have not developed such clear characteristics of entrepreneurs.

His success began with the creation of the popular radio soap *Baroni* that combines existing cultural elements in a new way. He created a novel broadcast format and bought his own airtime. His entrepreneurial activity began with the foundation of his media production company. From then on, he worked with contracts that define his rights to broadcast and to financial gains from advertisement and the sale of his products. His training in business and accounting was used effectively to manage his production company and radio station.

He invested his own money, accrued debt, found sponsors, and risked failure whenever he was convinced of his potential for success. From then on, he also had to resist his colleagues' envy and overcome major obstacles to financing projects. Jealousy about success implies that personalities like Mande Massa are more than just admired. Since he received his award, the public (his colleagues and other renowned people) have expected him to make financial gains, and many refused to support him.

> People do not even talk about jealousy. This is part of the problem. . . . Once you are successful, you have to battle. If you don't do this, they don't rest until they have brought you down. You have to battle, fight every day, you don't even settle down a minute, and when you are successful, the people think that you have everything, but in reality you have nothing. And instead of helping you, they search for ways to ruin you. I have lived through all this. Nobody gave me a single coin, neither the government nor private persons, nobody . . . I organize this big concert with debts if I can't find sponsors. (interview May 2013)

These social tensions are important issues but are generally not explicitly articulated. Mande Massa managed to overcome such difficulties and was able to realize his vision. In order to successfully complete his projects, he needed to persevere regardless of the costs and rely on a good nose for opportunities and persistence in his endeavors. His is driven by his conviction that his projects will have a positive impact on society and help to preserve the Mande traditional values. He is knowledgeable of what his audience appreciates and has the courage and strength to withstand social and financial pressures, at least for a certain time.

In this setting, Mande Massa is not only an inventor, he is also the entrepreneur who finds the means to realize his inventions and has the courage and charisma to achieve his visions. He invests his own means, takes credit, or finds sponsors, the latter of which being the more favorable form for financing projects. Sponsors, such as rich merchants or nominal godfathers and godmothers, seek involvement in projects as a means to exchange money for symbolic capital. The *Baroni* and the Mande Massa concert provide good opportunities for such an exchange, as sponsors receive advertisement space or even praise in front of a large audience while the entrepreneur has the advantage that such support does not have to be paid back. He assumes the risk in case of failure as well as a loss of his reputation and has to bear the tension that failure or success creates. When an entrepreneur is successful, he can reinvest the profit in further events and gains an immense increase in prestige.

The entrepreneur is indeed a socially ambiguous figure, perhaps more than the *dáwulatigi* and *tógotigi* that depend on the appreciation of their followers. In the urban and Muslim context, people in Bamako try to relegate much of the ambivalence of success to the extra-social domain (a gift from God, veiling feelings of jealousy) and not to explanations that are more widespread in other parts of West and Central Africa and explain power, success, and talent in a zero-sum game whereby it is assumed that when some have more they must have taken away from others, which often leads to extreme mistrust and social tensions that find their expression in power plays like accusations of sorcery and witchcraft (Fisiy and Geschiere 1996; Rowlands and Warnier 1988). Often various extraordinary skills are explained in these terms; excellent artists, performers, warriors, hunters, politicians, wealthy traders, and other influential individuals enjoy admiration but live under the constant risk of witchcraft accusations (Röschenthaler 2011: 414–417). Influential individuals such as African politicians have also been described as Big Men. Similar to the Melanesian Big Men—and occasionally Big Women—they need large crowds of followers who support them to raise the means required for their projects and constantly negotiate and fight on all fronts (Lindstrom 1984). The assemblage of economic wealth, occult knowledge, artistic skills, political renommée, and social acceptance by followers in one person, as used to describe Big Men, is no longer ascribed to the new and more individualistic "figures of success" that are portrayed by Banégas and Warnier (2001). Other scholars have highlighted similarities of Big Men with entrepreneurs (Martin 2013; Sykes 2007).

Mande Massa also mentioned jealousy and social tensions ("you need to battle every day") as well as the inevitable fact that attracting a large audience and potential sponsors draws means and success away from others and to his own venture. He shares this in common with Big Men and the industrial entrepreneur (who wants to attract customers with new products). The concepts of *tógotigi* and *dáwulatigi* are less ambivalent, less political, and more than merely economic. As some of the "figures of success" (Banégas and Warnier 2001), they are popular and celebrated individuals who are admired because of their respect for cultural values, wealth, and visible signs of success with which they surround themselves. Mande Massa displays some of these visible signs of success, which are due to his representation of the Mande king. He owns a whole range of expensive and exquisite *boubous* of shiny embroidered damask, and his "royalty" has become an embodied practice and finds expression in his entire habitus.

## CONCLUSION

This chapter has examined the evolution of Mande Massa's career in the period leading up to the launch of his own private radio station "Dakan, la voix du destin". Initially, Mande Massa was a newcomer in the media sector; he had to acquire all necessary skills on his own, using his talent as well as the opportunities provided by his traineeship at the radio station. He profited from his language skills, creativity, sense, and courage to create *Baroni*, a radio format comprising stories presented in episodes that differed from existing broadcasts. His popularity among his female audience and his social success were ahead of his financial gains. Despite his growing popularity, he worked for more than ten years without a fixed salary. This gradually convinced him to become an independent media entrepreneur with his own production company, projects, and sponsors, and eventually his own radio station.

His vision for his ventures, however, always reached beyond mere capitalist entrepreneurship in the sense of producing commodities or services to make money to reinvest in order to expand his enterprise. He used his skills to realize his social vision: ameliorate the situation of women in their compounds in the rapidly changing urban context and insecurity vis-à-vis social norms. Through his work he sought to preserve Mande traditional values and enable women to live more harmoniously in their often polygamous families. *Baroni*, the concert with the praise singers and artists, and the competition about the king's favorite wife are all based on these ideas and validate Mande culture and reassure women, all the while being acknowledged by the media. Mande Massa's success is based on the combination of cultural values from the past, his artist name, the role he embodies, and the popularity of the media he uses. With *Baroni*, he found a highly popular manner to communicate these issues and to master the art of knowing his audience's desires and passions. Thus he managed the split between the need for innovation in media production and the preservation of Mande values in an increasingly globalizing world.

Personalities such as Mande Massa are addressed in Bamanakan as *tógotigi* or *dáwulatigi*, terms that do not exactly connote "entrepreneurs" or "Big Men" but more closely reflect what Banégas and Warnier (2001) describe as "figures of success". Different from most of those described by Banégas and Warnier, he has a large followership that supports him. The terms *tógotigi* and *dáwulatigi* imply both entrepreneurial abilities and the capacity to attract crowds of followers but do not place them in the foreground. To a greater degree than *tógotigi*, which primarily reflects popularity, *dáwulatigi* implies that success can be based on any means available. Such ambivalence is also a characteristic feature of the industrial entrepreneur but is not evident in Mande Massa's biography. He has many of the abilities ascribed to a classical entrepreneur, such as creativity, courage, and the conviction to find money and achieve. He also has to fight the jealousy of other popular personalities and needs to win the support of a large audience as followers on a daily basis just like Big Men. He knows that he owes his success to his chanting audience: "We will die behind you, Mande Massa, we will never disappoint you". The huge amount of textiles he has been able to sell is visible proof of this support.

## NOTES

1. The material on which this chapter is based was collected during ethnographic field research in Mali, primarily in its capital Bamako between 2005 and 2013. I have known Mande Massa personally since 2010. I have discussed his career with him many times, both in person as well as during the crisis, on the phone, attended a concert, received his media products, and bought his textiles. In May 2013, additionally, the anthropologist and filmmaker Melanie Gärtner conducted and registered an interview with Mande Massa for me. I am grateful to both. My research in Mali was supported by the Cluster of Excellence 'The Formation of Normative Orders' at the Goethe University Frankfurt, in 2009, 2011, 2012, and 2013; and by the Vereinigung der Freunde und Förderer, the International Office, and the Stiftung zur Förderung der internationalen Beziehungen at the Goethe University Frankfurt in 2005, 2007, 2010.

2. See Dumestre (2011) (the characters of the International Phonetic Alphabet have been adapted for easier reading). Amselle (1987) describes such merchants in Bamako.

3. The figures of the poor inventor and the industrial entrepreneur who invests in the inventor's creations are closely connected (see Bude 1997). Janet MacGaffey's book title *Entrepreneurs and Parasites: the Struggles for Indigenous Capitalism in Zaire* (1987) refers to this notion.

4. In Mali, these were the newspaper *Le Soudanais* and Radio Mali, which was transformed into the radio and television station Radiodiffusion Television du Mali (RTM) in 1983, with Libyan and French support.

5. Radio Bamakan, Kledu, Guintan, Liberté, Djekafo, and Kayira became the most well-known radio stations in Bamako. In 2006, fifteen private radio stations were registered with the Union des Radios et Télévisions Libre du Mali (URTEL 2006; Radios in Mali 2013). In 2013, Bamako had twenty-two private radio stations in addition to the state-owned Office de Radiodiffusion Television du Mali (ORTM).

6. Africable was first launched in Paris in 1991 and Sidibe was a stakeholder. He later repatriated Africable to Bamako (Dioh 2009).

7. Bamako grew from a few hundred inhabitants in the 1850s to one million inhabitants in the 1990s. Over the last few decades its estimated population has increased to two millions (for a history of Bamako see Meillassoux 1969: 4–9; Villien-Rossi 1966; Philippe 2009).

8. The private radio station, Guintan—la voix des femmes—was founded in early 1995 by Ramata Dia.

9. The term is derived from *baro*, debates among groups of friends in the evening (Schulz 2002: 811–813). My interviewees contrasted *baro* with *sùmun*, the intimate conversation among couples or lovers in the late evening or night.

A vehicle for social criticism, *Koteba* is mostly staged in rural areas (Arnoldi 1995; Imperato 1994) but has also been brought to urban contexts (Meillassoux 1964).

10. *Dànbe* means honor, dignity, and reputation related to cultural values (Dumestre 2011); for moral and cultural Mande values see also Schulz (1999).
11. Tamani d'Or means "the golden drum". *Ntàman* or more often *ntàmannin* is a double-faced drum, held in the armpit, which *jèliw* (praise singers) manipulate with a bent stick (Dumeste 2011).
12. With BATEX-CI, a customer must order a minimum of five bales. In 2010, one bale was produced for 350,000 FCFA (about $730), and one set of cloths (wrapper, blouse, and head tie) was sold for 3,500 FCFA (about $7) (Röschenthaler 2015).
13. The Djekafo radio broadcasts are disseminated by branch radios also in Kayes and Mopti.
14. The show was held in Bamanakan and translated into French. The evaluation was done by the audience per SMS. Much importance was paid to the norms of preparing, eating, and behaving during the meals. For more on eating norms, see Dumestre (1996).
15. The film was planned to be released at the end of 2013.

## REFERENCES

Abu-Lughod, Lila. 2004. *Dramas of Nationhood: The Politics of Television in Egypt*. London and Chicago: University of Chicago Press.

Amselle, Jean-Loup. 1987. 'Fontionnaires et hommes d'affaires au Mali'. *Politique africaine* 26: 63–72.

Arnoldi, Mary Jo. 1995. *Playing with Time: Art and Performance in Central Mali*. Bloomington: Indiana University Press.

Askew, Kelly. 2002. *Performing the Nation: Swahili Music and Cultural Politics in Tanzania*. Chicago: University of Chicago Press.

Banégas, Richard and Jean-Pierre Warnier. 2001. 'Nouvelles figures de la réussite et du pouvoir'. *Politique Africaine* 82 (special issue: Figures de la réussite et imaginaires politiques), 5–21.

Barber, Karin. 1987. 'Popular arts in Africa'. *African Studies Review* 30, 3: 1–78.

Bourgault, Louise. 1995. *Mass-Media in sub-Saharan Africa*. Bloomington: Indiana University Press.

Bude, Heinz. 1997. 'Der Unternehmer als Revolutionär der Wirtschaft'. *Merkur* 51: 866–876.

Dioh, Tidiane. 2009. 'Mali: de Tripoli à Paris'. In: Tidiane Dioh: *Histoire de la télévision en Afrique noire francophone, des origines à nos jours*. Paris: Karthala, 137–144.

Dumestre, Gérard. 1996. 'De l'alimentation au Mali'. *Cahiers d'Études Africaines* 36 (144): 689–702.

Dumestre, Gérard. 2011. *Dictionnaire bambara-français*. Paris: Karthala.

Ellis, Stephen and Yves-Andre Fauré (eds). 1995. *Entreprises et entrepreneurs africaines*. Paris: Karthala-Orstom.

Falola, Toyin and Steven Salm. 2005. *Urbanization and African Cultures*. Durham: Carolina Academic Press.

Fardon, Richard and Graham Furniss (eds). 2000. *African Broadcast Cultures*. Oxford: James Currey.

Fisiy, Cyprian and Peter Geschiere. 1996. 'Witchcraft, violence and identity: different trajectories in postcolonial Cameroon'. In: Richard Werbner and Terence Ranger (eds). *Postcolonial Identities in Africa*. London and New Jersey: Zed Books, 193–221.

Gärtner, Melanie. 2008. ' "Milagros in Mali oder "die Wahrnehmung des Fremden" '. In: Mamadou Diawara and Ute Röschenthaler (eds). *Im Blick der Anderen. Auf ethnologischer Forschung in Mali*. Frankfurt: Brandes & Apsel, 22–47.

Imperato, Pascal. 1994. 'The depiction of beautiful women in Malian youth association masquerades'. *African Arts* 27, 1: 58–65, 95–96.

Jalloh, Alusine and Toyin Falola (eds). 2002. *Black Business and Economic Power*. Rochester: University of Rochester Press.

Keita, Mamadou. 1992. 'Reflections sur la presse ecrite'. *Politique africaine* 47: 79–90.

Lindstrom, Lamont. 1984. 'Doctor, lawyer, wise man, priest: Big-Men and knowledge in Melanesia'. *Man* (N.S.) 19, 2: 291–309.

MacGaffey, Janet. 1987. *Entrepreneurs and Parasites: The Struggles for Indigenous Capitalism in Zaire*. Cambridge: Cambridge University Press.

MacGaffey, Janet. 1998. 'Creatively coping with crisis: entrepreneurs in the second economy of Zaire (the Democratic Republic of the Congo)'. In: Anita Spring and Barbara McDade (eds). *African Entrepreneurship: Theory and Reality*. Gainesville: University Press of Florida, 37–50.

Martin, Keir. 2013. *The Death of the Big Men and the Rise of the Big Shots: Custom and Conflict in East New Britain*. Oxford: Berghan.

Meillassoux, Claude. 1964. 'The "Koteba" of Bamako'. *Présence africaine* (English edition) 24, 51: 28–62.

Meillassoux, Claude. 1969. *Urbanization in an African Community*. Seattle: University of Washington Press.

Myers, Mary. 2000. 'Community radio and development'. In: Richard Fardon and Graham Furniss (eds). *African Broadcast Cultures*. Oxford: James Currey, 90–101.

Philippe, Sebastien. 2009. *Une histoire de Bamako*. Brinon-Sur-Sauldre: Editions Grandvaux.

Radios in Mali. 2013. 'Rural community radios in Mali'. http://www.ictregulation toolkit.org/en/toolkit/notes/PracticeNote/3153, accessed 26 August 2013.

Röschenthaler, Ute. 2011. *Purchasing Culture: The Dissemination of Associations in the Cross River Region of Cameroon and Nigeria*. Trenton: Africa World Press.

Röschenthaler, Ute. 2015. 'Dressed in Photographs: Between Uniformization, Self-enhancement and the Promotion of Stars and Leaders in Bamako.' *Africa* 85, 4: 696–720.

Rowlands, Michael and Jean-Pierre Warnier. 1988. 'Sorcery, power and the modern state in Cameroon'. *Man* (N.S.) 23, 1: 118–132.

Schulz, Dorothea. 1999. 'In pursuit of publicity: talk radio and the imagination of a moral public in Mali'. *Africa Spectrum* 99, 2: 161–185.

Schulz, Dorothea. 2002. ' "The world is made by talk": female fans, popular music, and new forms of public sociality in urban Mali'. *Cahiers d'Études africaines* 168, 4: 797–829.

Schulz, Dorothea. 2012. *Muslims and New Media in West Africa: Pathways to God*. Bloomington: Indiana University Press.

Schumpeter, Josef. 1934. *The Theory of Economic Development*. Cambridge, MA: Harvard University Press.

Spring, Anita and Barbara McDade. 1998. *African Entrepreneurship: Theory and Reality*. Gainesville: University Press of Florida.

Sykes, Karen. 2007. 'The moral grounds of critique: between possessive individuals, entrepreneurs and big men in New Ireland'. *Anthropological Forum* 17, 3: 255–268.

URTEL 2006. 'Liste des radios libres opérationelles'. http://www.e-tic.net/etic/files/radios_mali.pdf, accessed 30 August 2013.

Villien-Rossi, Marie-Louise. 1966. 'Bamako, capitale du Mali'. *Bulletin de l'IFAN* 28 (serie B, 1–2): 249–380.

# 13 The Women Behind the Camera

## Female Entrepreneurship in the Southern Nigerian Video Film Industry

*Alessandro Jedlowski*

The producers of the Nigerian video film industry are generally perceived to be males. This chapter, however, highlights that a good number of women have successfully established themselves as entrepreneurs in the southern Nigerian video business, creating new spaces for female economic and social mobility in this sector. As my research shows, these successful female video producers all belong to the same generation; they were born in the 1970s and early 1980s. Most of their families come from the southern Nigerian high-middle class with hometowns in the southeastern part of the country. They were university graduates before they entered the industry, spent time studying abroad, and built up important transnational business connections, and they had initially followed the professional paths (in the university, banking, or commercial business sectors) their parents had suggested and later moved on to a self-confidently chosen alternative. They have a rather independent private life and manage to keep their private affairs beyond the reach of public attention. Although they belong to a group of influential elites, their biographies comprise autonomous choices and reflect headstrong determination, which makes them representatives of the ideal-type "self-made women". These women were able to accomplish their achievements because of their persistence and entrepreneurial skills, rather than inherited economic and social privileges. Their association with the Nigerian elite nevertheless facilitated their affirmation of autonomy and the respect that accompanies it.

In order to understand the specific economic and political context in which these women video producers have emerged as successful entrepreneurs, this chapter will first offer insight into the history of the Nigerian video industry and the economic transformations that the Structural Adjustment Policies of the 1980s provoked as well as the professional opportunities that women have envisaged for themselves in the Nigerian social fabric. I will then outline the professional careers of three celebrated female video entrepreneurs and conclude by presenting them as new entrepreneurial figures of success. As the Nigerian video phenomenon is highly diversified, including profound ethnic and regional differences, my focus in this chapter is on the section of the video film industry that produces videos in English and operates in southern Nigeria.[1]

The analysis of these women's life histories draws on a wide range of both ethnographic and secondary sources collected during a research project conducted between 2009 and 2012. The ethnographic materials were collected during fieldwork in Lagos, Nigeria, between early 2010 and mid-2011.[2] In Lagos, information was gathered during numerous informal conversations and guided interviews with industry practitioners and members of the audiences as well as through participant observation on film sets, at screening venues, and at distribution hubs. The secondary sources include newspapers, blog articles, documentary films, and television programs, and were collected in archives and libraries in both Nigeria and the United Kingdom and through online research.

## ENTREPRENEURSHIP IN NIGERIA'S ECONOMIC HISTORY

Female video entrepreneurs have created new spaces for economic and social mobility in present-day Nigeria, a country in which entrepreneurial activities remain "engendered in terms of access, control, and remuneration, [and] more men than women tend to be in the lucrative enterprises, especially in the formal sector, as owners and managers of large firms and small industries. Many (but not all) women tend to be in the smallest informal sector microenterprises" (Spring and McDade 1998: 15). Contrary to widespread opinions, however, entrepreneurial women are not unusual, particularly in precolonial times, as a number of scholars have documented.

Among the entrepreneurial individuals who established wide-ranging networks for the collection and distribution of trade goods on the coast and in the hinterland (Dike and Ekejiuba 1990; Inikori 2002; Lovejoy 1980) were a number of influential women. Among the outstanding figures was the merchant queen Omu Okwei of Ossumari (Olukoju 2002), Madam Efunporoye Tinubu of Abeokuta, Iyolade Efunsetan Aniwura, and Madam Omosa of Ibadan (Denzer 1994). The Yoruba social and political setting acknowledged women's economic importance by granting them prestigious titles and privileges. They became famous as large-scale entrepreneurs owning numerous slaves and often their own army to protect their trade caravans on journeys from the hinterland to the coast. Madam Tinubu also successfully fought wars with her army to support the king of Abeokuta. Yoruba women monopolized important industries and trades such as the production of *adire* textiles, indigo-dying, and pottery, industries that all women had an active role in at the time (Denzer 1994). Women in southeastern Nigeria were more involved in farm work but also had the opportunity to fill privileged economic positions and were successful traders and entrepreneurs (Chuku 1999; Coquery-Vidrovitch 2002). Particular institutions provided women with the powerful means to oppose male politics (Dike 1995; Ifeka-Moller 1975).

The ventures of these early entrepreneurs were risky; they invested means or worked on credit to achieve their goals and had to cope with high losses of means and prestige (or even their freedom) when their goods were captured or damaged. The activities of these well-to-do precolonial entrepreneurs were disrupted by British colonization, which perceived most entrepreneurs to be rivals to its economic and civilizing projects and led to the establishment of policies that contributed to the decline of local businesses (Nwabughuogu 1982). Women's roles in particular were reduced in the colonial setting and they were deprived of political influence (Amadiume 1987). This situation provided new opportunities for alternative individual success in the frame of state employment both during colonial times and following independence. Such figures of success included the bureaucrat, the civil servant, the government official, the intellectual, and the university graduate. In most sub-Saharan African countries throughout the 1960s and 1970s, these figures constituted the main models of economic and social achievement. Richard Banégas and Jean-Pierre Warnier emphasize (2001: 5–6) that the Structural Adjustment Policies of the 1980s effectively devaluated the political and economic importance of these social figures. In Nigeria, the application of Structural Adjustment Policies also led to the collapse of national television infrastructures and public entertainment facilities.

As Brian Larkin underscores, during the decades that preceded the introduction of Structural Adjustment Policies in Nigeria, "the state's role as employer was supplemented by its continual intervention in the economy" (2008: 179). The economic transformations that occurred throughout the 1980s, however, weakened the state's capacity to exercise this form of control. Public spending was radically reduced and the private sector privileged. Stability was replaced by ever-increasing forms of risk. The progressive affirmation of an "atomized capitalism" (Mbembe 2006), together with the devaluation of national currencies, the marginalization of the state in the administration of social services and economic infrastructures, the growing informalization of national economies, the worsening of national education systems, and the multiplication of armed conflicts, generated new itineraries of capital accumulation, and, consequentially, a set of new models of social achievement and economic success (Banégas and Warnier 2001; Ellis and Fauré 1995).

This is the context in which the southern Nigerian video industry emerged (see Barrot 2005; Haynes 2000; Larkin 2008). Critics and scholars commonly date the birth of the video industry to 1992, the year when *Living in Bondage*, the first straight-to-video movie to achieve remarkable commercial success, was released (cf. Haynes and Okome 1998). The birth, growth, and progressive consolidation of the video business brought to the fore a number of new professional figures connected to the world of filmmaking, which have assumed a particular social relevance over the past twenty years. The video industry's economy produces, according to some—rather unreliable but at least indicative—figures, between $200 and $300 million of annual revenues (*The Economist* 2006) and is the second largest employer in the country after the government (*The Economist* 2010). It created a large number of employment opportunities, ranging from the producer to the marketer,[3] the director to the cinematographer, the make-up artist to the stunt double, and the video rental shop owner to the video bootlegger.

Accordingly, the video business established itself as a highly popular and viable form of "entrepreneurship" for Nigerian youths, a platform within which social models of success and achievement have since been shaped and exposed to the public through the videos themselves as well as the large amount of "metacultural" products (news, blogs, fan magazines, etc.; cf. Urban 2001) that were produced and circulated in relation to the video industry. The Nigerian video business emerged as a form of entrepreneurship that is not only defined, as Janet MacGaffey would suggest, by "innovation and bold decision making" (1988: 38), but is also characterized by a specific capacity to "recycle" and "reassemble" already existing materials in order to "multiply the uses that can be made of documents, automobiles, houses, wood, or whatever, and [develop] the ability to put together different kinds of combinations of people with different skills, perspectives, linkages, identities, and aspirations" (Simone 2004: 214; see also Sundaram 1999).

The decline of the "administrative apparatus of the state and the expansion of the [informal] economy weakened the mechanism of male control over women" (MacGaffey 1987: 166; see also Coquery-Vidrovitch 1997: 5). As the list of women entrepreneurs mentioned by Nnamdi Madichie (2009) in his review of women's entrepreneurship in Nigeria over the past decades attests, a number of successful female entrepreneurs have once again emerged. In general terms, however, Nigerian women still have to cope with an atmosphere of strong gender discrimination in professional contexts. As Woldie and Adersua's quantitative research underlines, "the percentage of firms owned by women in Nigeria is [still] very low compared to their male counterparts" (2004: 85, 90). There are, nevertheless, examples of success.

## WOMEN IN THE SOUTHERN NIGERIAN VIDEO INDUSTRY

The three female entrepreneurs whose professional trajectories I will analyze below inhabit this context, which is characterized by both the emergence of new professional possibilities for women and the persistence of stereotypes and forms of discrimination. Compared to the success of other female entrepreneurs who have emerged in the past few years, these women's professional achievements have a particular sociocultural value because they take place within the entertainment sector, a sector of the economy that, while being particularly visible because of the place it occupies in national media and the public sphere, has always been treated as morally suspect in Nigeria as elsewhere in Africa. As the work of Bisi Adeleye-Fayemi highlights, for instance, women involved in theatre and television were often looked at by men with concern, and "families objected strongly to their daughters or wards having anything to do with such a 'wayward profession'" (1997: 126).

The success of the video industry as a business enterprise in general, and the work of these women in particular, not only counterbalance these ste-reotypes, they also transform the entertainment sector into "an avenue for women to achieve independence, wealth, and fame" (Bryce 2012: 72).

In the academic debate about the Nigerian video industry, the role of women has generally been underestimated. Articles that focus on the con-nection between women and the video industry tend to analyze the discourse about gender that videos produce and circulate. They see these videos gen-erally as propagators of the worst sexist and patriarchal stereotypes about women and their place in society (cf. Abah 2008; Evwierhoma 2008; see also Okome 2010). Some analysts have nuanced these criticisms by show-ing the variety and complexity of the gender discourse that videos circulate (Garritano 2000) by emphasizing that the video stories make new forms of female social mobility visible (even if often in a condemnatory tone, see Okome 2004) and by highlighting that through the representation of social injustices, videos have opened up a space for the elaboration of critical dis-courses about gender issues and the structure of Nigerian society in general (Bryce 2012; Oloruntoba-Oju 2006).[4] However, almost no attention has been given to the analysis of how the industry, as a form of business, has opened new spaces for women's economic and social mobility. Apart from the recently published introduction to the volume *Global Nollywood* in which Matthias Krings and Onookome Okome (2013: 15–16) emphasize the role women producers play in Nollywood, the industry has been gener-ally portrayed as a primarily male-run business in which women occupy a rather marginal position.[5] But, as I intend to emphasize in this chapter, this is only partially true; throughout the industry's history, and particularly over the course of the last few years, women have played an influential role.

In the past five to ten years, the southern Nigerian video industry has traversed a deep production crisis that activated important processes of transformation that are progressively transnationalizing and formalizing the industry's economy (Jedlowski 2012a, 2013a). Within this framework, the female entrepreneurs (Emem Isong, Stephanie Okereke, and Peace Anyiam-Osigwe) whose work I intend to analyze in these pages have held a pivotal position. I have chosen these three individuals because of their involvement in transforming the economy of the industry in recent times, a role that has given them pronounced visibility in national and international media. It is important to note, as Haynes and Okome (1998: 117) have indeed pointed out, that female producers and directors, such as Amaka Igwe, Lola Fani-Kayode Macaulay, Idowu Phillips, Franca Brown, Uche Osotule, Ameze Imarhiagbe, and Christyn Michaels, have been active in the industry since its early days.

Acknowledging their fundamental role as forerunners of female entrepre-neurship in this field, I will now analyze the work of three successful women whose work I consider representative of successful female entrepreneurship within the video industry in recent times. Thanks to their specific business strategies, they have gained pronounced social visibility and contributed to the construction of the collective imagination of women's social and economic success.[6]

## Writing the Recent History of the Nigerian Video Industry through the Experiences of three Female Entrepreneurs

As outlined above, the video industry has flourished since the 1990s and has indeed become one of the most important branches of the Nigerian economy. Around the mid-2000s, however, the southern Nigerian video industry entered a period of production crisis, which imposed a number of profound economic transformations (as the Nigerian press has repeatedly emphasized over the past few years, cf. Husseini 2009; Njoku 2009; Ekunno 2011). The crisis principally affected the section of the video industry that produces English language movies and was largely the result of the lack of a formal production and distribution system, the consequential incidence of piracy on the economy of the industry, and the impact of the introduction of new technologies (VCDs and DVDs to replace VHS tapes, internet, and satellite television) on the sustainability of the straight-to-video system of distribution that characterized the early years of the industry. Within this framework, the women whose experiences I depict below emerged as key figures due to the solutions they proposed and actuated in terms of the challenges imposed by the production crisis.

### Enem Isong

The first figure I want to present is Emem Isong, a scriptwriter, video producer, and distributor active in the industry since the mid-1990s, who is considered one of the most successful producers in Nollywood today. Precisely because of her success, of the three women discussed in this chapter, she is probably the one whose achievements had the strongest influence on the social conception of female success. Coming from a southeastern Nigerian upper-middle class family (her parents were civil servants), Isong studied theatre arts at Calabar University and, before realizing that filmmaking was her true passion, she started a career in the banking sector. A few years later, she moved to Lagos in order to begin her experience in the video business. As she admitted in her interview with me (Isong 2011), and in numerous interviews with local newspapers and fanzines (cf. Aduwo 2010; *City People Extra* 2011a), the beginning of her career as a producer was difficult; she faced numerous failures, had to borrow money from her family and friends, and waited years before being able to produce the film she had in mind. Nonetheless, by the end of the 1990s she had managed to create a name for herself, and over the course of the early 2000s, she became one of the most appreciated scriptwriters and producers in the industry. Her main contribution to the video industry's development, however, became evident, at least in my opinion, during the aforementioned production crisis period (from 2005–2006 onward). Some of the entrepreneurial strategies she applied during this period revealed themselves to be extremely success-ful, making her production company one of the few that were only margin-ally affected by the crisis.

First, as she understood that the production crisis had primarily affected the section of industry producing English language videos,[7] she began to diversify her productions and target local language film markets, particu-larly in her home-region, the Ibibio-speaking Akwa Ibom State in southeast-ern Nigeria. Furthermore, in order to reduce film budgets, she conceived an original production practice that developed a system where films were shot in two different languages (English and Ibibio) at the same time, that is, on the same set, with the same script, the same crew, and, at least partly, the same actors.[8] During my fieldwork, I shadowed the shooting of one of the first videos Isong produced using this technique (*Midnight Whisper/Idomo*, 2012) and I discussed the economic advantages of such a strategy with her. Although the budget for a straight-to-video film before the crisis was 5 mil-lion Naira (around $32,000), during my research it had fallen to around 2.5 million Naira ($16,000).[9] According to Isong, before the crisis, a film of this kind could reasonably expect to produce 50% profit, but such results had become much harder to achieve, as the average number of copies sold per film had fallen dramatically during the crisis. Accordingly, Isong maintained that by using the dual-language production strategy she could double the revenues of her releases, and thus counterbalance the effects of the production crisis. With only a minimal increase in production costs, she could almost double the number of official copies sold by addressing two different sections of the market: on the one hand, the rather multi-ethnic and urban English-speaking section of the Nigerian audience, and, on the other, a linguistically specific, culturally identifiable Ibibio section that was eager to consume entertainment products in their own language, which had been commercially unexploited by mainstream Nigerian entertainment entrepreneurs. If, as she emphasized during her interview (Isong 2011), an average film normally sold a maximum of 20,000 original copies during the production crisis, by applying the double-language strategy, she hoped to sell around 40,000 copies. As I mentioned earlier, Isong was already pro-ducing local language films as early as the beginning of the crisis (*Mfana Ibagha* in 2006; *Ekaete* in 2008; and *Uyai* in 2009) and thus had a clear perception of the economic potential of film releases that targeted small, linguistically specific segments of the audience. With the elaboration of the double-language production strategy, she further developed her company's production-diversification, confirming it as one of the most viable solutions to the economic impasse the industry had fallen into.

Complementary to this strategy, which targets small-scale, local sections of the video market as a solution to the industry's problems, Isong initiated a commercial strategy that was decisively oriented toward transnational audiences. When she realized—as many others in the industry had—that the lack of a structured distribution system was profoundly affecting the video economy and opening the gate for the circulation of illicit copies, she developed what could be defined as an informal windowing strategy.[10] In the most structured film industries, windowing systems are normally highly structured and formalized: films are released first in cinemas, then on the internet and satellite televisions, and finally on DVD. Within this framework, the geography of their circulation is precisely planned ahead of time. Because of the lack of such a structured system, Nigerian producers tend to lose much of their potential revenues to illicit networks of circulation. Often, a Nigerian video was (and still is) illegally duplicated in the days that follow its release on the Nigerian market, and then quickly sent (via internet and bootleg copies) to other African countries as well as to Europe, the United States, and the Caribbean. Acknowledging this evidence, Isong decided to plan a diversified release calendar for her new films, focusing first on the more formalized markets (such as the U.S. and Ghana) and leaving Nigeria at the bottom of the release calendar.[11] By doing so, she managed to protect what she considers her best market (the U.S.) from the interference of Nigerian bootleggers and thereby facilitated the rationalization of the transnational circulation of videos, which is likely to have important consequences for the economy of Nigerian video production.[12]

The application of these strategies pushed Isong to the forefront of the industry, making her face ubiquitous in the Nigerian entertainment press and TV programs. Thanks to its success, her production company continued to produce films regularly throughout the production crisis period and managed to attract the most well-known Nigerian actors (i.e., Genevieve Nnaji, Ramsey Nouah, Omotola Jalade-Ekeinde, Ini Edo, etc.) to star in its productions. In an industry that many believed was destined to fail, Isong's work became a synonym for success, defining the industry's new trends in terms of both economic strategies and aesthetic and narrative choices, becoming a model of achievement both within and beyond the industry's environment.

## Stephanie Okereke

Stephanie Okereke, the second female entrepreneur I want to focus on, can be introduced in relation to the tendency toward transnational audiences and formalized economic strategies I described above. Okereke started her career in the video industry as an actor in 1997 and, over the first part of the 2000s, became one of the most appreciated Nollywood stars. However, as she revealed in her interview (Okereke personal communication), she did not feel fully satisfied as an actor and therefore decided to study to be a filmmaker. As numerous other Nigerian directors have done in the recent past, she decided to study abroad and attended the New York Film Academy in Los Angeles. As soon as she completed her degree in 2008, she released her first feature film, *Through the Glass*. Bringing about a set of original distribution strategies, the film was released only in movie theatres, with no straight-to-video distribution, and the DVD release was launched only two years later. To Okereke's and most industry practitioners' surprise, the film was a sensational commercial success, marking a fundamental step in the recent history of the video industry. As I have illustrated elsewhere (Jedlowski 2012a), since the mid-2000s movie theatres have started to reappear in southern Nigeria.[13] While they had initially focused on foreign film distribution (mainly Hollywood), around the mid-2000s they began to screen Nigerian films with acceptable technical standards as well. Within this context, Okereke's film was the first to achieve real economic success, and thus clearly underscored the relevance of theatrical distribution strategies for the resurrection of the video film industry's economy. The success of *Through the Glass* indicated that a viable formal distribution channel was emerging at a time when many industry practitioners felt that the crisis was a consequence of the lack of a formalized distribution system.[14]

The success of the film, however, was not only related to the adoption of theatrical distribution strategies; a number of other Nigerian films had already been released in cinemas since the mid-2000s but none had managed to achieve a real commercial breakthrough. Hence, *Through the Glass*'s success was also the result of a number of specific choices that Okereke had made in relation to the construction of the film's narrative and the definition of production strategies. The film's plot and location are deeply connected to her experience at the New York Film Academy in Los Angeles; it is a light comedy shot in LA, with a primarily American cast and crew; the only Nigerian character is Okereke herself. It basically reproduces the plot and narrative construction of an average Hollywood film, with a bit of added Nigerian flavor. In many ways, its commercial success in Nigerian theatres was related to this aspect: the film met the tastes of the upper-middle-class audience that has access to the new multiplexes and is generally critical of mainstream Nollywood film styles while enthusiastically supporting Hollywood films and American-style television. More than any previous Nigerian theatrical release, Okereke's film offered a Nigerian version of Hollywood that could attract the wealthiest section of the Nigerian audience to the video industry, thereby creating new economic possibilities for the films' circulation. As most analysts have emphasized, Nollywood's video audience has been socially transversal since the beginning of the video phenomenon, but the larger percentage of video consumers belonged to the lowest segments of Nigerian society (see Haynes 2000; Okome 2007a). The production crisis created an impasse in the economic relations between the industry and its audiences and, as I emphasized earlier, the straight-to-video distribution model that had made Nollywood videos accessible for the lower sections of the Nigerian population ceased to be economically viable. Okereke's film offered a solution to this problem by displacing the film's targeted audience: from the lowest segments to the highest, from the poorer to the wealthier, that is, from those who could afford to buy a VCD copy of a new release to those who have the means to go to movie theatres a few times a month.[15]

This strategy marked a dramatic shift in the history of the Nigerian video industry, which has often been praised precisely for its capacity to create a local popular followership, but numerous critics and practitioners believe that this trend is only a short-term phase in the video industry's development, which might find new avenues for popular distribution in the future through the introduction of neighborhood movie theatres and increased internet circulation (see Jedlowski 2013a).

Beyond these debates, however, it is important to note Okereke's capacity to challenge social assumptions about her position as a woman in the video industry's environment, which has allowed her to acquire increased independence. Her dissatisfaction with her position in front of the camera as an actor, and her decision to become engaged in film direction and production, can be read as part of a move to assume direct responsibility over the film production process and, with it, over the film's narrative and aesthetic choices. The success she obtained made her choice visible and socially recognizable, and it subsequently imposed itself as model that confirmed that the role of the "woman behind the camera" can be a successful and rewarding one.

### Peace Anyiam-Osigwe

If Okereke's work and the production of *Through the Glass* ultimately put the emphasis on the viability of making the video industry migrate from straight-to-video distribution strategies to theatrical circulation, the work of the third female entrepreneur I will discuss here played an important role in transforming the international image of the Nigerian video industry by creating a globally visible platform for its celebration. Peace Anyiam-Osigwe is part of an extremely wealthy and influential Nigerian family. Her father, Emmanuel Onyechere Osigwe Anyiam-Osigwe, was a businessman and an influential figure in the development of the Nigerian oil industry. During his lifetime, he accumulated an immense fortune, which his sons inherited after his death in the late 1990s. Peace—as did her seven brothers—studied abroad; she began her career in the financial business, before getting involved in the video industry as a producer and television programmer. Her name, however, became internationally known when, supported by her family's foundation (the Aniyam-Osigwe Foundation, a philanthropic foundation that manages a percentage of the fortunes her father had left to his descendants), she created the African Movie Academy Awards in 2005. The annual award ceremony was modelled on the American Academy Awards (The Oscars), and provides the best African productions (in both digital and celluloid format) with the chance to compete for different categories of prizes (including best film, make-up, soundtrack, cinematography, and so on). Since its creation in 2005, the AMA Awards ceremony, which is held in Nigeria every year around April, has grown exponentially, and the 2012 edition was attended by Hollywood stars such as Morris Chestnut, Lynn Whitfield, Maya Gilbert, and Rockmond Dumbar. It was screened throughout the African continent by numerous regional and continental media and was covered by international television stations such as CNN and Al-Jazeera.

According to Peace Anyiam-Osigwe, the AMA Awards's mission is to present a modern and dynamic image of sub-Saharan Africa, something different from the image produced and circulated by older African cinema festivals such as the FESPACO in Ouagadougou and the Journées Ciné-matographiques de Carthage in Tunis. Since their establishment, these festivals have been influenced by Third Cinema theories and post-independence pan-African ideologies. They were sponsored by western funding agencies and had participated in circulating a mainly art-oriented, politically engaged type of cinema that was targeted at festivals rather than commercial distribution (see Şaul and Austen 2010). In contrast, the AMA Awards focus on locally funded film productions that aim at commercial circulation. Similar to other African cinema festivals, the AMA Awards places particular emphasis on the technical, aesthetic, and narrative qualities of films. Nonetheless, its primary objective is to emphasize the existence of dynamic and autonomous African film industries, which are economically successful and fully capable of competing with the standards set by film industries located elsewhere in the world. In this sense, the AMA Awards's organizers' focus on glamor, media visibility, and advertising seeks to highlight the existence of an Afrocentric commercial entertainment culture, which is autonomous and self-centered and does not need to be sanctioned by any external authority to be successful (i.e., the western funding agencies, foreign film festivals, western film critics, etc.), and whose capacity to achieve global visibility goes well beyond the position of marginality in which western exoticism has located African cultures since the colonial era (see Jedlowski 2013b).

The success that the AMA Awards have managed to achieve over the past few years increased the international visibility of the Nigerian and African video production phenomenon (Tutton and Purefoy 2010; Wenner 2009), and it has given an important boost to the creation of a continental and pan-African popular film culture with a shared star system and an increasingly interconnected economy. Furthermore, it has participated in the consolidation of the bridge that has, over the course of the last few years, increasingly linked the African corporate business sector (represented for instance by big telecommunication companies such as Airtel and MTN) and the entertainment industries. In this sense, the AMA Awards, and the work of Peace Anyiam-Osigwe, have created avenues for the Nigerian video industries' future growth, which are destined to further influence the transformation of the media landscapes in Nigeria and in other regions of the continent.

## Female Entrepreneurship in the Video Film Industry and the Emergence of New Figures of Success

The personal success of these three women, together with that of other female entrepreneurs active in the industry whose names I have mentioned throughout these pages, played an important role in creating new models of economic and social mobility for Nigerian women. As Banégas and Warnier (2001: 9) argue, defining how success is measured and sanctioned in a specific society is a complex analytical task. They stress that one possible starting point is the observation of how it is translated into specific forms of material culture, namely in specific strategies that pertain to the accumulation of economic and symbolic capital. In most African societies—and Nigeria is no exception in this sense—success is measured and shown by the acquisition of a set of material goods (expensive cars, fancy and big houses, imported top-brand clothes, and gadgets), which, through their symbolic value, provide the individual that acquires them a particular social status (Banégas and Warnier 2001: 9–10). The individuals that I have portrayed in this chapter all fit this discourse; their economic success is made socially visible through explicit strategies of material accumulation and display. However, in my view, this aspect is secondary in the definition of their success. The female entrepreneurs I describe do indeed accumulate and expose their material wealth, but their success is of heightened visibility and significance, particularly for their female followers and admirers, because of the autonomy and independence these women display vis-à-vis their male counterparts.

As outlined at the beginning of this chapter, a brief overview of their biographies illustrates that they all belong to the same generation; they were born during or just after the Nigerian oil-boom, in the 1970s and early 1980s. Furthermore, they all belong to the southern Nigerian high-middle class (apart from Peace Anyiam-Osigwe, who, as I evidenced earlier, comes from a wealthy family) and graduated from university before entering the industry. They have all spent at least one year studying abroad (either in the UK or in the U.S.) and have important transnational business connections. Their professional paths have taken a similar route, as they initially embarked on the careers their parents had envisioned for them (university, banking, and financial sectors) only to later move on to an independently chosen alternative. In their initial phase of entrepreneurship, they relied on social networks that provided access to credit and reassurance. Finally, most of them have a rather independent private life (at the time this chapter was written, they were either single or divorced; some of them, like Isong, were single mothers by choice) and managed to keep their private affairs away from the limelight. They surely belong to the elite, but their biographies are characterized by autonomous choices and stubborn determination. They are indeed representatives of an ideal-type of "self-made woman", who achieve success because of their own will and entrepreneurial skills rather than some inherited economic and social privilege (even if, of course, their belonging to the Nigerian elite helped them to affirm their autonomy and the respect associated with such a status).

Furthermore, their exposure in local and transnational media allows these women to be extremely visible social figures, a factor that easily transforms them into a model for younger generations of Nigerian women. Their faces, voices, words, and thoughts appear on an almost daily basis on Nigerian television programs, internet sites, fanzine magazines, or newspapers.

Contrary to female film stars, whose presence in the media is generally connected to gossip and sex scandals, the image of these women is always connected to representations of economic and entrepreneurial success. They therefore appear to be model women who did not need to use their bodies in order to achieve social recognition, and that managed to make it without—or rather beyond—the support of their fathers, brothers, and husbands. The informal discussions with audience members I conducted during my fieldwork as well as the web comments, the YouTube clips, and the printed interviews that circulate in abundance in the Nigerian public sphere confirm this point. These women's autonomy, freedom, and economic success still provoke some anxiety in a mainly male-centered society like Nigeria. For instance, rumors about lesbianism, sterility, and hidden family issues (abandoned children, broken marriages, betrayals, and so on) do occasionally appear in relation to these and other female figures.[16] But the fact that these women generally have a role behind rather than in front of the camera keeps them more protected than film actresses from the male chauvinism that characterizes popular discourses on female artists.

In fact, as Kate Henshaw-Nuttal, a famous Nigerian film star, attested during an interview reported in the documentary *Nollywood Lady aka Peace Mission* (2008), the video industry as a whole has progressively transformed and deconstructed these stereotypes, making the world of filmmaking an acceptable, and often highly desirable, professional environment for women. Kate Henshaw-Nuttal's account of her experience makes this point perfectly clear:

> When I told my dad I wanted to be a musician, he said: "No, you should go and study medicine". [Thus] I'm a medical microbiologist by profession, I graduated and all that, but then I left my degree somewhere in a box and I started acting. Back then, parents couldn't even conceive that their children wanted to act . . . but now everyone says: "Oh, my daughter loves your film! She wants to act!" Parents are actually coming and approaching me to ask: "Could you take my daughter, my niece through? We love your films, you guys are doing a lot for the image of the country!" And then young girls look up to you and say: "I like the roles that you play, they teach me a thing or two! You are always nice!" [and] I get a lot of text messages that say: "I want to be like you!"

The point Kate Henshaw-Nuttal underscores, the way opinions about the role of women in Nigerian entertainment industries has transformed over the past few years, drives this chapter to its conclusion. As I illustrated above, much of the literature that discusses the relationship between the Nigerian video industry and the position of women in the Nigerian society is based on content analysis of the videos it produces. Within this context, video representations of women (often stereotypical, sexist, and violent) have been condemned, and videos have been accused of exercising a bad influence on Nigerian society in general and on audiences' behavior in particular (see Okome 2010).[17] In this chapter, by focusing on successful examples of female entrepreneurship within the video industry, I have attempted to present a different scenario in order to highlight the complexities that define the interaction between the video industry and the transformations of gender issues in Nigeria. While agreeing to some extent with concerns about the representations of women that some Nigerian videos have generated, I have tried to move the focus beyond the content of the videos to the people who work behind the camera to produce them in order to analyze the ways the industry, as an economic enterprise, proposes new models of social and economic achievement for Nigerian women.

## NOTES

1. For an in-depth analysis and regional declinations of the Nigerian video phenomenon, see Barrot (2005), Haynes (2000), Krings and Okome (2013), and Larkin (2008).
2. This research was conducted as part of my Ph.D. project, which was sponsored by the University of Naples "L'Orientale". Warm thanks go to Jonathan Haynes and Sandro Triulzi for their supervision of my research and to Ute Röschenthaler for her contributions to the final version of this chapter.
3. "Marketer" is the term people normally use in Nigeria to refer to the video distributor.
4. For an analysis and interpretation of the specific forms of social political criticism of Nigerian videos, see also Haynes (2006), Larkin (2008, chapter 6), and McCall (2007). The debate about "gender" in Africa and the way African women have been represented in literature, popular culture, and academic research is extremely vast. For an introduction, see Cornwall (2005), and for an analysis of the representation of gender in West African popular culture, see Newell (1997).
5. While the names of a number of Nigerian female entrepreneurs, such as Amaka Igwe and Emem Isong, and female stars, such as Genevieve Nnaji and Omotola Jalade-Ekeinde, appear in numerous academic articles about the Nigerian video industry, the only articles that discuss the roles of women behind the camera directly are, to my knowledge, Okome's (2007b) transcriptions of his interviews with the controversial Pentecostal video producer Helene Ukpabio and with the successful video businesswoman, Emem Isong (Okome 2000), whose experience I discuss below. As they are primarily based on interview transcriptions, however, these articles do not produce any substantial attempt to interpret the way the industry, as a form of business, has created new models of social and economic mobility for Nigerian women. Whenever this issue is discussed, it takes the form of a discussion of video contents rather than an analysis of the video industry's economic environment (cf. Okome 2004; Künzler 2009).
6. In this chapter, I rely on Charles Taylor's definition of social and collective imaginaries as "the ways in which people imagine their social existence, how they fit together with others, how things go on between them and their fellows, the expectations that are normally met, and the deeper normative notions and images that underlie these expectations" (2002: 106; see also Strauss 2006).

7. As the figures released by the Nigerian Censors Board attest, during the production crisis local language film production remained stable, and in some cases increased, while English language film production progressively decreased as a result of the saturation of the video market and the economic collapse of numerous production companies active in this branch of the industry. For a comparative analysis of the impact of the production crisis on the different sections of the video industry, see Jedlowski (2012b).

8. A similar practice was also used in the early days of Hollywood, just after the introduction of sound recording technologies, but it lasted only for a few years because it was in the end more expensive than subtitling (see Vincendeau 1988).

9. The average budgets for the new wave of Nigerian films that target theatrical distribution is significantly higher (between $300,000 and $500,000; see also Jedlowski 2013a).

10. Within the world of film distribution, the terms "window" and "windowing" are normally used to indicate the way the circulation of a film is controlled in time and space in order to maximize the revenues.

11. The Filmmakers Association of Nigeria (FAN) comprises Nigerian filmmakers and distributors based in the U.S. After its intervention, the American market has become one of the more structured and reliable environments for the distribution of Nigerian videos in recent years. Currently, it accounts for up to a third of the revenues of an average Nigerian video release (Isong 2011; see also Jedlowski 2013a). Nigerian distributors equally consider Ghana, with its (at least partially) formalized video market, a reliable source of revenues (Ejike 2010; see also Meyer 2010).

12. Similar to Isong, Vivian Ejike, another successful female entrepreneur, started her career in the video industry after working a few years in the banking sector and obtaining a university degree (in French Studies at the University of Port Harcourt). She also worked with Isong for several years. In 2009, she released the video *Silent Scandal*, which, thanks to Ejike's specific production and distribution strategies (higher budget, use of both Ghanaian and Nigerian stars, earlier release in Ghana in order to beat the competition of Nigerian bootleggers), became the most successful straight-to-video release in English since *Osuofia in London* (2003), selling 100,000 copies in its first week of release (Ejike 2010), a considerable success in 2009 when the industry was still in crisis.

13. Cinema-going culture had almost disappeared in the southern region of the country as a result of the wave of privatization that followed the application of the Structural Adjustment Policies and the increase of social insecurity in large Nigerian cities. The first new multiplex cinema opened in Victoria Island, Lagos, in 2004.

14. Interestingly enough, the two films that have bettered the box-office records set by *Through the Glass* in the years that followed its release were also produced by female producers. *Ije, the Journey* (2010), produced and directed by Chyneze Anyaene, became the most successful Nigerian film released by grossing almost 60 million Naira (around $380,000) in the first three weeks of screening in Nigerian cinemas. The following year, *The Return of Jenifa* (2011), produced by the Yoruba star Funke Akindele, created a new record by grossing 10 million Naira ($65,000) in just one week of screening, becoming one of the fastest grossing Nollywood releases of all time.

15. The price for an original copy of a Nollywood film is around 200 Naira ($1.50), while tickets for the cinema are sold for around 1,500 Naira (almost $10). See also Jedlowski (2012a).

16. An example of such rumors can be found in a report on Isong's production company and the group of female actors she casts regularly in her films. The

fanzine reports, and by reporting insinuates, that "it was rumored sometime ago that there could be more than just mutual understanding among these stars since they are all females" (*City People Extra* 2011b: 4).

17. The debate on the effect of media content on audiences' behavior is vast and complex (see, for example, Moores 1993; Bryant and Oliver 2009). However, much of the literature on the representation of women in Nigerian videos tends to imply a rather linear (and, in my view, controversial) relationship between film content and viewers' behavior.

## REFERENCES

Abah, Adebayo. 2008. 'One step forward, two steps backward: African Women in Nigerian video films'. *Communication, Culture & Critique* 1: 335–357.

Adeleye-Fayemi, Bisi. 1997. 'Images of women in Nigerian television'. In: Karin Barber (ed). *Readings in African Popular Culture*. Bloomington: Indiana University Press, 125–131.

Aduwo, Bola. 2010. 'Emem Isong: the story behind the glory'. Published on the Blog *Nollywood uncut*. http://www.nollywooduncut.com/nollywood-celebrity-interviews/81-emem-isong-nollywood-movie-producer, accessed 20 May 2012.

Amadiume, Ifi. 1987. *Male Daughters, Female Husbands: Gender and Sex in African Society*. London and New Jersey: Zed Books.

Banégas, Richard and Jean-Pierre Warnier. 2001. 'Nouvelles figures de la réussite et du pouvoir: introduction au thème'. *Politique Africaine* 82: 5–21.

Barrot, Pierre (ed). 2005. *Nollywood: Le phénomène video au Nigeria*. Paris: L'Harmattan.

Bryant, Jennings and Mary Beth Oliver. 2009. *Media Effects: Advances in Theory and Research*. London: Routledge.

Bryce, Jane. 2012. 'Signs of femininity, symptoms of malaise: contextualizing figurations of 'woman' in Nollywood'. *Research in African Literatures* 43, 4: 71–87.

Chuku, Gloria Ifeoma. 1999. 'From petty traders to international merchants: a historical account of three Igbo women of Nigeria in trade and commerce, 1886–1970'. *African Economic History* 27: 1–22.

City People Extra. 2011a. 'Emem Isong: "why I left banking for film making"'. Lagos: City People Media Group, 2–3.

City People Extra. 2011b. 'How her new clique changed the movie industry'. Lagos: City People Media Group, 4.

Coquery-Vidrovitch, Catherine. 1997. *African Women: A Modern History*. Boulder: Westview Press.

Coquery-Vidrovitch, Catherine. 2002. 'African businesswomen in colonial and post-colonial Africa: a comparative study'. In: Alusine Jalloh and Toyin Falola (eds). *Black Business and Economic Power*. Rochester: University of Rochester Press, 199–211.

Cornwall, Andrea. 2005. *Readings in Gender in Africa*. Oxford: James Currey.

Denzer, LaRay. 1994. 'Yoruba women: a historiographical essay'. *International Journal of African Historical Studies* 27: 1–40.

Dike, Chike (ed). 1995. *The Women's Revolt of 1929*. Proceedings of a National Symposium to Mark the 60th Anniversary of the Women's Uprising in South Eastern Nigeria, N.G.A., Lagos.

Dike, Kenneth and Felicia Ekejiuba. 1990. *The Aro of South-eastern Nigeria, 1650–1980: A Study of Socio-Economic Formation and Transformation in Nigeria*. Ibadan: Ibadan University Press.

*The Economist.* 2006. 'Nollywood dreams: Nigerian films are so successful that the government wants to get involved'. http://www.economist.com/node/7226009, accessed 27 July 2006.

*The Economist.* 2010. 'Lights, camera, Africa: movies are uniting a disparate continent, and dividing it too'. http://www.economist.com/node/17723124, accessed 16 December 2010.

Ejike, Vivian. 2010. Personal Communication. Lagos: 22 December 2010.

Ekunno, Mike. 2011. 'Nollywood and the new cinema'. *Next*, 2 January 2011.

Ellis, Stephen and Yves Fauré. 1995. 'Introduction'. In: Ellis, Stephen and Yves Fauré (eds). *Entreprises et entrepreneurs africains*. Paris: Karthala, 5–33.

Evwierhoma, Mabel. 2008. 'Women through the eye of the camera: the aesthetics challenge of Nigerian films'. In: Foluke Ogunleye (ed). *Africa through the Eye of the Video Camera*. Manzini: Academic Publishers, 125–132.

Garritano, Carmela. 2000. 'Women, melodrama, and political critique: a feminist reading of *Hostages, Dust to Dust* and *True Confession*'. In: Jonathan Haynes (ed). *Nigerian Video Films*. Athens: Ohio University Press, 165–191.

Haynes, Jonathan (ed). 2000. *Nigerian Video Films*. Athens: Ohio University Press.

Haynes, Jonathan. 2006. 'Political critique in Nigerian video films'. *African Affairs* 105, 421: 511–533.

Haynes, Jonathan and Onookome Okome. 1998. 'Evolving popular media: Nigerian video films'. *Research in African Literatures* 29, 3: 106–128.

Husseini, Shaibu. 2009. 'Nollywood 2008: stuck in the middle of nowhere'. *The Guardian Nigeria*, 23 January 2009: 24–25.

Ifeka-Moller, Caroline. 1975. 'Female militancy and colonial revolt: the women's war of 1929, Eastern Nigeria'. In: Shirley Ardener (ed). *Perceiving Women*. London: Malaby Press, 127–137.

Inikori, Joseph. 2002. 'The development of entrepreneurship in Africa: South-Eastern Nigeria during the era of the trans-Atlantic slave trade'. In: Alusine Jalloh and Toyin Falola (eds). *Black Business and Economic Power*. Rochester: University of Rochester Press, 41–79.

Isong, Emem. 2011. Personal Communication. Lagos: 10 January 2011.

Jedlowski, Alessandro. 2012a. 'Local language films and the reverse side of the production crisis'. *Weekly Trust*, 30 June 2012. http://weeklytrust.com.ng/index.php?option=com_content&view=article&id=9736&catid=57&Itemid=154.

Jedlowski, Alessandro. 2012b. 'Small screen cinema: informality and remediation in Nollywood'. *Journal of Television and New Media* 13, 5: 431–446.

Jedlowski, Alessandro. 2013a. 'From Nollywood to Nollyworld: processes of transnationalization in the Nigerian video film industry'. In: Matthias Krings and Onookome Okome (eds). *Global Nollywood: Transnational Dimensions of an African Video Film Industry*. Bloomington: Indiana University Press, 25–45.

Jedlowski, Alessandro. 2013b. 'Nigerian videos in the global arena: the postcolonial exotic revisited'. *The Global South* 7, 1: 157–178.

Krings, Matthias and Onookome Okome (eds). 2013. *Global Nollywood: Transnational Dimensions of an African Video Film Industry*. Bloomington: Indiana University Press.

Künzler, Daniel. 2009. 'The figure of success as content and consequence of the video film industries in southeastern Nigeria and Ghana'. Paper presented at the conference 'Nollywood and Beyond', Mainz, 13–16 May 2009, 1–25.

Larkin, Brian. 2008. *Signal and Noise: Media, Infrastructure and Urban Culture in Northern Nigeria*. Durham and London: Duke University Press.

Lovejoy, Paul. 1980. *Caravans of Kola: The Hausa Kola trade, 1700–1900*. Zaria: Ahmadu Bello University Press Limited.

MacGaffey, Janet. 1987. *Entrepreneurs and Parasites: The Struggle for Indigenous Capitalism in Zaire*. Cambridge: Cambridge University Press.

MacGaffey, Janet. 1988. 'Creatively coping with crisis: entrepreneurs in the second economy of Zaire (the Democratic Republic of Congo)'. In: Anita Spring and Barbara McDade (eds). *African Entrepreneurship: Theory and Reality*. Gainesville: University Press of Florida, 37–50.

Madichie, Nnamdi. 2009. 'Breaking the glass ceiling in Nigeria: a review of women's entrepreneurship'. *Journal of African Business* 10: 51–66.

Mbembe, Achille. 2006. 'On politics as a form of expenditure'. In: Jean Comaroff and John Comaroff (eds). *Law and Disorder in the Postcolony*. Chicago: Chicago University Press, 299–336.

McCall, John. 2007. 'The Pan-Africanism we have: Nollywood's invention of Africa'. *Film International* 5, 4: 92–97.

Meyer, Birgit. 2010. 'Ghanaian popular video movies between state film policies and Nollywood: discourses and tensions'. In: Mahir Şaul and Ralph Austen (eds). *Viewing African Cinema in the Twenty-first Century: FESPACO Art Films and the Nollywood Video Revolution*. Athens: Ohio University Press, 42–62.

Moores, Shaun. 1993. *Interpreting Audiences: The Ethnography of Media Consumption*. London: Sage.

Newell, Stephanie. 1997. *Writing African Women: Gender, Popular Culture, and Literature in West Africa*. London: Zed Books.

Njoku, Benjamin. 2009. 'Nollywood is dying: interview with Francis Onwochei'. *The Vanguard*. 21 February 2009, 36.

Nwabughuogu, Anthony. 1982. 'From wealthy entrepreneurs to petty traders: the decline of African middlemen in Eastern Nigeria, 1900–1950'. *The Journal of African History* 23, 3: 365–379.

Okome, Onookome. 2000. 'Naming, suffering and women in Nigerian video films: notes on the interview with Emem Isong'. *Nduñode: Calabar Journal of Humanities* 3, 1: 43–56.

Okome, Onookome. 2004. 'Writing the anxious city: Images of Lagos in Nigerian home video films'. In: Okwui Enwezor *et al.* (eds). *Under Siege: Four African Cities. Freetown, Johannesburg, Kinshasa, Lagos*. Ostfildern-Ruit: Hatjie Cantz Publisher, 315–336.

Okome, Onookome. 2007a. ' "The message is reaching a lot of people": proselytizing and video films of Helen Ukpabio'. *Postcolonial Text* 3, 2: 1–20. http://journals.sfu.ca/pocol/index.php/pct/article/view/750/419.

Okome, Onookome. 2007b. 'Nollywood: Spectatorship, audience and the sites of consumption'. *Postcolonial Text* 3, 2: 1–21. http://journals.sfu.ca/pocol/index.php/pct/article/view/763/425.

Okome, Onookome. 2010. 'Nollywood and its critics'. In: Mahir Şaul and Ralph Austen (eds). *Viewing African Cinema in the Twenty-first Century: FESPACO Art Films and the Nollywood Video Revolution*. Athens: Ohio University Press, 26–41.

Oloruntoba-Oju, Taiwo. 2006. ' "Dèdè n dẹ ku ikú n dẹ Dèdè": fe/male sexuality and dominance in Nigerian video films (Nollywood)'. *Stichproben. Wiener Zeitschrift für kritische Afrikastudien* 11: 5–26.

Olukoju, Ayodeji. 2002. 'The impact of British colonialism on the development of African business in colonial Nigeria'. In: Alusine Jalloh and Toyin Falola (eds). *Black Business and Economic Power*. Rochester: University of Rochester Press, 176–198.

Şaul, Mahir and Ralph Austen (eds). 2010. *Viewing African Cinema in the Twenty-first Century: FESPACO Art Films and the Nollywood Video Revolution*. Athens: Ohio University Press.

Simone, AbdouMaliq. 2004. *For the City Yet to Come: Changing African Life in Four Cities*. Durham and London: Duke University Press.

Spring, Anita and Barbara McDade. 1998. 'Entrepreneurship in Africa: traditional and contemporary paradigms'. In: Anita Spring and Barbara McDade (eds). *African Entrepreneurship: Theory and Reality*. Gainesville: University Press of Florida, 1–36.

Strauss, Claudia. 2006. 'The imaginary'. *Anthropological Theory* 6, 3: 322–344.

Sundaram, Ravi. 1999. 'Recycling modernity: pirate electronic cultures in India'. *Third Text* 13, 47: 59–65.

Taylor, Charles. 2002. 'Modern social imaginaires'. *Public Culture* 14, 1: 91–124.

Tutton, Mark and Christina Purefoy. 2010. 'Stars shine at African Oscars'. *CNN International*. http://edition.cnn.com/2010/WORLD/africa/04/30/african.movie. awards/index.html, accessed 30 April 2010.

Urban, Greg. 2001. *Metaculture: How Culture Moves Through the World*. Minneapolis: University of Minnesota Press.

Vincendeau, Ginette. 1988. 'Hollywood Babel: the multiple language version'. *Screen* 29, 2: 24–39.

Wenner, Dorothy. 2009. 'Showtime in Nigeria'. *Die Zeit*, 12 June 2009. http://www. zeit.de/2009/25/Nigeria.

Woldie, Atsede and Adebimpe Adersua. 2004. 'Female entrepreneurs in a transitional economy: businesswomen in Nigeria'. *International Journal of Social Economics* 31, 1/2: 78–93.

# 14  You Have to Be Brave and Fearless

## Video Film Entrepreneurs' Practices and Discourses in Tanzania

*Claudia Böhme*

The arrival of video film in post-socialist Tanzania opened up new entrepreneurial opportunities for many artists who over the last few decades have established a major film industry in Tanzania. Using Nollywood as a model,[1] hundreds of young Tanzanians shifted from the media and fields like theatre or literature to the audiovisual medium of film to tell their own stories in Kiswahili, entertain, and make a living. Among them are directors, producers, mobile video vendors (*machinga*[2]), video shop, library, and cinema owners, and movie translators. This also holds true for the piracy business, a sector that has created thousands of jobs in the video filmmaking's shadow industry.

When I talked to video film practitioners, they explained the film business as a special working field, as its main product, film, is a medium of a fantastic and imaginary space. The films often revolve around individual success or failure and are, as Birgit Meyer (2001) has described for Ghana, connected to the hopes and dreams of their makers. Those who enter the film business are driven by the hope of making the transition from a small-time actor, director, or video film seller to a big entrepreneur, a *mjasiriamali wa filamu*.

*Mjasiriamali*[3] is the common Swahili term for entrepreneur; it comprises *mjasiri*, a brave and fearless person, and *mali*, wealth. The term is also historically related to local conceptions of Big Men, like the "power brokers" in the nineteenth century who, as Felicitas Becker (2004) describes, established themselves as "sultans" and "chiefs" in the region through their personal abilities as leaders and traders. Colonial rule, however, demolished the networks of these power brokers by forcefully shifting loyalties and driving internal competition (Becker 2004: 8). After independence and the creation of a socialist state under Julius Kambarage Nyerere, self-reliance and innovative problem-solving were promoted, while urban-based entrepreneurs were considered "bloodsuckers" and a threat to *Ujamaa* (socialism) (Brennan 2006). In Tanzania at that time, the only way to participate in private business and trade was the growing black market (Boner 2011; Tripp 1997). After the economic crisis in the 2000s, which resulted in a growth in the informal market and the resultant adjustment programs, entrepreneurs were reevaluated as part of a competitive private economy (Boner 2011: 18–19). Accordingly, the concept of *mjasiriamali* has undergone a major shift over the course of the last century; furthermore, as the definition below shows, the term has assumed similarities to western conceptions of entrepreneurship and apparently lost its former political dimension. Through new media like film, advice literature,[4] and the internet, local understandings have become mixed with globally circulating conceptions, stories, and imaginations of entrepreneurship. These new media have offered not only multiple possibilities for entrepreneurial activity,[5] but also platforms for discussion and interaction. The Tanzanian video filmmaker and critic Bishop Hiluka wrote an article on video film entrepreneurship on his personal blog in September 2011. At the beginning of his article, he explains the term entrepreneurship in Swahili as follows:

"UJASIRIAMALI" [Entrepreneurship] is the ability and goal of a person or people to think, to create and to bring about a new possibility for economics/production and to enter the market without fearing competition or the available restrictions and the problems that can occur. An entrepreneur is someone with the faith to risk something, an inventor, a clever person who is able to discover and to use different economic chances, the one who loves efficiency and better quality of artistic work, he should not be of the habits to stir up and destroy the regulations of agreements and plans. Again an entrepreneur is said to be someone who loves to look for and receive various information, who sets goals, who sets plans and follows them, he shouldn't be a dependent but someone who believes and has the ability to convince and has a network. (Hiluka 2011, my translation)

Hiluka has taken courses at the University of Dar es Salaam Entrepreneurship Centre (UDC) and read several books on the topic.[6] His definition clearly shows some of the main characteristics of the concept of a classical "Schumpeterian" entrepreneur as an independent visionary investor looking for new possibilities without fear of risk. In contrast to Schumpeter's notion, however, a video entrepreneur is at the same time a creator and an investor. Additionally, Hiluka points to the love of creating a better quality of artistic work (Bude 1997). All this distinguishes an entrepreneur from normal businesspeople, whose daily activities do not produce major changes, new technologies, art genres, and so on, although there is no agreed upon definition of how the term is used in the literature on entrepreneurship (Spring and McDade 1998).

In the same article, Hiluka takes a very critical stand against the development of Tanzanian film entrepreneurship. He questions why most individual actors in the film business have yet to achieve financial success despite the large growth and high popularity of video film production, complaining: "They live a beggar's life!" He further argues that most just "sell their faces"; they become famous without earning anything. In addition to the library and video cinema owners who are said to be pirating films and are considered a threat to the industry, blame is primarily placed on the shoulders of the big film distributors. Hiluka continues: "By the time a film is ready, the only thing left to do is to sit on your hands and talk to the distributor so that the film will be distributed! No matter how much he [the filmmaker] will be paid!" Hiluka corroborates his argument with the case of a young filmmaker who had desperately tried to obtain lucrative deals for his films but was unable to compete with the established structures of distribution (Hiluka 2011). As Hiluka's blog article shows, becoming a successful entrepreneur is one of the major discourses within the Tanzanian video film scene.

In this chapter I want to examine the practices and discourses associated with video film entrepreneurs.[7] I will illustrate that the industry is not only divided between filmmakers and producers or distributors but also between very different entrepreneurs who have successfully conquered specific economic niches on different scales of the video film business. By looking at the careers of these actors, I will provide insights into the varieties, characteristics, and specificities of video film entrepreneurship in Tanzania.

Like the video film industries themselves, scholarly interest has produced an enormous output of academic work on the topic. Video films, at first mainly from West Africa, have been studied as forms of expression with a potentially subversive character (Haynes 2003, 2007; McCall 2007; Okome 2007a); as medial transcriptions and visualization of older ideas and forms of mediation between humans and transcendent powers (Behrend 2003; Meyer 2003; Wendl 2004); as Pentecostal propaganda (DeWitte 2003; Okome 2007b); as the forms of appropriation of films of foreign origin (Adamu 2007; Krings 2005; Larkin 1997); and as expressions of a parallel modernity (Larkin 1997). The entrepreneurial side of the video film business has yet to be given satisfactory attention.

With the growth of the video film industry and the coinciding increased film revenues and salaries for filmmakers, increasing numbers of young Tanzanians not only try their luck at becoming a famous actor or director, they also dream of being a film producer, that is, a video film entrepreneur who produces and distributes his own and other people's video films. As the business has become gradually more competitive, there has been a marked growth in discourses on power and belonging, exploitation, and the fair distribution of profits. The video film industry has created different localized practices in production, reception, and distribution, new elites and hierarchies, and dependencies between actors.

This chapter begins with an overview of the evolution of entrepreneurial activity in the video film business in Tanzania. Using three video film entrepreneurs as examples, my goal is to provide a deeper insight into their life histories and careers, and the difficulties against which they had to fight when establishing their businesses.

## A "SMALL MEDIUM" WITH A BIG IMPACT: THE ROOTS OF VIDEO FILM ENTREPRENEURSHIP

The idea to produce video films and develop a locally based industry in Tanzania was fostered by the reception of Nollywood as a successful model for African film production (see also Krings 2010). As Jonathan Haynes has shown, in Nigeria the video boom was paradoxically the product of an economic breakdown, and video films reflected the resulting poverty (Haynes 2000: xv) and uncertainty (Barber 2000: 262). In a time when going to the cinema was too dangerous because criminality had risen rapidly, the possibility of watching a film at home was a reassuring alternative. The Nigerian video film industry took off from this state of emergency and brought about an unexpected boost in the cultural as well as the informal sector. "Like the automobile (also increasingly imported from Asia), the video camera has given African entrepreneurs an entrée into domestic markets and a personal autonomy impossible with 'lumpier' early film technologies" (Austen and Şaul 2010: 7).

In Tanzania, the impact of the crisis has not resulted in the same level of insecurity as in Nigeria. However, the 1980s and 1990s were economically challenging because of the failing economic politics in the *Ujamaa* era under president Nyerere and the resultant structural adjustment programs that the IMF and the World Bank had initiated. These economic and political changes also impacted the popular arts and media sector.

Ali Hassan Mwinyi, Tanzania's second president, known for his liberal politics, exemplified by his nickname "Mzee Ruksa" (Mr. Allowed), made the introduction of video in the mid-1980s possible by loosening the former import ban on video technology (Smyth 1989: 396) and the later introduction of TV and the legalization of private broadcasting in 1994. Established entrepreneurs seized the opportunity and expanded their businesses. The famous media mogul, Reginald Mengi, is a good example; he used the fortune he had amassed producing ballpoint pens to launch the independent TV station, ITV, five years before the government's station was created, as the owner of the IPP Media Group in Tanzania (Makura 2008: 162–181). Video films from abroad that began circulating in Tanzania were enthusiastically received by both businessmen, who began to distribute pirated copies to audiences that ranged from the young urban poor to the emerging middle class. Films from Hollywood, Hong Kong, and India were most popular. The local reception of globally circulated video films and TV programs connected Tanzanian viewers with the transnational flows of media and made them part of a "mediascape" and new "imagined worlds" (Appadurai 1996: 33). The mass import of video equipment led to a technological revolution that fostered a (video) cassette culture that replaced popular audio production, similar to what Peter Manuel (1999) describes for the music cassette business in India. The video medium enabled artists to conserve and reproduce their work and thereby video film sales provided them with the ability to work independently and make a living.

Politicians and cultural workers considered video films that often focused on love, sex, horror, and action a cultural threat and a reflection of the failures of the class enemy; all the same, these small media were difficult to control.[8] The introduction of the video film fostered tremendous changes when popular cultural and economic practices in the media industry shifted from the audio focused radio play and popular theatre's live stage performances characterized by interaction with the audience to the new medium. The new medium was also, however, connected to established practices and social spaces. Accordingly, a network of producers and distributors emerged with specific roles, duties, and hierarchies for the mass production of video films.

## BRINGING CINEMA TO THE PEOPLE: THE VIDEO SHOW ENTREPRENEUR

The introduction of video film and TV in the 1990s contributed to the bankruptcy of the big cinema houses owned by Indian businessmen in Tanzania (see Brennan 2005: 510; Smyth 1989: 396). The decentralization and democratization of media also, however, fostered the creation of alternative spaces for viewing film and opened up new entrepreneurial possibilities. So-called video shows that were located in every quarter of a town or village spread like wildfire, as many people could not afford their own TV or VHS player. The video cinemas are creatively arranged self-made places. The projectionists show video films of different origins in small simply equipped rooms with a TV set and VCR for a reasonable entry fee. The architecture of these spaces varies from very simple wooden constructions with walls of Jute or plastic bags to mud houses with grass roofs and solid cinema houses.

The video shows offer mixed movie programs, ranging from Hollywood and particularly martial arts action movies, Indian classics, and Nigerian films to, since the rise of the Tanzanian video film industry, Swahili movies as well. The increasing popularity of local movies led to a decline in the popularity of Nigerian movies, which have by now almost been replaced by Tanzanian films.[9] In the early days, the absence of a TV in a household could have explained why Tanzanians went to video shows; but today, as the ratio of TVs and video players per household has increased especially in urban areas, this reason is no longer applicable. Today, Tanzanians go to video shows for various reasons. First, from an economic perspective, Swahili movies that are sold in the market for 5,000 Tsh[10] (about $3) on VHS and for 2,500 (about $1.50) on DVD are screened in a video show for only 100 Tsh (5 cents) per film for adults and only 50 Tsh for children, and are therefore more economically feasible options. More importantly, as Laura Fair (2009) argues about former cinema theatres, video shows play a role as a social space. The late Venny Karuguna, owner of the Maoniko video show in Magomeni Makuti, explained it to me as follows:

> You know entertainment is where people gather. You can sit at home with enough beer in your fridge, but if you are alone it isn't much fun.

But if you go to the bar crowded with people you have fun. So that's why people come here to the show, not that they don't have a TV, but they are coming because it means something to them.[11]

After the last cinema house, the Avalon, was closed in 2002 (Brennan 2005: 510), video shows were the only public "cinemas" accessible for ordinary citizens within the quarters of Dar es Salaam. In 2003 and 2007, Muslim Jaffer, a Tanzanian businessman and entrepreneur of Indian origin, opened two new multiplex cinemas, the New World Cinema and the Century Cinemax in the Mwenge quarter in northern Dar es Salaam, which primarily show Hollywood and Bollywood films for a better off and predominantly Indian audience. In contrast, video shows offer a cheaper alternative to these unreachable spaces and function as a "cinema of the poor", that is a parallel cinema.[12] Due to their different audiences, programs, and roles in creating semi-intimate publics (Appadurai 1990; Gunner 2005; Schulz 2002), these cinema cultures are also sometimes discussed along the ethnic lines of Tanzanians of Indian origin, *wahindi*, and "Africans", *waafrika*. In the following example, I will focus on a video show that I visited regularly in 2008 to illustrate the particularity of this entrepreneurial space and show that the video shows are not only a valuable business for their owners but also create social semi-public spaces, especially for young males in the quarters.

## THE MAONIKO VIDEO SHOW AND SPORTS CENTER

While looking for a place to carry out participant observation in January 2008, I came to know Venny, the owner of the Maoniko video show in Magomeni Makuti in Dar es Salaam. Venny was an old skinny limping man dressed in very simple clothes and on first sight he would not fit the image of a successful entrepreneur. Nevertheless, that he was an entrepreneur became clear during my many visits to the show and when he told me his story.

Venny Karuguna was born on 20 December 1955 in Kagera, Bukoba District in northeast Tanzania. He joined the military when he finished high school and later worked for the Association of Tanzanian Farmers (*Shirika la Wakulima wa Taifa*). While he was studying at Dar es Salaam University, a twist of fate brought him back to his village when both his parents passed away. When he came back to Dar es Salaam in 1988, he had to start anew and tried to make a living selling coffee and as the owner of a *daladala*, a local bus. With the money he was able to save, he rented a room and the start-up equipment for a new business. When I asked him why he shifted his business and opened a video cinema in 1994, he explained:

I decided to open a video show because of the situation of commerce at that time. The rules regarding trade and commerce were very strict, so I thought working in the service sector was better than doing trade. The situation was so bad for doing trade that you couldn't sell anything.

> And if you think how the government had prohibited commerce with abroad, if I hadn't done the other businesses it would have been really difficult.[13]

Another important reason was that Venny had been a long-term fan of popular cinema and was an expert in diverse cinema cultures. At the beginning, Venny showed mainly Indian and American films, but adapted his program accordingly when Nigerian movies entered the country at the end of the 1990s and Tanzanian movies from 2003 onwards.

The Maoniko Video Show is located on a dusty little street in Magomeni Makuti on the main road to Sinza in Dar es Salaam next to a small kiosk. The cinematic space is only identifiable from a simple blackboard that depicts the daily program, and the attached covers of the movies that are currently shown, with written commentaries in chalk, such as *unyama kali* ("very brutal"), *kali sana* ("hot"), *ya kusisimua* ("thriller"), *filamu mpya ya kibongo* ("new Tanzanian movie") (Figure 14.1).

The video show originally opened at around nine in the morning and closed at eleven or twelve at night, but after some time, the local authorities prohibited film screenings in the morning to prevent pupils from going to the cinema instead of going to school. During weekdays, there is a fixed schedule of Hollywood action, Indian classics, Swahili movies, and sometimes football. In the short breaks in between, people watch music videos on the private television station East African TV, or the very popular comedy show, *Ze Comedy*. On the weekend, when there is more time for screening, primarily Indian and Swahili movies are shown.

Venny was the head of a small private company. He had two assistants who helped him to collect the entry fee, to chase away children who remained sitting or found their way into the room without paying, and with the technicalities of screening, including inserting the video cassette and rewinding and fast-forwarding the cassette to the beginning of the movie. Similar to big cinemas, mobile snack vendors sold ice cream or local snacks like roasted chicken feet to the audience while the film played. A mobile trader offered coffee in between the breaks on a small wooden bench in front of the cinema where moviegoers could get some fresh air and chat with their neighbors.

The screening room was a 15 meter square brick-built room without windows. In the back of the room, Venny had built wooden benches with different heights so that everybody could have a good view, and mats were laid on the floor in the front of the benches for the smaller children. Two ventilators provided fresh air and one electric bulb offered some light during the breaks. The TV and the VHS were set on a table in the front.

The viewers came from the neighborhood, mainly children and young men between five and twenty years of age as well as a few housemaids with small children, and they all knew each other. The audience was divided into the more quiet people sitting on the benches and the ones on the floor, who

*Figure 14.1*    Maoniko Video Show (Photo: Claudia Böhme)

commentated loudly during the film and acted as film critics. Accordingly, the video shows resembled the spaces and practices of oral story telling that Uta Reuster-Jahn (1999) described in her study of storytelling in southern Tanzania.

During my research, I visited the Maoniko Video show once or twice weekly between January and April 2008. My first visits were greeted with negative outbursts, such as "what is the *mzungu*[14] doing here?", "where did you get the *mzungu* from?", or "we are all going to sell!" Sitting next to me, Venny defended me. Soon I became an integral and respected part of the cinema's audience. I soon realized that the video show was much more than a room where people watched movies; it was a social space where young people gathered and the screened films functioned as an arena where the audience could learn and discuss. It reminded me of a school or youth center. But more than that, watching movies in the video show was a daily ritual where people shared a form of "communitas" (Turner 2005) as a temporary community detached from the regular societal structure of the quarter. Entering the show, referred to as *"nenda kuzama"* ("go and dive") in Swahili, watching the movie, and coming out of the cinema resembled the stages of a rite of passage. For Venny, the video show was a good business with a satisfying daily income of approximately 12,000 Ths (about $10) a day, from which he was able to make a living and be counted as a respected businessman in the neighborhood.

Several studies on the Tanzanian history of cinema highlight the role of wealthy entrepreneurs of Indian origin, like the cinema pioneer Hassanali Adamji Jariwalla in Zanzibar at the turn of the nineteenth century (Brennan 2005; Fair 2009; Reinwald 2006), followed much later by Muslim Jaffer, in successfully building up cinema business in Dar es Salaam. Is Venny a cinema entrepreneur like his colleagues in the celluloid and nowadays Multiplex business? His willingness to risk, his innovative ideas, and his economic investment in finding his niche surely make him an entrepreneur, albeit on another scale. When politics were unfavorable for trade, he saw the opportunity and took the risk of shifting his business, recognizing the missing space for film and the need for it. Using the small start-up capital from his former businesses, he bought video equipment and rented a room. Several years later he was not only the head of a successful company but, as he was among the first to start a video show, with his many followers he was able to establish a new economic sector, the Tanzanian video cinemas.

## FROM THEATRE TO VIDEO FILM ENTREPRENEUR

A second group of video film entrepreneurs illustrates how video film producers become Big Men through the accumulation of wealth in the video film industry. As Siri Lange (2002) describes for popular theatre, in the time of transition from a socialist to a capitalist system, state sponsored cultural troupes became privately owned businesses. Directors had the financial means to produce theatre plays and then stepped into harsh competition with the remaining government based group, Theatre One Tanzania (TOT).

> [T]hese entrepreneurs are regarded as "big men" in their communities, running businesses with 30–60 employees and owning their own houses, but they are still members of what we may label the lower

middle class, living in Swahili-type housing in "Swahili" suburbs and only dreaming of possessing a vehicle. Captain Komba is an exception from this rule, since the CCM has provided him with a personal car and the troupe with a minibus and small lorry. (Lange 2002: 120)

When video film became available, theatre practitioners, such as the famous popular theatre comedy actors, the late Mzee Small, Bi Chau, and King Majuto, began to record their sketches on film. An Indian businessman, Babu, helped them distribute their cassettes and earn an extra income to supplement the low wages paid at local TV stations.[15]

Other video film pioneers turned the medium into a money-making business when they began filming and editing weddings or birthday documentaries that they sold to their clients, including Chrissant Mhengga. He shifted from photography to video film and founded his company, Small Productions, in 1996. Later, he became one of the well-known directors of TV soap operas and video films with his company, Mega Production.

However, as these early video films were poor-quality comedies, Tanzanians preferred to watch Nigerian movies which, since the turn of the century, were brought to Tanzania by travelling businessmen. People praised Nigerian movies as truly African and felt that it was easier to identify with them than with movies from abroad (see also Krings 2010). Nigerian movies functioned as a kind of economic and cultural stimuli, as they fostered in Tanzanians the idea of making their own movies and building their own video film industry. Tanzanian artists from various backgrounds turned to video film production and founded art groups as production units for their films. Soon people talked about a coming *mapinduzi ya filamu ya Kiswahili*, a "Swahili film revolution", coined by the writer and filmmaker Sultan Tamba, with its final goal of victory over Nigerian films and the creation of a filmmaking plant.

As a private business enterprise based on the production of films and with its own aesthetics, video films challenged the cultural politics of Tanzania. Unlike the earlier artists' role of performing the nation, as was the case with dance and drum, *ngoma,* and *taarab*-music during Tanzania's socialist era (Askew 2002; Edmondson 2007), video filmmakers were above all free from state control.

## INDIAN ENTREPRENEURS AND DISCOURSES ON EXPLOITATION

As Vijaya Ramachandran and Manju Kedia Shah (1999) illustrate, minority and non-indigenous ethnic networks have experienced substantial growth in sub-Saharan Africa. This is also true for the long-term Indian entrepreneurship in East Africa, where Indians and Tanzanians of Indian origin have played a major role in diverse businesses as well as in the video film industry.[16] Since the beginning of cassette-based music production, they have established a production and distribution system for local artists, and with the coming of the video film, they were ready to expand their business.[17] Filmmakers like Sultan Tamba and Mussa Banzi started working together with two Indian-owned companies, GMC[18] and Wananchi Video Production.

In its formative year, 2003, the industry consisted of only three distribution companies: Wananchi Video Production and GMC, which belong to the same family of owners, and Game 1st Quality, owned by Mtitu Game. GMC kicked off its productions with the hip-hop video film *Girlfriend* in 2003, which was a huge success. The two companies, GMC and Wananchi, soon had a monopoly over video film distribution and hired filmmakers with their actors. But due to the filmmakers' low earnings and a lack of transparency in accounting, talks of exploitation gained ground. The common statement, *Wahindi wanatunyonya* ("the Indians are exploiting us"), was connected to the discourse of the Indian exploiter and bloodsucker, which was fostered during Tanzanian socialism (see also Brennan 2006). Five years later, they produced at least five movies per week and the format changed from VHS to VCD and DVD, as increasing numbers of Tanzanians bought DVD players. Further distribution companies, like Kapico (Kayumba Promotion International Company) and the now leading Steps Entertainment Ltd, have since entered the market. In subsequent years, filmmakers have tried to make themselves independent from the big distribution companies by circulating their movies on their own or setting up their own companies. With better pay and working conditions, the Indian-led Steps attracted many filmmakers and today has the de facto monopoly in distribution. In 2007, the price of DVDs and VCDs dropped from 8,000 Tsh ($5) to 2,500 Tsh ($1.60) to combat street vendors, *machinga,* who sell pirated copies for a third of the original price. The crackdown on video film pirates hides the fact that many of today's producers were involved in piracy before they went into "legal" production.

The video film business has attracted artists and entrepreneurs from different economic sectors, such as the former theatre practitioners who became independent from TV stations by producing video films; TV workers like Chrissant Mhengga who shifted from photography to film and began establishing small scale studios; and Indians or Tanzanians of Indian origin who took over production and distribution. The next example illustrates how one of the most successful video film producers in Tanzania localized the Nigerian model and made Tanzanian film production a big business in its own right.

## FROM MISSIONARY TO FILM PRODUCER

The Tanzanian gospel music producer and dealer of Nigerian films, Mtitu Game, entered film production in 2005 as an "African" businessman who joined the mainly "Indian" producers. Game established his own production unit and only distributed his own productions. This strategy differed from GMC and Wananchi, who not only contracted filmmakers and their actors but also bought movies from independent groups. Developing a distinct film aesthetic and content, he established himself as one of the most successful Tanzanian video film producers.

Mtitu Gabriel was born in the Southern Highlands of Tanzania in 1972 into a family of farmers. He attended schools in Tanzania and Kenya and discovered his passion for film in the mission school when he watched Charlie Chaplin films that were shown by a German priest. He reflected on his first contact with the film medium at a time when Tanzania did not yet have TV:

> At that time there was no modern technology and all these things. The first time when you watched a movie you were hypnotized, I mean you were so happy and that's the way I learned to love movies. I thought to myself ok that's what you call cinema; it was still black and white at that time. We didn't have TV, which was only introduced quite recently.[19]

As best pupil in secondary school, he received a scholarship and went to study in Luxembourg. Later, he studied international relations and psychology in Luxembourg and Amsterdam and worked as a Baptist missionary. As cinema was forbidden for priests, he followed his passion once a month when films were screened in the churches in Luxembourg. When he returned to Dar es Salaam, he visited local cinemas in the city center, such as Empire, where he watched movies like the American *Commando* with Arnold Schwarzenegger.

To earn a living, he worked with different companies in Nairobi, Tanga, and Dar es Salaam before deciding to become an independent businessman. When he travelled to Nigeria as a representative of African Missionaries in 2001, he saw his chance in the blossoming Nigerian film industry, Nollywood. He fostered contacts with Nigerian film marketers at the famous Idumota market in Lagos and established a network of business partners. As the only distributor who legally imported Nigerian films on VHS and later VCD to Tanzania, Game was able to import up to 3,000 VCDs from Nigeria to Tanzania a week. Using his contacts with video film traders in neighboring countries, he also sold videos to Zambia, Mozambique, Malawi, and DR Congo. The high popularity of Nigerian films soon inspired Tanzanian artists to make their own films in Kiswahili. Game had to reduce his business when the local video film industry expanded and the Tanzanian Shilling lost value followed by rising import taxes (Krings 2010: 75).

Game became interested in becoming a media producer himself in 2002 when his Chinese-Japanese friend Robert Lee invited him to Kobe, Japan. Impressed with the Japanese work ethic, he decided to stay there and attend a media school to study audiovisual and music video production. After his

return in February 2003, he opened his own music and video production studio in Dar es Salaam, specializing in gospel music. When the first
Tanzanian video films entered the market, he had very limited knowledge
about the production of feature films. To educate himself, he took part in
international film workshops in Hong Kong, Singapore, the Philippines,
and the United States (Fullsail University and New York University), until
he was able to hold workshops and teach filmmakers himself. He started
to distribute Swahili video film comedies in cooperation with the Kaole
Sanaa Group and the small company, Mega Video. Initially, his goal for
joining local production was to disseminate religious messages via film
like he had done through gospel music. He wanted to join film and music
to create a multilayered message for the promotion of his gospel songs in
the films.

With the three popular actors from the Kaole Sanaa Group, Blandina
Chagulla, the late Steven Kanumba,[20] and Vincent Kigosi, known from
TV serials on Independent Television (ITV), he released his first video
film, *Johari,* in 2005 with his newly founded company Game 1st Quality
(Figure 14.2). The film depicts the story of a love triangle in which the young
Johari is caught between two men, the poor but honest Hans and the rich,
philandering, and violent businessman Jack. When Johari finally decides
on Hans, she realizes that Jack has infected both her and Hans with HIV.
At the end of the film, Jack is healed by joining a church and becoming a

*Figure 14.2*   Mtitu Game on set (Photo: Claudia Böhme)

born-again Christian with plans to work as a missionary in Swaziland and leaves Johari and Hans the sum of 5 million Tsh (about $4,200) and his car.

The film was enthusiastically received by Tanzanians from different backgrounds and made the actors the most well-known film stars in Tanzania (Böhme 2014). With *Johari* and the films that followed, Mtitu Game and his crew were able to develop a specific film aesthetic with stories set in luxurious urban settings with indoor scenes in splendidly decorated living rooms, his gospel music soundtrack, and striking sound effects that mark dramatic points in the films that depict the life of the rich and successful, not only to appeal to their audience by offering an escape and desire for a better life but also to show its dark sides. The moral decay of the characters is visible through the display of their verbal and physical violence. It is, as Brian Larkin has described for Nigerian movies, an "aesthetics of outrage", "a narrative based on continual shocks that transgress religious and social norms and are designed to provoke and affront the audience" (2008: 184). According to Matthias Krings, the relation to Nigerian films can be described as a mimetic relationship through which filmmakers try to adopt an "aura" of Nollywood in their own films (2010: 85). When Mtitu Game started film production with Tanzanian and Nigerian actors and directors with the film *Dar2Lagos-4-reunion* in 2006, he finally reconnected with his former entrepreneurial activity and brought the two film industries together. He therefore not only established himself as the only producer and distributor of Tanzanian-Nigerian films, but was also said to have brought local film production to a higher level.

Like the video film entrepreneurs discussed above, it was the attraction and high popularity of audiovisual media that encouraged Game to shift his businesses. It was the audiences' preference for movies with local content that encouraged the seller of Nigerian films to become a producer of Tanzanian films. Fusing the two industries' aesthetics and styles with tales of religious morality and occupying his own genre of Tanzanian films, Game successfully established himself as one of the most popular producers vis-à-vis the Indian entrepreneurs. Today, he is the director of a big media production company and lately also a media school[21] that offers training and chances for entrepreneurial advancement for many young actors and film producers. His entrepreneurial spirit is not only evident in the risk he took to localize the highly popular Nigerian genre and transform it into a Tanzanian version; it is also found in his innovative spirit to merge the two industries.

## FEMALE VIDEO FILM ENTREPRENEURS

While many women have made the move from an unknown actress to a popular film star with a valuable income, female video film and media producers remain a minority in Tanzania.[22] The first female video film

producers were part of the upper middle class with a favorable family background. Dorothy Kipeja, the managing director of Tripod media, founded
her company in 2003 under the supervision of her mother at the age of
twenty-two while she was still attending school in the U.S. In 2006, she
graduated with a BA from the South African School of Motion Picture and
Live Performance. She started her business with music videos and documentaries, starting with the production of two video clips by the famous Bongo
Flava singer, Lady Jay Dee. Her growing success encouraged local and international organizations to work with her, including UNICEF, Family Health
International (FHI), the mobile phone company, ZAIN, and *Wanawake na
Maendeleo* (WAMA).[23]

Her company's main office is located in one of the wealthier quarters of
Dar es Salaam, far from the production and distribution areas of downtown.
When I visited the company in 2009, it had fourteen employees. Her first
video film, *Najuta mie* (*I regret*), did not receive much publicity. By 2009,
she had released eight more Tanzanian video feature films. Her own film,
*Simu ya Kifo* (*Murder by Call*), produced in 2007, was based on the late
Faraji Katalambula's 1965 novel that Kipeja remembered reading in school.
She hired another author, the late Hammie Rajab, to write the screenplay
and direct the movie, which was shot in Tabora with a crew of twenty and a
relatively big budget for Tanzania of forty million Tsh (about $30,000). The
film premiered in the Little Theatre cinema in Oyster Bay, Dar es Salaam. In
addition to the problem of piracy, which had led to mistrust in her production unit, Kipeja also had to challenge male domination as a young female
producer, particularly during the production of her own film.

While Kipeja had a very privileged background and exclusive role working mainly in film production, Lucy Francis Komba, working on the ground,
had more literally to fight her way into the male dominated business. Born
in 1976 as the daughter of a soldier from Songea and a police officer from
Musoma in southern Tanzania, she left school in 1995 with an O-Level
(SSC in the U.S.). She was trained as a secretary in a state-owned school
and received a diploma in Informatics with the IT Company, Softech. She
opened her own stationery shop and worked in a shop in the city center of
Dar es Salaam for two years before she was hired by the High Court.

While she was in school, Lucy Komba (Figure 14.3) had already started
designing, acting, performing acrobatics (*sarakasi*), and practicing karate
even though her father forbade her from participating in these "male businesses" and beat her when he found her practicing. When she told her friend,
the director and actor Tuesday Kihangala, about her love for acting, he called
her to join the Fukuto Arts Group. Longing to be a leader herself, she soon
left the group with some of the actors and founded her own art group, Dar
Talent. When she produced her first comedy, she called the aforementioned
pioneer of film production Chrissant Mhengga asking for help. He advised
her to join the Kaole Sanaa Group in Dar es Salaam. With Kaole she acted
in four TV-serials for Independent Television (ITV), among them the classic,

*Figure 14.3*   Portrait of Lucy Komba (Photo: Deogratias Daffi)

*Jahazi* (*The Dhow*), with the famous actress Blandina Chagulla. But as she was commonly cast in negative roles, such as a prostitute or a death-bringing wife, she was not able to attain the celebrity status of her colleagues.[24]

In 2006, she decided to make her own movies with the help of the already-established filmmaker Mtitu William. She produced her first film, *Utata* (*Problem*), with the help of William's colleague, John Kallage, with a budget of three million Tsh (about $2,400), and was able to sell the master in 2007 for seven million Tsh (about $5,600) to the distribution company, Steps Entertainment. When the film was released, people claimed she had stolen the story from the U.S. action classic, *Double Impact*,[25] starring Jean-Claude Van Damme. Similar to *Double Impact*, *Utata* is a twin story, but in contrast to the former, it tells a totally different version of a mother who leaves one of her twins in the hospital and the twins finally meet later in life. Discourses about originals, copies, and filmic authenticity are very common in Tanzania and filmmakers are often accused of stealing stories from Nigerian films especially. As such, authenticity and originality make important markers for the acceptance of one's success in the film business. Lucy Komba explained that in her opinion the accusation of copying was simply a form of bullying because she was one of the first female directors and producers:

> You can respect and despise somebody at the same time. There are men who hated me when they learned that I am a producer and didn't even

greet me. But later on they realized their stupidity and greeted me but we did not work together. When I advised them to make a film they wouldn't listen to me. They just couldn't accept that I can also make good movies. They used to say "You haven't done well, let us show you how to do it!"[26]

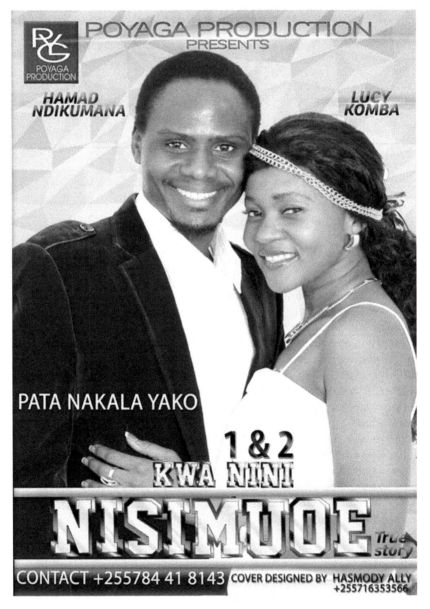

*Figure 14.4*   Cover of the film *Nisimuoe* by Lucy Komba

With her next film, *Yolanda,* Lucy Komba told a story she had witnessed during her time working at the court. The story focused on a woman who is cheated out of her inheritance by her husband's relatives after his death. As this represents a common problem in Tanzania, the film was a great success, especially with female viewers who could easily identify with the suffering of Yolanda. This time she could cover the costs of production of six million Tsh with an output of ten million Tsh when she sold the film to Steps. After *Yolanda* she was able to produce two additional films, *Vice Versa* and *Ama Zako Ama Zangu (Tit for Tat),* which she distributed with the help of Steps before she established her own company, Poyaga Productions (Figure 14.4).

She experienced a personal setback in 2008 when her newborn son's father suddenly left her at the height of her success. With the help of her relatives and friends, however, she was able to produce and distribute her next film, the two part *Cleopatra,* independently, marking the beginning of a successful family business. *Cleopatra* is the story of a young woman, who, against all odds, is able to become a film actress.

Lucy Komba's career development from a small-time actress and court secretary to a leading film producer shows how, in making use of a long-term passion for film, she has made her way in the industry. With a longing for entrepreneurship already exemplified in building her own art group, she conquered a male-dominated business and, when compared to her male colleagues, was able to offer a truly female perspective for the predominately female video film audience. Initially despised and disrespected by male filmmakers, she was persistent enough to survive in the business. In making use of a network of relatives, she made herself independent of established producers and distributors. The high appreciation of the audience, and later of other film producers, finally proved her entrepreneurial ability. These examples show how women have started to actively conquer their own spaces for social mobility and economic success (see also Jedlowski, this volume). While most of them come from a privileged background it is also their strong will, the ability to fight gendered restrictions, and the creation of new social networks that make female entrepreneurs transform their supposedly weak standing into real female power.

## CONCLUSION

The new video film medium and the possibility of making films with a low budget have opened up new opportunities for Tanzanian entrepreneurs. Artists from different areas have taken independent film production as a valuable business strategy and means of negotiating and discussing critical social issues. The film industry, with its different branches of production, consumption, and distribution, opened up a variety of activities for entrepreneurs. Among the first to explore such avenues were people like Venny

Karuguna, who in filling the gaps of the closed cinema houses brought cinema to the people. His small-scale business is valuable not only because it generates a satisfactory income for Venny, but also, as I have illustrated above, it creates a social imaginary space for young Tanzanians that fosters their self-reflection of their own dreams of success. When I returned to Dar es Salaam in 2009, I found out that Venny had passed away. The video show was still running under the direction of one of his young workers. The life of Venny marked by the shifts in Tanzanian history represents the *kupanda na kushuka*, "the ups and downs of life", in Tanzania, which denotes the flexibility small-scale entrepreneurs need to creatively adjust to new political and economic circumstances. Venny was confronted with various restrictions, particularly the lack of financial and technical resources as well as the threat of government institutions, to make the space of the video show conform to legal regulations.

Producers like Mtitu Game are on the other side of the spectrum of entrepreneurial businesses by occupying a niche and becoming one of the most popular and successful producers in Tanzania, creating jobs for hundreds of actors and technical staff. Mtitu Game's career trajectory is one of a stable rise of a Tanzanian businessman who fruitfully connected a Lutheran gospel to film production. It depicts the entrepreneur as a cultural mediator with a specializing force that challenged the de facto monopoly of Indian producers and his colleagues' claim of copying Nigerians.

As the example of Lucy Komba illustrates, female film producers still have to fight their way in a male dominated business. Becoming an artist is not considered a suitable career-choice for women in Tanzania, and if, as did Komba, a woman does indeed become a producer, she is subjected to the envy of her male counterparts. Lucy Komba resisted her father's beatings, the verbal and psychological violence inflicted by those who resented her, as well as the power strategies used by the big distributors.

In all three cases, the audience finally acknowledged and proved the entrepreneurs' success: Venny in a space where the less well-off youth in the quarter can watch and enjoy movies, Game for the possibility of admiring Tanzanian stars vis-à-vis their Nigerian counterparts, and Lucy Komba for a female perspective in the stories of the movies. While piracy was part and parcel of the availability of movies in video cinemas, for producers like Game and Komba it is one of the biggest challenges in the business.

When talking to people about successful film entrepreneurs, they often explained the reason for success by being gifted with *kipaji* ("talent"), *ujanja* ("cleverness"), or *baraka* ("blessing"). The premises as well as the visual outcomes of success, money, and status symbols are often related to the politics of the belly (Bayart 1993), the unjust or illicit means of accumulation, corruption, sugar daddy's or mummy's, or occult economies and *uchawi* (sorcery), similar to what the discourses on the ethnic networks of Indian businessmen show. The culture and practices of gossip are most salient in the many newspaper scandals created around successful film producers. Despite the ongoing gossip on conspicuous production, the Tanzanian film entrepreneurs show how, according to the Swahili tradition, they were able to appropriate foreign influences and ideas and integrate them into local practices. The Tanzanian video film entrepreneurs were able to appropriate the model, frame, and structure of the Nollywood video film production and successfully translate and localize it, creating their own local networks, films, language, and aesthetics. While the discourse of imitating and mimicking other film industries has not yet become silent, it has become clear that, as their films are deeply rooted in the cultural practices of the region, the Tanzanian film entrepreneur is as different from his Nigerian colleagues as the films they are producing.

In the aforementioned blog post, Bishop Hiluka, himself a video film entrepreneur, has drawn the attention of the Tanzanian public to this fast growing economic sector and the many upcoming young artists who aspire to be entrepreneurs themselves. His recollections about a filmmaker who failed in the industry point to the restrictions and limitations of entrepreneurial activity and the dangers associated with a further monopolization in the area of production and distribution.

As I have illustrated above, the video film entrepreneur cannot be understood using the prevalent descriptions and interpretations of classical entrepreneurship. While they might share the common willingness to take a risk and the innovative power to build up a private enterprise in various economic circumstances, the video film entrepreneur is far more of a dream worker and mediator between different cultures and practices closely linked to the imaginary and revolutionary potential of the film medium.

## NOTES

1. The entrepreneurial side of the African video film business is a neglected topic. An exception is Birgit Meyer (2001), who explored the relationship between Ghanaian video film entrepreneurs and the discourses about successful figures in the movies. Nigerian and Ghanaian video films have received major scholarly attention but with a focus on the movies' content and the discourses they foster in society.
2. The name relates to a region and ethnic group in southern Tanzania. Migrants who came from there to Dar es Salaam in the 1980s are said to have started this kind of mobile trading (Liviga and Mekacha 1998: 8–9).
3. Also *mwekez* ("investor"), *mwaminishi* ("a make-believer, inspirator").
4. For example, the booklet by Kasiliwa (2011), the title of which translates from Swahili as "Entrepreneurship: the way to financial success . . . understanding the way to get rid of poverty" (Dar es Salaam: Assemblies of God).
5. See also Grätz 2013 (the Special Issue "New media entrepreneurs and changing styles of public communication in Africa").
6. Email communication, 26 November 2013.
7. This chapter is based on long-term fieldwork carried out between 2006 and 2010 in Tanzania's video film industry. Research involved taking part in the

production, consumption, and reception of movies as well as in the work of film related organizations.

8. For the revolutionary potential of small media, see Sreberny-Mohammadi (1990) and Sreberny-Mohammadi and Mohammadi (1994).

9. Additionally, Tanzanian film translators translate foreign language films into Swahili, thereby replacing the formerly necessary live commentators (see also Krings 2009, 2010). By retelling the film, the "translators" actively bridge movies' language and cultural gap.

10. Tsh refers to the currency Tanzanian Shillings.

11. Interview with Venny Karuguna, Dar es Salaam, 23 January 2008.

12. The number of video shows in Dar es Salam is much higher in poorer neighborhoods when compared to quarters where the middle and upper classes live. There is not a single video show in the city center.

13. Interview with Venny Karuguna, Dar es Salaam, 23 January 2008.

14. *Mzungu* ("the one who wanders around") is the common description for "white" Europeans or Americans.

15. According to Siri Lange (2002: 152, note 107), Mzee Small paid the cameraman the sum of 100,000 Tsh (about $160), but was only able to do so by selling advertising time to the company Kosha Soap for 150,000 Tsh (about $250).

16. On the Indian community in Tanzania, see also Nagar (1996), Kiem (1993), Morris (1956).

17. See also Reuster-Jahn and Hacke (2011) for the case of Bongo Flava.

18. Global Sounds, Mamu Stores, and Congo Corridor.

19. Interview with Mtitu Game, Dar es Salaam, 17 September 2009.

20. Steven Kanumba died in April 2012 at the age of twenty-eight.

21. See http://www.game1stquality.co.tz/, http://www.ssimcollege.com/ (accessed November 2014).

22. Well-known examples are Rita Paulsen, managing director of Benchmark Productions and creator of the popular TV-show Bongo Star Search (BSS) Tanzania and Joyce Kiria and Salama Jabir, both presenters at East Africa TV (EATV).

23. Interview with Dorothy Kipeja, Dar es Salaam, 11 March 2008; see also http://www.thecitizen.co.tz/magazines/25-woman/1944-she-has-set-a-mark-in-tanzanias-entertainment-industry.html (accessed 13 January 2013).

24. Interview with Lucy Komba, Dar es Salaam, 23 September 2008.

25. Directed by Sheldon Lettich, USA 1991.

26. Interview with Lucy Komba, Dar es Salaam, 23 September 2008.

## REFERENCES

Adamu, Abdalla Uba. 2007. *Transglobal Media Flows and African Popular Culture: Revolution and Reaction in Muslim: Hausa Popular Culture*. Kano: Visually Ethnographic Productions.

Appadurai, Arjun. 1990. 'Topographies of the self: praise and emotion in Hindu India'. In: Lila Abu-Lughod and Catherine Lutz (eds). *Language and the Politics of Emotion*. Cambridge: Cambridge University Press, 92–112.

Appadurai, Arjun. 1996. *Modernity at Large. Cultural Dimensions of Globalization*. Minneapolis: University of Minnesota Press.

Askew, Kelly. 2002. *Performing the Nation: Swahili Musical Performance and the Production of Tanzanian National Culture*. Chicago and London: Chicago University Press.

Austen, Ralph and Mahir Şaul. 2010. 'Introduction'. In: Mahir Şaul and Ralph Austen (eds). *Viewing African Cinema in the Twenty-First Century: Art Films and the Nollywood Video Revolution*. Athens, Ohio: Ohio University Press, 74–91.

Barber, Karin. 2000. *The Generation of Plays: Yoruba Popular Life in Theater*. Bloomington: Indiana University Press.

Bayart, Jean-François. 1993. *The State in Africa: The Politics of the Belly*. London: Longman.

Becker, Felicitas. 2004. 'Traders, "big men" and prophets: political continuity and crisis in the Maji Maji rebellion in Southeast Tanzania'. *The Journal of African History* 45, 1: 1–22.

Behrend, Heike. 2003. ' "Call and Kill". Zur Verzauberung und Entzauberung westlicher technischer Medien in Afrika'. In: Erhard Schüttpelz and Albert Kümmel (eds). *Signale der Störung*. München: Wilhelm Fink Verlag, 287–300.

Böhme, Claudia. 2014. 'The rise and fall of a Tanzanian movie star: the case of Steven Kanumba'. In: Matthias Krings and Uta Reuster-Jahn (eds). *Bongo Media Worlds: Producing and Consuming Popular Culture in Dar es Salaam*. Köln: Rüdiger Köppe, 185–210.

Boner, Elizabeth. 2011. *The Making of the "Entrepreneur" in Tanzania: Experimenting with Neo-liberal Power through Discourses of Partnership, Entrepreneurship, and Participatory Education*. Ph.D. thesis, University of California, Berkeley. http://escholarship.org/uc/item/6cj0p3dh, accessed 9 August 2014.

Brennan, James. 2005. 'Democratizing Cinema and Censorship in Tanzania, 1920–1980'. *The International Journal of African Historical Studies* 38, 3: 481–511.

Brennan, James. 2006. 'Blood enemies: exploitation and urban citizenship in the nationalist political thought of Tanzania, 1958–75'. *Journal of African History* 47: 389–413.

Bude, Heinz. 1997. 'Die Hoffnung auf den "unternehmerischen Unternehmer". Über wirtschaftliche Eliten'. *Universitas* 52: 850–858.

De Witte, Marleen. 2003. 'Altar media's living word: televised charismatic Christianity in Ghana'. *Journal of Religion in Africa* 33, 2: 172–202.

Edmondson, Laura. 2007. *Performance and Politics in Tanzania: The Nation on Stage*. Bloomington and Indianapolis: Indiana University Press.

Fair, Laura. 2009. 'Making love in the Indian Ocean: Hindi films, Zanzibari audiences, and the construction of romance in the 1950s and 1960s'. In: Jennifer Cole and Lynn Thomas (eds). *Love in Africa*. Chicago: Chicago University Press, 58–82.

Grätz, Tilo. 2013. 'New media entrepreneurs and changing styles of public communication in Africa: introduction'. *Journal of African Cultural Studies* 25, 1: 1–13.

Gunner, Liz. 2005. 'Introduction: African imaginaries and transnational spaces'. *African Studies* 64, 1: 1–7.

Haynes, Jonathan (ed). 2000. *Nigerian Video Films*. Athens, Ohio: Ohio University Center for International Studies.

Haynes, Jonathan. 2003. 'Political critique in Nigerian video films'. African Affairs 105 (421): 511–533.

Haynes, Jonathan. 2007. 'Nnebue: the anatomy of power'. Film International 5, 4: 30–40.

Hiluka, Bishop. 2011. 'Ujasiriamali sekta ya filamu umedhoofishwa makusudi . . . ' *Kulikoni* 9 September 2011. http://bishophiluka.blogspot.com/2011/09/ujasiriamali-sekta-ya-filamu.html, accessed 3 March 2012.

Kasiliwa, Robert. 2011. 'Ujasiria mali. Njia na Namna ya Kufikia Mafanikio ya Kifedhea . . . elewa Jinsi ya Kuwekeza Ondoa Umaskini (Entrepreneurship: the way to financial success . . . understanding the way to get rid of poverty)'. Dar es Salaam: Assemblies of God.

Katalambula, Faraji. 1981 (1965). Simu ya Kifo. Nairobi: EALB/KLB.

Kiem, Christian. 1993. 'Die indische Händlerminorität in Ostafrika. Ursachen und Verlauf eines ungelösten Konflikts'. *Sociologus* 43, 2: 146–167.

Krings, Matthias. 2005. 'Bollywood/Kallywood. Mediale Transfers und populäre Videos in Nigeria'. In: Gereon Blaseio, Hedwig Pompe, and Jens Ruchatz (eds). *Popularisierung und Popularität*. Köln: Dumont, 303–317.

Krings, Matthias. 2009. 'Turning rice into pilau: the art of video narration in Tanzania'. *Intermédialités* 4 (Electronic version, edited by Vincent Bouchard, Ute Fendler, and Germain Lacasse). http://cri.histart.umontreal.ca/ cri/fr/INTERME-DIALITES/interface/numeros.html, accessed 16 September 2011.

Krings, Matthias. 2010. 'Nollywood goes east: the localization of Nigerian video films in Tanzania'. In: Mahir Şaul and Ralph Austen (eds). *Viewing African Cinema in the Twenty-First Century: Art Films and the Nollywood Video Revolution*. Athens, Ohio: Ohio University Press, 74–91.

Lange, Siri. 2002. *Managing Modernity: Gender, State, and Nation in the Popular Drama of Dar es Salaam*. Ph.D. thesis, University of Bergen.

Larkin, Brian. 1997. 'Indian films and Nigerian lovers: media and the creation of parallel modernities'. *Africa* 67, 3: 406–440.

Larkin, Brian. 2008. *Signal and Noise: Media, Infrastructure, and Urban Culture in Nigeria*. Durham und London: Duke University Press.

Liviga, Athumani and Rugatiri Mekacha. 1998. *Youth Migration and Poverty Allevation: A Case Study of Petty Traders (Wamachinga) in Dar es Salaam*. Dar es Salaam: REPOA.

Makura, Moky. 2008. *Africa's greatest Entrepreneurs*. Johannesburg: Penguin.

Manuel, Peter. 1999. *Cassette Culture: Popular Music and Technology in North India*. Chicago: University of Chicago Press.

McCall, John. 2007. 'The pan-Africanism we have: Nollywood's invention of Africa'. *Film International* 5, 4: 92–97.

Meyer, Birgit. 2001. 'Prieres, fusils et meurtre rituel. Le cinema populaire et ses nouvelles figures du pouvoir et du succes au Ghana'. *Politique Africaine* 82: 45–62.

Meyer, Birgit. 2003. 'Visions of blood, sex and money: fantasy spaces in popular Ghanaian cinema'. *Visual Anthropology* 16: 15–41.

Morris, Stephen. 1956. 'Indians in East Africa: a study in a plural society'. *The British Journal of Sociology* 7, 3: 194–211.

Nagar, Richa. 1996. 'The South Asian diaspora in Tanzania: a history retold'. *Comparative Studies of South Asia, Africa and the Middle East* 16, 2: 62–80.

Okome, Onookome. 2007a. 'Nollywood: spectatorship, audience and the sites of consumption'. *Postcolonial Text* 3, 2. http://postcolonial.org/index.php/pct/article/view/763/425.

Okome, Onookome. 2007b. *Women, Religion and the Video Film in Nigeria: Glamour Girls 1&2 and End of the Wicked: Theatre, Performance and the New Media in Africa*. Bayreuth: Institute for African Studies, 157–181.

Ramachandran, Vijaya and Manju Kedia Shah. 1999. 'Minority entrepreneurs and firm performance in sub-Sahara Africa'. *Journal of Development Studies* 36, 2: 71–87.

Reinwald, Brigitte. 2006. ' "Tonight at the Empire": cinema and urbanity in Zanzibar, 1920s to 1960s'. *Afrique & Histoire* 5: 81–109.

Reuster-Jahn, Uta. 1999. *Mwera Ndango. Untersuchung einer afrikanischen Erzählgattung (Südost-Tansania)*. Köln: Rüdiger Köppe.

Reuster-Jahn, Uta and Gabriel Hacke. 2011. 'The Bongo Flava industry in Tanzania and artists' strategies for success'. Working Papers of the Department of Anthropology and African Studies of the Johannes Gutenberg University Mainz, 127.

Schulz, Dorothea. 2002. ' "The world is made by talk": female fans, popular music, and new forms of public sociality in urban Mali'. *Cahiers d'Études africaines* 168, XLII-4: 797–829.

Smyth, Rosaleen. 1989. 'The feature film in Tanzania'. *African Affairs* 88, 352: 389–396.

Spring, Anita and Barbara McDade. 1998. 'Entrepreneurs in Africa: traditional and contemporary paradigms'. In: Anita Spring and Barbara McDade (eds). *African Entrepreneurship: Theory and Reality*. Gainesville: University Press of Florida, 1–34.

Sreberny-Mohammadi, Annabelle. 1990. 'Small media for a big revolution: Iran'. *Politics, Culture and Society* 3, 3: 341–371.

Sreberny-Mohammadi, Annabelle and Ali Mohammadi. 1994. *Small Media, Big Revolution: Communication, Culture, and the Iranian Revolution*. Minneapolis und London: University of Minnesota Press.

Tripp, Aili Mari. 1997. *Changing the Rules: The Politics of Liberation and the Urban Informal Economy in Tanzania*. Berkley: University of California Press.

Turner, Victor. 2005 [1969]. *Das Ritual. Struktur und Anti-Struktur*. Frankfurt am Main: Campus.

Wendl, Tobias. 2004. 'Wicked villagers and the mysteries of reproduction: an exploration of horror movies from Ghana and Nigeria'. In: Rose Marie Beck and Frank Wittmann (eds). *African Media Cultures: Transdisciplinary Perspectives*. Köln: Rüdiger Köppe, 263–285.

# 15 Investiture and Investment of a Prominent Singer
## The (Ad)venture of the Youssou Ndour Head Office

*Ibrahima Wane*

In Senegal, musicians were the first artists to become businesspeople. Youssou Ndour is one of the emblematic figures of this evolution, and some of his songs express how he himself experienced this development. "Xalis" ("Money" in Wolof),[1] one of his first original compositions, is a very evocative example. His verses highlight the socioeconomic dimension of artistic work. The singer has always understood his metier as an occupation that on one hand provides pleasure for his audience and on the other provides a living for the artist. This vision has guided Youssou Ndour's approach and his trajectory as he developed a career as a musician and made himself a name as a captain of industry. He has created an enterprise based upon the ideas his own songs convey using the basic resources he was able to secure from his artistic activities' revenues. Starting from this correlation between the repertoire of the singer and the realizations of the economic entrepreneur, I chose to make use of art discourse to examine the way in which the figure of the entrepreneur is constructed, the roles that he chooses to play, the management style he has adopted, and the obstacles he had to face in a context that is characterized by limited state intervention in the development of cultural industries.

### THE INTERSTICES OF CULTURAL POLITICS

The cultural politics of independent Senegal closely follow Senghor's conception of development. For Léopold Sédar Senghor, the poet and art critic who governed the country from 1960 until 1980, the project of society is only viable when it takes into account the interaction between culture and economy:

> In the view of the Senegalese Government, the way to cultural development lies through economic development, and vice versa. While economic growth, on the one hand, frees man from certain material contingencies, thus affording him more leisure for and making him more receptive to the things of the mind, cultural development, on the

other hand, allows of the expansion of the individual's intellectual and artistic personality, thus preparing him for the tasks to be carried out in connection with economic planning. (Mbengue 1973: 22–23)

This central idea is best summarized in the well-known phrase "culture is the beginning and the end of development".[2] In the course of the realization of this vision, art occupies a strategic position as an instrument of construction of national and black African identity and also as a privileged channel of the vulgarization of state policies. Senegal was therefore one of the first African countries to create a ministry exclusively dedicated to "cultural affairs" shortly after the first Festival Mondial des Arts Nègres carried out under Senghor's auspices in 1966. The country has from very early been furnished with various modern cultural institutions: the arts school, the Théâtre National Daniel Sorano, the Musée Dynamique, the manufacture of decorative arts, the national archives of Sénégal, regional cultural centers, les Nouvelles Editions Africaines (which was created together with Côte d'Ivoire and Togo), and so on.

The same cultural setting has gained strength in other West African countries, such as Ghana and the neighboring countries of Mali and Guinea, whose leaders have subscribed, as Léopold Sédar Senghor did, to socialism. In Ghana, President Kwame Nkrumah, who has, since he assumed office, acknowledged the role of popular music in the fight for independence, the consolidation of national unity, and the promotion of African culture, has distinguished himself through several projects that favored the world of music during his term in power. He created a recording studio, offered fellowships to musicians and to dance groups, and so on (Collins 2009/2010: 82). After achieving independence, Guinea followed suit. President Sékou Touré, who attached great value to "cultural independence", focused on music, as it was supported by the Parti Démocratique de Guinée (PDG) during their time in power and began to

> disband a plethora of dance orchestras and vocal groups, in vogue under the colonial regime, which confined their performances to slavish renditions of tangos, waltzes, fox-trots, swing music and other rhythms imported from Europe and the Caribbean. (The Ministry of Education and Culture of the Republic of Guinea 1979: 80)

New orchestras were created which were

> prepared to research and advance *our* musical cultural heritage. This was in accordance with the approach adopted by the PDG, which imposed on them a sacred obligation to draw their inspiration solely from the wealth of epic and popular folk traditions, which was henceforth to be rid of alien contrivances. These were the folk traditions that had come into existence and been performed during the numerous periods

of relaxation, struggle, distress, labour, moral grandeur or growth of awareness experienced by our people. (Ibid.: 80)

The authorities also provided a recording studio for the national radio, La Voix de la Révolution, and a label, called Syliphone, which held the monopoly of the release and distribution of records. In Mali, too, the large orchestras that emerged were dependent upon the public sector, including the national orchestra, the Ambassadeurs, the Rail Band, and the regional orchestras (Counsel 2003).

This state patronage is different from the model the Senegalese state adopted. The Senghor government did not interfere with the production process, and at the onset of independence, entertainment music was not a preoccupation for the authorities, as they left it completely to the private sector. The state therefore did not directly influence the orchestras, and these cultural entities were created without any political intervention. The state only had under its auspices the elements of the Théâtre National Daniel Sorano, the Troupe Nationale Dramatique, the Ensemble National de Ballet, and the Ensemble Lyrique Traditionnel. Other artistic groups were not subjected to direct state pressure, even when they profited from the studios and being broadcast on national radio, which was indispensable for all those who wanted to produce and diffuse their artwork.[3] The production of records was, in contrast to visual/graphic arts[4] and films[5] for example, which benefitted from various institutional support, completely beyond the care of the state and was instead in the hands of foreigners in Paris or Senegal, such as the Frenchman Louis Fourment, who is the founder of the label N'Dardisc, and the owner of the record magazine *La Radio Africaine*, which is situated in Dakar Plateau.

In the second decade of independence, the Senegalese state neither returned to the freedom of creation nor did it seek to subjugate music. Instead, it expressed a desire to contribute to enhancing the performance of the orchestras and engrain them more directly in local traditions, since their repertoires largely remained dominated by their adoption of Afro-Cuban pieces. The state took on several initiatives to realize this project. The ministry of culture, for example, promoted the creation of a Senegalese national committee of music in 1971.[6] This body consisted of professionals and was responsible for considering the problems of this sector and taking measures to make them more dynamic, i.e., organizing festivals, competitions, and so on. It was also this context, in which the Bureau Sénégalais du Droit d'Auteur (BSDA) was created, which was supposed to protect the artists' rights in their work and defend their material and moral interests. Additionally, a fund was created for helping artists in need and for the development of culture. It had the objective to encourage creativity by providing awards to artists for their original work and to innovative cultural associations.

The debates about how to create authentic Senegalese music led to the idea of creating an orchestra "that consisted of employed musicians who could, free from the fears of the constant search of money and even in spite of mediocre productions, engage in long research on Senegalese and African music more generally" (Seck 2005: 89).[7] The Orchestre National du Sénégal, created in 1980 under the auspices of the Minister of Culture, was understood as a melting pot in charge of reproducing exactly the two-part project of rooting and opening, which had been so important to the President of the Republic.

This demonstration of interest was not tied to investment in the cultural industries. Instead, it was followed by a time of empty accounts due to the repercussions of the Structural Adjustment Programs in the 1980s and 1990s, a budgetary scarcity that even led to the shutdown of the Musée Dynamique, the Archives Culturelles du Sénégal (ACS), and the Centre d'Etude des Civilisations (CEC), among others. At that time, state patronage retreated into the background with a focus on new priorities (Sylla 1998: 1). The neoliberal policies that the government adopted followed the dictum "less state is a better state" and rather relied on private initiatives. This restriction of the state intervention has as a corollary in the cultural sector the enlargement of the field of intervention of the artists who would in this way benefit both from enjoying more liberties and taking on more responsibilities.

## SHEDDING THE FIGURE OF THE ARTIST

The economic crisis that reached its climax at the end of the 1970s due to factors such as the worldwide recession caused by the petrol crisis and climate change, including the recurrent droughts in the Sahel, led to considerable social restructuring. It greatly eroded, for example, the prestige of civil servants and university graduates, who had previously symbolized social stability and success in the eyes of a popular strata of society (Banégas and Warnier 2001: 5). The buying power that civil servant salaries had guaranteed decreased due to inflation and the myth of university diplomas began to lose its attraction at the end of the 1970s, as higher education, which had previously promised a brilliant career in the public sector, no longer guaranteed a position in the administration. Furthermore, universities had released hundreds of jobseekers onto the market, and they later ended up forming an "association of unemployed diploma holders". To combat this problem, the government began to redirect them toward the creation of small and medium-sized enterprises (SME), particularly in the baking, transport, and import/export sectors, and vegetable gardening (Niane 1991: 52; Sall 1986), which led to the opening of other trajectories for social promotion. To date, such trajectories have been completely beyond classical reference models for social ascent and the secrets for rising to the heights in social hierarchies. Artists form an integral part of this new category of social ascent.

Until the 1970s, two figures had dominated the musical scene. The traditional singer, a griot by birth, provided the donor, to whom he was attached, with nobility. A griot reached a career peak by joining the Théâtre National Daniel Sorano. By reaching this level, these singers were able to make gains on two levels: first by performing as a praise singer for certain personalities, and second, as an artist of national importance, both of which brought a certain level of material prosperity, the external signs of which are the villa, the car, a well-furnished cloak room, regular pilgrimages to Mecca, and so on. In Mali, a similar model prevails, where divas such as Tata Bambo Kouyaté, Fanta Damba, and Kandia Kouyaté work under the auspices of generous patrons (Diawara 2003: 199). By contrast, modern musicians involved in the entertainment sector were less engaged in social imperatives. Consequently, a reputation as nonchalant drunkards was attached to these artists that depicted them as consuming their irregular revenues in exaggerated acts of spending (Benga 2002: 297).[8] When Youssou Ndour emerged on the scene, this image faded away in favor of his image as a stable worker who doubles as a social leader, thereby becoming the idol of thousands of young people.

Born in 1959 in Médina, a popular neighborhood adjacent to Dakar's city center, the son of a craftsman and a griotte (a female praise singer), Youssou Ndour developed an early interest in becoming a singer. His father, however, was concerned by the musician's lifestyle and reputation, and firmly opposed his son's choice, trying to keep him in school as long as possible before he finally surrendered to his son's stubbornness.

After attending the music academy of Dakar, Youssou Ndour began his professional career in 1976 with the Star Band, one of Senegal's biggest orchestras.[9] After three years, he created the Etoile de Dakar with other former members of the Star Band. He later left the group, following a series of internal disagreements, and went on to form the Super Etoile with some members from the Etoile de Dakar in 1981. He is still with this group today.

This trajectory allowed him to work with different orchestras that were hired by powerful nightclub patrons and to live the experience of being a member of a group created by musicians themselves who decided to stand on their own feet and share the concert revenues. These experiences sensitized him to questions about leadership. Youssou Ndour was also able to show his belief that artists had the right to have ambitions and to refuse to allow others to delimit his horizon and confine him to a particular destiny. This conviction is reflected in some of his compositions, such as the song "Donkasigi" ("The Peak"),[10] in which he declares that from his point of view each human being has the right of aspiring to reach the peak.

Youssou Ndour assumed the characteristics of an entrepreneur similar to the figure that Joseph A. Schumpeter described, an actor with the ambition to take the initiative and the will to innovate (McDaniel 2005: 486). Accordingly, he moved on from being a band member to adding a larger dimension to his professional activities. In 1982, he decided to organize his orchestra as an enterprise. He rented an apartment in which he established his offices and a rehearsal room, making the beginning of his company, the Société Youssou Ndour et Super Etoile. Among its more than thirty employees were musicians, technicians, the manager, and the administrative staff (Moindjié 1986: 14). The evolution of his enterprise also represented a means for the singer to compensate for the challenges he faced at the beginning of his career when he had resisted the objections of his father who wanted his first son to become employed in an institution. In an interview with the magazine *Réussir*, he recalled:

> When I began to earn a bit of money, after having paid my bills, I said to myself: I will now look for an office with which I can convince my father that a musician, just like a lawyer or a banker, can work in an office. (Ndour 2006: 6, my translation)

In the following year, he became the producer of the music cassettes of Super Etoile. At the same time, Ndour became interested in another element of the musical business when he rented what became one of the most well-known nightclubs of Dakar, the Thiossane Night Club.[11] This enabled him to organize his own concerts and recruit a faithful fan base. Subsequently, he expanded his sphere of influence and increased his autonomy when he created an even more ambitious organization, the Société Africaine de Promotion Musicale (SAPROM), in 1985, with the help of a friend, an expert in accountancy. Through the creation of this society, which was responsible for organizing Super Etoile shows, producing his cassettes, and managing his property (musical equipment and vehicles of transport), he was further able to professionalize his venture and acquire competence in the domains of administration, management, and accountancy. This process was driven by his decision to remain—in contrast with most other famous African artists who have moved to Europe or the United States—in Senegal and reinvest the profits he made in western markets in local show-business.

Youssou Ndour confronted another weakness of Senegalese music when he opened his recording studio, Xippi, in 1991, using royalties from his record company, Virgin, (Arnaud 2008: 111), and bank credit facilitated by the state.[12] By opening this new facility, he was able to break the early 1980s rule that musicians went to France to produce their music. He later attached another important unit to the studio, which enabled the production and duplication of cassettes (Xippi Inc). Xippi ("open eyes"), which is at the same time the name of the first album that was produced in the studio, offered, according to its owner, the advantage of working in a Senegalese ambiance and also reduced the production costs. Ndour completed his expansion by establishing another record company, Jololi ("clochette"), in 1995, after the release of the album *The Guide*, whose single "Seven Seconds" won him a golden record (Lahana 2005: 119).

With this "empire", the artist was able to reach and surpass the status of a role model of individual success. This talented artist did not only succeed through his metier to climb to the elite level and reach down the climbing pole to others; he was also able to modify the physiognomy of his sector of activity and influence trajectories, thereby positioning himself among the powerful actors who have influenced a transformation in socioeconomic realities. With his engagement, this artist follows his intention to fully play his role in the national development, as he has proclaimed since the publication of his song "Xaley Réew Mi" ("The Country's Youths"),[13] in which he promises that he, and other people like himself, will do everything possible to render the country prosperous.

The singer made his contribution to nation-building through his message and also by joining his actions with his words. His activities as well as his (artistic) work concern many sectors of society. Hence, in the late 1990s, the leader of Super Etoile turned his interest toward the media, which is closely linked with the show-business world. He establishes the Groupe Com 7 in 1998, together with two businessmen. The company consisted of a radio station, three daily newspapers, and a printing press, and gradually evolved in the context of the development of private media that emerged in the 1980s under the initiative of professional journalists who had formerly been part of the state media (Paye 1992: 370–371). The creation of private newspapers that produced diverse information weakened and later superseded the partisan press, as political parties found large arenas for expression in these independent organs. The liberalization of the airwaves and the audiovisual media ten years later, from 1994 onward, encouraged the creation of multimedia enterprises.

Youssou Ndour is aware that the media, which form another component of the culture industry, are not necessarily financially profitable;[14] he is also aware, however, that they can constitute an efficient supplement for both the activities of the artist and the businessman. They are not only a powerful support for the promotion of musical products but also a means to influence political, economic, and social spheres. After four years of associative collaboration, he distanced himself from his associates due to internal differences about how Com 7 should be managed, and he launched his own media enterprise, the Groupe Futurs Médias, in 2002, that at present comprises a radio station (RFM), a daily newspaper with general information (*L'Observateur*), a television station (TFM), and a printing press. These different enterprises are united under the holding Youssou Ndour Head Office (YNHO).[15]

## THE STYLE AND THE STAFF OF THE CHIEF OF THE ORCHESTRA

Youssou Ndour unites both the activities of an artist and of a patron. In his function as the principal stakeholder, he is also the director of the enterprises he founded: he is president of the Groupe Futurs Médias and manager of the YNHO. His, as he likes to emphasize, "responsible and competent collaborators" take on much of the daily management tasks (Ndour 2006: 8). Ndour only elaborates his ideas in instances such as the Conseil d'Administration, but leaves it to the specialists to put them into practice. These indications express the pride of the self-made man who did not bother to undergo long periods of study to get everything under the authority of diplomas. Youssou Ndour therefore is in the habit of sending those who are interested in knowing more about the function of his enterprises to those who are responsible for the respective departments, emphasizing that they have the required profile.

His insistence on the quality of his staff is no coincidence, as many among them are his close relatives and childhood friends. This situation suggests that family solidarity and trust in relationships can be highly appreciated human values. Personal relationsships' interference in professional responsibilities can also, nevertheless, be disadvantageous for the enterprise. Youssou Ndour has distinguished himself with a management procedure that seeks to reconcile these two parameters. He decided to support his close relations and friends and implemented a system of professionalism in his business at a time when local show-business had yet to become structured and was only able to attract and employ artists and sound technicians. At the beginning of this venture, for certain tasks he could only count on individuals for whom he felt a certain affection and mutual trust. In exchange, Ndour committed himself to finding the means for his faithful companions to gradually study and acquire the capacities needed to fully take over the professional tasks. Accordingly, almost all his brothers and sisters were engaged in the music world at a very early stage.[16] Boubacar Ndour became the first director of the record company, Jololi, and is currently the program director of Télévision Futurs Médias; initially, Ngoné Ndour directed Xippi Inc., and then Jololi before she created the label Prince Arts with two of her brothers; Matar Ndour (better known as Ndiaga) was a technical director first and then became the Director of the TFM; and Birane, Youssou Ndour's first son, is the Vice Director of the Groupe Futurs Médias.

This configuration situates Youssou Ndour in his own enterprise as the family head, a role that the oldest often fills when they are required to replace the parents from a certain age onward, as the song "Taaw" ("The Eldest") expresses.[17] The relationsships and interactions that the patron has with his collaborators make it difficult to distinguish between his role as director of his enterprise, the leader of his orchestra, and the family head. Furthermore, his status as businessman is not without effect on his image as an artist, and in the majority of cases confusion stems from the latter rather than the former. Despite the fact that his talent is nearly universally accepted in Senegal, his role as a director of an enterprise is often subjected to criticism. Regardless of whether they are right or wrong, his detractors see his hands behind every step his companies take. For example, the media focused on Youssou Ndour when Jololi had a conflict with an artist. Rumors also point to Youssou Ndour as soon as any part of Groupe Futurs Médias faces a problem, even though journalists are supposed to work as fully independent agents. Hence, in 2006, when the daily *L'Observateur* published compromising information about the President of the Republic's son, the relationship Youssou Ndour had with the high state authorities was automatically affected and his television project was blocked for two years.[18]

As Youssou Ndour plays many different roles, he also has to fight on several fronts: while he tries to remain on the forefront of the artistic scene to keep his despisers on tenterhooks (who see in him essentially a businessman who is only interested in money) on one hand, he also has to do everything to keep his enterprises going and rescue them from weak conditions (above all the state, its tax collectors, etc.) and the Bureau Sénégalais du Droit d'Auteur on the other hand.

## THE BREACH OF THE MUSIC INDUSTRY: WHEN THE *NDAANAAN*[19] LOSES HIS VOICE

Youssou Ndour had pushed until the beginning of the 2000s his career as an artist and was crowned with several distinctions in addition to maintaining his entrepreneurial activities that generated dozens of employees. Due to these achievements, he was celebrated by his equals of the Confédération Nationale des Employeurs du Sénégal (CNES, the National Confederation of Employers) after he won golden records in Europe[20] in 1994. His performance and his leadership are also celebrated by various academic institutions. In Dakar in 2007, Ndour, the creator of the album *The Guide* (*Wommat*)[21] was made Docteur Honoris Causa (honorary doctor) of the Institut Africain de Management (IAM). He is the patron of the godfather of the Faculté Civilisations, Religions, Arts et Communication that was created in 2010 by the Université Gaston Berger at Saint Louis, which is Senegal's second university. In the following year, the University of Yale in the U.S. also awarded him the title of an honorary doctor. When his invitations to the podiums of excellence multiplied, however, his enterprises became more and more obscure, as the reality of local show-business was not always pleasant. As the music industry emerged from a sector that is dominated by informality, its pioneers faced obstacles that were difficult to conquer. Because of their status and the notoriety of their founder, they have to be strict about the administration's rules (paying of taxes, social benefits for employees). In exchange for their cooperation with the state's rules, they cannot, however, expect protection from the state, as it does not take any repressive measure against injurious malpractices of wheeler-dealers seriously. Producers and sellers of counterfeited products, for example, profit immensely from the government's inaction; thousands of illicit copies that enter the country from abroad and swamp the Senegalese market are complemented with copies fabricated by local pirates. The creation of a national brigade to fight piracy[22] in 2007 was not able to cease such practices. This service, with limited strength and logistics, is only able to show symbolic results with the occasional confiscation of duplicated materials. The number of pirated products has managed to suffocate the record companies to the point that they are no longer able to sell more than a symbolic number of CDs.[23] In the end, Youssou Ndour was forced to realize that all his efforts were unable to produce the results he had been hoping for because of this unhealthy environment. In this context, it is not by coincidence that Youssou Ndour reinterpreted the song "Sama Doom" ("My Son/My Daughter")[24] to remind listeners of the proverbial formulation that when ten people dig, ten others pile up, which creates a lot of dust but no hole.

The ravages of piracy have exposed the weakest element of the music industry, its distribution. As music sales are not able to reach small market stalls,[25] the pirates have taken over the job of making artistic production accessible to the consumers when they take it to the streets, to all the junctions of the big cities, via the young ambulant sellers who appropriate a large part of artists' usual clientele. In this way, they constitute a new type of entrepreneurs who create their market niche in the shadow of the culture industry. Another factor that has contributed to undermining the efforts of professionals in music production is the dematerialization of music. The evolution from the cassette to the CD in the early 2000s has already unnerved many actors; information and communication technologies have also contributed to a feeling of unease among production companies. The proliferation of the new communication technologies (mobile phones, mp3) and the diversification of technology that allows the easy copying and transporting of music (hard disks, USB sticks, etc.) has benefited the pirates, who have profited far more than creators and producers. The ease by which an individual can copy artwork has complicated the control of artistic production and decreased the potential for investors to earn a living.

Jololi's shutdown, together with other record companies that were all obliged to close their doors,[26] illustrates the fragility of private cultural enterprise, the reason for which is the absence of a veritable policy of support for investment in the cultural sector. The state, which has to date lacked any concern for supporting artistic and cultural activities in its GNP (gross national product) is still not aware of the potential for art to contribute to the creation of employment and wealth.[27] Accordingly, the cultural sector remains imprisoned by a conception that is focused on arts' vocation of play, education, and identity.

## CONCLUSION

When Senegal reached independence, the production of records was one of the few sectors of cultural life left completely in the hands of private initiative. The structural adjustment policies and the withdrawal of the state from various sectors of activity, which have become the norm two decades later, confirm this tendency. Musicians are not only autonomous and independent from state power; they also have countless possibilities to extend their reach in the industry. They are expected to create their own opportunities and develop their own metier. Accordingly, they find themselves in the position of acting as the principal investors in the domain of musical infrastructure. A prominent example, Youssou Ndour, has positioned himself as one of the leading figures of the music industry through the creation of several companies that cover multiple aspects of show-business (recording, industrial production, event management, etc.). His conceptualization of music and art as a means of socioeconomic promotion and development is at the center of his repertory. He has inspired imitators up until the hip-hop movement. From the end of the 1990s onward, the initial reaction of the leaders of the hip-hop movement was to develop production infrastructure (studio, sound equipment, etc.) as soon as their revenues (rewards, royalties, and revenues from copyright) reached a sustainable level. These entrepreneurs share a common experience, as their enterprises serve the needs of the founders themselves, guaranteeing their autonomy and enhancing their performance. Subsequently, other artists have also benefited from these enterprises, as they ameliorated the artists' creative environment and, at the same time, created employment. The entrepreneurial artist did not begin his venture with an obsession to make profit, even though he counted on the profitability of his investments to ensure the continuation of the enterprise. His ability to innovate and transform also includes fighting against the institutional environment's constraints, which illustrates the need for cultural enterprises to find a firm footing in the economic fabric. The precariousness of the musical industry means, that artists like—paradoxically—Youssou Ndour, who was the locomotive of the music industry over the course of the 1990s, is currently identified with only one of his media companies, Futurs Médias, as he had to give up almost all his other cultural enterprises. Ironically, Youssou Ndour's becoming a minister did not reverse this tendency.[28]

The economic malaise of the late 1970s and the following disengagement of the state have stimulated private initiative and spurred the evolution of show-business. The equation of the de-materialization of artistic productions with the rise of piracy, which is the major preoccupation of the 2000s, has pushed the cultural entrepreneurs to find alternatives and adjust to the new conditions.[29] As such, artists are investing in more lucrative sectors (such as property, automobile, transport, agro-industry, etc.) in their attempts to support their musical activities, which are, after all, their sources of achievement and legitimacy. The art that was the capital for the foundation of the music enterprises has become in such a situation a receptacle for the resources that are generated with the new gap in the market. Meanwhile, musicians have proved their social usefulness and their effectiveness by contributing a great deal to raising public awareness about the inner workings of politics, and have mobilized people to engage in their future, foster the spirit of citizenship, and promote political change through their songs (Ndiaye and Sy 2003; Savané and Sarr 2012).

## NOTES

1. This was the Etoile de Dakar orchestra's lead single (the hit) from their first record, *Xalis*, released in 1979.
2. Président Senghor's message was delivered to the nation on 3 April 1966, the day before the sixth anniversary of Senegal's independence. The celebration of this national holiday almost coincided with the inauguration of the First Festival Mondial des Arts Nègres (from 1 to 24 April 1966).
3. The national radio is able to record on magnetic bands, which later can be used for the writing of a record. In the 1970s, some private individuals offered the same service. The most well-known is Moussa Diallo, manager of the nightclub Sangomar in Thiès, about 70 km from Dakar. With a four-track tape recorder, this technician has recorded the tapes of the majority of Senegalese orchestras that were prominent from 1970 to 1980.
4. The support of the visual or graphic arts was done, for example, by purchasing the artwork that formed part of the state's private art collection, by organizing large exhibitions of Senegalese art abroad, and through the subventions that received those artists who worked under the influence of the Négritude and who were subsumed under the name "Dakar School".
5. The state tried to control the organization and administration of the film industry with the creation of the Société Nationale de la Cinématographie (SNC) and the Société Sénégalaise d'Importation, de Distribution et d'Exploitation Cinématographique (SIDEC).
6. The Comité National Sénégalais de la Musique is a local section of the Conseil International de la Musique (CIM), which works under the auspices of UNESCO.
7. Professor Assane Seck has twice occupied the post of Ministre des Affaires Culturelles (1966–1968 and 1978–1981).
8. At that time, singers complained in some of their compositions about the lack of consideration, above all from the parents of the young women whom they court or whom they wish to marry. Ouza Diallo, for example, called on the adults to be more open and understand that the artists are human beings that obtain their livelihoods through honest means (Ouza, *Musiciens*, 45 tours, 1976).
9. The Star Band de Dakar was founded in 1959 by Ibra Kassé, who was at the same time the owner and manager of the nightclub, Miami, where the orchestra regularly performed. Over the course of the 1960s and 1970s, numerous big shots from the Senegalese music scene appeared on its stage (Pape Seck, Abdoulaye Mboup, Médoune Diallo, Mar Seck, Doudou Sow, Thione Seck, etc.) as well as stars from other African countries (the Gambian singer Laba Sosseh, the Nigerian saxophonist Dexter Johnson, the Liberian trumpet player Bob Amstrong, the Guinean drummer and singer Amara Touré, The Togolese guitar player Barthélémy Attisso, etc.).
10. The song, "Donkasigi", figures on the record, *Nelson Mandela*, released in 1985.
11. Nightclubs are the only gap in the market that attracts investors. In the 1970s, some businessmen ventured into this sector. Adrien Senghor, Ousmane Diagne, and Dame Dramé jointly opened the Club Baobab in 1970. The famous Baobab Orchestra emerged from this and survived longer than the nightclub and is still in existence to date. El Hadji Ndiouga Kébé opened the club Sahel in 1974, after which the popular band was named that performed in this location.
12. He bought and restored the first modern studio established in Senegal, the Golden Baobab, which was opened in 1979 by Francis Senghor, the musician

and son of the late President of the Republic, Léopold Sédar Senghor, but who had an ephemeral existence. Dakar's second studio, Studio 2000, was founded in 1981 by El Hadj Ndiaye, the professional photographer who later on became a cultural entrepreneur with partners from Switzerland.

13. This song forms part of the cassette *Bekoor* (1985).
14. The majority of the Senegalese dailies cost 100 FCFA (about $0.25). This price far from covers the costs of production and the other charges that are connected with running the newspaper. The weak advertisement market is not able to fill this gap.
15. YNHO includes other structures as well, such as Birima, which is a micro-credit system destined to support small enterprises which receive credit without interest and deposit. They receive the credit on the basis of their verbal engagement and trust that they will repay their debt. This institution is called the "Bank of the Poor" after a song by Youssou Ndour ("Birima", which forms part of the cassette *Lii* that was released in 1996) that he created in 2008 and which was dedicated to a precolonial hero who is a symbol of courage and honor. In the holding YNHO, the Joko project (the contact, the connection) is also sheltered, which is named after another record. It was initiated in partnership with Hewlett Packard and the Société Nationale de Télécommunications (SONATEL) with the objective to make the information and communication technologies available to economically disadvantaged youths by establishing internet cafes, offering training in webmastering, and by telemarketing.
16. Ngoné took part in a two-year training course in sound engineering at the School of Audio Engineering in London before she returned to Dakar to dedicate herself to music production. Matar trained himself as a sound technician when he came in contact with the foreign engineers Youssou had collaborated with. Boubacar became acquainted with audiovisual technology during his time in the U.S. Birane Ndour holds a Bachelor in Business and Administration that he obtained from the American Business School at Paris. Two members of the family, Aby and Ibrahima, Youssou's sister and brother, chose the stage as their field. Aby is a singer and brought the choirs of Youssou Ndour to success for several years before she began a solo career. Ibou studied programming and arrangements for two years. He became a pianist and plays with Super Etoile and other artists.
17. This song is found on the album, *Immigrès/Bitim Rew* (1984).
18. TFM has regained the authorization to broadcast in May 2010.
19. "A great artist" in Wolof.
20. After he received his golden records in 1994, Youssou Ndour was nominated to perform the official hymn at the World Cup opening ceremonies in 1998 in France. He was elected the African artiste of the century by the magazine Folk Roots in 2000. He won a Grammy award in the United States in 2005. In 2007, *Time Magazine* listed him among the hundred most influential personalities of the world.
21. *The Guide (Wommat)* is the CD that contains "Seven Seconds", a duet with Neneh Cherry, who helped Youssou Ndour win the golden record.
22. The Brigade Nationale de Lutte contre la Contrefaçon was created by presidential decree following the Association des Métiers de la Musique du Sénégal (AMS) and the Coalition Interprofessionnelle des Producteurs et éditeurs de Phonogrammes du Sénégal's (CIPEPS) lively protests as they worked out an action plan that culminated in a demonstration in town. The Brigade Nationale de Lutte contre la Contrefaçon is attached to the Department of the Interior.
23. In the 1990s, an artist such as Youssou Ndour was able to sell up to 100,000 copies, but today, it is difficult to even sell 5,000.

24. "Sama Doom" appeared for the first time on the cassette *Jamm—La Paix* (1986) and was published again in 2009 on the CD *Spécial fin d'année Plus*, which is a remix of some of these songs.

25. In the 1960s and 1970s, when vinyl emerged on the music scene, there were music shops in the city center of Dakar, such as La Radio Africaine, La Disquerie, Musiclub, and the Disco Club. At the beginning of the 1980s, with the arrival of the cassette, the producers began to distribute their products at the market stalls to reach more customers. This inspired some businessmen to gradually specialize in the distribution of music and later become producers themselves.

26. Jololi ended its activities in 2007. Origines (a record company that was created as part of Pyramide Culturelle du Sénégal [PCS], a private structure that comprises several units, among them Studio 2000 and the television channel 2STV) and KSF Productions (founded by Talla Diagne, a distributor who became one of the largest Senegalese music producers in the 1990s) were also unable to survive this situation. The labels that were created by music stars, such as Baaba Maal (Yoff Productions) and Oumar Pène (Diamono Productions) for the production of their own work and the promotion of young talents have disappeared from the cultural landscape as well.

27. To date, no official statistics exist that would support evaluation of the influence of the cultural sector. The Ministry of Culture signed an agreement with the Agence Nationale de la Statistique et de la Démographie in 2011 with the objective of trying to put an end to this situation.

28. After the creation of the citizen's movement in 2011, Youssou Ndour was willing to run in the election for the president in Senegal. His candidature was, however, not officially accepted by the Conseil Constitutionnel because of administrative reasons. He then campaigned for the opposition for the departure of President Abdoulaye Wade. After his defeat, the singer and businessman was nominated Minister of Culture and Tourism in April 2012 by Macky Sall, who won the elections. Six months later, he became the Minister of Tourism and Entertainment. Since September 2013, Youssou Ndour has been an advisory minister for the President of the Republic.

29. After closing down Xippi and Jololi, Ngoné Ndour created Prince Arts in 2008 with her brothers Ibrahima and Matar, a label of more humble dimensions, which connects the phonographic production with the organization of shows and the production of television broadcasts. Despite the difficulties, for her it is out of the question that she would stop being an artist, as she is someone who has grown up with music (interview with Ngoné Ndour, April 2011).

## REFERENCES

Arnaud, Gérald. 2008. *Youssou Ndour, le griot planétaire*. Paris: Editions Demi-Lune.

Banégas, Richard and Jean-Pierre Warnier. 2001. 'Nouvelles figures de la réussite et du pouvoir'. *Politique Africaine* 82: 5–21.

Benga, Ndiouga Adrien. 2002. 'Dakar et ses tempos. Significations et enjeux de la musique urbaine (c. 1960-années 1990)'. In: Momar-Coumba Diop (ed). *Le Sénégal contemporain*. Paris: Karthala, 289–308.

Collins, John. 2009 [2010]. 'Highlife and Nkrumah's independence ethos'. *Journal of Performing Arts* 4, 1: 82–91.

Counsel, Graeme. 2003. 'Cultural policy and music in Mali'. *Africa Quarterly* 43, 4: 36–51.

Diawara, Mamadou. 2003. *L'empire du verbe et l'éloquence du silence*. Cologne: Rüdiger Köppe.

Lahana, Michelle. 2005. *Youssou Ndour, la voix de la Médina*. Paris: Patrick Robin Editions.

Mbengue, Mamadou Seyni. 1973. *Cultural Policy in Senegal*. Paris: UNESCO.

McDaniel, Bruce. 2005. 'A contemporary view of Joseph A. Schumpeter's theory of the entrepreneur'. *Journal of Economic Issues* 39, 2: 485–489.

The Ministry of Education and Culture of the Republic of Guinea. 1979. *Cultural Policy in the Revolutionary People's Republic of Guinea*. Paris: UNESCO.

Moindjié, Ali. 1986. *La création musicale moderne au Sénégal. Difficultés du secteur*. Grande enquête de fin d'études, Dakar: Centre d'Étude des Sciences et Techniques de l'Information (CESTI), Université Cheikh Anta Diop de Dakar.

Ndiaye, Mamadou-Abdoulaye and Alpha-Amadou Sy. 2003. *Les conquêtes de la citoyenneté. Essai politique sur l'alternance*. Dakar: Editions Sud Communication.

Ndour, Youssou. 2006. 'J'ai investi des milliards dans ce pays . . .' (interview). *Réussir* 4: 4–9.

Niane, Boubacar. 1991. 'Des énarques aux managers (Notes sur les mécanismes de promotion au Sénégal)'. *Actes de la Recherche en Sciences Sociales* 86–87: 44–57.

Paye, Moussa. 1992. 'La presse et le pouvoir'. In: Momar-Coumba Diop (ed). *Sénégal. Trajectoire d'un État*. Dakar: CODESRIA, 331–377.

Sall, Issa. 1986. *Chômage des diplômés de l'enseignement supérieur et sénégalisation de l'emploi*. Grande enquête de fin d'études, Dakar: Centre d'Etude des Sciences et Techniques de l'Information (CESTI), Université Cheikh Anta Diop de Dakar.

Savané, Vieux and Baye Makébé Sarr. 2012. *Y'en a marre. Radioscopie d'une jeunesse insurgée au Sénégal*. Paris: l'Harmattan.

Seck, Assane. 2005. *Sénégal. Émergence d'une démocratie moderne (1945–2005)*. Paris: Karthala.

Sylla, Abdou. 1998. *Arts plastiques et Etat au Sénégal*. Dakar: IFAN Cheikh Anta Diop.

# Contributors

**Claudia Böhme** is a post-doc researcher and lecturer at the Chair of Anthropology at the University of Trier, Germany. Her areas of research are cinema and media cultures in Tanzania and East Africa. Her work has appeared in the books *Listening to Africa: Anglophone Literatures and Cultures* (Winter, 2012), *Genre Hybridization: Global Cinematic Flows* (Schüren, 2013) *Global Nollywood* (Indiana University Press, 2013), *Bongo Media Worlds* (Rüdiger Köppe 2014), *Trance Mediums and New Media* (Fordham University Press, 2014), and in *Africa Today* and the *Journal of African Cinemas*. She is one of the editors of the online journal *Swahili Forum*.

**Joseph Hill** has a Ph.D. in Anthropology from Yale University and is assistant professor of anthropology at the University of Alberta. He previously taught at the American University in Cairo and the University of Rochester. His research focuses on Sufi Islam as it relates to gender, forms of knowledge, authority, and performance. Since 2001, Hill has conducted ethnographic research on the global Fayḍa Tijāniyya Sufi movement, especially among the movement's members in Senegal and Mauritania. He also examines the rise of performance genres such as hip hop and Sufi dance as controversial yet effective vehicles for drawing young people into the religious community.

**Alessandro Jedlowski** is a Marie Curie/Cofund post-doctoral fellow in anthropology at the University of Liège (Belgium) and a member of the Centre for the Study of Contemporary Africa of the University of Naples "L'Orientale" (Italy). His publications include the book *Nollywood: L'industria Video Nigeriana e le sue Diramazioni Transnazionali* (Liguori, 2014), and the articles "Small Screen Cinema: Informality and Remediation in Nollywood" (*Journal of Television and New Media*, 2012) and "On the Periphery of Nollywood: Nigerian Video Filmmaking in Italy and the Emergence of Intercultural Aesthetics," in *Postcolonial Italy: Challenging National Homogeneity* (Palgrave McMillan, 2012).

**Karen Lauterbach** holds a position as associate professor at the Centre of African Studies, University of Copenhagen. She is also attached to a research program on charismatic Christianity in Africa at the Centre for Theology. She has done research on Congolese refugee churches, spiritual economies, and the politics of access to assistance in Uganda. Among her publications are: "Becoming a Pastor: Youth and Social Aspirations in Ghana" (*Young* 18.3, 2010), "Spiritual Gifts and Relations of Exchange among Congolese in Kampala, Uganda," in *Religion and Development—Nordic Perspectives on Involvement in Africa* (Peter Lang, 2014), and "Religion and Displacement in Africa: Compassion and Sacrifice in Congolese Churches in Kampala, Uganda" (*Religion and Theology* 21.3–4, 2014).

**Rebekah Lee** is senior lecturer in History at Goldsmiths College, University of London. She has published on various aspects of the social and cultural history of South Africa. Her research interests span issues of gender, migration, urbanization, health, religion, identity, and material culture. Her *African Women and Apartheid: Migration and Settlement in Urban South Africa* (IB Tauris) appeared in 2009. She is presently writing a book on death and memory in modern South Africa. In 2012, she directed a film documentary on the funeral industry in contemporary South Africa (*The Price of Death*), which won the 2013 Richard Werbner Prize for Visual Ethnography at the Royal Africa Institute's International Festival for Ethnographic Film.

**Olivier Atemsing Ndenkop** is a journalist and research fellow in the Department of Philosophy of the University of Yaoundé I in Cameroon. He is series editor for the publisher Action Sociale Africaine and has worked for several Cameroonian dailies. He is also the author of *L'Affaire Albatros. Enquête sur un Avion à Scandales* (forthcoming). Since November 2013 he has become a member of the Collectif Investig'Action (Brussels), where he is currently in charge of *Journal de l'Afrique*.

**Inès Neubauer** studied Social and Cultural Anthropology at the Goethe University Frankfurt, Germany. Her book *Prostitution in Bamako—Akteurinnen Zwischen Geld und Moral* (Brandes & Apsel, 2014) analyzes discourses and social dynamics of prostitution in Bamako/Mali. She has worked as a consultant for GIZ (German international cooperation and development agency) and is presently working on a Ph.D. thesis on consumption and development in Africa.

**David O'Kane** is a graduate of the National University of Ireland and of Queen's University Belfast, where he conducted doctoral research on land reform and nationalism in Eritrea. He has taught and researched in Eritrea, Ireland (north and south), Russia, the United Kingdom, and New

Zealand. Since 2011, he has been a senior research fellow in the research group "Integration and Conflict along the Upper Guinea Coast" at the Max Planck Institute for Social Anthropology, Halle, Germany. His current research focuses on educational policy and post-civil war reconstruction in Sierra Leone.

**Silke Oldenburg** is senior lecturer at the University of Basel, Switzerland. She holds a Ph.D. in Social Anthropology from Bayreuth University, Germany. Her research centers on political anthropology, youth, gender, generation and belonging, media and journalism, urban anthropology, and everyday life in contexts of protracted violent conflict. Her regional focus is on the Great Lakes Region and on the Andes. She has published "Under Familiar Fire: Making Decisions in the 'Kivu crisis' 2008 in Goma, DR Kongo" (*Africa Spectrum* 45.2, 2010) and is the author of the forthcoming monograph *Growing Up in Goma: War, Youth, and Everyday Life in Eastern Congo.*

**Ute Röschenthaler** is professor of Social and Cultural Anthropology at the Johannes Gutenberg University Mainz, Germany, and member of the Cluster of Excellence "The Formation of Normative Orders" and the research program "Africa's Asian Options" at Johann Wolfgang Goethe University, Frankfurt. She has extensive field experience in Cameroon, Nigeria, and Mali and works on cultural mobility, the emerging markets in Africa and its trade networks with the Global South, entrepreneurship, branding, media and advertisement in the urban context, and intellectual property rights. Her recent books are *Purchasing Culture: The Dissemination of Associations in the Cross River Region of Cameroon and Nigeria* (Africa World Press, 2011) and *Copyright Africa: How Intellectual Property, Media and Markets Transform Immaterial Cultural Goods* (Sean Kingston Publishing, 2015, edited with Mamadou Diawara).

**Marko Scholze** obtained a Ph.D. in Social Anthropology from the University of Bayreuth for his thesis on Tuareg engagement in tourism in the north of Niger. In addition to acting as academic coordinator at the Institute for Ethnology at Johann Wolfgang Goethe University, Frankfurt (since 2008), he has published on tourism and cultural heritage in Niger, Mali, and North Africa. His publications include *Moderne Nomaden und fliegende Händler: Tuareg und Tourismus in Niger* (LIT, 2009).

**Dorothea E. Schulz** has previously taught at Cornell University, Ithaca, and Indiana University, Bloomington, and is currently a professor in the Department of Cultural and Social Anthropology at the University of Cologne, Germany. She has published widely on media practices and public culture in Sahelian West Africa, gender studies, and Islam in West Africa. Her new research project addresses Christian-Muslim relations and questions of religious pluralism in Uganda. Her publications include *Perpetuating the Politics of Praise: Jeli Praise, Radios, and the Politics of Tradition in Mali* (Koeppe, 2001), *Muslims and New Media in West Africa* (Indiana University Press, 2012), and *Prayer in the City* (Transcript Publishers, 2012, with Patrick Desplat).

**Antoine Socpa** obtained a Ph.D. in Social Anthropology at Leiden University in 2002. He is currently affiliated with the Department of Anthropology, University of Yaounde I in Cameroon. His research interests include health and development, politics, citizenship, food security, migration, and trade networks between Asia and Africa. In addition to his book *Democratization and Autochthony in Cameroon* (LIT, 2003), he has published several articles in international journals. He is the General Secretary of the Pan African Association of Anthropologists (PAAA), Coordinator of the Cameroon Association of Anthropologists (CAA), and Manager of the Centre for Applied Social Sciences Research and Training (CASS-RT).

**Abdoulaye Sounaye** received his Ph.D. in Religious Studies and Anthropology from Northwestern University, USA, and currently works as a research fellow at the Zentrum Moderner Orient Berlin. His research interests include Islam in Niger and West Africa, secularism, religion and gender, Islamic revival, political Islam, Islam and development, Islamic knowledge economy, and religion and media practices. He is currently working on a book manuscript that deals with appropriations of the sermon as a particular religious genre among the Sunnance, a Salafi group in Niger. His most recent article, "Mobile Sunna: Islam, Small Media and Community in Niger," was published in *Social Compass* 61.1 (2014).

**Ibrahima Wane** is senior lecturer at the Department of French at the University Cheikh Anta Diop of Dakar (Senegal), where he teaches African oral literature. His present research interests focus on poetry and popular music in West Africa. He is the author of numerous publications on the relationship between artistic production and social and political transformations. His most recent publications include "Figures et Parures d'une Parole: Le Chant de Ndiaga Mbaye" in *Au Carrefour des Littératures, (Afrique-Europe)* (Karthala, 2013) and "Afrique 1950: Pas et Phases d'une Musique Cosmopolite" in *Great Black Music* (Actes Sud, 2014). He is also the director of several film documentaries on immaterial cultural heritage in Senegal, among them *Yela, Melodies of Memory* (Lydel Com., 2008).

# Index

For Product Safety Concerns and Information please contact our EU
representative GPSR@taylorandfrancis.com
Taylor & Francis Verlag GmbH, Kaufingerstraße 24, 80331 München, Germany